Who Killed Tom Thomson?

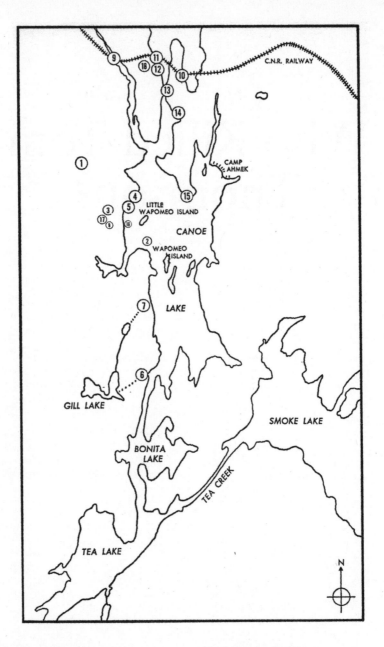

1. Original Thomson gravesite
2. Thomson's body recovered
3. Mowat Lodge
4. The Trainor cottage
5. The Blecher cottage
6. Gill Lake portage
7. Alternate Gill Lake portage
8. George Rowe's cabin
9. Canoe Lake train station
10. Mark Robinson's house
11. Joe Lake Station
12. Original Portage Store
13. Joe Lake dam
14. Favorite camping site of Thomson's
15. Thomson cairn (also a favorite Thomson camping site)
16. Thomson's canoe recovered
17. Post Office (former Hospital building)
18. Algonquin Hotel

Original Map by William T. Little. Revisions made by Brandon Little.

Who Killed Tom Thomson?

The Truth About the Murder of One of
the 20th Century's Most Famous Artists

John Little

Skyhorse Publishing

Skyhorse Publishing books may be purchased in bulk at special discounts for sales promotion, corporate gifts, fund-raising, or educational purposes. Special editions can also be created to specifications. For details, contact the Special Sales Department, Skyhorse Publishing, 307 West 36th Street, 11th Floor, New York, NY 10018 or info@ skyhorsepublishing.com.

Skyhorse® and Skyhorse Publishing® are registered trademarks of Skyhorse Publishing, Inc.®, a Delaware corporation.

Visit our website at www.skyhorsepublishing.com.

10 9 8 7 6 5 4 3 2 1

Library of Congress Cataloging-in-Publication Data is available on file.

Cover design by Rain Saukas

Print ISBN: 978-1-5107-3338-1
Ebook ISBN: 978-1-5107-3341-1

Printed in the United States of America

To the memory and efforts of Mark Robinson,
Blodwen Davies, and my father Bill Little.

CONTENTS

"To the living we owe respect, but to the dead we owe only the truth."

—Voltaire

PREFACE

The Little family has enjoyed (perhaps "enjoyed" is not the best word to use) an odd sixty-plus-year relationship with the Tom Thomson saga. I say "odd" because, after all, it's not everybody whose father has held the bones of Tom Thomson in his hands.

This event occurred on an overcast day back in the fall of 1956 when my father, Bill Little, along with friends Jack Eastaugh, Leonard Gibson, and Frank Braught, unearthed human remains while digging on the periphery of a very small and rather obscure burial ground within Algonquin Provincial Park in southeastern Ontario, Canada. Local tradition had indicated that the body of the iconic artist had been buried here on July 17, 1917. But, the tradition continued, a mere two days after the burial, the artist's family had contracted the services of an undertaker from Huntsville, a small town located approximately thirty-eight miles to the southwest, to retrieve the body and return it to the family plot in Leith, another small town located almost 181 miles southwest from the artist's original gravesite. The Huntsville undertaker's task had been a challenging one, as it had required that he dig through five to six feet of soil, remove both an oak casket and rough box, and then transfer a terribly decomposed corpse from its original casket into a metal one. The metal casket would then have to be soldered to seal it for transport by train to its final destination. The undertaker would later go on record that he then reburied the oak casket and rough box in the original grave from which he had removed them.

Making his task even more daunting was the fact that the undertaker had eschewed all help from the local populace, indicating that he preferred to work alone. That he chose to do so in the dead of night during the height of the mosquito and black fly season certainly raised a collective eyebrow from the denizens of the Canoe Lake area but, as they weren't involved with the exhumation, and were probably quite content with this fact, it had been generally assumed that the undertaker had done his job and that the transfer of Tom Thomson's body had taken place and that it had subsequently been laid to rest within the Leith Pioneer Cemetery of the Leith Presbyterian (now United) Church. Consequently, thirty-nine years later, when news broke that Thomson's original grave was still occupied, a series of shockwaves spread across the nation.

In the ensuing weeks, newspapers throughout Canada reported on the discovery and, ultimately, the attorney general's office stepped in to render a conclusion on the skeleton that had been found within the unmarked grave of the little cemetery next to Canoe Lake. Based upon their examination, the attorney general's office had concluded that these were not the bones of Canada's most famous artist, but of an indigenous person who had, somehow, found his way not only into Thomson's original grave, but also into what was left of the artist's original casket. As the reader can well imagine, such a pronouncement served to raise more questions than it answered. And, indeed, such answers as were proffered by the government as to how such a thing could have happened required such mental gymnastics to accept that many Canadians flatly refused to believe it, and loudly began to question, for the first time, just where Thomson's body was actually buried.

And that was just the matter of where the artist's body had been interred! Even more intriguing was the manner in which he died, which has been fraught with controversy ever since his body was found floating in the waters of Canoe Lake on July 16, 1917. Thomson had barely been in his (first) grave when the rumors began to fly—he had committed suicide; there was a love triangle and he was killed by his jealous rival; he slipped and hit his head on a rock and drowned; he was murdered by a cottager over a disagreement about World War I. And those were just the rumors that appeared in the first half of the last century. The second half brought more statements and allegations, such as that the artist was drunk and fell out of his canoe and drowned, or that a lodge owner had killed him over a debt. If ever there could be said to have been anything that was truly "a riddle wrapped in a mystery inside an enigma," the Tom Thomson case was certainly it.

Twelve years after the attorney general had weighed in on the matter, my father was approached by the nation's television station, the Canadian Broadcasting Corporation (CBC), and asked if he would assist them with research they were then conducting for a documentary on the late artist. He obliged their request and the television program entitled *Was Tom Thomson Murdered?* was viewed by millions of Canadians, and served to once again fan the flames of national interest in the matter of the artist's death and final resting place. Sometime during his work with the CBC, a large publishing house had learned of my father's research into the matter of Thomson's death and burial, and approached him with the idea that rather than allow all of his research materials to languish, he should coordinate his archive materials into a book that would throw further light on the mystery. My dad spent the next year writing *The Tom Thomson* Mystery, (quite literally, as he wrote the entire manuscript by hand and then had my older sister Sally type it out to submit to the publisher). And much to my father's surprise, when the book was published by McGraw-Hill in 1970 it quickly became a national best-seller. The embrace of his book by the Canadian public revealed that my father was not alone in his belief that there was something quite suspicious about how the artist had met his end and where his body had been laid to rest.

All of the above took place during a period of time that extended from four years before I was born until I was ten years old and, consequently, I grew up with Tom Thomson as part of the family discourse. Indeed, I can't remember a year when the subject of Tom Thomson wasn't discussed within our family and, whenever we ventured out on a canoe trip, it was usually to Algonquin Provincial Park, where the mystery of the artist's death and burial would once again assume center stage. My father had even felt obliged to pack me off to Taylor Statten's Camp Ahmek on Canoe Lake the summer I was fifteen years old; the very spot where the Thomson drama had played out. In looking back, it strikes me that the specter of Tom Thomson was omnipresent throughout my childhood, like a ghost that needed to be exorcised.

This reached a critical tipping point for me during the early 1990s, when new testimony and archive materials that had not been available to my father when he had written his book became available through various provincial and national archives. Prior to this there had been testimony from people who had known Thomson personally that had been published in the books of authors such as Harold Town, David Silcox, Ottelyn Addison, and Joan Murray. Buoyed by the content of this bounty of material, I decided to conduct some research of my own into the matter by attempting to track down and interview anyone I could find who had actually known Thomson. Starting upon such a quest three quarters of a century after the death of the artist was certainly a foolhardy enterprise, as all of those who had been close friends and contemporaries of Thomson during the final year of his life had for the most part passed on, leaving me access only to those who were the children of those who had known the artist (and consequently who were quite young when they had met him), or those who had known other people who had known Thomson that lived and worked within the Canoe Lake area at the time of his death. Nevertheless, even those who had but minor roles in the Thomson drama had interesting pieces of the puzzle to share, and once these had been pressed into place they revealed a far more complete picture of the final days of Tom Thomson than had been afforded previously.

Thus, 1990 proved to be an interesting year in this regard, as I was able to speak with a number of fascinating people, including conducting what would prove to be the last interview ever given by A.J. Casson, who was at that point in time the last surviving member of Canada's most famous band of landscape artists known collectively as the Group of Seven. Many members of the group had known Thomson quite well, and so I was hopeful that they might have shared with Casson some insights regarding what they knew about his passing. This was also the year that I had made the acquaintance of a ninety-year-old former trapper and Order of Canada recipient Ralph Bice. Bice had lived and worked in Algonquin Park most of his life and, as I had been told by certain people in the Muskoka area, he was "the man" to speak to if one wanted to know the "truth" about Tom Thomson. As someone who had already amassed a great deal of data on the late artist, I was anxious to pick the brain of this venerable gentleman.

I should note that we in the Little family had grown up with the belief that Tom Thomson was a stand-up guy; indeed, he was a Canadian icon who was everything a Canadian icon should be, shy of being an NHL player. However, it wasn't long into my conversation with Bice that quite a different portrait of the artist emerged. According to the old trapper, Thomson had a reputation throughout the park for being, in his words, "a drunken bum." That assessment, I must admit, caught me completely off guard. And while my guard was down, the trapper delivered another numbing left hook to my consciousness with his statement that Thomson (a.k.a. "the drunken bum") was also a rake, a man who was known to lead women on in the false hope that he would marry them. And then the trapper delivered what he believed was the coup de gras to Thomson's character; that Thomson not only "couldn't paint unless he had a bottle of gin," but was also bombed when he had simply fallen out of his canoe and drowned on that fateful summer day back in 1917. Oh yeah, and he wasn't much of a canoeist either. In short, everything I had grown up believing Thomson to be—a man of temperance, a gifted artist, a soft-spoken gentleman, and an expert canoeist—was wrong. It was like speaking to somebody from a different planet where down was up and forward was backward. To Bice's way of thinking, there had been altogether too much fuss made about the man whose paintings are considered to be, in some circles at least, "the visual equivalent of our national anthem." Granted that such a statement, voiced by the author David Silcox, might be a little over the top, reflecting as it does nothing but a mid Ontario-centric point of view (no one, for example, from the East or West Coasts of Canada, sections of land that border the Atlantic and Pacific oceans respectively, could feel that Thomson's paintings perfectly capture for them what it means to be "Canadian"), but it does accurately reflect the esteem in which Thomson is held by a vast majority of Canadians. But one couldn't count the old trapper in amongst that group. As he put it to me that day:

> The one thing that's bothered me is that there is a cairn built to the memory of Tom Thomson—there's even a lake named after him! Why in the world can't they let it die? Stop all this! You know, he was gone for fifteen years before they started to make a big thing out of him. When Frank Mason, my brother-in-law, went down there [Canoe Lake] to teach in 1932, everybody would tell you about Tom Thomson— "Oh he was drunk and fell out of a canoe." Everybody considered and heard that he was so drunk . . . and Harold Town found out, you know who Harold Town is? He wrote

a book about the artist, and he said, "there's no doubt in the world that he stood up in the canoe to relieve himself [when he died]." I had a man here this morning, he said, "Oh I understand that his trousers were open and maybe his penis was out when he fell."

The old trapper neglected to mention how his morning's guest had come by this rather intimate bit of information, as no statement that has survived from any of those who were present when Thomson's lifeless body was pulled from the water on that fateful July day back in 1917 had ever testified to this. Nevertheless, Bice had voiced his assertions as if the matter were not open for debate.

His mention of Harold Town being the primary support for his beliefs in this matter certainly brought back memories. Town, along with the aforementioned David Silcox, had authored a book entitled *Tom Thomson: The Silence and The Storm* that had been published thirteen years previously. I remembered the book, as well as their statement within it that "the large majority of drowned canoe fishermen are found with their flies open." Apart from the grammar of the sentence (a "large majority"—is there such a thing as a "small majority"?—and what exactly is a "canoe fisherman"—one who fishes for canoes?), I had issues with the authors' assertion, particularly since they had not cited any studies on the matter as evidence (as if there has ever been such a study conducted on the position of pant zippers on drowned canoe fishermen!). Nevertheless, Town and Silcox had presented this as being a categorical fact; that the artist had been drunk, stood up in his canoe to urinate, lost his footing, fell and hit his head on the gunwale of the canoe, and then toppled into the water and drowned. Case closed. An impressively sweeping conclusion that was completely free of any supporting evidence. To my way of thinking, the authors' assertion was easy to dismiss—and yet here was Bice, a man who (unlike Town and Silcox) had actually been in Algonquin Park when Thomson had met his fate, supporting their contention.

Still, the testimony I had read from those who had been present when the artist had gone missing and when his body was found did not square with what either Bice or the authors of *The Silence and the Storm* had contended. The reason, I soon discovered, was that the old trapper with whom I was conversing had never met Thomson during all of his years in the park. Indeed, he claimed that the closest he had ever come to the artist was when Thomson had once walked past him at a regatta at Joe Lake in 1915. The trapper then confessed that he hadn't been in the Canoe Lake region of the park when Thomson went missing, nor when the artist's body had been recovered from the water. And yet only a week or so before our get-together Bice had written a letter to the editor of a local newspaper in which he lambasted the artist's character in much the same way that he had with me that day. This is not to suggest that Bice possessed no knowledge of consequence regarding the artist, but it quickly became evident that what knowledge he did possess had been acquired second-hand; i.e., from the recollections of others who had known the artist personally, and that quite a lot of his information regarding the artist's death had evidently been acquired from individuals such as the author Harold Town, who had been thirty-seven years shy of drawing his first breath when the artist had died.

I recall leaving Mr. Bice's house that day feeling quite frustrated that my interviewee possessed no more knowledge about Thomson than anyone else who had read *The Silence and the Storm* and had taken the authors' statements about his death at face value. Many years later I would discover that my preliminary disappointment with Bice would prove to be incredibly shortsighted, as when I eventually transcribed my interview with him I discovered that he had actually been a veritable fount of information about the secondary players in the Thomson drama, most of whom he knew quite well. And one statement he had made to me that day held particular significance. We had been discussing the possibility that Thomson had been murdered (Bice did not believe this) and when I suggested that Park Ranger Mark Robinson, the man who had been charged by the government to investigate the matter at the time, had been firmly of the opinion that foul play was involved, the old trapper waved off the suggestion. "Well, if he thought that there was foul play involved then he should have contacted the police at the time," he snorted. "Then this whole mystery would have been solved long ago and they would have known if he was murdered." On that point we were both in concurrence as not only had the police never been called in to investigate Thomson's death at the time that it occurred, but from my vantage point the only people who had ever taken the time and trouble to investigate the artist's death were writers, and their literary offerings over the decades had only brought before the Canadian public a morass of conflicting conclusions on the matter—but this is as it must be whenever writers pretend to be detectives. Such disparate viewpoints served to further muddy the water and only evidenced proof that a proper police investigation into the Thomson case had been sorely lacking from the beginning. However, the fact that the police were not involved in 1917 did not mean that they could not be involved today.

Granted, the matter of Tom Thomson's death represents the coldest of cold case files, but there does exist evidence, and a fair measure of it, that would at least provide an investigating officer trained in such matters with the information necessary to render an informed opinion on whether the artist's death was simply an accidental death via, say, drunken urination while standing up in a canoe, or something far more sinister. And certainly any conclusion based upon the experience of such a person (or persons) would be far more meaningful and infinitely more valuable not only to Thomson's legacy, but also to Canadian history than would be the random opinions of various scribes who possessed little to no knowledge or experience in matters of criminal investigation and forensic science.

To this end, I was fortunate to connect with two detectives from the Ontario Provincial Police (OPP), Daniel Mulligan and Scott Thomson (the latter of whom, it is rumored, is a distant relative of the late artist), who both expressed a willingness to review the facts of the case, and to offer me their professional opinion on the matter. However, now having secured the involvement of the two detectives, the real work began. Both detectives told me that they required all of the pertinent data regarding the death of the artist, which entailed my scouring the archives for all of the testimony from people who knew Thomson and who were also present when the tragedy at Canoe Lake went down in July 1917. Once this material had been amassed, it then had to be arranged in a certain sequence so that a timeline of sorts could be laid out. Consequently, I organized the materials as if a death had just been called in to a local police detachment—e.g., a body was discovered—where? Who discovered it? What was his or her statement regarding the matter? (That was file one.) What was the condition of the body when it was found? (File two) Who saw the deceased on the last day of his life? What was said? Where was he going? How was his mood? Did he seem anxious or depressed? (File three) Was there anybody who might have wished to harm the victim? Did he have any known enemies? If so, whom? (File four) All told, I prepared over seventeen such files for the detectives. And, to my surprise, all of the questions indicated above, and many more that would arise during the detectives' analysis of the case, had answers in the form of testimony from parties who were there at the time of Thomson's death. None of the original source material that contained this testimony could be edited; i.e., all of it—from the fawning praise of Thomson's patron, the Toronto ophthalmologist Dr. James MacCallum, to the disparaging words of the old trapper Ralph Bice—had to be weighed and examined critically. Ditto for the evidence supporting the various theories that had been advanced over the past one hundred years regarding how Thomson had met his fate—from accidental death by drowning, to suicide, to foul play, to the belief of Town and Silcox that a combination of alcohol and standing up in a canoe to urinate caused his death. Once this material had been collected and organized under these various "case files," it was then turned over to the two detectives for their professional analysis. The conclusions reached by the detectives in this matter represent something unique in the Thomson literature: a police detective's professional opinion as to how the artist met his death.

Additional material presented in this book that represents another first in the Thomson literature is as follows:

- The opinion of the First Nations Band of Golden Lake. In 1956 when the Crime Lab and Attorney General's office of Ontario concluded that the human skeleton found in Tom Thomson's original grave in Algonquin Park was that of a native or half native, they then did a most peculiar thing. Rather than returning the newly identified bones to the natives, they instead placed them in a cardboard box and reinterred them in Thomson's original grave. To the author's surprise, I found out that no one had ever bothered to contact the Algonquins for their insight and opinion on the Thomson case. And so, this grievous oversight has now been corrected and the Algonquins First Nations people speak on the matter for the first time.
- New testimony supporting the contention that a lodge proprietor in Algonquin Park may have been Thomson's killer is

brought forth. Until now, a woman named Daphne Crombie was the only one to make such a claim. Now, Muskoka artist Doug Dunford reveals testimony that he was privy to that suggests that members of the Group of Seven might also have been aware of this.

- Testimony from the aforementioned Order of Canada recipient and long-time Algonquin Park guide Ralph Bice that reveals new insights about a late-night card game and drinking party that occurred hours before the artist went missing.

- The potential role of Thomson's alleged drinking binges in the matter of his death, along with the marital infidelities of certain members of the Canoe Lake community where Thomson lived during 1917.

- Testimony from Blanche Linton (nee Packard), a young woman who worked at the Algonquin Hotel in 1917 and who was one of the few to see the artist on the last day of his life, and what Thomson's fellow guides (he occasionally worked as a fishing guide) suspected to be the cause of his death.

All of this evidence has been brought together for the first time, in addition to material obtained from diverse archive sources (and added to the fifty-plus years of research that my late father conducted) and presented for analysis to detectives Mulligan and Thomson. Their conclusions represent the closest thing we will ever get to a definitive answer to the one hundred-year-old mystery of how Tom Thomson met his end.

DRAMATIS PERSONAE

To appreciate the details of the story that follows, it is helpful to have a snapshot of both the venues and cast of characters that appear in the drama:

THE TERRAIN

Algonquin Park: A huge parcel of land owned by the provincial government of Ontario. Covering a distance of 2,955 square miles and containing over 2,400 lakes and over 745 miles of streams and rivers, the park sits between Ottawa and Georgian Bay in Southern Ontario. It was established in 1893 and is the oldest provincial park in Canada. Its proximity to major cities such as Toronto and Ottawa and certain cities within the United States that border Ontario, such as Buffalo, resulted in it being one of Canada's most popular vacation and tourist attractions. While a highway runs through it today, in 1917 it was a true wilderness that was only accessible by train to people traveling from the city.

Mowat: A small village that slowly came into being as a result of a logging boom that started in the Canoe Lake region of Algonquin Park in the 1830s. White Pine was the primary lumber of choice and there was lots of it in Algonquin Park. Logging continued through into the 1860s and was augmented in 1881 when the Canada Central Pacific Railway came through the region. By 1897, the timber baron J.R. Booth had established the Arnprior, Parry Sound and Ottawa railway, which provided additional arteries into the park. With the railway came the opportunity for settlement for the lumbermen and their families, as well as the railway workers. This settlement became the village of Mowat, named in honor of Sir Oliver Mowat, who was the Premier of the province of Ontario from 1872 to 1896. The village of Mowat was a lumber mill town that included lodgings, small stores, and a hospital. The population eventually grew to five hundred, making it then the largest town in Algonquin Park. By 1898, a small school was established for the children of the local residents and thirty students were enrolled. However, the lumber industry gradually began to decline, and, by 1914, the year-round population had dwindled to 150. Mowat soon became a ghost town and, by 1918, its year-round population had dropped below forty-eight.

Mowat Lodge: A pair of adjacent lumber bunkhouses within the village of Mowat that eventually became a tourist lodge. The bunkhouses were originally built to provide accommodation for the lumbermen who worked for the Gilmour Lumber Company operation at Canoe Lake. When the company went bust around the start of the twentieth century, the buildings were abandoned. In 1913, John Shannon Fraser decided to convert the two abandoned bunkhouses into an inn for tourists and Mowat Lodge was born.

Algonquin Hotel: An inn for tourists that predated Mowat Lodge. The Algonquin Hotel was erected on the shores of Joe Lake in 1908 to accommodate tourists who were arriving into the park by train. A train station was built just in front of the hotel, and Tom Mernill, who opened the hotel, maintained its seasonal operation up until Edwin and Molly Colson purchased it from him in 1917. The Colsons would also open an outfitter's supply store near the hotel.

Algonquin Park Headquarters: Shortly after the railway was put through, and after the park achieved national park status within

Canada, a Park Headquarters was established first at Canoe Lake, but later moved to Cache Lake. The park superintendent was Peter Thomson, who was replaced in 1898 by George W. Bartlett. Under Bartlett, an attempt was made to make the park self-reliant. It was at this point that short-term leases were granted between the Provincial government and various tourist inns, camps, and cottages.

THE PEOPLE

Tom Thomson: A landscape artist who grew up near Owen Sound but lived most of his winters in Toronto. From spring until late fall he would live in Algonquin Park, either at Mowat Lodge (or occasionally at the Trainor cottage if they were absent from the area) and the rest of the months he would spend camping out in a tent. He found semi-regular employment as a general handyman and as a guide for fishing parties. Thomson was thirty-four years old when he first came to Algonquin Park in 1912 and would return each spring until his death five years later.

George W. Bartlett: The superintendent of Algonquin Park. Bartlett wielded ultimate authority within the park on behalf of the province of Ontario, and employed upwards of twenty-seven rangers to assist him in the task of enforcing and contracting leases, prohibiting poachers from operating, and encouraging tourism to the area.

Mark Robinson: One of the many park rangers who worked under Bartlett's supervision. He was a naturalist who in time would come to know the area like the back of his hand, in addition to being a veteran of World War I. He would become one of Thomson's few friends within the park and was the one entrusted by Bartlett to investigate the artist's death on behalf of the province of Ontario.

George Rowe and *Lowrey Dickson*: Two guides who plied their trade primarily for Shannon Fraser at Mowat Lodge. They shared a cabin together on Canoe Lake for a number of years, but later built their own cabins apart from one another in the region. They were friends with Thomson, but also competitors for guiding jobs with him.

Shannon and *Annie Fraser*: The proprietors of Mowat Lodge during the time that Thomson came to the park. Shannon delighted in his job as owner of the lodge, but was known as a bit of a yarn teller. His wife Annie was by all accounts very friendly and popular with both the residents on Canoe Lake and the guests of Mowat Lodge.

Edwin and *Molly Colson*: The proprietors of the Algonquin Hotel and the first Portage Store in the region. Edwin Colson had been a park ranger prior to running the Highland Inn on Cache Lake. His wife Molly had been trained as a nurse, which endeared her to the small population in and around the Mowat area.

Dr. Goldwyn Howland: A medical doctor and professor of neurology at the University of Toronto, who had rented a small summer cottage on an island in Canoe Lake when Tom Thomson's body was discovered. He was the one who first saw it bob to the surface of the lake.

Dr. Ranney: A coroner from North Bay who had been called in to handle the inquest after the death of Tom Thomson.

The Trainor Family: A family from Huntsville, Ontario that had a small cottage on Canoe Lake that was located just up from the shoreline in front of Mowat Lodge. The family consisted of Hugh Trainor, a former lumber company foreman, his wife Margaret, and two daughters Marie and Winnifred. One of the daughters,

Winnifred, was said by some to have been engaged to Tom Thomson at the time of his death.

The Blecher Family: An American family from Buffalo who had a summer cottage on Canoe Lake next door to the Trainor cottage. The family consisted of Martin Blecher Senior, his wife Louisa, and two adult children, daughter Bessie and son Martin Junior. The family had a long-standing feud going with Tom Thomson at the time of the artist's death.

TIME LINE OF THE
THOMSON STORY

Saturday, July 7, 1917. Candian landscape artist Tom Thomson writes and posts a letter to his patron in Toronto, Dr. James Mac-Callum. Thomson attends a party later that evening at a guide's cabin. Alcohol is consumed and a fight breaks out between Thomson and a local cottager (Martin Blecher Junior). The cottager threatens Thomson.

*Sunday, July 8, 1917—*1:00 p.m. Tom Thomson paddles away from the dock in front of Mowat Lodge and heads south on Canoe Lake.

    3:05 p.m. Thomson's overturned canoe is spotted about a half mile south from his point of departure by Martin Blecher Junior and his sister Bessie. They do not investigate.

Monday, July 9, 1917. Thomson's abandoned canoe is located floating upside down behind Little Wapomeo Island. It is brought over to either Mowat Lodge or the Blecher family's boathouse.

*Tuesday, July 10, 1917—*9:15 a.m. Park Ranger Mark Robinson is notified by Shannon Fraser (and perhaps also Charlie Scrim) about the discovery of Thomson's abandoned canoe. Robinson heads to Canoe Lake to investigate the matter.

Wednesday, July 11, 1917—Sunday, July 15, 1917. Mark Robinson and others begin a search for the missing artist, checking the portages, islands, and land routes that Thomson had been known to travel.

Monday, July 16, 1917—9:00 a.m. Tom Thomson's body is spotted floating 125 yards off shore to the south of Little Wapomeo Island by Dr. Goldwyn Howland, a man who had rented a cabin on the lake that weekend. The body is towed to a point of land by two guides in their canoe. Mark Robinson is notified of the discovery by Charlie Scrim. He, in turn, notifies the park superintendent who then sends for a coroner from North Bay. The body is left in the water overnight tethered to the branch of a fallen tree.

Tuesday, July 17, 1917. After repeated attempts to reach the Thomson family by telegram without success, Mark Robinson decides that Thomson must be buried immediately. The body is transferred to Wapomeo Island and embalmed. The body is buried in the early afternoon in a little cemetery that sits some distance to the northwest of Mowat Lodge. The coroner arrives later that evening. He conducts an inquest into Thomson's death without having opportunity to view the body. The inquest starts at midnight and concludes at approximately 1:30 a.m. Based on the evidence, the coroner concludes that the artist died an accidental death due to drowning.

Wednesday, July 18, 1917. Winnifred Trainor, acting on behalf of the Thomson family, secures the services of an undertaker from her hometown of Hunstville to exhume the artist's body from its grave at the cemetery at Canoe Lake and transfer it into a metal casket that is then soldered shut. The undertaker arrives on the evening train, and waves off any help with his task. By himself he digs through six feet of earth, removes the oak casket and rough box from the grave, transfers Thomson's body into the metal casket and solders it. All of this taking place within a span of three hours.

Thursday, July 19, 1917. The steel casket is brought to the Canoe Lake train station sometime after 12:30 a.m. It goes out on the evening train en route to Owen Sound.

Friday, July 20, 1917. The casket arrives in Owen Sound on the evening train and is placed in the undertaker's establishment where it remains until morning.

Saturday, July 21, 1917. The casket is interred in the cemetery of the United Church in Leith, Ontario.

Summer 1930. Mark Robinson shares his views on the matter of Thomson with Bill Little; i.e., that the artist did not die an accidental death by drowning and that his body was never removed from the little cemetery at Canoe Lake.

October 1956. On a sketching expedition at Canoe Lake, Bill Little and a friend, Jack Eastaugh, visit the little cemetery to do some painting. While there, Robinson's words return to them and the two men decide to test the ranger's hypothesis. They return the next morning with two friends and dig in the spot that the ranger had indicated was Thomson's original gravesite. They find the remains of an oak casket and pine rough box. Within what's left of the casket they find human remains that match the description of Tom Thomson. They notify a local doctor who, in turn, notifies the Attorney General's department about their discovery and the Attorney General's office dispatches two men to exhume the grave and examine the bones.

October 1956. Word gets out to the press about the discovery. The Thomson family expresses its wish to have the investigation shut down. The Attorney General's office shuts down the investigation and declares that the bones found within Thomson's original grave and casket are those of an indigenous person. The bones are reburied in the grave from which they were exhumed and a small white cross is erected.

PROLOGUE

1972. Canoe Lake. My father and I are standing atop what we believe is Tom Thomson's grave in Algonquin Park. My father has a familiarity with this place that few can appreciate. He shares with me his belief that Tom Thomson lies buried beneath our feet under four and a half feet of soil. "How did he die, Dad?" I ask. He tells me the story. Who knows, maybe he thinks that I'll pass it on to my kids one day.

It's a story that will serve to grip me throughout childhood and into my adult life. It's frustrating that there has never been a definite resolution to it. There are some who think this is for the best. A good thing. It's a damned good mystery, after all, and who doesn't enjoy that? I have always had trouble equating the premature death of a man as being on par with cognitive entertainment. I can't help but think that Tom Thomson, a man who valued truth in art and, one would guess in life as well, might think that the matter of how he lost his life warranted something more than the casual speculations of those who think it's a good thing that the matter never be looked into in any meaningful way for fear of spoiling a good mystery.

In my darker moments, however, I must concede that I sometimes believe that the mystery of Thomson's death will never be fully solved—but that doesn't mean that one shouldn't try. I felt my enthusiasm returning once more during the researching and writing of this book—just one more run through of the facts; maybe something missed before will come to light. There has to be a way to solve the mystery of Thomson's death and where his body is buried. I humbly respect the fact that brighter minds than mine have racked their brains trying to undo the Gordian Knot that is the Tom Thomson mystery and, to date, all have come up empty, and that only a fool would consider an attempt to solve the mystery one hundred years after the fact. And so, I proceed.

Recognizing that the term "writer" is not a synonym for "detective," it is my intention to present the material that I gathered for the Ontario Provincial Police detectives (with whom I connected to attempt to solve the case) in a manner that will reveal a factual and fascinating story, but I shall leave the conclusions, where and if they can be drawn, to the professionals in such matters. This is not to suggest that I have not raised questions of my own regarding certain points in the narrative that heretofore have not been examined very thoroughly, but for the most part I have resisted the temptation of most writers to lead the reader to a particular conclusion and have endeavored to keep my thumbprint off the telling of the story. Some of the testimony presented herein has been brought forth previously to the public by various authors over the years; but, as the reader will soon discover, what this same testimony suggests to professional detectives who decipher such evidence for a living is another matter entirely.

However, before the detectives can enter our narrative, we must first venture back in time to 1917, and a very different Canada than the one we know presently. Robert Borden, who had succeeded Wilfrid Laurier as Canada's prime minister, was then in his sixth year as head of the nation; a nation that found itself embroiled in the third year of World War I. Borden had by this point pledged half a million soldiers to the war effort, but the volunteers had dwindled as Canadians soon realized that there wasn't going to be a swift resolution to the conflict overseas. (Borden also had the dubious distinction of having introduced income tax to Canadians to help the war effort. It was meant to be a temporary measure, but, as history will record, it was anything but.)

The premiere of the province of Ontario was a man by the name of William Howard Hearst, a temperance devotee and one of the pillars of the Methodist Church. Hearst's government had passed the Ontario Temperance Act (OTA) in 1916, which, like the income tax legislation, had been introduced as a temporary war-time measure. The OTA made it illegal for anyone in Ontario to possess and consume beer or liquor outside of one's home, and to this end Hearst's government had shut down all of Ontario's bars, taverns, clubs, and liquor stores. So pervasive was the effect of the OTA upon the culture of the time that, to the majority who took it seriously, those who consumed alcohol at a rate similar to what one might observe today during an evening of watching a sporting event with friends, would be considered alcoholics or derelicts; occupying the bottom rungs of the ladder of respectable civilized society. The OTA would run for eleven years, from 1916 until 1927, at which point the provincial government would assume total control over the lucrative business of alcohol sales within the province by creating the Liquor Control Board of Ontario (LCBO)—which has controlled the sale of alcohol in the province to this day.

On April 12, 1917, the right to vote in municipal and provincial elections was extended to women in Ontario for the first time. The four western provinces had made the move to extend the franchise to women in 1916, but it was still a year away from occurring in Nova Scotia, two years away for New Brunswick, and four years still in the future for Prince Edward Island. Quebec would be the last to fall into line, requiring another twenty-three years to elapse before women were allowed to have their say in municipal and provincial elections.

The date of July 1, 1917 had been a significant one, as the nation had celebrated its fiftieth Dominion Day—an important milestone to be certain, but also a cause for some insecurity as it underscored the fact that Canada was but a mere babe on the world stage. The country hadn't yet had sufficient time to develop its own unique culture and identity and, to a large extent, can still be accused of clinging to the European way of doing things. Canada was still several months away at this point from the establishment of what would eventually become its primary national sporting institution—the National Hockey League.

Algonquin Park, established in 1893, had by 1917 already been long promoted as a vacation destination and tourist getaway, enticing those from the cities, particularly Toronto and Ottawa, to head north in order to enjoy the unsullied wilds that the province of Ontario had to offer. Even Ontario's neighbors to the south, residing in the states of Michigan and New York, had been enticed to cross the border to relax in the tranquility of the park's clean air, sparkling lakes, and abundance of flora and fauna that were not to be found in their congested urban centers. For this reason, the appeal of the park, then as today, was not lost on many city dwellers who had grown tired of the drama that attends the mart of economic strife and gain that plays out daily upon the stages of the nation's major cities. Such people longed for a little down time in a more relaxed environment and viewed the park as a balm for their troubled souls. These urbanites boarded trains that headed north from Toronto on the Grand Trunk Railway Line. After several hours in rail cars they eventually reached Scotia Junction, just north of Huntsville, and there they would switch trains to continue east into the park. Canoe Lake Station was among the first stops within the park and was quite close to two tourist lodges, thus making it the stop of choice for those who were coming into Algonquin Park for the first time. Canoe Lake itself was (and remains) a modest sized lake, featuring a shore length of approximately thirteen and a half miles and a surface area of approximately six and a quarter miles.

During the week of July 10 through July 16, 1917 the area in and around Canoe Lake was pleasant in terms of its temperature, averaging a little over 17°C (62.6°F) most of that week, with inter-mittent rain. And, on the morning of July 16 the weather held forth the potential of being even more agreeable. No clouds intruded into the morning sky and the mercury had started heading north on its way to a weekly high of 26.1°C (78.98°F).

For one particular tourist and his daughter, the morning of July 16 had started out with the promise of being a wonderful day. But the day had just begun, and what it brought with it would not only serve to lay the foundation for one of Canada's greatest myster-ies, but also haunt the father and daughter for the rest of their lives.

Chapter One

A BODY RISES

I t's an eerie thing to contemplate; a severely decomposed and badly bloated corpse slowly rising from the depths, until it ultimately breaks the surface of a calm lake during the early morning hours, just as the mist is starting to lift. After eight days of submersion, the bacteria generated by its decomposing flesh had evidently produced sufficient gases to cause the corpse to shift from its murky resting place thirty feet below the water's surface and begin its ascent.

Goldwyn Howland, a medical doctor and professor of Neurology at the University of Toronto, had awakened early on the morning of July 16, 1917 in a small cottage that he had rented on Statten's Island. Statten's Island (now known as Little Wapomeo Island) is a small island, situated near the northwestern shore of Canoe Lake, which had originally been leased from the government by Taylor Statten, a man employed by the national YMCA as the Boy's Work Secretary, but who was away that month at a YMCA training school in Massachusetts. Howland had arrived in the park only the night before, bringing with him his young daughter, Margaret. The pair had been looking forward to some father and daughter time together over the coming week and had already enjoyed a little fishing and canoeing on the evening of their arrival. Above all for the good doctor, he had been most welcoming of the kind of mental relaxation that being in a rural environment had always seemed to induce. On this particular morning he decided to let his daughter sleep in; there would be no shortage of outdoor things to do once she awoke and these, combined with the fresh air and sunlight, would tire her out quick enough. Not wanting to disturb her slumber, Howland stepped outside onto the small veranda at the front of the little cottage and was immediately taken with the splendor of his new surroundings. Having arrived the evening before, he hadn't had the opportunity yet to see the sights of the lake in the morning sunlight. His view from the front door allowed him to take in all the northern section of Canoe Lake and, although it was still early, the sun was already beginning to shine brightly through a cloudless sky. Looking several hundred yards to his right he could see what is now called Wapomeo Island, and looking directly across the lake from the cabin he could spy Hayhurst Point, a small isthmus that cuts into the northern portion of Canoe Lake. While it featured a steep rock face, there was a trail that led to the top that would afford a tremendous view of the lake. Yes, that might be a good spot for he and his daughter to visit today. The doctor sat down on the steps next to the front door of the cabin, content in the thought that it was shaping up to be a great day. And then it happened.

He had been looking toward a point of land just west of Wapomeo Island when suddenly something broke the placidness of the lake's surface. The object appeared to be about 400 yards away and immediately caught the doctor's attention. It looked too big to be a loon, and far too motionless to be an otter or a beaver. Even more peculiar was the fact that, whatever it was, it hadn't moved since it came to the surface of the lake. Howland strained his eyes to make out what the object might be. There were intermittent flashes of color, flecks of brown and gray, which revealed themselves in between the crests and troughs of the waves—but the object was too far away for him to make out its true identity with any degree of precision. Intrigued, Howland walked down to the shoreline of the island for a closer look. The extra thirty yards he gained from doing so did nothing to bring the object more clearly into focus. He shrugged his shoulders and walked about the shoreline for a bit, looking at the natural beauty that surrounded him from different points on the little island, but every now and then taking a look back at the object that still hadn't moved in the water.

As the doctor was just about to return to the cabin his peripheral vision picked up on something else: two men in a canoe paddling south down the center of the lake. The men were the local guides George Rowe and Lowrey Dickson and, from the doctor's vantage point, they appeared to be heading in a direction that would eventually bring them within a hundred feet or so of the object. It occurred to the doctor that if he could hail these men they would be able to make a positive identification of the bobbing object, and thus settle what had now become a gnawing curiosity for the physician. Howland quickly walked out to the end of a small dock that jutted some twenty feet out from the island and called out to the men to secure their attention. Upon hearing a voice, both guides lifted their paddles from the water and looked in the direction that the sound was coming from. Once the doctor had secured their attention he pointed toward the object that was still bobbing in the water and asked if they would take a look at it for him.

"Sure thing!" Dickson replied, and then tapping his partner on the back with his paddle, said, "Probably a loon."[1] Rowe wasn't sure if Dickson was talking about the man on the dock that was yelling and waving his arms, or the object that he just now spied floating in the water about 300 yards southwest of them. Dickson had also spotted it, and the guides presently decided to change their course to move in and investigate.

It wasn't long before both men realized that the object they were closing in on was definitely not a loon; however, they were not yet close enough to rule out its being a dead animal. Animal carcasses floating in the lake were certainly not unusual, particularly when the ice melted in the spring. But this was mid-summer, which would make such an occurrence something of a rarity. As the bow of the guides' canoe continued to cut through the water, the object that lay before them slowly began to come more clearly into focus and, as it did, a sense of uneasiness began to rise in both men. Rowe, the man in the bow,[2] would have been the first to discern that the object they were approaching was clearly clothing of some sort— grayish in color—perhaps someone's laundry had blown into the lake from one of the cottage clotheslines. But as the canoe verged nearer he would have discerned that this article of clothing also had hair. And as they drew closer they would have observed something bluish gray in color protruding from beneath the clothing that looked like a human hand. It would now have been evident to both men that the object that they were rapidly closing in on was not some cottager's wayward laundry but rather a human body—but whose body? In 1917 the population in the Canoe Lake region was small, perhaps thirty to forty people year-round, and everybody knew each other well. The only person who had been reported missing was the seasonal resident and part time guide, Tom Thomson—but that was eight days ago and everybody believed he had been lost or stranded in the woods. Indeed, the woodland was where all of the search parties had concentrated their efforts when attempting to locate him.

The guides ceased their paddling and allowed their canoe to glide in alongside the body. One can only hope that the corpse was floating face down[3] as its state of decomposition would have been startling. Later reports indicated that the putrefaction had advanced to the point where the flesh was detaching from its hands[4] and the limbs and face were severely swollen.[5] While it's likely that both men would have suspected the identity of the body that they now found themselves looking down upon, its condition was such that making a positive identification would have proven difficult.

Both of the guides had known Thomson well. Indeed, the three had gotten together to have a few drinks and play some cards only nine days prior at Rowe's cabin. Rowe had also been Thomson's guiding partner on several occasions when the pair had taken tourists out from Mowat Lodge for an afternoon of fishing and sight seeing. But the object that Rowe was looking at presently didn't look anything at all like the man he had partied and guided with. Visions of Thomson, and of the clothes that he typically wore on those occasions, now began to trickle through the old guide's consciousness, bringing with them the grim realization that Tom Thomson was dead. Rowe turned around from his position in the bow of the canoe to face Dickson, and witnessed a look of silent anguish on his friend's face.

"What is it?" yelled Dr. Howland from the end of the dock.

He received no reply from either man.

"What is it?" he yelled again, the urgency in his voice snapping both Dickson and Rowe from their reverie.

"It's a man!" yelled Rowe. "It's Tom Thomson!"[6]

The name meant nothing to Howland. But a dead body floating less than five hundred yards from where both he and his daughter were vacationing was certainly a cause for alarm. The body had to be removed from its proximity to the island.

"Do you have a rope?" he yelled.

Rowe looked puzzled. "What do you want us to do with it?"

There was no way Howland wanted the corpse brought to the little island that he and (particularly) his daughter were presently occupying. He quickly scanned the horizon for the next nearest point of land from where the body was floating. An outcropping of shore, about five hundred and thirty-eight yards due south, would make do for the time being.

"Tie your rope around the body and tow it over to shore!"[7] Howland yelled, gesturing toward a point of land that would come in time to be called Gillender's Point, named after Hannah Gillender, from England, who would purchase the property in 1925 with her friend Annie Krantz from Philadelphia. But that was still eight years away; in 1917 the small point sat empty and was unnamed. The doctor then yelled to the men to leave the body in the water once they reached the shore, as removing it would only accelerate its rate of decomposition.

An apocryphal story that has endured throughout the years has it that when the doctor and his daughter had gone out onto the lake for a little fishing on the evening they had first arrived at Canoe Lake, Margaret had snagged her fishing line on something, and, after attempting to free her line to no avail, her father had simply cut it loose from the object it was snagged on, and the two had paddled back to the island. The object that the daughter was believed to have snagged her line on was later presumed to have been the body of Tom Thomson, as the body would be spotted the next day floating in and around the very location where she had caught her line the night before. This may be one of those rare occasions when an apocryphal story turns out to be true, as when my father asked Dr. Howland's daughter Margaret about this anecdote many years later she replied that this did indeed describe the situation as she remembered it.

Upon reaching Gillender's Point the guides paddled into an area that was sheltered by large stones and tree stumps. Quickly scanning the shoreline, they spotted a large tree that had toppled into the water from the shore, a portion of its trunk lay submerged in the water with some of its gnarled branches jutting upward into the air. One of these branches would suffice as a temporary hitching post of sorts, allowing the guides to release the end of the rope that had been tied into their canoe and secure it to the tree branch. The other end of the rope would remain firmly attached to Thomson's corpse, thus securing the already rather fragile body in the shallow waters. The guides knew without the doctor telling them that their next step would be to notify the authorities, which, in the Canoe Lake area, was the Algonquin Park Ranger Mark Robinson.

Robinson had been a park ranger since 1907, save for a brief absence in 1915-1916 when he had been overseas fighting in World War I. There he had been an officer with the rank of major, had been wounded, and subsequently discharged. In the spring of 1917 it was a considerably frailer Mark Robinson who found himself back in Algonquin Provincial Park. He was now fifty years old, still fit and capable, but the war and his injury had weakened him considerably. Nevertheless, Robinson had returned to his duties as if he had never been away, these included overseeing the influx of tourists that came and went by train at both the Canoe Lake and neighboring Joe Lake stations, as well as making specific rounds at various points throughout the park to check for poachers.

Robinson was a naturalist and an expert canoeist, and he and Thomson had developed a mutual respect over the past several years that they had known each other. Whenever the artist had a question about where to find a particular type of tree or what season a specific color would be predominant in the park, it was Robinson's council that he sought. And when Thomson had first been reported missing it was Robinson who had led the search parties to look for him. Thomson had been more than just a seasonal park resident to the ranger; he had been a friend and, consequently, breaking the news to him would not be something either of the guides was looking forward to.

The shoreline where the guides had beached their canoe and out from which Thomson's body had been moored, lay several hundred yards to the south of several cottages and Mowat Lodge, an inn for tourists that was located just off the northwestern shore of Canoe Lake. Word of the discovery had by this time travelled back to the lodge and, at some point, Charlie Scrim, a part-time guide who had been staying at the lodge and who had also been a friend of Thomson's, had either volunteered or had been dispatched to inform Mark Robinson of the morning's discovery. Further learning of the news that morning were the summer cottagers Martin Blecher Junior and his neighbor, Hugh Trainor, and shortly thereafter the pair had hopped into Blecher's motorboat and headed over to the point of land where the guides were now safeguarding the body.

After about a twenty-minute paddle north along Joe Creek, Charlie Scrim had reached the Joe Lake Dam. Here he pulled his canoe from the water and carried it on his shoulders along a short path that led to the Joe Lake Narrows, a small basin of water that lay just above the dam. He placed his canoe back into the water and made a beeline to Mark Robinson's cabin. The ranger's cabin was situated on the northeast corner of this small body of water and just south of the Grand Trunk Railway tracks, which ran atop the bank that separated the narrows from Joe Lake. When Scrim reached the ranger shelter house that was Mark Robinson's home he quickly beached his canoe and, without bothering to knock, charged into the ranger's cabin. Tears were streaming down his cheeks.

"They found Tom's body!" Scrim exclaimed.

"What?" Robinson asked, incredulously.

Scrim repeated his statement and then provided what details he knew about the morning's discovery. The ranger felt as if he had just been kicked in the stomach—hard. He had worked himself almost to the point of exhaustion over the past week, walking and canoeing all around the Canoe Lake region in the hope of locating the missing artist. The news from Scrim had, in an instant, revealed that his labor had been for naught.

Looking at the man now crying before him, Robinson would have noted a cruel irony, as the primary reason that Thomson had decided to stay on at Canoe Lake that summer had been out of concern for Scrim, who had not been well.

"I'm not going back to fire ranging," Thomson had told the ranger only a few months previously.

"Why Tom?" Robinson asked, as he had known that the artist had spent the previous summer fire ranging in Achray and, as far as he knew, the artist had enjoyed the experience.

"Well, Charlie's not long to be with us," Thomson had replied. Indeed, Scrim had long been suffering from tuberculosis and the prognosis was not encouraging. Thomson then added, "It's little as we can do to try to make his life as happy as can be, so I'm not going up north. I'm going to stay down here. I'll take out a guide's license to make him think that I'm not doing it on his account." Then the artist added, "I'll do all I can," and asked Robinson if he'd do likewise. The ranger replied that he would do what he could.[8] Thomson had feared that Scrim might not live out the summer, and so wanted to be around in order to spend what little time was left with his friend. In an unforeseen twist of fate, it would prove to be Thomson who would not live to see the fall.

Robinson shook the memory from his head and returned to business. He obtained what information he could from Scrim, and then made use of the phone service that interconnected the various ranger cabins throughout Algonquin Provincial Park with Park Headquarters. Within minutes, he was speaking with the park superintendent, George W. Bartlett. Bartlett was a respected man in the park, and not only for his sense of fairness and administrative abilities, but also for his toughness. There is an anecdote about Bartlett's capacity in the latter category that was related to the author by the former guide and trapper Ralph Bice:

There's a story about Bartlett that nobody much knows. He used to be a lumber scaler, and because he was so rough, so good at handling men, they sent him to the park. But one time, I think in Muskoka, over on the east or west side of Parry Sound, they were having trouble in the lumber camp. The men just wouldn't do what they were told, so they sent for Bartlett. His father had been a pugilist—a heavyweight—and Bartlett had decided that he was going to take the bunch on. And Bartlett said, "I need two men to keep them [the lumber men, rumored to be around thirty in number] off my back"—and the three of them cleaned up that lumber camp!

I heard this from my father, and the man that told my father was one of the men who was sent in to keep the men off Bartlett's back. He said he never saw such a thing in his life—he said they would run at Bartlett, and one poke here and one poke there, and the men were unconscious on the ground.[9]

In short, Bartlett was a man who was very much in charge, and he had the respect of all the park rangers under him, Mark Robinson being no exception. As the phone service within Algonquin Park only interconnected the various ranger cabins with Park Headquarters, any messages that needed to be sent either into or out of the park had to be sent via telegraph or letter, a circumstance that would prove to be an exceptional source of irritation to the Thomson family over the immediate days to come.

Bartlett instructed Robinson to handle the investigation of the Thomson case on behalf of the government. For his part, the superintendent indicated that he would immediately wire for the nearest coroner, who happened to be based out of North Bay, and would also telegraph the Crown County Attorney for any additional instructions.[10] Now tasked with his immediate duties, Robinson knew that he would need to view the body for himself in order to confirm to his satisfaction that it was indeed that of Thomson.

Nodding goodbye to Scrim, the ranger walked out from his cabin and down to the shoreline, where he eased his canoe into the water of the Joe Lake Narrows and began heading south. After carrying his canoe on his shoulders as he walked the short path around the Joe Lake Dam, he set it down within the waters of Joe Creek. Robinson was an accomplished canoeist and he made good time along the creek, finally coming out at the northern tip of Canoe Lake. From there he made his way over to the western shore, paddled past the small row of cottages and south past Statten's (Little Wapomeo) Island and finally over to the point of land where Thomson's body was presently floating in the shallows.

By the time he had beached his canoe a small crowd of people had already gathered on the shoreline. He looked out at where the corpse was floating and noticed that somebody had placed a blanket over its head and torso. This had been done for two reasons; first, to serve as a barricade of sorts between the body, which was now rapidly decomposing under the hot summer sun; and second, to attempt to quell the powerful stench that was now emanating from the corpse.

"Who covered the body?" the ranger asked.

"We did, Mark," replied Hugh Trainor, gesturing to himself and Martin Blecher Junior.[11]

The ranger knew most of the parties present quite well, having dealt with them in one manner or another for several years. Hugh Trainor had been the foreman of the now defunct Gilmour Lumber Company, a job that had required him to be almost as tough as Bartlett and, by some accounts, he was. Martin Blecher Junior was a twenty-five-year-old American cottager, who lived in Buffalo most of the year but had, for the last several years, spent his summers cottaging at Canoe Lake with his sister and parents. Robinson was also aware that there was some discord between the Blecher family and Thomson during the summers of 1914 and 1915; however he didn't know if the feud had continued during his absence for the War effort in 1916. The ranger was particularly familiar with the two old guides George Rowe and Hugh Lowrey Dickson, the latter of whom everybody referred to by his middle name of Lowrey. Both men were year-round residents on Canoe Lake and, when they were sober, were regularly employed for guiding and handiwork jobs at the various lodges and hotels in the area, particularly Mowat Lodge. All of these men were familiar to the ranger with the exception of Dr. Howland, who had joined the men on shore just prior to Robinson's arrival.

"Who first spotted the body?" asked Robinson.

"I did," Dr. Howland replied.

"And who are you?" Robinson asked.

Howland gave the ranger his name and occupation.

"At about what time did you first notice it?"

"I was sitting just at the front steps of the cabin over there and saw something rise in the water. It came up in a straight line from the island to this shore. It was about 9:00 a.m."[12] The ranger took down the information in a note pad, along with additional data on Dr. Howland, such as his address in the city. Robinson then looked across at Rowe and Dickson who were standing opposite him.

"Did either of you make an identification?"

"Yeah. We're both pretty sure it's Tom," said Rowe.

Robinson nodded grimly, and then looked out at the object that was half hidden beneath the blanket, bobbing with each passing wave. He knew what had to be done next—and he wasn't looking forward to it.

Robinson waded out from shore a short distance to where the body was anchored. He reached out and took a hold of a corner of the blanket and, after a deep breath, pulled it back to reveal the dead man's head and torso. He had seen death before—his memories of the war were still freshly imprinted on his mind—but he wasn't prepared for this. The skin was bluish gray; the eyes and tongue in the corpse would most likely have been protruding. The flesh had already begun to peel away from certain parts of the body, and its face, neck, and limbs were grotesquely swollen. Indeed, the seams of the gray woodsmen shirt that clothed the upper body of the corpse had been strained to capacity. Robinson knew the clothing, the hair color, and the general features of the body well enough to make a positive identification. A wave of stench from the decomposing flesh washed over him and he quickly threw the blanket back over the corpse. He'd seen enough.

"Do you recognize the man?" he heard Howland ask.

The ranger nodded without looking back at who had asked the question.

"Yes, it's Tom Thomson."[13]

During his search for the artist the previous week the ranger had been fueled by the belief that his friend would be found alive. But now both the week and that belief had passed. It was clear that Thomson was dead and wouldn't be coming back again. A thought briefly flashed through Robinson's mind that maybe he should have dragged the lake for the body, as the Mowat Lodge proprietor Shannon Fraser had suggested to him eight days previously when he had delivered the news that the artist's canoe had been found floating upside down in Canoe Lake.[14] Doing so would have saved everybody a lot of time and effort and it was now evident that the woods hadn't been where Thomson had disappeared to during his absence. Robinson knew by the level of decomposition that had already occurred that the body would have to be buried soon, but he also knew that before this could happen the coroner would need to arrive and examine the body. And, in the ranger's opinion, he couldn't get there fast enough.

Robinson made his way back to shore and rejoined the group. He knew that he would have to return to his cabin to await the coroner's arrival, which he anticipated occurring sometime later that evening. Although he hated leaving his friend's body, he knew that there wasn't anything more he could do about the situation and, looking out at the blanket that was undulating with the waves, he realized that it really didn't matter much to Tom Thomson at this point. Robinson instructed the guides to leave the body in the water until the coroner arrived. Better to leave Tom where he is, he thought, it will all be over soon enough.

The ranger informed the men that he would be back in touch with them soon and pushed his canoe out from shore to begin the long paddle back to his cabin. It must have seemed surreal to him: Tom Thomson, dead. Various moments from his interactions with the artist over the years must have come flooding back to him. There was that time five years previously when he had first set eyes on Thomson at Canoe Lake Station. The ranger had been on the lookout for poachers who were then in the habit of taking the train into the park under the pretense of being tourists, only to then cut out into the bush to ply their illegal trade of trapping animals. As Robinson had been observing the people milling about the platform on that particular day, a thirty-four-year-old Tom Thomson had stepped off the train. He was, in Robinson's words, "a tall, fine-looking young man with a packsack on his back." The packsack might have looked suspicious, indicative of a very brief stay. Most tourists who came into the park brought valises that contained a week's worth of clothing. Thomson, by contrast, was traveling very light indeed. As Robinson was observing the demeanor of the new arrival, one of the railway men from Canoe Lake Station approached him and, slyly gesturing toward Thomson, said, "There's your man."[15] Robinson nodded, and then approached the young man. Discreetly taking him aside, the ranger asked the artist some standard questions about what his business was in the park. It turned out that Thomson wasn't looking to poach furs, but rather for an affordable place to stay. The ranger would have smiled at that memory, and at the fact that only a day or so later he would again be approached, this time by the section foreman, Charlie Ruttan, who had cautioned him, "Look Mark, if I was you I'd keep my eye on that chap that come in the other night."

"Why, is there anything strange about him?" Robinson had asked.

"Well, he had three sticks stuck up, and a bit of board on it and he was dabbing bits of paint on it. I don't know what he was doing."

"Well," Robinson had asked, "is he an artist?"

"A what?"

"An artist."

"What kind of a thing is that?"

Robinson had attempted to explain to the foreman what an artist was, but to no avail.

"Well," Ruttan had replied, "I don't know what kind of a thing an artist is, but I'd watch him anyway."[16]

Thomson had never been understood here, thought the ranger. Indeed, four years after his first meeting with Robinson, the situation had apparently remained the same, causing the artist to write to his patron, Dr. James MacCallum: "The natives can't see what we paint for."[17]

Thomson had also been viewed with some measure of disapproval by the local guides, who—with good reason—had viewed the younger man as their chief competition for a limited quantity of summer and fall guiding jobs.[18] Thomson was certainly an attractive choice, at least compared to some of the guides. He was good looking and younger than most of his guiding rivals. He was also somewhat traveled, having lived in the United States for a brief period of time, he was articulate and musical (his instrument of choice being the mandolin), reasonably well-read and a talented landscape artist to boot. In addition, he was an excellent canoeist and seasoned fisherman. In short, for tourists, particularly from the United States, who were to spend several days in the company of a guide, he would have been a logical first choice as opposed to, say, someone who had never been out of Ontario and had little common ground to share with prospective clients. Yes, Thomson had certainly stood out from the local population, try as he might to have blended in.

And then there had been that time in 1915 when Robinson had invited a group of female schoolteachers from his hometown of Barrie to head north for a week in the park. They had stayed at Mowat Lodge and there they had met Thomson. One of the girls had asked the artist how he had kept his clothes clean when he was out camping and painting so much. Thomson smiled and replied that he simply removed his clothes, trailed them behind his canoe for a while and then dried them on a rock.[19] This caused the girls to blush. Later that same week Thomson had startled the women again with his radical ideas on freedom between the sexes. He told them that he didn't believe in double standards for men and women; that it should be the same for all. If, for example, a girl wished to smoke, she had as much right as a man to do so. All of the girls considered this to be progressively radical thinking at the time.[20]

Robinson arrived at the end of Joe Creek, lifted his canoe up and out of the water for the brief portage that circumnavigated the dam and then paddled the remaining distance to his cabin. The cabin itself had been a ranger stationhouse since 1911,[21] and its proximity to the Grand Trunk Railway line, Joe Lake Station, and the Algonquin Hotel provided quick and easy access to one of the main arteries of entrance and egress to the park. Many were the times that Thomson would paddle up Joe Creek to visit with the ranger in his cabin. He often would show Robinson his "boards," small paintings he had created while out in the wilds that he would later hope to work up into full canvases. The thought that those get togethers would never happen again served to break the ranger free from his sentimental thoughts. Robinson pulled his canoe up onto the shore in front of his cabin, and then straightened up, sighed, and stretched his arms in order to get some blood circulating into his hips and back. Although it was only early afternoon, it already seemed like it had been a long day. He slowly ambled up the short path to his cabin where he settled in to await the coroner's arrival on the evening train.

In the interim another Canoe Lake resident, the Mowat Lodge proprietor Shannon Fraser, had also learned of the news regarding Thomson's fate and decided that he should notify the artist's family of the tragic discovery made that morning. Apart from running Mowat Lodge, Fraser was also the postmaster for Canoe Lake. A tall man of strong Scottish stock, with bright red hair and a gift of the gab, Fraser, rather paradoxically for a man in the letter business, had never been particularly adept at writing. As a consequence, he hastily composed the following rather ambiguously worded telegram and sent it to the attention of Thomson's father, John Thomson:

> Canoe Lake, Ont.
> July 16, 1917
> J Thomson
> Owen Sound
> Found Tom this morning.
> —JS Fraser[22]

The Thomson family had been in a state of high anxiety for six days, ever since receiving a telegram from Fraser the previous Tuesday, July 10 informing them that Tom's canoe had been found floating upside down in Canoe Lake. They, like Robinson, had earnestly clung to the belief that he was alive, but perhaps injured somewhere in the woods around Canoe Lake, or marooned on one of its islands. Fraser's present telegram did little to quell their anxiety, and instead served to raise more questions than it answered.

The passage of time has left it unclear as to whether it was Fraser or Robinson who originally sent for the undertakers. While Robinson was certainly the man in charge of the Thomson affair, given that Fraser ran the post office at Canoe Lake and that an invoice for the undertakers' services was later sent to his attention, the directive might well have come from his hand. In any event, at approximately 8:00 p.m. on the evening of July 16, two undertakers—Robert Flavelle and Michael Roy Dixon, from the nearby towns of Kearney and Sprucedale, respectively—had arrived in the park by train, bringing with them a hardwood coffin and rough box. Dixon had been trained as an embalmer, and it was likely that he had been the one to contact Flavelle, who was a furniture dealer by trade, but who also sold caskets and served as the local undertaker for the Almaguin Highlands region of the province. Dixon also happened to be Mark Robinson's cousin[23] and, thus, a family connection of sorts existed that was probably, if not largely, the reason why he had been contacted for the job. According to Dixon:

> When I arrived at Joe Lake Station I was met by Mark Robinson, ranger. His first question was, "Is the coroner from North Bay on the train?" He was not and I informed him I could do nothing without a death certificate.[24]

Without a coroner, and without a death certificate, there could be no action taken by the undertakers that evening, which meant that Thomson's body would have to remain in the water overnight. It was decided that the undertakers would stay the night in the hope that the coroner would be arriving on the morning train. Dixon chose to stay with his cousin Mark Robinson[25] at the ranger's cabin, while Flavelle opted to rent a room at one of the local lodges.

Meanwhile, back on the shoreline, Rowe and Dickson had also received the news that the coroner had been absent on the evening train. Not wanting to leave Thomson's body unattended, the two guides decided to spend the night watching over it. They lit a fire and slept that evening by the shore, which could not have been pleasant with the calm of the summer's night interrupted by the sound of Thomson's corpse scrubbing up against the branches of the tree it was tethered to with each passing wave.

Chapter Two

THE BODY IS EXAMINED AND BURIED

The guides were awakened early the next morning by the sound of voices and the familiar dissonance of a canoe being dragged up over a rocky shore. Wiping the sleep from their eyes, the two men looked up to see Mark Robinson and the two undertakers now standing next to them. They further noticed that a casket and rough box had also made the trip to their campsite.

The ranger had brought some bad news however; the morning train had come and gone and the coroner from North Bay had not been on it. The coroner's absence had not been well received by Robinson, as the strong odor of decay that was now emanating from Thomson's body was making it obvious that an immediate burial was now a matter of some urgency—flies were beginning to gather on the corpse.[1] According to Rose Thomas, whose parents Edwin and Emily Thomas ran the Canoe Lake Train Station, word had already circulated that, "He was so decomposed that . . . they just had to do something about it. He had a lot of black hair, and they said there was just a little black tuft of it [left] because he was so badly decomposed."[2] Another day of keeping the body tethered to the limb of a tree while the hot summer sun, the flies, the maggots, and the water combined to strip it, hour by hour, of any semblance to something human, was proving more than the ranger's conscience could abide. Besides, the body still needed to be examined, and the longer this was put off, the less likely any evidence as to the cause of the artist's death would be discovered.

When it was discovered that the coroner had failed to show that morning, Shannon Fraser made one last attempt to contact the Thomson family to find out what they wanted done with the artist's body. He sent out a telegram, this time to Thomson's brother-in-law, Tom Harkness:

> Canoe Lake via Algonquin Park,
> Ont. July 17, 1917
> T.J. Harkness, Owen Sound
> Tom Thomson drowned in Canoe Lake. Wire immediately
>   what to do.
> —J.S. Fraser[3]

In the event that the first telegram missed its mark, a second one, sent by A.E. Needham, was sent to the attention of Thomson's older brother George:

> Algonquin Park, Ont. July 17, 1917
> George Thomson
> Owen Sound
> Tom Thomson drowned in Canoe Lake.
> Body found. Now awaiting burial there.
> —A.E. Needham[4]

The fact that these telegrams have survived indicates that the Thomson family had received them, but given their shock at the news, the absence of a direct telephone service into the park, and the speed with which things were now proceeding at Canoe Lake, it is clear that there was a delay in their reply. Consequently, once it was clear that the coroner had not been on the train that had pulled out from

Joe Lake Station on the morning of July 17 Mark Robinson was faced with a difficult decision to make; should he sit and wait, thus permitting his late friend's body to continue to decompose in the waters of Canoe Lake until the coroner eventually arrived and/or the Thomson family got in touch with him, or should he act upon the recommendation of both the undertakers and Dr. Howland and move to bury the body immediately?

Not wanting to overstep his authority on such a sensitive matter, Robinson sought council from Superintendent Bartlett. Placing a call from his cabin, the ranger informed his superior of the coroner's absence on the morning train, the condition of Thomson's body, and also what the doctor and the undertakers had advised in support of an immediate burial. But Robinson had his own more poignant reasons for wanting Thomson buried sooner rather than later.

"Look, Mr. Bartlett, Thomson was my friend," Robinson began, "and I hate to think of him lying there. It's not right."

To his surprise the gruff former lumberman was sympathetic to his plight.

"I agree with you," Bartlett replied, however the superintendent didn't have an alternative. It would be impossible to bury the body without a death certificate, and only a coroner could issue such a document.

The ranger continued to press his case gently but firmly, reminding Bartlett that his position of superintendent carried with it certain other capacities and powers, one of which made him the *ex-officio* coroner for the park. Consequently, all that the ranger required was the superintendent's sanction and Thomson could be buried that very afternoon.

"There are two undertakers here," explained Robinson. "They have a coffin and a case for a coffin, and we can take his body out and do the best we can with it anyway."

Bartlett thought the matter over. After all, he wanted the matter resolved as quickly as the ranger did. Finally, he issued his directive: "You go right down, take that body out of the water, and have the undertakers fix it up as well as they can and then have it buried over in the little cemetery."[5]

The little cemetery to which he referred was an unofficial graveyard that lay on a hillock that was set back a fair distance behind Mowat Lodge. Headstones marked but two graves within the cemetery; one was that of a mill hand, James Watson, originally from Parry Sound, who had died in 1897 (he had been killed at the Gilmour lumber mill on his first day at work), while the other grave belonged to a young boy, Alexander Hayhurst, who had been buried in 1905 at the age of eight years, a victim of diphtheria. And now, with Bartlett's decree, Tom Thomson's grave would be the third. But before any burial could take place, Bartlett would have to sign an official death certificate. According to Dixon:

> [Robinson] got in touch with Mr. Bartlett, the superintendent of the park, and he sent over a certificate of accidental death by drowning. As superintendent, he said, he was *ex-officio* a coroner.[6]

Bartlett signed the certificate of death, which despite his never having viewed the body, cited the cause of Thomson's death as "accidental death by drowning." The body had been found in the water, after all, and so it was highly probable that the artist had met with an accident while on the water and had drowned. For the moment, determining exactly how Thomson had met his end was not Robinson's priority; he believed, being the good Anglican that he was, that his first obligation to his late friend was to ensure that he was given a proper Christian burial. And, now armed with the death certificate signed by his superior, Robinson possessed the full authority to carry this out. Unless he heard otherwise from the Thomson family over the next several hours, it was his intention to have this done as quickly as possible.

Despite the superintendent's in absentia declaration that Thomson had died accidentally from drowning, as Robinson stood on the Canoe Lake shoreline that morning he decided that he wanted Thomson's corpse to be inspected for any signs of foul play prior to turning it over to the undertakers for interment. As Dr. Howland, the man who had first spotted the body, also happened to be a trained medical man, it suggested to the ranger that he would be the obvious choice to perform such an examination.[7] The fact that Howland wasn't trained as a coroner did not pose a problem to Robinson's way of thinking. The plan now was to examine Thomson's body, embalm it, and then bury it that afternoon.

After conferring with the doctor and the undertakers, it was decided that more work space was required than what was afforded them on the narrow shoreline at Gillender's Point, and so the decision was made to transport Thomson's body directly east across the water to the northwest corner of Wapomeo Island, which would provide both the necessary space and privacy for what was to follow. "We came over, took the body, [and] we brought it over here across from Gillender's Point, around onto the point of Big Wapomeo," recalled Robinson.[8] Dixon also recollected that, "we brought the body to the island and [there] proceeded to embalm it."[9]

Once the body had been safely delivered to Wapomeo Island, the two guides, together with the undertakers, assisted the ranger in removing Thomson's corpse from the water. Robinson had secured two timber planks, which he had placed across some reasonably level rocks on the shore of the island and, once the body was removed from the water, it was laid upon the wooden slats.[10] The body had become so badly decomposed that the slightest touch on one of its many blisters would have caused the skin to fall off, and attempting to lift it from the water solely by its limbs might well have resulted in the limbs detaching from the corpse. Instead, the undertakers fitted a canvas shroud beneath the body and then, with four men each taking hold of a corner of the shroud, they gently lifted it up out of the water and placed it upon the two planks that Robinson had provided.[11] The ranger then gave the okay for Howland to step in and begin the post mortem.

In order for the doctor to adequately inspect the body, its clothing had to be removed and, once this had been done, Howland recorded the following notes, which would later be entered into evidence during the coroner's inquest:

- A man aged about forty years.
- In advanced state of decomposition.
- Face, abdomen and limbs swollen.
- Blisters on limbs.
- A bruise on right temple, size of 4" long.
- No other sign of external marks visible on body.
- Air issuing from mouth.
- Some bleeding from right ear.[12]

Mark Robinson's diary entry for this day supported the doctor's analysis, with the exception of the location of the bruise on the temple:

Tuesday, July 17: Dr. Howland examined body at my request. We found a bruise on left temple about four inches long. Evidently caused by falling on a rock. Otherwise no marks of violence on body.[13]

Howland and the undertakers then proceeded to determine if there was any water in the lungs of the corpse and, according to

Robinson, "there was no water in the lungs."[14] It was at this point that the ranger made an additional observation that would disturb him for the rest of his life:

> Around the [body's] left ankle there was a fishing line wrapped 16 or 17 times. . . . And Roy Dixon asked me if I had a sharp knife, and when I said I had, he said, "Will you just remove those strings?" And I did, and I counted them—that's why I know there was 16 or 17. I have it in my diary or notebook just exactly how many there were. I let them drop down, while at the time Dr. Howland and the undertakers were probing to find if there was water in the lungs . . . but across the left temple there was a mark, it looked as if he had been struck with the edge of a paddle, just up across the left temple.[15]

In an interview Robinson would later grant to the author Audrey Saunders in 1944, he indicated that the line that he had removed from Thomson's leg was a cotton fishing line, and that it totaled fifteen feet in length. After cutting it free, Robinson reported that he gathered it up and burned it along with other debris from that morning.[16] The undertaker Roy Dixon confirmed the existence of the fishing line in a newspaper interview in 1956:

> There was a fishing line wrapped around his legs. The fish line was ordinary cord line and it certainly was not knotted or tied. It was scrambled around his legs in a haphazard fashion.[17]

Robinson disagreed with Dixon's recollection on this point:

> This [fishing line] was wrapped on as carefully, right around and around and around. Now that wasn't tangled up all

over—there's a report that his legs were tangled up in a fishing line—that's not so.[18]

If the line around Thomson's ankle was indeed a cotton or cord one, then it was what is known as a "twisted" or "braided" line or hand line—which is not at all like the thin nylon lines we're more commonly used to seeing for fishing in modern times. In fact, such a line is more like a small rope. According to the sales literature that comes with such lines:

> Braided fishing line is made up of many thin fibers woven into a very strong fishing line . . . braided lines are very abrasion resistant, some manufacturers claim up to 15x (yes, fifteen times) the abrasion resistance of steel wire! This is very important when fishing on rocky terrains where there are various sharp objects that can snap nylon line easily.[19]

Why would there be corded line around Thomson's left ankle? The ranger was nonplussed. Moreover, Robinson had fished with Thomson in the recent past and he didn't recognize the line as being one that Thomson owned.[20] Still, as Dr. Howland had now finished his examination and the undertakers were standing by, this wasn't really the time to interrupt the proceedings with additional inquiries that would only postpone what now needed to be done.

As Howland stepped away from the body, Dixon and Flavelle were given the nod to proceed with the task of getting Thomson's body ready for the grave. They began their rather challenging task by washing down the corpse. This was done primarily in the belief at the time that doing so would keep the men safe from any bacteria that might be present on the decomposing flesh. As rigor mortis would have been absent from the body after thirty-six hours, and as Thomson had presumably been dead for several days at this point, there existed no reason for them to massage or manipulate the limbs in an effort to return joint laxity to the corpse. However, something had to be done about the severe bloat of the body, otherwise it would never have been able to fit within the constraints of the casket. To remedy this situation, the undertakers moved to aspirate the internal organs of the body and to infuse it with embalming fluid. As this was Dixon's specialty, he quickly set about his task by first cutting an incision into the right carotid artery and right jugular vein of the corpse and then injecting the artery with embalming fluid. This resulted in an expulsion of congealed blood and interstitial fluid from the jugular vein. At this point he would have administered a formaldehyde-based fluid via a gravity pump, i.e., by holding the bottle of embalming fluid higher than the hose leading out of it so that gravity would deliver the bottle's (or in Thomson's case, the bottles') contents into the corpse. Dixon may well have used more than one injection point on the body, given the level of decomposition present, in which case the axillary, brachial and femoral arteries, along with the ulnar radial and tibial vessels, would also have been opened.

The embalming fluid having thusly been administered, the undertakers continued their efforts to reduce the extreme swelling of the corpse. This was accomplished by making a small incision two inches above and two inches to the right of the navel, and then inserting a trocar (a three-edged cutting/draining tool) into the stomach and chest cavities in order to puncture the hollow organs and aspirate their contents of gas and fluid. The abdominal incision would normally have been closed via sutures, but given the fragile condition of the flesh on the corpse, any attempt at suturing would have proven fruitless, and so the puncture points on the body would have been left as they were.

The undertakers' efforts had been a success as Thomson's corpse had now returned to more-or-less normal dimensions. As its level of decomposition had negated the option of a viewing, there existed no need to reclothe the corpse. And so Flavelle and Dixon simply proceeded to wrap the body in the same canvas shroud in which it had been lifted from the water and fitted the shrouded body into the casket.[21] With the most unpleasant part of the task now behind them, the men closed the casket lid and transferred the coffin onto a small barge that would normally have been deployed to transport work materials and supplies to the various islands on the lake.[22] With the casket now aboard, the barge began its trek across the water to a landing point next to the Blecher cottage that was used by most of the cottagers on the lake, as well as Mowat Lodge.

By the time the barge reached its destination and pulled in alongside the small dock, Hugh Trainor's daughter Winnifred, who was beside herself with grief, had already ventured from her cottage and stood prepared to meet the watercraft. Winnifred, according to various sources, had been either one of the artist's girlfriends or his fiancée. A.Y. Jackson, who had been one of Thomson's closer friends in the art world, would share with my father that Thomson had in fact been engaged to Trainor, and that Thomson had even booked a cabin for two weeks that forthcoming August at Bella Lake Lodge (now Billie Bear Lodge), a small campground situated just outside of Huntsville, for their honeymoon. At this point in the narrative, however, the exact nature of the couple's relationship is irrelevant, apart from the fact that Miss Trainor evidently felt a sense of claim over the late artist. According to Charles Plewman, who had been a guest at Mowat Lodge during this time:

> Miss Winnie Trainor, Tom's girlfriend from Huntsville, whose parents had a cottage on Canoe Lake in front of the lodge, appeared on the scene and demanded the right to see the remains, saying that there must have been foul play, as she was certain that Tom didn't drown by accident in a small lake like Canoe Lake. This, Mark Robinson stoutly refused

to grant (The body had been in the lake about eight days and was not very presentable).[23]

After turning away Miss Trainor, Robinson and the undertakers removed the casket from the barge and placed it upon a buckboard that had been brought down to the shoreline by Shannon Fraser. The wagon had been hitched up to two horses and, with the coffin now aboard, Fraser turned the wagon around and headed back to Mowat Lodge. In the interim, Rowe and Dickson had been dispatched to dig a fresh grave at the little cemetery.[24]

All things considered, Robinson had done a respectable job in organizing the *ad hoc* funeral on such short notice and, over the next hour or so, a small group of people began to gather in front of the lodge to prepare for what would be a small, but dignified, country funeral. Once all the attendees had assembled, Fraser gave a slight snap on the horses' reins, which started the wagon rolling its way along a narrow dirt road that led toward the little cemetery. The cortege fell in behind.

Those known to have been in attendance that day included Mark Robinson, Shannon Fraser and his wife, Annie, of Mowat Lodge, Hugh Trainor and his wife, Margaret, along with their daughter Winnifred, Mr. and Mrs. Ed Colson, who ran the Algonquin Hotel that Thomson used to frequent, the guides George Rowe, Lowery Dickson and Charlie Scrim, Mr. Charles Plewman of Toronto, and Martin Blecher Junior, along with his sister Bessie, and their parents, Louisa and Martin Martin Blecher Senior, the latter being assigned to act as lay minister over the proceedings.

The buckboard eventually came to a stop at the foot of a gentle slope where Fraser, with the assistance of three other men, lifted Thomson's casket from the floor of the hearse and up onto their collective shoulders. Slowly the procession made its way along a pathway that led to the freshly dug grave. Once at the gravesite

Mark Robinson handed Martin Blecher Senior his copy of the *Anglican Book of Common Prayer*,[25] from which the cottager began to read Psalm 203.13-17, which concludes:

> For as much as it hath pleased Almighty God of his great mercy to take unto himself the soul of our dear brother here departed, we therefore commit his body to the ground; earth to earth, ashes to ashes, dust to dust; in sure and certain hope of the Resurrection to eternal life, through our Lord Jesus Christ; who shall change the body of our low estate, that it may be like unto his glorious body, according to the mighty working, whereby he is able to subdue all things to himself.

Plewman would later recall Thomson's burial as being "a sad and forlorn affair,"[26] with the gloomy weather only adding to the dark emotions that colored the day. According to Plewman:

> The sky was overcast and the rain was falling. It had all the earmarks of a backwoods funeral. . . . The group that huddled around the graveyard was small, something like 12 or 13. No one from his immediate family was present, nor were any of the pals with whom he had painted. As for a minister there was none. The Stattens, whose cabin was nearby, were absent, apparently away, and unaware that the funeral was taking place, as were, I imagine, his other friends. Mark Robinson, the park ranger, appeared to be in charge. On the surface it looked as if he had not been in touch with the family since locating the body or had received any instructions on what to do with the remains. I have since been told that there was a delay in reaching the family.[27]

At the conclusion of the impromptu service, Thomson's casket was lowered into the ground and the mourners dispersed, save for the two guides, George Rowe and Lowrey Dickson, who remained behind to fill in the grave. Nothing about the service that day gave any indication that they were burying a national icon. Indeed, according to Charles Plewman, "From what I had witnessed that day, he might as well have been Algonquin Park's 'Unknown Man.'"[28]

Chapter Three

THE INQUEST

When the funeral service concluded, Shannon Fraser retraced his way along the cemetery path back to his wagon. As he walked, any sense of sadness that he might have experienced during the service gradually began to give way to anger.

Not one member of the Thomson family had seen fit to attend their family member's funeral. For that matter, not one of them had even bothered to answer either of his telegrams over the past week. And then there was the fact that he had personally spent money out of his own pocket when the artist had first been reported missing, paying the guides George Rowe and Lowrey Dickson to assist with the search. Thomson's family, by contrast, had done nothing.

And while Thomson may have been somewhat of a black sheep to his family—after all none of his family members had ever seen fit to visit him in the park during the past several years that the artist had been coming there to paint—Fraser nonetheless had held out hope that the Thomson family might at the very least have responded to his telegrams. Perhaps more importantly from the lodge owner's perspective, he had allowed himself to entertain the hope that the artist's family might even have offered to compensate him for his out of pocket expenses in doing what he could to try and find their missing relative. Repayment was important to Fraser as, with the war on, not as many tourists were heading north that summer, which made predictable income anything but, and he still had bills to pay. And then there was the fact that his brochures for the lodge had indicated that it was "a family resort," with "2,000 lakes and streams." Once word got out that one of these lakes was now spitting up dead bodies out of its depths it would certainly put the kybosh to those looking to get away from the city for a little family recreation. All in all, the past two weeks had not been good ones for the harried lodge owner. The rain was still falling, which only served to darken his mood further.

Once he had returned to his buckboard, Shannon helped his wife up and into the wagon, before climbing up and sitting down on the wet front seat next to her. He slowly turned the wagon round and once again snapped the reins to get the horses moving in the direction of Mowat Lodge. As the buckboard rolled along the muddy road that led back to the lodge, the idea came to Fraser that he should give the Thomson family a piece of his mind. Nothing nasty, mind you; after all, everybody grieves in his or her own way and, of course, there certainly would be no repayment of expenses if he pissed them off. Nevertheless, he was going to at least make them aware of what he and the locals had had to endure over this ordeal in their absence.

Briefly bringing the wagon to a stop at the front of the lodge and helping Annie down, Fraser then climbed back aboard, took up the reins and started the horses moving forward toward a hill that lay a little further south. His destination now was the Canoe Lake post office. Fraser knew it well, as the building had once been "Camp Mowat," the predecessor of Mowat Lodge. Prior to that, the building had served as the hospital for the now defunct Gilmour Lumber Company, and it had also been the Fraser family's home when they had first arrived in Algonquin Park.

The Frasers had moved to the park in 1907 from Kingston, Ontario and were an extended family consisting of Shannon, his wife Annie, their three-year old daughter Mildred, Shannon's mother Anne, and Annie's father Joseph Stewart. Fraser had taken over as

Canoe Lake postmaster from Robert Galna in 1908, and it was a job that held considerable appeal to him. Fraser was gregarious by nature, and his duties as postmaster allowed him to make two trips a day to the Canoe Lake Train Station to pick up and deliver mail, and, of course, hobnob with any tourists who stepped off the train. This latter perk was important to him, as it provided him with an opportunity to let all interested parties know that reasonably priced accommodations were available at his lodge. In fact, it had been during one such stop at Canoe Lake Station in 1912 that Fraser had first met Tom Thomson. Mark Robinson had been present on that day and, indeed, had been the one to make the introductions between the artist and the lodge owner.

"I would like to find a place to stay, where I could get a good bed and good eats," Thomson had said.

"Well, the Algonquin Hotel is a short distance away," replied the ranger, gesturing along the railroad tracks leading east. "That's about a quarter of a mile away. And there's also Mowat Lodge, about a mile and a half distance. It's run by a man by the name of Fraser, and they provide good meals and excellent beds."

"I think that's the place for me," the artist had replied. "How far away did you say?"

"Mile and a half."

The ranger looked over and noticed that Shannon Fraser was now standing on the train platform a short distance away from where he and Thomson were talking.

"Mr. Fraser's right here—I will introduce him to you."

Robinson motioned for the lodge owner to come over to where he and Thomson were standing and relayed the artist's desire to seek accommodation in the area.

Fraser looked Thomson up and down before stating, "Well, I think we can make room for you. We're pretty well filled but we'll try and provide some room for you some place."

According to Robinson, Mowat Lodge was far from full that day, having only two guests, but such was Fraser's way. Thomson thanked the lodge owner and threw his backpack into Fraser's buckboard. The pair then headed south along the old country road toward Mowat Lodge.[1]

By 1913, the number of tourists who were coming into Algonquin Park looking for accommodation had increased, and the enterprising Fraser had quickly concluded that more money could be made if he had more rooms to rent. As a result, he arranged to take possession of a pair of bunkhouses that sat on the old Gilmour Lumber property that were situated just down the hill from his home.

The bunkhouses had been left over from a time when the lumber company had been a going concern at Canoe Lake, but that was now enough years in the past to be nothing but a memory. While the Frasers had done a little bit of work on the bunkhouses, there really wasn't much to the lodge. The ground floor of one of the buildings was converted into a long living room, the floors of both bunkhouses were then painted, and the large living room was furnished with leather chairs and padded loveseats. All of the guestrooms were situated on the second floor, and the lodge was heated primarily by box stoves, along with one small fireplace.[2] By 1916, Fraser had added a coat of whitewash to the buildings and connected the two bunkhouses together by building a verandah between them and—voila!—Mowat Lodge was born.

While the lodge had a certain rustic charm, not all of the guests felt that it was the "resort" that Fraser's advertising and letterhead had led them to believe. Jack Wilkinson, who lived in the area at the time, recollected that:

> Well old Shannon, you know, he used to build it up quite a lot . . . They'd all get down there expecting to see the Chateau Laurier. They would get in there and see an old

converted lumber camp. They were kind of put off a little bit, you know.[3]

Nevertheless, Fraser enjoyed operating the much larger lodge (the two buildings joined together had a combined length of 170 feet) and his gregarious nature, along with his wife Annie's considerable culinary skills, quickly endeared the pair not only to their lodge guests, but also to quite a few of the locals, as the Frasers would often sell meals to cottagers in addition to their guests.

For many years after having moved his family into the lodge proper, Fraser had continued to use his family's former home as the post office for the Canoe Lake community. And after the horses had pulled up to his former homestead on this day, Fraser stepped down from the wagon and walked up the short path and into the building. Upon entering he quickly set pen to paper to write a missive to Tom Thomson's father. He kept it brief and to the point, but made sure that it contained little comfort for the Thomson family patriarch:

Mowat, P.O., Ontario
Mr John Thomson, Owen Sound

Dear Sir:
We found your son floating in Canoe Lake on Monday morning about nine o'clock in a most dreadful condition. The flesh was coming off his hands. I sent for the undertaker and they found him in such a condition . . . he had to be buried at once. He is buried in a little graveyard overlooking Canoe Lake, a beautiful spot. The Dr. found a bruise over his eye and thinks he fell and was hurt and this is how the accident happened.

Yours Truly,
J. S. Fraser[4]

Now satisfied that he had not-so-subtly reminded the family that he was their man in the park for information on this matter, Fraser stamped the letter and placed it within his coat pocket and then walked back outside to the buckboard. With a tug on the reins the two horses turned and followed what by now was a familiar road heading east from Mowat Lodge and then north along another road that led to the Canoe Lake Train Station. Once there, Fraser delivered his letter in amongst whatever other mail happened to be heading out from Canoe Lake that afternoon.

In the meantime, Mark Robinson had returned to his cabin. He hadn't been there long when he received a call from Superintendent Bartlett indicating that the coroner from North Bay would—finally—be arriving later that night on the evening train.[5] Robinson would have had mixed emotions upon receiving this news; on the one hand, the coroner's arrival would bring an official end to the whole affair that had been consuming him so much over the past eight days; but on the other hand, the body had already been buried, so how significant could the result of such an inquest be? He was soon to find out.

The coroner had boarded the train leaving North Bay at 2:10 p.m. that afternoon (Tuesday, July 17) for Algonquin Park.[6] The hours ticked by until dusk. It was a little before 8:00 p.m.[7] when Robinson heard the familiar sound of the train whistle blowing from about a mile away, which prompted him to exit his cabin and make his way the short distance along the tracks to Joe Lake Station. As the locomotive slowly eased its way to a stop, Robinson watched as the tourists stepped down from the passenger cars, looking to see who among them could be the man that he needed to connect with. Finally, Dr. Arthur E. Ranney stepped off the train. Ranney was a stout, powerfully built man with a full goatee and dark piercing eyes; it would not have taken Robinson long to pick him out from amongst the other passengers that evening. The ranger stepped forward from the crowd and introduced himself.

"We'd been expecting you last night," Robinson said.

Ranney seemed genuinely surprised by the statement and explained that he had wired the day before with his intentions to arrive Tuesday evening.[8] The two men chatted briefly before walking the short distance to Robinson's cabin where the coroner was invited to spend the night. After providing Ranney with what he knew to be the details of the case, Robinson suggested that the pair should stop in at the nearby Algonquin Hotel, where Ranney could interview Edwin and Molly Colson, two people who had met with Thomson on the last day of his life. Ranney agreed with Robinson's suggestion and the two men then left the cabin and made their way back over the tracks to the hotel.

The Algonquin Hotel sat atop a small hill that was situated just behind the Joe Lake Train Station, making it one of the first stops on the Grand Trunk Railway line that brought passengers into Algonquin Park from the east or west. There was a short path that led from the back of the train station directly up to the hotel, which made it convenient for guests from the city to travel in comfort virtually to the hotel's front door. The Algonquin Hotel was a little on the rustic side, but it had twenty rooms and three bathrooms, and also featured two large screened-in porches that delighted its guests. While it was not as upscale as the Highland Inn on nearby Cache Lake, it was still a considerable step up from Mowat Lodge.

As the ranger and coroner entered the hotel they were greeted by the Colsons, who then invited them into the dining area where tea was served. Edwin had been a park ranger prior to getting into the hotel business, which had always made it easy for Robinson to relate to him. Molly had originally been trained as a nurse, and had served the Canoe Lake community for many years in that capacity, first as the local mid-wife, and later in the role of community doctor. She had married Edwin in 1907, the same year that the Frasers had moved to the park, and the two had for a time taken over the management of the Highland Inn on Cache Lake near where Superintendent Bartlett was headquartered. The spring of 1917 proved to be a momentous one in the Colson's lives, however, as they had just purchased the Algonquin Hotel, and had also opened up an outfitting store just down from the hotel that sold supplies to anyone who sought to camp and canoe within the park.

Both Ranney and Robinson listened to what the Colsons had to say regarding their interaction with the artist on the day that he went missing.[9] Their testimony had been brief, as they had only spoken with Thomson for a short time that morning. Glancing at his pocket watch, Ranney noted that it was now after 10:00 p.m., and announced that he needed to start the official proceedings as there were more people to be interviewed and it was his intention to wrap the whole matter up that evening so that he could return to North Bay first thing in the morning.

As the coroner had not eaten prior to getting on the train that day, he was no doubt delighted to learn that a large dinner was awaiting him at the Blecher cottage at Canoe Lake. And since he would be coming to their cottage to eat, the Blecher family had also kindly offered the coroner the further use of their cottage to host the inquest. Both offers were welcomed by Dr. Ranney, and it was quickly decided that both he and Robinson would depart for the Blecher cottage immediately, have dinner, and then take the Blechers up on their generous offer to make use of their cottage for the inquest, which was centrally located for the majority of the people who would be called upon to provide testimony. During his discussion with Robinson, the coroner was surprised to learn that there would be no corpse for him to inspect that evening, and, indeed, that Thomson's body had already been embalmed and buried earlier that afternoon, but he was nonetheless confident that this would not present a problem and that the inquest could and should proceed.

"Mr. Blecher provided a first-class dinner," Robinson would later recall, "and everything went on swimmingly as far as that part was concerned."[10] After the repast, the ranger then set to work rounding up those individuals whom he considered to have been the most knowledgeable regarding Thomson's final hours. Toward this end he had collected Dr. Howland, who had first spotted the body and who had examined it at the island; Martin Blecher Junior, who, along with his sister Bessie Blecher, had been the first to spot Thomson's overturned canoe shortly after the artist had gone missing; Shannon Fraser, who was believed to be the last person to have spent time with Thomson on the morning of his disappearance; and Hugh Trainor, who owned the cottage just next door to the Blechers, and whose family had known the artist well. Just as the inquest was about to commence, Robinson realized that the guide George Rowe was absent. As Rowe had been one of the two guides who had retrieved Thomson's body from the lake, his presence would be required. Robinson quickly set out to collect him and the pair then returned to the Blecher cottage. Surprisingly, Lowrey Dickson, the other guide involved in the retrieval of Thomson's body, was omitted from the gathering that evening.[11] And while it is not indicated in any of the surviving correspondence, it is presumable that Martin Blecher Senior and his wife Louisa would have been present at the inquest as well, as it was their cottage that played host to the event.

When word eventually trickled out about the choice of venue for the inquest, there was grumbling within certain factions of the Canoe Lake community.[12] To these people, the Blecher cottage seemed a highly inappropriate locale for the inquest to take place, as it had been known throughout the community that the Blechers had held no affection for the artist. Moreover, there existed the possibility that holding such an event within the walls of their cottage, with all members of the Blecher family present, might well serve to influence the proceedings somewhat. George Rowe, for example, had been present during a heated argument that had transpired between Thomson and Martin Junior the night before the artist went missing, but it would be uncomfortable presenting this recollection within the cottage and in the presence of Martin Junior and his family. Recounting this incident might well have been interpreted as suggesting that the young man had something to do with the artist's death, for which there was absolutely no evidence. Moreover, Rowe was smart enough to realize that bringing this matter up might well lead to the opening of a line of inquiry that would have revealed the quantity of drinking that went on within the old guide's cabin that evening—and this was definitely not something that Rowe (or Dickson or Fraser) would have wanted brought to the attention of a government official such as Dr. Ranney during a period of enforced prohibition. Besides, Rowe was savvy enough to understand that the coroner was the professional in such matters, and, consequently, he would be the one to decide what happened to Thomson. A guide's opinion on such a sensitive medical matter was irrelevant. Any grumbling about either the venue for the inquest or its ultimate conclusion would come much later. For the moment, the inquest was taking place at the Blecher cottage, and it got underway at midnight.[13]

As Dr. Ranney had never had the opportunity to inspect Thomson's corpse, he solicited Dr. Howland's opinion regarding how it presented upon examination.[14] As Howland was a trained medical man, his testimony assumed a position of preeminence during the inquest. He presented it in the form of the following sworn statement:

Canoe Lake

July 17-17

Dr. G.W. Howland qualified medical practitioner of Toronto,
 Ont. Sworn,

Said:

I saw body of a man floating in Canoe Lake Monday, July 16th,
at about 10 A.M., and notified Mr. George Rowe, a resident, who
removed the body to shore. On 17th, Tuesday, I examined the
body and found it to be that of a man aged about 40 years in
advanced state of decomposition, face, abdomen and limbs swollen,
blisters on limbs, there was a bruise on right temple size of 4" long,
no other sign of external marks visible on body, air issuing from
mouth, some bleeding from right ear, cause of death drowning.

(Sgd). Gordon W. Howland,
M.R.N.A.C.P.[15]

The doctor's sworn statement would prove controversial many years
later when, in 1931, the author Blodwen Davies would reach out
to Dr. Ranney requesting information regarding the content of his
official report on the Thomson case. To her surprise, and to this
day, no such report has ever been found within the public records at
North Bay or Queen's Park. Nevertheless, Ranney did claim to still
have in his possession his notes from the night of the inquest, and
these he provided to Miss Davies:

Dear Miss Davies,

Received your letter asking for information from standpoint
of coroner. This occurred in 1917, 14 years ago, and naturally
you must admit the circumstances are not fresh in my memory
but, upon looking up my notes, I am able to give you the
information you require.

The body was in such a state of decomposition when found that it had to be buried as quickly as possible. The body was thoroughly examined by Dr. G. W. Howland, qualified medical practitioner of Toronto, before inquest, who gave me a full description of the condition of the body; there was only one bruise on the right side of head, temple region, about 4 inches long, this, no doubt, was caused by striking some obstacle, like a stone, when the body was drowned. Dr. Howland swore that death was caused from drowning, also the evidence from the other six witnesses points that the cause of death was drowning. Those who were present at the inquest were as follows: Dr. G.W. Howland, Miss Bessie Blecher, Mr. J.E. Colson, Proprietor Algonquin Park Hotel, Mr. J.S. Fraser, Proprietor Mowat Lodge, Canoe Lake, Mr. Mark Robinson, Park Ranger, Mr. Martin Blecher, tourist, and Mr. G. Rowe, Resident guide. Hoping this information will help you. I am

Yours very truly,
A.E. Ranney[16]

However, on June 8, 1931 Davies found herself in receipt of quite a different letter, this one written to her by Thomson's elder brother George. In with his letter Thomson had included "a copy of the coroner's finding at the inquest which we hold in his [Dr. Ranney's] own handwriting," and which read as follows:

July 17, 1917
Body of Tom Thomson, artist, found floating in Canoe Lake, July 16, 1917. Certified to be the person named by Mark Robinson, Park Ranger. Body clothed in gray lumberman's shirt, khaki trousers and canvas shoes. Head shows marked swelling of face, decomposition has set in, air issuing from mouth. Head

has a bruise over left temple as if produced by falling on rock. Examination of body shows no bruises, body greatly swollen, blisters on limbs, putrefaction setting in on surface. There are no signs of any external force having caused death, and there is no doubt that death occurred from drowning.

GW Howland,
538 Spadina Ave, Toronto[17]

The reader will already have noted a contradiction as to which side of Tom Thomson's head the bruise was said to have been located. Such a contradiction is hard to square apart from the coroner simply misinterpreting Howland's testimony, just as it would appear he misinterpreted his name as being "Gordon" rather than "Goldwyn" in the sworn statement cited above.

If we look for corroborating testimony taken at the same time regarding the location of the bruise on Thomson's head, we find that Robinson's diary entry from July 17, the day when Thomson's body was physically examined by Howland, supports the contention that the wound was located on the left side of Thomson's temple:

[Tuesday] July 17, 1917. . . . Dr. Howland examined body at my request. We found a bruise on left temple about four inches long, evidently caused by falling on a rock. Otherwise no marks of violence on body.[18]

It should further be noted that missing from Ranney's notes (and his handwritten statement regarding Dr. Howland's testimony from the Thomson family) is the report of bleeding from the right ear, which Howland's earlier sworn testimony had indicated.[19]

It has not come down to us through the years if Mark Robinson had been asked any direct questions at all during the inquest; presumably he was. If so, they may well have been similar to the ones that Miss Davies posed to him in 1930, which would have provided some additional context regarding Thomson and his death:

Question: Was there anything wrong with his heart?
Robinson: There may have been but I scarcely think so, as he could throw up his canoe and go uphill over portages without any trouble.

Question: How deep was the water in which Thomson was found?
Robinson: About 30 feet.

Question: How far was it from shore?
Robinson: 125 yards.

Question: Was his fishing rod and line found?
Robinson: No.

Question: Do you think it was his own line which was wound around his ankle?
Robinson: It might have been his own line, but not his regular fishing line.

Question: Did you see a mark on his forehead and if so what was it like?
Robinson: A slight bruise over the left eyebrow.
Question: Were his paddles found?
Robinson: One was found tied in his canoe as for portaging.

Question: Was his knife or anything else missing from his person?
Robinson: Not as far as I know.[20]

The others who were in attendance that evening were likewise called upon to offer their testimony in regard to what they knew about the artist's activities on the last day that he was seen alive. Such testimony as exists will form the content of a later chapter, however for our purposes presently we know that Dr. Ranney would have learned that Thomson was somewhat of a loner who was inclined to paddle off by himself for days and weeks at a time to paint and fish. Indeed, Shannon Fraser, who was one of the last people to have spoken with the artist on the day that he disappeared, recalled that Thomson had indicated that he was heading out for a short fishing trip to a nearby lake. This would have been at approximately 1:00 p.m. on Sunday, July 8. The coroner would further have learned that the Blecher siblings had spotted Thomson's overturned canoe floating near Wapomeo Island at 3:05 p.m. that same afternoon. Eight days later Thomson's corpse bobbed to the surface of the lake, not far from where his overturned canoe had first been spotted. Dr. Howland's testimony, as we've seen, revealed that his examination of the body indicated no evidence of foul play in his estimation, and the bruise on the artist's temple needn't be looked at with any degree of suspicion, as all it suggested was that the artist had somehow come to bump his head at some point prior to his death. All of this taken together suggested to Ranney that the deceased, a man who habitually liked to venture out on his own, had met his end most likely due to a fall, perhaps on or near a portage, which saw him hit his head on a rock (hence the bruise), and then roll into the water and drown.

There is no indication that the fishing line that was discovered wrapped sixteen or seventeen times around Thomson's left ankle was given any consideration, and may not even have been introduced as evidence during the inquest. If it was, Dr. Ranney did not see fit to include it in any of his notes that survived from that evening. Nothing in the testimony that Dr. Ranney heard that night suggested to him that the cause of Tom Thomson's death was anything other than what Superintendent Bartlett and Dr. Howland had already indicated. As Robinson would later recall, "Almost before we had time, Dr. Ranney [said], "Clearly a case of accidental drowning—accidental drowning is the verdict!"[21] The ranger added that only the guide George Rowe had attempted to voice a protest regarding the coroner's decision, but it was quickly shot down by Dr. Ranney:

> One of the old guides [George Rowe was the only guide in attendance that evening] started to remonstrate a little, but [Ranney announced], "The case is closed!" So there's the way it went.[22]

The inquest, from start to finish, had lasted a little more than an hour and a half. At 1:30 a.m., Martin Blecher Junior offered to give the ranger and the coroner a ride back to the Joe Lake Dam in his motorboat and his offer was readily accepted. Robinson recollected that the time was about 2:30 a.m. when he and Ranney were let out at the dam. Both the ranger and the coroner then walked the short distance to Robinson's cabin and retired for the night. As Ranney had to catch a train back to North Bay that morning the men caught about three and a half hours of sleep before arising at 6:00 a.m. Robinson prepared a quick breakfast for them and then walked with Ranney to Joe Lake Station.[23]

If Robinson was strangely silent during the inquest (particularly given his outspokenness on the matter over the years to come), it may well have been due to the harried pace at which things had proceeded. There had been the disappearance of Thomson and the search that followed; once the body had been discovered, the ranger's primary focus had been on getting it buried; the cause of death he left to the medical authorities to figure out. But once the verdict had come down, and the ranger had time to think about the matter and consider some of the testimony he had received and some of the things he had seen on the day that Thomson's body was pulled from the water, he began to have grave doubts about the validity of the official verdict rendered at the inquest. Such doubts might well have surfaced by the next morning, as during their walk to Joe Lake Station the coroner suddenly turned to the ranger and reiterated, "It's a case of accidental drowning." Robinson shrugged. "It was no use trying to say anything. That was settled as far as that was concerned."[24]

Little was said between the two men as they waited for the train to arrive. And when it did, Ranney simply nodded, climbed aboard and returned home to North Bay. Mark Robinson would never see him again.

Chapter Four

THOMSON'S LAST DAY

The morning of Sunday, July 8, 1917, had started out overcast. An east wind was blowing and with it came a fine rain.[1] Perhaps it was the overcast weather, or the late-night card game at George Rowe's cabin the night before where everybody imbibed a little too much, that caused Thomson to sleep in that morning. In any event, it was late that morning when he rolled out of bed. Given the activities of the night before, a night in which he had almost come to blows with one of the partiers, he felt surprisingly good.[2]

Thomson had been staying at the Trainor cottage since the spring of that year, and also during the summer whenever the family was absent, as it afforded him more privacy than Mowat Lodge did as of late. The Frasers, he believed, had been going through his mail when he was not around, and this was an intrusion that he would not countenance.[3] He left the bedroom and walked into the main room of the cottage, where he could look out the window onto Canoe Lake. He could see that it was still raining out, and the dark clouds didn't look like they would be going away anytime soon. Thomson made his way over to the washstand and basin in the cottage where he then shaved and brushed his hair. Given the dreary weather, the artist put on a heavy gray woolen lumberman's shirt, a pair of khaki trousers and white canvas shoes.[4] He knew that he needed to paddle up to the Algonquin Hotel that day and get some supplies for a forthcoming canoe trip he had planned. He had already decided that he would wait and see how he felt and how the weather was later that afternoon before deciding if he would leave for his trip that day. In any event he was hungry and, as it was still morning, he knew that if he went over to Mowat Lodge he could probably still get breakfast there. He left the Trainor cottage and ventured west along a path that led to Mowat Lodge.

Annie Fraser had been busying herself in the kitchen when Thomson entered the main room of the lodge. He casually made his way over to the dining area, pulled out a chair and sat down at one of the tables. Annie quickly spotted her guest and, having long been familiar with his preferences, started in preparing a breakfast that she knew he would like. Bringing the food over to his table, Annie struck up a conversation and the two chatted for a while.[5] When both the meal and the conversation ended, Thomson then lit a cigarette, rose from the table and stepped outside onto the veranda.[6] He again checked the skies and scowled. The miserable weather showed no signs of letting up.[7] He took a long drag on his cigarette and placed his hands on the veranda railing. The veranda interconnected the two former bunkhouses and was sheltered by a breezeway, and so Thomson knew that he could stay dry there a while until, hopefully, the weather improved.

He hadn't been outside long when he was joined by Shannon Fraser and the two men began conversing about what they planned to do that day—when and if the rain cleared. It is unlikely that Thomson would have shared with Fraser that his plan was to head out on a lengthy canoe trip, as he had grown somewhat resentful of the Frasers as of late, believing that they were a little too interested in his affairs.[8] For his part, Fraser mentioned that he had arranged with the Colsons to borrow a boat from them, which he had hoped to obtain that afternoon to rent to one of his guests, but that the Colsons had left it on the shore of the Joe Lake Narrows. This would require him to get some help to carry it around the Joe Lake Dam and put it into Joe Creek. The artist nodded and told Fraser that he would definitely help him with the chore. According to Fraser:

> Sunday morning he says to me, "I will go up with you and help [you] lift a boat over the Joe Lake Dam."[9]

Thomson then indicated that he would be heading up to the Algonquin Hotel shortly and that he would be happy to take Shannon up with him in his canoe, which would require them to put in at the Joe Lake Dam near where the boat Fraser wanted to secure was beached. Taking advantage of help when it was offered, Fraser nodded in agreement and it was then decided that they should leave presently. The pair then made their way down the steps of the veranda and made their way east past the chip yard towards the access point next to the Trainor cottage where Thomson's canoe was waiting. The two men climbed in, pushed off from shore and began paddling north. Fraser would later recall that the rain was still coming down furiously:

> So we went up and it was raining hard and he [Thomson] was wet through.[10]

The damp weather had become a considerable source of irritation to the artist as, like most of us, Thomson was not a fan of black flies and mosquitoes,[11] which had been seemingly omnipresent that summer, and prevented him from spending any meaningful length of time outdoors painting or fishing as they would beset him in swarms. The spring had proven to be cold and wet and, as a result of the weather and the bugs, Thomson had effectively shut down his painting in late spring (what is generally considered to be his last painting, "After the Storm," was painted in the late spring of 1917) and had found employment throughout May and

June doing handyman jobs, as well as a little bit of guiding when the opportunity presented itself. It was his intention to start up his painting again sometime over the next several weeks, in between some fishing and canoe trips that he had planned throughout the remaining weeks of July and the month of August.[12]

Thomson had loved fishing ever since he had been a small boy growing up on his parents' farm in Leith. The farm had abutted Georgian Bay where there was no shortage of great fishing to be had and as he grew older his passion for fishing continued unabated and, by all accounts, he had grown into a very skilled and passionate fisherman. It's interesting to note that despite his well-earned renown for his painting skill, there exist no photographs taken of the artist at his craft. By contrast, almost every photograph that has come down to us from Thomson's time in Algonquin Park (a period of time that paralleled his ascendency as an artist) feature him engaged in some manner of fishing (e.g., posing with a catch of fish, tying a casting fly onto his line, fly fishing by a waterfall, and sitting in a canoe with his fishing rod by his side). Even a good number of still photographs that he took, along with several paintings that he created, feature catching (or caught) fish as their motif. It would appear that fishing was his true passion; art just happened to be something that he was good at and that brought in some much-needed money from time to time.

Fraser and Thomson continued north on Canoe Lake until the lake branched out in two directions; heading left would take them along Potter (or Corkscrew) Creek, which would lead to Canoe Lake Station; heading right would take them along Joe Creek, which would lead them to the Joe Lake Dam. The men swung right when they reached the split in the lake, as the dam was where Fraser had been told the Colsons had left the boat he intended to pick up. Apart from helping Fraser, however, paddling to the Joe Lake Dam was the route Thomson would need to take in order to visit the

Algonquin Hotel, which was just a short walk north from the dam. The hotel was where he knew he could pick up certain supplies that he would require for his forthcoming fishing trip.

He had been planning the fishing trip for some time now, the starting point of which was going to be South River, a destination that, if he was traveling there by canoe, would have required him to paddle the better part of eighty-one miles northwest from Canoe Lake. He had paddled to South River before, in July or August of 1915, shortly after he had purchased a new Chestnut Canoe and silk tent.[13] However, on this trip he was to be met at South River by Park Ranger Tom Wattie,[14] and from there the two friends had planned to head across to Temagami, a municipality some 175.5 miles northeast from Canoe Lake, that featured over 2,485 miles of canoe routes and some of the best fishing in the province. Certain of Thomson's camping equipment—a tent (manufactured by Abercrombie and Fitch), a sleeping bag, a fold-up cot, and a pair of waterproof pants—he had already sent on ahead by train to South River several days earlier.[15]

In preparation for the fishing trip Thomson had already accessed certain of the food supplies that he would require from Mowat Lodge, but he still wanted a good supply of bacon and Shannon Fraser evidently didn't have it in sufficient quantity to suit his purposes. He had tried to convince Fraser to purchase pigs three months previously, writing to his brother-in-law Tom Harkness:

I have been talking to the people here at the post office about pigs. Have been advising them to get about 6 or 8 small ones and keep them till fall, which they could do without much expense and hang them up for the winter. . . . Supposing they decide to try it out, what would they have to pay for the pigs and where would be the place to send for them—and could they be shipped by express or freight any distance?[16]

We're not sure what Harkness replied but, whatever it was, we do know that as of July of that summer no pigs had been purchased by the people at the post office, chief of whom was the man Thomson was paddling with on this particular morning, as Fraser was the man who ran the post office. The thought that he would soon have all of the supplies he needed served to lighten the artist's mood somewhat, as did the fact that the rain was beginning to ease off.

Unlike Thomson, Mark Robinson had risen early that morning and had enjoyed breakfast in his cabin with his eleven-year-old son John (nicknamed "Jack"), who had come to the park from Barrie to visit with his father. The Robinson children had always looked forward to the summer months in Algonquin Park, as there was never a shortage of outdoor activities such as swimming, fishing, canoeing, camping, and wildlife spotting. The ranger hadn't been awake long that morning when he had received instructions from park headquarters to travel down the railway line to Source Lake, where he was to inspect some lumber that had been cut and piled. Robinson decided to take Jack with him for company on the excursion that morning.

The rain was still falling and a strong northeast wind had picked up, causing Robinson to wrap his coat around the boy as the pair made their way along the railway track to their destination. When they arrived at Source Lake, the ranger looked over the timber and, finding nothing problematic, returned with his son and the section foreman to Joe Lake Station.[17] After saying some hellos to the station staff, the Robinsons made their way back to the cabin where the ranger then set about preparing an early lunch for he and his son.

The rain had stopped by the time that Thomson and Fraser had arrived at the base of the Joe Lake Dam. Both men quickly exited the canoe and pulled it up on shore. They walked the short distance up the path that led to the Joe Lake Narrows. Upon reaching the top of the path they were met by the Colsons, who took them the short distance to where they had pulled the boat up onto shore. As Fraser stopped to inspect the boat, Thomson and the Colsons proceeded north along the path towards the Algonquin Hotel. Looking out across the narrows from the window of his cabin, Robinson spied the trio walking along the path on the opposite shore and watched as they eventually turned onto a footpath that led directly up to the Algonquin Hotel. Once they left the main path they disappeared in amongst the trees and fell out of Robinson's field of view. The ranger then sat down with his son to enjoy their lunch.[18]

Thomson was no stranger to the Algonquin Hotel, having guided for its guests on occasion. Guiding, however, was just one of the jobs that Thomson worked at while in the Park. During the spring and early part of the summer of 1917, Thomson had taken on a number of general handyman jobs in order to earn some much-needed money. He had already planted gardens for Lowrey Dickson, the Trainor family, and the Frasers at Mowat Lodge.[19] However, he enjoyed guiding as it was nowhere near as tedious as general handyman labor, and the hotel guests were always keen to fish, which allowed him to indulge in his favorite pastime—with the added bonus of getting paid for it. The tourists typically would arrive in full force during August (after the black flies and mosquitoes had died down) and September (to see the Fall colors), and in anticipation he had already taken out a guide's license in April of that year.[20] He also expected to further supplement his income during the autumn months by selling a few of his paintings to his guiding clients as well as to the odd guest that would be holidaying at one the various lodges in the area.

On this particular morning at the Algonquin Hotel, seventeen-year-old Blanche Packard was starting her shift as a waitress in the guide's dining room. She was familiar with Thomson, having first witnessed him painting by the Algonquin Hotel. Molly Colson had told her at the time that he was a painter who sometimes did odd jobs for them. Packard had also been aware that the artist would sometimes barter these paintings at the Algonquin Hotel for supplies such as bacon and bread.[21] These were not large canvases, but rather small oil paintings that Thomson had painted on eight by ten-inch wooden panels that featured various landscapes he had observed throughout the park. As Packard began her daily task of setting up tables, Molly Colson entered the hotel with the artist in tow and called out, "Tom wants some grub!"[22] Spotting Packard, she told her to head out to the hotel's walk-in icehouse and retrieve a slab of bacon. When Packard brought it into the kitchen and laid it on the counter Molly then pulled forth a carving knife and cut off a weighty slice. She turned to Thomson and asked, "Will that do you?"

Thomson nodded and replied, "Yes, I'll be back within twelve to fourteen days."[23]

When Thomson's brother George would arrive at Canoe Lake shortly after learning that Tom had gone missing, he had likewise been led to believe (probably from the Colsons, and contrary to what Shannon Fraser would later indicate at the inquest) that Thomson wasn't simply going away for a day's fishing, but rather "had prepared for and laid in provisions enough for a two or three week cruise."[24] This corroborates Packard's testimony and, indeed, there is evidence in a letter written the day before he disappeared that Thomson had been planning to set out on several canoe trips over the remaining summer months (one presumably with Wattie):

> [I] have done some guiding for fishing parties and will have some other trips this month and next, with probably sketching in between . . . [25]

Like Wattie (and unlike Fraser), the Colsons and certain of their staff were thus aware that Thomson was preparing to leave on an extended expedition. Packard further recollected that the Colsons had been fond of Thomson and that, "Mrs. Colson particularly was always asking if he had this or that little comfort at his cabin. She mothered him and was often heard to ask, 'Do you need anything Tom?'"[26]

To earn the food that he would be receiving that morning Thomson had spent a portion of the previous week nailing clapboards onto the hotel kitchen.[27] He had made a point of saving some of the end pieces of the boards he had been cutting that week with the intention of using them as panels for the paintings he had anticipated doing during the weeks and months to come.[28] It would evidently be these panels that Thomson's brother George would later collect from the Trainor cottage and send to Dr. MacCallum from the Canoe Lake post office on July 19, 1917.[29]

Packard had admired the artist's paintings, some of which had been on display in the Algonquin Hotel that summer, and she remembered one painting in particular of a waterfall that had caught her eye, which the Colsons had hung up on display in the guide's dining room. Most of the guests at the Algonquin Hotel were Americans, and often groups of four or five went together with two guides for extended tours of the park. Packard remembered that whenever the guides were short staffed, the call usually went out to "get Tom!"[30] Thomson had been in the habit of stowing his food supplies in a packsack that he would wear and, according to Packard, after he had put his newly acquired supply of bacon in it, along with some freshly baked bread and butter, she had witnessed him slip it on and buckle it up that morning at the Algonquin Hotel.[31]

In the summer of 1944, while conducting research for her book *Algonquin Story*, author Audrey Saunders had the good fortune to interview Molly Colson about her interaction with the artist on the morning of July 8, 1917. Saunders had evidently picked up on a rumor that both Thomson and Fraser had been drinking, and had even given a drink to "Old Mr. C" that morning.[32] Given that Edwin Colson wasn't of sufficient antiquity to be given such a sobriquet, the reference was most likely made about Edwin's father John, who also lived at the Algonquin Hotel. Saunders decided to inquire of Mrs. Colson about the validity of the rumor. Molly Colson denied it. When asked if Thomson could have been drinking that morning, Molly had replied that there was no alcohol on Thomson's breath[33] and that in the hour and a half that had elapsed from when he left her hotel until he was seen leaving Mowat Lodge he "couldn't get tight in that time."[34] Also worth noting is that Molly Colson further recollected that Thomson had fifty dollars on him,[35] a not insubstantial sum in 1917. This is an intriguing revelation, as when Thomson's body was pulled from the waters of Canoe Lake eight days later the amount of money that he had on his person had been reduced to sixty cents.[36]

And while Thomson was not believed to have consumed any alcohol that morning, Packard reported that she had made a snack for the artist, along with a pot of tea, which the artist had shared with Molly Colson in the kitchen. After finishing his tea, Thomson said his goodbyes and left the hotel.

At about this time Mark Robinson once again looked out from the window of his cabin and witnessed Thomson coming back down the path from the Algonquin Hotel. He was met at the end of the path by Shannon Fraser who, now having finished with his inspection of the boat, had come to collect Thomson to help him lift it over the dam.

Emily Thomas, who was the wife of Edwin Thomas, the foreman for Canoe Lake Station, also recalled seeing both Thomson and Fraser around noon that day:

We saw him pass the [Canoe Lake] Station Sunday noon with Shan Fraser, went past the section house, hot sultry day, fine rain. That was July 8, 1917. We spoke to them on their return. . . . Had left the canoe at Joe Lake Creek.[37]

Sometime after Robinson and his son had finished their lunch, and presumably sometime after Thomson and Fraser had returned from their excursion to the Canoe Lake Section House, the ranger had ventured out onto the porch of his cabin where he had witnessed the pair walking along the portage path across the Joe Lake Narrows from him down to where Thomson had left his canoe at the Joe Lake Dam. Perhaps this is when Thomson had helped Fraser lift his boat over the dam. Evidently the two men saw Robinson, as they waved to him.[38]

Robinson may then have busied himself with other matters, as when he eventually looked out toward where the men had been heading he noticed that Thomson now had a fishing rod in his hand and had cast a line into the water by the dam. Thomson's activity at the dam immediately piqued the ranger's interest as he had had a friendly fishing competition on the go with the artist over the past several weeks:

> There was a big trout below Joe Lake Dam and both of us had been trying to get it. We'd had it hooked different times and both of us had failed to catch the fish; [Thomson] was making his own bugs and I was using any contrivance I could. . . . and we both were trying to play the game that way, but neither of us got the fish.[39]

Robinson quickly grabbed his binoculars to see if Thomson was having any luck:

> I was standing watching them. I took my [field] glasses out to see if Tom was going to have a try for the trout, and he was pointing out something to Mr. Fraser, and I made up my mind Tom was going to try for the trout, and I guessed he'd get it that time. I ran down to the shore, up the path up by my

side [of the Joe Lake Narrows] and I sat down looking down on the two fellows down below me—Tom casting. Presently, he got the trout on [his fishing line] and it played, at least I thought he was going to land it, but it got away.[40]

Robinson would learn later from Shannon Fraser that at this point Thomson in a half joking sort of way had said, "Well, Shannon, I guess I'll go down to Tea Lake Dam, or to West Lake or to Gill Lake, and I'll catch a big trout and I'll bring it home and I'll put it on Mark's doorstep; he'll think I've got the fish."[41] Robinson, for his part, believed that neither man had seen him looking down on them:

And I sat right above them looking at them. Well, Tom hadn't seen me, I sat still and as he went up onto the bank and turned, Tom looked back and I waved to him. "Howdy," he says. That's the last time Tom Thomson spoke to me.[42]

In one of life's great (if typical) ironies, Robinson would later recount that the trout that had so successfully eluded both he and Thomson's efforts to catch it would eventually be caught by an American tourist, who had never caught a trout before, on his very first cast.[43]

After failing to land the trout, Thomson and Fraser walked down the path beside the Joe Lake Dam to where they had left Thomson's canoe. The men then slid the canoe into the water, climbed in, and proceeded to paddle south down the creek and out into Canoe Lake.[44] Once the pair hit Canoe Lake they put in at the Mowat Lodge dock. Thomson then walked over to the Trainor cottage where he picked up some additional fishing tackle that he had stored there, while Fraser went up to the lodge to collect some supplies that Thomson had requested for his fishing trip. It wasn't long before Fraser returned to the dock, bringing Charlie Scrim with

him. The men brought with them the items that Thomson had requested, including a tightly fastened one-gallon can of maple syrup
and a one-and-a-half-pound jar of jam.[45] In later taking a statement
from Scrim, Robinson's notes indicated what items Thomson had
opted to take with him that day:

- One small tin pail (three pints)
- One pound of rice
- One can of sugar (about one pound)
- Two pounds of flour
- A half-dozen potatoes
- A small frying pan
- A split bamboo fishing rod, along with reel, line, and land-
  ing net.[46]

The bamboo rod was one that Thomson used for casting.[47] Such
a quantity of supplies was consistent with what the artist would
normally take with him on a two or three-week trip as so indicated
in a letter that the artist had sent to Dr. MacCallum two months
previously when the pair were contemplating going on a fishing trip
that coming June:

> You can get any extra blankets or stuff from Fraser and I
> have all the supplies including 1 gallon maple syrup, pail of
> jam, plenty bacon, potatoes, bread, tea, sugar, all kinds of
> canned stuff, tents, canoes, cooking outfit, plates etc. I tried
> to get some chocolate and failed, have no Klim [powdered
> milk], & no coffee. That I think is everything we need for
> two or three weeks, including Williamson.[48]

In an audio recording made of Mark Robinson in the early 1950s,
the ranger revealed that Fraser had also brought down to the dock a

loaf of bread and an extra supply of bacon for Thomson to take with him on his fishing trip that day. According to the ranger, Fraser had wrapped these items up in a rubber sheet for the artist.[49] As Thomson had just acquired a supply of bacon from the Colsons that morning that was believed sufficient to last him for a week or two, there wouldn't exist a need for any "extra" bacon. It is more likely that Fraser had simply gone up to the lodge to get a loaf of bread and a rubber sheet in which to wrap up some of the supplies that Thomson would be taking with him that day.

Packing his supplies into the canoe, Thomson then turned to Fraser and said, "I will go down to West Lake and get some of those big trout. And I will be back either tonight or tomorrow morning—don't worry if I am late getting back."[50] Those, presumably, were the last words that Tom Thomson ever spoke. The lodge owner watched as Thomson untied the painter that connected his canoe to the Mowat Lodge dock, and then climbed in and began paddling south towards the Gill Lake Portage, which lay ahead of him by a distance of a mile and a half. Fraser also recalled seeing Thomson letting out his copper fishing line while paddling through the narrows between Gillender's Point and Wapomeo Island.[51] Fraser then turned and walked back up to the lodge.

Mark Robinson, who was in charge of investigating the artist's disappearance, would later state that several people who were staying at Mowat Lodge also witnessed the artist's departure that afternoon.[52] One of these people was of course Thomson's friend Charlie Scrim, who related to Robinson that the artist had not taken a hat or a coat with him on that afternoon, and had been wearing a heavy gray woolen lumberman's shirt, khaki trousers, and white canvas shoes.[53] According to Dr. Ranney's notes from the inquest, these were the exact same articles of clothing that Dr. Howland had testified were found to be on Thomson's body when it was recovered from the water eight days later.[54]

Chapter Five

PROBLEMS BEGIN

I should like to break off from our narrative of the story at this point to examine some of the problems that have already surfaced regarding the testimony we have been exposed to thus far.

THE LAST WALK

As the reader will recall, Emily Thomas had reported that she had witnessed both Tom Thomson and Shannon Fraser walking past the Section House for Canoe Lake Station around noon on Sunday, July 8. The Thomases and their cousins, the Wilkinsons, ran the Canoe Lake Train Station and all lived together in the upper level of the train station. Emily's daughter Rose, and Rose's cousin Jack Wilkinson, who were ten and five years of age respectively on the day in question, both corroborated Emily Thomas's testimony during an interview that they granted the Algonquin Park Archives in 1976.[1]

This is an important but very curious piece of testimony; important in the sense that it provided more sets of eyes that had seen the artist on the last day of his life; and curious as the Section House that Mrs. Thomas and her relatives referred to was located about a half mile west of Canoe Lake Station, which itself was a quarter mile west of where Thomson was when at the Algonquin Hotel that morning. If Thomson had gone to the hotel solely to secure provisions for his forthcoming canoe trip, and also to help Shannon Fraser lift a boat over the Joe Lake Dam, there existed no reason why he and Fraser would have opted to take a walk west from the hotel along the tracks for three quarters of a mile, only to then promptly turn around and walk the same distance back to Thomson's canoe at the Joe Lake Dam. Given that the weather had cleared up by this time and Thomson had a fishing trip to get started on that was a considerable distance north of Joe Lake, a lengthy walk with Shannon Fraser would not have been on his dossier for that day.

There is no evidence that either Thomson or Fraser had picked up anything at all from the Canoe Lake Section House, and both men had other things they needed to get on with, which made their time somewhat limited. And so we are left with the fact of a one and a half mile round trip walk that was entirely purposeless.

THE ALCHEMY OF FISHING LINE

Dr. Robert P. Little, a camper and one-time guide in Algonquin Park, knew Thomson and the Frasers quite well. In speaking with Annie Fraser about Thomson's activity on the final day of his life, Little was told that:

> Mr. Fraser last saw him as he was letting out his copper fishing line while paddling through the narrows to the right of the twin islands.[2]

This is an interesting observation, as if Fraser noted that the fishing line that Thomson had been using in the hour or so prior to his death was made of copper, then how would a cotton braided line end up being wrapped around the artist's left ankle when his body was pulled from the water? Certainly Fraser would know a copper line when he saw one as he would have been quite conversant with all manner of fishing lines, having set up innumerable fishing trips for guests at his lodge over the years. Moreover, he would have been very familiar with the fishing tackle that Thomson regularly employed as he had seen firsthand Thomson fishing in and around Mowat Lodge for the previous five years and, indeed, had seen the artist load his fishing tackle, including whatever lines he was using, into his canoe when Thomson left for his fishing expedition that afternoon. There is no answer to this question that isn't mere conjecture and so we are left to ponder just how a copper line could morph into one made of cotton.

LAST WORDS

There is also something odd regarding the testimony that we have regarding Thomson's alleged last words to Fraser: "Don't worry if I am late getting back."[3] And these are peculiar words—after all, Fraser wasn't Thomson's parent; why would he care what time the artist returned? Fraser, of all people, knew that Thomson was but a temporary lodge guest who, according to Robert Little, "usually camped out when the weather permitted, from April till the first snowfall in October or November and he was perfectly at home in his gypsy tent."[4] Moreover, Thomson had been staying at the Trainor cottage prior to his absence—not Mowat Lodge. The summer months were the busiest ones at the lodge, with Fraser looking after his guests and securing whatever services for them that he could. That he would worry that a semi-seasonal lodge guest (Thomson had stayed in Achray, not Canoe Lake the summer before) might be late getting back from a day of fishing, especially when it was not unusual for the artist to be out for days or weeks at a time, or that Thomson himself would attempt to pacify such a concern by telling Fraser not to worry if he was late getting back, seems highly out of character for both men.

A TWO-WEEK SUPPLY OF GROCERIES FOR AN AFTERNOON OF FISHING

And then there was Thomson's alleged statement: "I will go down to West Lake and get some of those big trout and I will be back either tonight or tomorrow morning."[5] This is what Shannon Fraser indicated to Dr. James MacCallum shortly after Thomson's burial. He made a similar statement to Mark Robinson. And it is these statements that have been the basis for the belief that the artist had been merely out for an afternoon or overnight fishing expedition when he met with the accident that claimed his life. Such a brief excursion, however, would not have required much in the way of provisions, perhaps just Thomson's fishing rod, landing net, and bucket. One can envision that an evening meal of lake trout and perhaps a breakfast early the next morning (if he decided to camp out that evening) might require some additional food supplies, to be certain, but would it really require one pound of rice, one pound of sugar, two pounds of flour, six potatoes, a loaf of bread, a gallon of maple syrup, a pound and a half of jam, and an "extra supply of bacon"? Such a supply of groceries seems to be considerably in excess of what would be necessary for an afternoon of fishing.

Based on the information that George Thomson had obtained when he had arrived in the park soon after his brother's disappearance, there had been no question that on the last day his younger sibling had been seen alive he had "laid in provisions enough for a two or three week cruise."[6] He clearly had learned first hand of the quantity of supplies his younger brother had with him on the day that he was last seen from people who had either spoken with the artist to learn of his plans or who saw what he had packed into his canoe. As George Thomson was staying at Mowat Lodge he would have had opportunity to speak with the two men who brought his brother's supplies down to the dock for him, namely Charlie Scrim and Shannon Fraser, as Scrim was a guest at the lodge and Fraser was its proprietor. Such a stock of supplies as Thomson was said to have left with that afternoon strongly suggested to George that the artist was probably leaving to meet up with somebody. As Thomson's sister Elizabeth Harkness would recall:

> When [George Thomson] came back from his first visit to Canoe Lake [when Tom Thomson had first been reported missing] he told us that the Frasers had shown him a statement of Tom's affairs (with them) concerning the last few weeks, including the things he bought that Sunday to take with him, namely cold half raw potatoes, pancake flour, etc., so when we heard this we came to the conclusion he had met with a party and would be all right.[7]

But if Blanche Packard and George Thomson's testimony is accurate; i.e., that Thomson had not been leaving for an afternoon of fishing, but rather had been heading out for a lengthier canoe trip, then why would he have said to Fraser, "I will be back either tonight or tomorrow morning"? And if Thomson did indeed intend to only go out for an afternoon of fishing, then why did he pack into his canoe such a quantity of supplies that he wouldn't need for such a venture? Such would only represent needless items that he would then have to carry over the Gill Lake Portage. Surely if he was only heading out for a few hours of fishing in order to play a joke on Mark Robinson, and then planned on departing on his two-week canoe trip after his return, it would have been more practical to a seasoned canoe tripper such as Thomson to simply leave his supplies at Mowat Lodge until he returned either later that evening or the next morning.

Moreover, the only trip of such a magnitude that we know Tom Thomson had planned at this point was the one in South River with

Tom Wattie. And if the artist was intending to leave for South River, it would have made more sense to have brought his supplies with him to the Algonquin Hotel that morning and then leave directly from Joe Lake—rather than return to Canoe Lake, pick up his supplies, and then paddle back to Joe Lake and continue on from there. Had he intended to take the train to South River, it likewise would have made more sense to load both his canoe and his supplies onto the train that would have departed from Canoe Lake Station or Joe Lake Station, rather than paddle back to Mowat Lodge, pack his supplies into his canoe, and then take them out with him for an afternoon of fishing.

Perhaps Thomson's statement to Fraser at the Joe Lake Dam earlier that day about his heading out for an afternoon of fishing solely to play a joke on Mark Robinson may well have been a wry joke itself. But then if the artist was heading out to South River to hook up with Tom Wattie for a two-week fishing trip, why was he reportedly last seen to be heading south towards the Gill Lake Portage when South River was the better part of eighty-one miles away to the north? Given that the source of the information regarding Thomson heading off for an afternoon of fishing was Shannon Fraser, while everyone else who had contact with the artist on the last day of his life indicated that he was heading off for a two-week fishing trip, it's difficult to know whom to believe in the matter. Certainly, such contradictions were perplexing to the Thomson family, causing Tom's sister to state:

Why Fraser put up the bread and butter yarn puzzles me. He is certainly ignorant and without principle. His whole story beginning to end is a muddle of contradictions. What is the underlying meaning of it all is what I would like [to know].[8]

CAMPING WITHOUT A TENT

The inconsistencies don't end here, however. The reader will recall that the day before Thomson disappeared he had complained in a letter to MacCallum that the black flies and mosquitoes were much worse than he had experienced in any year since he had been in the park. And yet, if the bugs were that bad that summer, why would he choose to send on his sleeping bag and tent to South River prior to his departure? He certainly would have known that he would need to camp out for at least two nights while en route to meeting up with Tom Wattie. Moreover, whether he was camping out while paddling to South River or simply camping out overnight after an afternoon of fishing in one of the lakes west of Canoe Lake, it seems inexplicable that Thomson would be willing to do so without the shelter provided by either a sleeping bag or a tent, the absence of which would essentially have left him no protection at all against these insects. It's clear that Thomson owned both a tent and a sleeping bag, and it's also clear that neither of these items were found to be among his personal affects when these were returned to his family from Mowat Lodge after his death, which supports the contention that he had shipped them to Wattie in South River at some point prior to his demise.

Perhaps rather than canoeing to South River (as he had done previously in the summer of 1915), he instead was planning on taking the train. If so, that would negate the need for his camping out overnight en route. But again, if this was the case why was he last seen with a two-week's supply of groceries packed into his canoe and heading in the opposite direction from the Canoe Lake Train Station?

THE TIME OF DEPARTURE

The testimony is also contradictory regarding the exact time that Thomson had pulled away from the Mowat Lodge dock. We find, for example, that Shannon Fraser had telegraphed Dr. James Mac-Callum on Tuesday, July 10 (the day Thomson's overturned canoe had been reported to Mark Robinson, and two days after he was last seen alive) that he had been present when Thomson left his dock at "Sunday noon" (i.e., 12:00 p.m.).[9] However, two days later, on Thursday, July 12, Fraser wrote a letter to MacCallum that indicated he had seen the artist leave the dock at "one o'clock"[10]— a difference of one hour. Mark Robinson's notebook from 1917 indicated that his investigation into the matter had Thomson leaving "Fraser's dock after 12:30 p.m.,"[11] which is anything but precise (how long after—five minutes after? Thirty minutes after?). According to what Robert P. Little had learned directly from Annie Fraser, Thomson had "left with his lunch [as we've seen, the quantity of groceries he was said to have taken with him would constitute quite a "lunch" indeed] at about 1:00 p.m."[12] Recollecting the event without his notes some thirty-five years later, Robinson stated that Thomson left the dock at "1:30 by Mr. Fraser's evidence [from the inquest]."[13]

Based upon the testimony thus presented, Tom Thomson was last seen leaving the Mowat Lodge dock on Sunday, July 8, sometime between 12:00 p.m. and 1:30 p.m. An hour and a half is quite a disparity in trying to construct an accurate timeline. Nevertheless, that space of time at least provides a window within which we know that the artist had set off on his final paddle. And as Thomson's upturned canoe was reportedly spotted at 3:05 p.m.[14] that same Sunday afternoon by both Martin and Bessie Blecher, Thomson would have had to have met his fate sometime between 12:00 p.m. and 3:05 p.m.; that is to say, within a window of three hours and five minutes from the time he pulled away from the Mowat Lodge dock.

FISHING IN THE AFTERNOON

Also troubling is that a fisherman of Thomson's experience would be heading out to fish in the middle of a hot July afternoon. Certainly a knowledgeable fisherman such as Thomson would have known that the best time for catching fish is either at dusk or in the early morning; Thomson heading out to fish around 1:00 p.m. in the afternoon would fly in the face of his own considerable experience both as a fisherman and as a guide for fishing parties. This is not to suggest that fish can't be caught in the afternoon, but rather that it is less likely to happen at that time of the day.

THE LOCATION OF THE ACCIDENT

When Thomson's canoe had been recovered both of his paddles were found lashed onto the thwarts of the craft in position to portage,[15] so the artist could not have been paddling at the time that he suffered his accident. This evidence is suggestive that the accident occurred either when Thomson was preparing for or during a portage; i.e., on land, not water.

This, indeed, had been the belief of Dr. Howland, as he had indicated that the bruise on the artist's temple was suggestive of his having struck his head on a rock or a stone—and there would certainly be no rocks or stones for him to bump his head on in the middle of the lake. However, if he met with his accident on land, we are puzzled by how his body ended up being submerged in thirty feet of water and out 125 yards from shore. Adding to this confusion is the fact that both his canoe and his body were found between a half-mile and a mile, respectively, north of the two closest portages, suggesting that the artist never made it to either one of them.

There are several portages leading off of Canoe Lake to lakes such as Smoke, Tea or Gill. However, given that Thomson was paddling along the west bank of Canoe Lake when last seen it is believed that he was heading to one of two portages that led to Gill Lake. Both of these portages are located on the west shore of the lake (about a mile, and a mile and a half, respectively, from the Mowat Lodge dock). For Thomson to paddle the mile, or mile and a half, to one of these portages would have taken him perhaps fifteen to twenty minutes, and yet his overturned canoe was first spotted on the west side of Canoe Lake, between Statton's Island (now Little Wapameo Island) and Bertram's Island (now Gilmour Island), which, according to Mark Robinson (who would have paddled that route far more often than Thomson),would have been somewhat less than a half mile from his point of departure.[16] When Robinson considered where Thomson's overturned canoe had been found relative to the portage he was heading to on that day he expressed surprise:

> An east wind was blowing and his canoe could not have been there under ordinary conditions.[17]

Despite Thomson's canoe and body being found the better part of a mile north of the Gill Lake portage, if we assume for the moment that he did, in fact, make it there safely and met with an accident close to shore that caused his canoe to then drift back out into the lake, the wind should have carried it to the south east, and yet it was found floating upside down in the north-west portion of the lake. If Thomson had fallen and hit his head while portaging, both his canoe and body should have been found on the portage trail, not in the water. If he had fallen on the shore prior to making it to the portage, then his fishing rod, landing net, frying pan, tin pail, axe, and some of his supplies would have easily been visible either on shore or within very shallow water. Instead, they were never seen again. And if he met his accident while crossing a portage, why would some of his supplies still be in the front of his canoe rather than buckled onto his person? Again, according to Robinson:

> His provisions and kit bag were in the front end on the canoe when found.[18]

Shannon Fraser wrote on July 12, 1917 (two days after the canoe was found) words that confirmed Robinson's recollection:

> At three o'clock his canoe was found floating a short distance from my place with both paddles tied tight in the canoe, also his provisions were found packed in the canoe. The Canoe was upside down.[19]

Robinson's testimony above is the only mention of a "kit bag" being found, and the only provisions that the ranger recalled finding in the artist's canoe when he turned it over that day were a one-gallon can of maple syrup, a one-and-a-half-pound tin of jam, and a rubber sheet.[20] None of the other items Thomson took with him on that day were ever seen again.

And when Thomson's body eventually came to the surface of the lake, it did so about 125 yards due north of Gillender's Point in approximately thirty feet of water in a direct line between that point of land and Little Wapomeo Island.[21] As Mark Robinson was heard to remark:

> And where was Tom Thomson from half past one to something after three, which would be another hour and a half, in travelling about, well, hardly half a mile? There was something fishy.[22]

QUO VADIS?

And then there is the issue of where exactly Thomson had been heading off to when he left the Mowat Lodge dock that afternoon. The testimony from the Frasers (and from Mark Robinson in interviewing Shannon Fraser) regarding his destination that day is anything but consistent, having him setting out to visit one of several different lakes:

- "Tea Lake Dam, or to West Lake or to Gill Lake"—Mark Robinson (recollecting what Shannon Fraser had told him)[23]
- "He made preparations to go to Tea Lake Dam to fish"—Robert P. Little (recounting what Annie Fraser had told him)[24]
- "When we got down to the dock he said, 'I will go down to West Lake and get some of those big trout and I will be back either tonight or tomorrow'"—Shannon Fraser[25]

Given that all of the above testimony regarding where Thomson was heading off to on that final day came from the same source—Shannon Fraser—it is odd that it is so contradictory. In reviewing the above accounts, two indicate that the artist was heading to the Tea Lake Dam or to West Lake, and one indicates a potential destination of Gill Lake. While this is somewhat confusing, in the final analysis it probably doesn't matter, as Thomson never made it to any of these lakes, and perhaps not even to a portage that would have led to one of them.

THE CAPSIZED CANOE

As we have seen, Annie Fraser told Dr. Robert P. Little that Shannon Fraser had watched Thomson "letting out his copper fishing line while paddling through the narrows to the right of the twin islands."[26] Even this statement is odd as it means that Fraser had continued to stand on his dock and watch the artist paddle down the lake for the better part of ten minutes following Thomson's departure. For a man who had a lodge to run and guests to look after during his busiest time of the summer, that is a considerable period of time to spend watching someone paddle down a lake. And then, almost as soon as Fraser would have looked away, something beset the artist as it was at this very location that Thomson's overturned canoe would be spotted roughly two hours later by Martin and Bessie Blecher.[27] As they did not see a body floating near the canoe, we can safely conclude that Thomson was already at the bottom of Canoe Lake at this point. They also didn't report seeing any of the artist's supplies floating near the upturned canoe.

Even the location where the upturned canoe was first spotted is inexact. Mark Robinson told the author Audrey Saunders in 1944 that the Blecher siblings had passed the canoe about halfway between the Mowat Lodge landing and Wapomeo Island.[28] According to Robinson's diary for Tuesday, July 10, however, the Blechers had reported that they had first spotted the canoe floating upside down between Statton's Point and Bertram's Island on Sunday afternoon,[29] which would have placed it further to the south east. Shannon Fraser had written in a letter dated July 12 that the canoe had been first spotted "a short distance from my place [Mowat]."[30] Robinson would then attempt to put a sharper point on the overturned canoe's location by futher telling Audrey Saunders that the canoe was first spotted "a little east of Big Wapomeo Island,"[31] which is in a different section of the lake than where Fraser had indicated he had last seen Thomson letting out his copper trolling line. Annie Fraser believed that the Blechers had first spotted the canoe "near the far end of the second twin island (belonging to Mr. Bertram and Mr. Pirie),[32] which would have placed it further south than either Fraser or Robinson had recollected.

The reader will note that in each of these versions the Blecher siblings did not stop to investigate the watercraft that they had observed but merely noted its presence as they proceeded on their way to the Tea Lake Dam. This was said to have been at 3:05 p.m. on Sunday, July 8.[33]

More confusion follows as to where the canoe ended up after this point. The Blechers told Robinson that upon their return from the dam the canoe was no longer in the spot where they had first observed it and so they simply headed back to their cottage.[34] However, Robert P. Little claimed that Annie Fraser had shared with him the fact that the Blechers not only saw the canoe on their return, but that "they towed Tom's canoe back to Mowat Lodge and put it in their boathouse."[35] This testimony is ambiguous as to which boathouse the canoe was placed in—the Blechers' or one belonging to Mowat Lodge. In either case this testimony is directly at odds with what Mark Robinson, who had been tasked with investigating the matter, recalled. According to Robinson, the canoe wasn't discovered until the next day (Monday), after it had floated in behind Little Wapomeo Island.[36] Robinson recollected in 1953 that Charlie Scrim had been the one to tell him that the Blechers had found the canoe floating behind Little Wapomeo Island.[37] Emily Thomas supported Little's testimony that the Blechers had towed the canoe to the Fraser's on Monday, July 9, recollecting that, "Martin Blecher saw the canoe floating, he went out and took it to Fraser's."[38]

Thomson's canoe, then, wasn't retrieved and (perhaps) deposited in the Blecher or Mowat Lodge boathouse until some time on Monday, despite it having been seen the day before. Things become even more bizarre at this point. The Blechers would most certainly have recognized the overturned canoe as belonging to Thomson, as the artist had painted it a unique dove-gray color, which made it stand apart from every other canoe in the park. And yet their reason for not telling anyone that they saw the canoe floating upside down in the water on Sunday afternoon was that they believed it was a canoe that had slipped its moorings from a local lodge. They didn't hold this belief long, however, as they certainly were of the opinion that it was Thomson's canoe when they happened upon it either upon their return from Tea Lake on Sunday or at some point on Monday, as they saw fit to either bring it to Mowat Lodge (where they knew the artist stayed from time to time) or (for some reason) to their own boathouse. No mention is indicated that the canoe they towed to shore was not the same one they had spotted abandoned on Sunday afternoon. And when the overturned canoe was brought to the attention of Shannon Fraser (presumably on the Monday), he saw fit to make mention of this to Emily Thomas at the Canoe Lake Train Station, but did not bring the matter to Mark Robinson's attention until the next day (Tuesday, July 10).[39] Robinson recollected in both typed and audio recorded testimony that he had first been told the news of the discovery of Thomson's overturned canoe by Charlie Scrim, however his daytime diary for Tuesday July 10, 1917 indicates that he was informed of the discovery by Shannon Fraser (perhaps it is possible that both men came to his cabin to break the news):

> *[Tuesday] July 10, 1917:* Morning wet and cool. Mr. Shannon Fraser came to house about 9:15 a.m. and reported that Martin Blecher had found Tom Thomson's canoe floating upside down in Canoe Lake and wanted us to drag for Mr. Thomson's body.[40]

And so by the time that Robinson finally became involved, Thomson's capsized canoe had been known about by some people in the Canoe Lake community for the better part of three days.

THE MISSING PADDLE

And then there is the issue of how many paddles were found in Thomson's abandoned canoe. It is common practice for canoeists to have two paddles, one would be what they would use to paddle their watercraft with, the other being essentially a "spare" that could be used in the event the "working paddle" should break or get lost. The spare paddle also was handy if one were to go out paddling with a friend as he or she could use it to assist in the paddling. In addition, if both paddles were tied onto the thwarts in a canoe they could be set in such a position so as to rest perfectly upon the canoeist's shoulders when he flipped the canoe up over his head to carry it over bushland trails that served to interconnect various waterways.

Shannon Fraser had indicated in a letter to Dr. MacCallum on July 12 that when Thomson's overturned canoe had been discovered it was noted that both of his paddles (the working paddle and the spare) had been tied in tightly.[41] This was echoed by the *Owen Sound Sun* in an article it ran about the missing artist that was published on July 13 that stated, "A later telegram stated that when the canoe was found the paddles were strapped to the thwarts."[42] Another paper, the *Globe*, reported on July 17 that, "Mr. Thomson was last seen at Canoe Lake at noon on Sunday, and at 3.30 in the afternoon his canoe was found adrift in the lake, upside down. There was no storm, only a light wind prevailing, and the fact that both paddles were in place in the canoe as if for a portage, adds to the mystery."[43] And finally, Mark Robinson who, along with the guide Charlie Scrim, were the ones that examined the contents of the canoe once it had been retrieved, stated, "I'm the man that took that canoe and turned it over and examined what was in the canoe; there was none of his equipment in it—even his little axe was gone—and the paddles were tied in for carrying."[44]

All of the above reports indicate that both of Thomson's paddles (both the spare and the working paddle) were present in the canoe when it was discovered. However, Mark Robinson would go on to state in the same interview that, "His paddle that he used in paddling was not there. If he'd had it with him, we never found it afterwards."[45] This statement was made during an audio recording conducted with the ranger in 1953, but he had also made mention of this observation in a handwritten response to a question posed to him by Blodwen Davies in 1930:

Question: Were his paddles found?
Robinson: One was found tied in his canoe as for portaging.[46]

So which was it—were two paddles found within the canoe or only one? Clearly, to Robinson's way of thinking, one of the paddles was missing. Both George Rowe and Mark Robinson had shared with my father the fact that Thomson had always used an ash paddle when canoeing, but this particular paddle was not in his canoe when Robinson and Scrim had examined it that day. Both men had then searched the shoreline of Canoe Lake in an attempt to locate it, but the ash paddle was never recovered. In addition, Robinson, to his surprise, found that the paddle/s that were tied to the thwarts of Thomson's canoe had been tied in so amateurishly that he had to cut them free with a knife, leading the ranger to believe that Thomson, who was a perfectionist about such things, could not have been the one who had tied them in. This was a view that was shared by the guide Norman Linton, who claimed he had been present at the time the canoe had been examined.[47]

It's hard to know what to make of this. Why would somebody steal Thomson's paddle and tie another one into his canoe? Some have postulated that Thomson was struck in the head with a paddle, perhaps his own paddle, and consequently it either broke during contact or had blood evidence on it that required it to subsequently be disposed of. The broken paddle was then replaced by the culprit. But this surely is pure speculation.

In any event, once Robinson had cut the paddles free from Thomson's canoe, he then inspected the watercraft for anything that might provide a clue as to what had happened to the artist. There was no damage indicated on the canoe itself, and tucked in the bow of the canoe were only a few of the supplies that Thomson was said to have taken with him.[48] If there had been an impact of the canoe with an object in the water that resulted in the artist being thrown from the craft or if he had fallen with his canoe while starting a portage, then, at the very least, the supplies that had been tucked under the bow should have been knocked free from where they had been stowed, and there should have been some evidence of a collision on or near the bow of the canoe itself. If the artist had fallen on a rocky shore while on a portage, for example, presumably his canoe would have fallen on the rocks as well, and so damage, or at least some scuffed paint, should have been present. No such damage was indicated.

The above points represent just some of the problems and inconsistencies one encounters in examining the details of the Tom Thomson case. Unfortunately, there will be many more problems that follow.

Chapter Six

THE SEARCH

After he had examined Thomson's canoe, Mark Robinson reported to Superintendent Bartlett, who immediately gave the ranger instructions to search the woods and surrounding areas at Canoe Lake to see if he could locate the missing artist. Robinson was confident that, while Thomson's abandoned canoe had been found in the water, Thomson himself was either stranded on one of the islands or perhaps nursing a broken leg on one of the portages.

The ranger set out to look for Thomson on Wednesday, July 11—a full twenty-four hours after he had first learned of the discovery of Thomson's abandoned canoe and three full days since the artist had last been seen. To assist him with the search Robinson had recruited Park Rangers Albert Patterson and E. Geitz, as well as Martin Blecher Junior. The latter proved to be an expeditious choice as he was one of the few people on Canoe Lake who owned a motorboat.

The men began their exploration along the southwest shoreline of Canoe Lake, particularly the areas in and around the two portages that led into Gill Lake, one of which had been the destination that Thomson had last been seen heading toward on the day that he went missing.[1] Upon arriving at the first of the two portages, the men set out on foot over the path that led to Gill Lake. Their search turned up no evidence that the artist had been there; i.e., no indication that a canoe had been pulled up on shore, no footprints along the portage trail, no sign of someone having suffered an accident, and not a trace of his missing paddle. They then got back in Blecher's motorboat and drove the better part of a mile further north to the main portage into Gill Lake. Once again, they came up empty. For the first time Robinson began to let worry cloud his thoughts; he had been positive that Thomson would be found reasonably safe and sound on or near the shore of one of these portages. That there was no evidence that he had arrived at either one left him flummoxed.

The next day (Thursday) the artist's elder brother George Thomson arrived at Canoe Lake. He and his wife had just started a vacation, leaving their home in New Haven, Connecticut to visit with George's family in Owen Sound when the news had reached the Thomson household that Tom had gone missing.[2] Acting on behalf of the family, George had left his wife behind with his parents and caught the next train out to Algonquin Park to investigate the circumstances surrounding his younger brother's disappearance. To placate George Thomson, Robinson didn't take part in the search that day, opting instead to take Tom's sibling along with him to speak with several people who might have some knowledge as to where his brother may have gone.[3] With Robinson otherwise engaged that day, the other rangers had continued the search. Working on a hunch, Robinson reached out to another ranger, Albert Patterson, asking him to go take the train west to Scotia Junction, and then south into the town of Huntsville to see if Thomson was there.[4] He knew that Thomson had friends in that town and so the artist might well have gone there to visit with them. But still, the fact that he had found some of Thomson's supplies still in his empty canoe was ominous. Something just wasn't right about the situation.

Shannon Fraser was also busy during this period, composing yet another letter that he would send to Thomson's patron, Dr. James

MacCallum, in which he revealed the details of his last meeting with the artist:

Mowat P. O.
July 12, 1917

Dear Sir.
Tom left here on Sunday about one o'clock for a fishing trip down the lake and at three o'clock his canoe was found floating a short distance from my place with both paddles tied tight in the canoe. Also his provisions were found packed in the canoe. The Canoe was upside down. We can find no trace of where he landed or what happened to him. Everything is being done that can be done. His brother [George Thomson] arrived this morning.
Will let you know at once if we find him.

Yours Truly,
J. S. Fraser[5]

Fraser had, of course, sent a telegram to MacCallum about Thomson's canoe being found two days previously; this most recent missive simply provided a few more details, but was primarily an update that the artist was still missing.

On Friday morning Robinson left George Thomson behind to take part in an aggressive search for the missing artist, which began with he and his son Jack paddling south on Canoe Lake to Bertram's Island, which had been—according to one account at least—the closest point of land to where Thomson's upturned canoe had first been spotted. Given that the ranger was still of the opinion that the artist's canoe had simply gotten away from him, it seemed a logical location to explore. After a thorough

search of the island had turned up nothing, the pair then paddled along the western shoreline of the lake, hoping that bent
brush or some of Thomson's missing supplies might be spotted and, thus, provide some indication of where he might be.[6]
The pair proceeded via portage to some neighboring lakes that
lay to the southwest and, finding no sign of the missing artist,
they then walked north along the Gilmore Road for half a mile
before heading west for another mile.[7] There was still no sign of
Thomson.

Robinson and his son then proceeded north, eventually hap-
pening upon a large beaver pond, which they circumnavigated and
then headed south to Gill Creek, and from there proceeded west
into Gill Lake. While at Gill Lake they spotted Colson's canoe "or
canvas boat"—perhaps the one that Fraser had borrowed to rent
to his guests and that the Blechers had heard had slipped its moorings.[8] What it was doing in a small lake to the southwest of Canoe
Lake that required a portage to access is anybody's guess, but it
most certainly precluded it from being the one that the Blechers
had noticed floating upside down on Canoe Lake the previous
Monday afternoon. Apart from this boat, there was no evidence
of any person having been in the Gill Lake vicinity in quite some
time. The father and son then decided to call it a day.

On their way back to their cabin they stopped in at Mowat
Lodge and brought George Thomson and Shannon Fraser up to
speed on what their search that day had yielded.[9] They also put in
briefly at Lowrey Dickson's cabin on the western shore of Potter
Creek to compare notes with both Dickson and a fire ranger by the
name of MacDonald who, likewise, had been out searching for the
artist that day.[10] From there the pair headed north up Joe Creek
until they reached the ranger's cabin.

The next morning (Saturday) Ranger Patterson had returned
from his recognizance mission to Huntsville and checked in with

Robinson. The news was bleak; Thomson had not been seen in that town for quite some time. Robinson spent the remainder of the day resting in his cabin and meeting the trains, while Patterson returned to his cabin at Moose Lake.[11]

At this point George Thomson had been in Algonquin Park for two days and, despite extensive searching by Robinson and the others, there had still been no sign of his younger brother's whereabouts. The fact that all of his brother's haunts had been investigated to no avail, along with the fact that George had left his new bride behind in Owen Sound with his parents while he had travelled to the park, was beginning to weigh heavily upon him. Besides, he only had a few days of holiday time left before he had to get back to his job in the States. Consequently, he decided that sitting around the lobby of Mowat Lodge in the hope that his brother might eventually turn up seemed to him a waste of his time, particularly when there were other people who were far more familiar with the local terrain than he was who were already out checking all of the places that Tom would most likely be. All in all, he knew that there was little more for him to do at Canoe Lake:

> I was then living in New Haven, Conn. And happened to be home on a short vacation when word came of the finding of Tom's canoe. I was obliged to return to work with little opportunity of investigating conditions surrounding his death.[12]

Apparently, some of the locals weren't impressed with how George Thomson had utilized his time while in the park. From their perspective, he preferred to stay within the comfortable confines of Mowat Lodge while other people, who shared no family connection with Tom Thomson, expended considerable time, effort, and money in the attempt to locate his missing brother. Shannon Fraser, writing in 1917, opined that:

> George Thomson ought to be the last one to say anything as he came up here and did not do anything to find Tom's body; did not even get men to grapple, [he] went back home and left everything for me to do, and the people were talking about him wondering if he had no money.[13]

At some point during Thomson's disappearance, Dr. MacCallum had evidently reached out to Shannon Fraser, asking him to do what he could to help locate the artist and offering to cover any expenses. In writing to MacCallum seven months later, Thomson's sister Elizabeth informed him that:

> When George was at Canoe Lake the first time Fraser showed him your telegram offering to pay expenses. George told him not to send any bill to you; that a family could not accept a kindness of that kind.[14]

Fraser, sensing an opportunity to recoup his out of pocket expenses, politely nodded to George in agreement—and then sent MacCallum a bill anyway. In the meantime, the press from the artist's hometown had gotten wind of Thomson's disappearance and had published the following article on page one of the *Owen Sound Sun* newspaper:

TOM THOMSON'S CANOE FOUND ON CANOE LAKE
Owen Sound Sun, July 13, 1917
Efforts Being Made to Find Him Since Sunday Last—Is a Noted Artist.

A telegram from Canoe Lake, Algonquin Park, received by his parents, Mr. and Mrs. John Thomson, 4th Ave. E., on Tuesday announced that a canoe belonging to their son, Thomas Thomson, the well known Toronto artist, had been found on the lake and no trace of Mr. Thomson could be found. He had arrived at Canoe Lake on Saturday and the canoe had been found the following day. Mr. Geo. Thomson, of New York, a brother of the missing man, arrived here on Tuesday and left for Canoe Lake on Wednesday morning, arriving there yesterday morning and a search is now being made for any trace of the young man. A later telegram stated that when the canoe was found the paddles were strapped to the thwarts, which might indicate that the canoe had drifted from its moorings and left Mr. Thomson marooned on one of the islands. The search was proceeded with all speed. . . . Mr. Thomson is very well known here and everyone will hope that he will be found safe and well. The other alternative is not pleasant to consider but should it be found that he has been drowned, Canada will have lost one of her most accomplished landscape artists, and a thorough gentleman.[15]

Robinson hadn't read this newspaper article, but even if he had he would not have shared its pessimistic conclusion. He had remained undeterred in his conviction that he was going to find his missing friend alive. To this end, save for the day spent with George Thomson, the ranger had spent almost every day that week exploring the woodland and surrounding lakes. During these travels he had walked, canoed, blown his "Vimy" whistle and even fired shots in the air from his rifle—but all to no avail.[16] In the meantime, Superintendent Bartlett had sent an additional four rangers to explore the southeast side of Canoe Lake as well as the area in and around the Tea Lake Dam.[17] As indicated earlier, Shannon Fraser had even contributed to the search for the missing artist, having apparently paid to send the guides Lowrey Dickson and George Rowe, in addition to a fire ranger ("Mr. McDonald") out to search for Thomson over a three-day period.[18]

By the end of the week Robinson was exhausted and, despite resting on Saturday, he couldn't shake the dull but steady fatigue that had persisted most of that day and on into the evening. He was just starting to doze off when the phone rang in his cabin. It was Superintendent Bartlett, who wanted to be brought up to date on how the search was proceeding. Bartlett knew that his ranger was pushing himself a little too hard. After all, Robinson was not a young man anymore and it was known that his experience in the war had weakened him considerably. Bartlett cautioned the ranger to take it easy.

"Look Mark, you must be tired travelling so much."

Robinson sighed. "I am but I can still travel more. I'd like to find Thomson. He must have broken a limb, or broken his leg, or fallen someplace and injured himself. But I've walked all over the bush, I've fired shots and I've blown my whistle. He knows my signal and the whistle as well as anyone does and I cannot find a trace of him." To Robinson it was inconceivable that the artist would have come to any grief on the water. He was too good a swimmer and too accomplished a canoeist.

Bartlett, however, pressed home his point. "Take a rest tomorrow, Mark."[19]

Robinson told his superintendent that he would but, of course, he didn't. Instead the ranger woke up early on Sunday, July 15, and patroled the east and north shores of Canoe Lake in a further attempt to locate his friend.[20] Again, he found no trace of Thomson and, dejectedly, he returned to his cabin for the night. The ranger drew a deep breath and resolved to get up early the next morning "to go out determined to find him on Monday."[21]

Thomson would in fact be found on Monday—floating face down in thirty feet of water.

Chapter Seven

"CONSIDERABLE ADVERSE COMMENT"

As hard as it may be to comprehend for Canadians today (as Algonquin Park and Tom Thomson have become almost synonymous over the decades) the passing of Tom Thomson carried with it very little impact in 1917. Indeed, almost as soon as Dr. Ranney had returned to North Bay, life at Canoe Lake went back to normal; the tourists continued to arrive into Algonquin Park, the guides continued to ply their trade, and the hotels in the area continued to enjoy a thriving business. One less guest at Mowat Lodge, in the bigger picture, simply meant one more room to let. What is easy to overlook in the matter is that during his lifetime Tom Thomson was virtually unknown outside of the Toronto art world. As Charles Plewman would later recall:

> At this point it is hard to realize how few were the people who had even heard of his death in 1917. I was back at Canoe Lake in 1921, four years later, but no one up there was talking about Tom Thomson. He seemed "forgotten."[1]

And there was a reason for this: to put it bluntly, Canada had more important things to focus on. In 1917 the country was then in the third year of World War I and, consequently, the news of a little-known landscape artist and handyman being found dead in a body of water within a remote provincial park in central Ontario paled in comparison to, say, the news of the Battle of Vimy Ridge, which had been fought just three months prior to Thomson's death. Mothers and fathers who had their sons torn from their lives by the war were of course more inclined to invest their sympathies elsewhere. It is only leisure that begets speculation on matters outside of the home, and there was very little leisure time to be had while World War I was being contested.

That being said, there did exist a small number of people back at Canoe Lake who had known the artist personally who had been impacted by his death, and who considered the manner in which the inquest had been conducted as being utterly facile—and they weren't shy about voicing their disapproval. Indeed, so vociferous were the naysayers that Robinson had felt compelled to make the following entry in his daily diary:

> [Wednesday] July 18, 1917—There is considerable adverse comment regarding the taking of the evidence among residents.[2]

As we've seen, certain parties within the community had not been pleased with the choice of venue. When Blodwen Davies was conducting research for her biography on Thomson in 1930, many of the people who had been in the Canoe Lake region in 1917 were still accessible. Even thirteen years after the tragedy she was able to pick up on hard feelings that still lingered amongst the residents. She had been told, for example, that the Blecher family had served cigars and beer to the attendees during the inquest.[3] That beer should be served during a time of what was supposed to be government enforced temperance to the attendees of an official inquest might have struck certain members within the Canoe Lake community as being highly inappropriate, particularly given the solemnity and sobriety that such an occasion warranted. After all, this was supposedly an official inquest into the death of a person from within the local community, not a gentleman's club get together. Mark Robinson had been aware that Martin Senior had beer in his cottage since June 30, as he had been the one who had cleared it for him at the train station. At the time the older Blecher had indicated to the ranger that it was "for personal use" only,[4] which had been the condition for its clearance, but during the night of the inquest there he was serving it up to everyone in his cabin.

The word that had trickled its way south to certain of Thomson's friends in Toronto such as A.Y. Jackson was that it had been "a very careless inquest."[5] Jackson believed that the apparent apathy of it all was "perhaps influenced by the feeling that he [Thomson] was of no importance as a painter and probably up there to avoid military service. . . . It could have been a heart attack and they did not take the trouble to find out. . . ."[6] While Robinson did not subscribe to the notion that the artist had suffered a heart attack,[7] he did agree with Jackson on the haste with which the inquest had been conducted.[8]

As we shall see in due course, the ranger never was accepting of the "accidental drowning" verdict but perhaps even more telling is the fact that neither were the majority of those who took part in the inquest in the early morning hours of July 18. Ed Colson, for example, had shared with his kitchen staff that certain of the guides had suspected foul play.[9] Mark Robinson believed likewise.[10] Martin Blecher Junior was of the opinion that the artist had committed suicide,[11] while his sister Bessie presumably would have been of the same opinion on the matter as her brother (however, as we have no evidence for her opinion on the subject we shall have to classify it as "unknown"). Shannon Fraser was said to have subscribed to the suicide theory as well.[12] Dr. Howland's report had indicated that the death was due to drowning.[13] We don't know if George Rowe subscribed to the same foul play theory that certain of his guiding friends embraced, but we do know that he did not believe that Thomson's death was due to "accidental drowning."[14] If Hugh Trainor agreed with his daughter Winnifred, then he would have been of the opinion that the artist had met with foul play.[15] However, as it has not come down to us what the patriarch of the Trainor family believed, we shall also have to classify his opinion on the matter as "unknown."

In reviewing the above it is little wonder that a sense of general dissatisfaction began to disseminate so soon after Dr. Ranney's decision had been rendered—perhaps only one of the eight members of the inquest had actually subscribed to it.

And that one person, Dr. Goldwyn Howland, would come in time to have his doubts about his statement at the inquest that the artist had died an accidental death by drowning (a statement that Dr. Ranney had largely based his verdict on). In correspondence exchanged between Dr. Howland's daughter Margaret and my father during the 1960s, she revealed that:

> My father, the late Dr. Howland, in subsequent discussion, mentioned the fact that there was a possibility that the drowning of Tom Thomson was not accidental.[16]

From the perspective of such people, the existence of a bruise on the artist's temple warranted serious consideration, rather than the hasty assumption that he had—for the first time in his life—simply fallen while traversing a portage and hit his head on a rock. Even Thomson's elder brother George, for example, and quite in spite of the coroner's ruling, had been troubled by the report of his brother's head wound:

> I think the revealing statement in the [coroner's] finding is that of the bruise over the left temple, which I believe rendered him [Tom] unconscious so that drowning ensued.

Of course it is hard to say what caused the bruise. It probably was an accident—though it is possible to have been foul play.[17]

Mark Robinson, likewise, once he had time to consider what had transpired, came to view the coroner's conclusion with a fair measure of skepticism if not outright contempt. In a letter written to a member of the Thomson family shortly after the tragedy, Shannon Fraser shared some of the misgivings he had heard from other people around Canoe Lake:

The verdict was death due to drowning. . . . However several people have said to me "it was no accident . . ."[18]

Winnifred Trainor had been among the first to suspect foul play[19] and, according to those who were on friendly terms with her, such as the old trapper Ralph Bice, she maintained this suspicion well into her later years.[20] Granted, in September 1917 there is evidence that she had, for a while at least, attempted to entertain the coroner's official conclusion. Reporting on a meeting that she had with Trainor, Thomson's sister Margaret had indicated that:

I asked her if she thought anyone had harmed Tom and she said, "No." Her theory was that he had fallen on the rocks and slipped into the water.[21]

Trainor, however, may have just been saying this to put Margaret Thomson at her ease, as she had been convinced (when she had confronted Robinson on the day of the funeral) that foul play must have been involved. And there were others who knew Thomson that cast an unbelieving eye upon the coroner's conclusion, particularly those who had guided with the artist. Quite apart from the bruise discovered on Thomson's temple or the fishing line that had been found wrapped suspiciously around one of his ankles, there existed another odd discovery, this one involving how Thomson's paddles had been tied into his canoe. Admittedly, it may have been an oddity only in the minds of the guides and certain of the park rangers who not only knew Thomson, but who themselves happened to be seasoned canoeists.

We have already seen that when the artist's overturned canoe had been pulled from the water Mark Robinson and the guides had been surprised at the manner in which Thomson's paddles had been lashed onto the thwarts. According to Blanche Packard, who had worked at the Algonquin Hotel that summer, the guides had told her, "It wasn't Tom's lashing."[22] The guide Norm Linton, Blanche's future husband, and also a man who claimed to have seen the artist's canoe when it had been pulled from the water, had also confided in her that, "Tom wouldn't be carrying a canoe with his paddles roped like that!"[23] According to Linton, the way Thomson's paddles had been tied had struck him as peculiar, almost shoddy, as the artist had been a perfectionist in such matters. "Even the cramper pan had to be kept just so," he recalled.[24]

So why would a perfectionist like Thomson tie his paddles into his canoe in such an uncharacteristically sloppy fashion? Blanche Packard further recalled that on the morning that Thomson had last been seen alive she had witnessed him buckle on his packsack,[25] and the fact that it wasn't on his body when it was pulled from the lake had struck her as curious:

> If, according to the theory, he stumbled while carrying the canoe, he should have been wearing this pack containing his food, and it should have been on the body when it was found. However, his old brown pack was never recovered,

nor were the rest of his supplies or his painting gear. All the guides who learned of the story agreed that the facts of the case were such as aroused their suspicions.[26]

"ACCIDENTAL DEATH BY DROWNING" REVISITED

To the minds of those who held such suspicions, if Thomson did, in fact, suffer an "accidental death by drowning," then certain things should have been easily explained. One theory advanced in support of the accidental death by drowning contention over the years had been that Thomson's canoe must have unexpectedly collided with something on the lake, such as a rock or a stump, which had caused the artist to pitch forward and strike his head, presumably somewhere on the canoe itself, lose consciousness, and topple into the water and drown. Indeed, this is the conclusion put forth by the author Gregory Klages in his book *The Many Deaths of Tom Thomson*. The problem with such a scenario is that his paddles were tied in for portaging, and he could not have been out paddling on the lake without access to his paddles. So Thomson simply falling out of his canoe in the middle of the lake couldn't have happened, nor could a collision have taken place as, if he wasn't paddling, his canoe wouldn't have been moving in order to collide with anything.

Furthermore, Thomson paddled a cedar strip canoe; if he had collided with an object such as a rock or a log with sufficient impact so as to cause him to be propelled forward and hit his head hard enough to be knocked out, then there should have been some indication of such a high impact collision on the canoe itself. However, not one of the people who inspected the artist's canoe after pulling it from the lake noticed that it had been damaged in any way. Not even something as minor as a paint scrape on the canoe was ever reported, and the canoe was inspected by seasoned canoeists such as Mark Robinson, who would have been looking for anything that would offer up a clue as to what had happened to the artist that might have aided in his search for him.

THE BAD JUDGMENT THEORY

Other theories advanced in order to lend support to the accidental death by drowning theory have it that while en route to the portage that he was paddling to that day, Thomson had stood up in his canoe to urinate, lost his balance and fell and hit his head on the gunwale (the wooden edges that line the open portion of a canoe), lost consciousness, and then toppled into the water and drowned. I will pass for the moment on the viability of a scenario wherein a person who is paddling a canoe while suddenly overtaken by an urge to relieve his bladder would first feel compelled to tie both of his paddles securely to the thwarts of his canoe before answering nature's call. Such a fantastic theory first found its way into print via the authors Harold Town and David Silcox in their book *Tom Thomson: The Silence and the Storm* in 1977. What makes such a statement so fascinating is that, apart from "zero" evidence to support such a contention, it could only have been made by a person (or persons) profoundly unfamiliar with canoes. Canoes are a very intuitive watercraft, and thus incredibly sensitive to the slightest movement one makes. It is almost impossible to hit your head in a canoe when standing up because the slightest movement will cause the canoe to pitch out in the opposite direction from which you are falling and it would be out from underneath you before you could strike your head on any part of it. Plus, a seasoned canoeist such as Thomson, who was only paddling a short distance of perhaps a mile or a mile-and-a-half to a nearby portage, would have only needed to hold in the urge to relieve himself for perhaps fifteen to twenty minutes at the most and, if that proved too long, he could have paddled into land at any point on his excursion that day as he was never more than a hundred yards off shore. Had he really needed to go to the bathroom that urgently; i.e., within five-to-ten minutes of leaving the Mowat Lodge dock, he had every opportunity to empty his bladder prior to setting out that day, as he had been at the Trainor cottage to collect his fishing tackle just before to his departure, and the outhouse on that property would have provided him the opportunity he required.

THE INEBRIATION THEORY

And finally there was the theory that he was drunk that afternoon and lost consciousness while paddling and simply fell out of his canoe and drowned, or that he was similarly inebriated as he was preparing to portage. In the latter scenario, the artist was supposed to have misjudged his step and slipped, hitting his head on a rock, and fallen into the water. Presumably his body would then have been carried out into the lake by the current, where it later sank. The problem with both of these theories is that, despite the statements of Town, Silcox, and Bice, there is no evidence that Tom Thomson was drunk on the morning that he was last seen alive. Indeed, the artist had been seen by at least seven people on the morning that he left (Molly and Edwin Colson, Blanche Packard, Shannon Fraser, Charlie Scrim, Mark Robinson, and Mrs. Edwin Thomas) and not one of them reported, either at the inquest or afterward, that Thomson had been inebriated. Indeed, Molly Colson quite specifically stated that there was no smell of alcohol on his breath and that he couldn't possibly have gotten drunk in the short time that passed from when she last saw him until he left the Mowat Lodge dock.[27]

What makes such a scenario even less likely to have occurred is that if Thomson's motor skills had been so grossly impaired by alcohol consumption so as to see him lose consciousness and fall out of his canoe within a half mile of the Mowat Lodge dock, such a condition would not have gone undetected by the people who saw him that morning. Moreover, if he had been that severely impaired (to the point where he was unconscious a mere five-to-ten minutes after he left the dock at Mowat Lodge) he certainly would have had trouble even getting into his canoe to leave that day, and most likely would not have made it out even ten yards from the dock, let alone the mile and a half necessary to reach the portage.

THE UNCHARTED WATERS THEORY

Of the various theories advanced for accidental death by drowning, the most plausible would seem to be that of collision. That is, that the artist had made a crucial mistake in his navigation and ended up making impact with a partially submerged log or rock that resulted in his being knocked unconscious so that drowning ensued. Let us neglect for the moment the facts that his canoe showed no sign of having impacted anything and that both of his paddles had been tied into his water craft. For such a scenario to play out, we would have to accept that Thomson had been, in effect, caught by surprise when his canoe suddenly rammed into either a large rock or a stump en route to the portage that day. This is an incredible supposition, however, given that Thomson had paddled this exact same route to the Gill Lake Portage as a matter of routine ever since he had first started canoeing in the Park in 1912—a period of five years. He evidently knew the lake well enough to guide tourists to and from this particular portage dozens of times without incident over several years. That he would suddenly forget the presence of a big rock or stump seems, if not impossible, at least highly unlikely. That

Thomson would hit his head off a rock at the Gill Lake Portage is also hard to fathom, as the access point to the portage does not feature large rocks for one to either slip on or strike one's head against. The shore is primarily gravel and, again, was a portage that Thomson had used countless times over the years that he had paddled on Canoe Lake.

A HIGHLY REGARDED CANOEIST

What had been particularly hard to square in the minds of those who knew the artist's habits well, such as Mark Robinson, was that a canoeist of Thomson's caliber should simply fall out of his canoe and drown. According to Robinson:

> [Thomson] had the reputation of being one of the best canoe men in the country and only a few days before [he went missing] . . . he and Charlie Scrim went right out the other side of Big Wap [Wapomeo Island] there; rescued two canoe loads of people. I forget whether there was more than five, I think there were about five people in them. They had both upset in the storm, and Charlie [Scrim] and Tom pulled out and went over and they succeeded in landing them on Big Wap—saved their lives. . . . I just mention that to show that he was a first-class canoe man or he wouldn't have done that.[28]

Robinson was not alone in this belief. Even seasoned guides such as Norm Linton, who had guided with the artist on several occasions, held Thomson's canoeing skills in very high regard:

> He [Thomson] could weather any gale with any man I've ever seen on the water.[29]

Even prior to 1917 Thomson had developed a positive reputation for his canoeing skills. His sister Louise Henry recollected a time when Thomson had returned home to Owen Sound in 1912:

> Tom had just come home from the North for a few days, and there was a young artist with him whose name was Broadhead. He told Mr. Henry about some very interesting experiences they had had in the North Country. One story he told was of a very narrow escape he and Mr. Broadhead had while running a rapids with the canoe pretty well loaded with supplies and their season's sketches. The canoe struck on a submerged rock and they lost most of their best sketches, most of their supplies, and came very nearly losing their lives. Mr. Broadhead said that if Tom had not been such an expert canoeman, they both would have been lost.[30]

When this incident was reported in the September 27, 1912 edition of the *Owen Sound Sun* newspaper, it was revealed that the two men had also capsized their craft on Green Lake, a result of a sudden cloudburst swamping their canoe. "However, they didn't lose anything and recovered the canoe as both the men are expert swimmers." Interestingly, the same article indicated that during this particular canoe trip both Thomson and Broadhead had paddled and portaged their way into Canoe Lake for the first time. If ever an unexpected rock or deadhead should present itself to be a dangerous obstacle, one would think that Thomson's first time on the lake (rather than several years later once he had become exceedingly familiar with it) would be when such a collision might have occurred. However, no accidents were reported.

Thomson's ability to survive capsizing his canoe in both the rapids and tempests of unfamiliar lakes had already been established. However, on the final day of his life when he paddled away from the Mowat Lodge dock, the weather was clear and there were no rapids to encounter or sudden cloudbursts to contend with. Moreover, Thomson was paddling upon a lake that he was by this point in time very familiar with, and he also presumably made it to a portage that he was also very familiar with. In addition, Thomson was a fit man with no health issues that could have contributed to his demise. Indeed, his sister Louise had once written about the exceptional stamina of her late brother:

> I remember one night he faced a blizzard and walked 10 miles to a party. On another occasion he walked to Meaford, about 20 miles away, rather than bother with a horse and buggy, although Father begged him to take them.[31]

As the reader will recall, when Robinson had been asked whether Thomson had any troubles with his heart, he had replied, "I scarcely think so, as he could throw up his canoe and go uphill over portages without any trouble."[32]

AN EXCELLENT SWIMMER

If Thomson had never learned to swim, then the official verdict of "accidental drowning" might have been easier to accept. However, in recounting Thomson's swimming skills, his childhood friend from Leith, Alan Ross, stated that, "he was one of the best swimmers of all the boys around Leith, and some of them were pretty good."[33] Ed Godin, who shared fire-ranging duties with Thomson in the summer of 1916 in Achray, never said much about Thomson, but he did feel obliged to mention that, "he was a very good swimmer."[34] Robinson supported Ross and Godin's opinion in this matter, testifying that:

> Tom Thomson was a first class swimmer in every respect. . . . and there wasn't a better swimmer in this country. Mr.

> [Taylor] Statten never produced a man who could swim bet-
> ter, I don't think, at his camps [Camp Amek and Camp
> Wapomeo].[35]

Perhaps the most compelling testimony to be put forth regarding
Thomson's aquatic skill came from Irene Ewing, who was a girlfriend of Winnifred Trainor's and who was also a friend of Thomson's. She was eighteen years of age at the time of Thomson's death,
but she vividly recalled a time when:

> Winnie and I were seated on the porch looking out over Ca-
> noe Lake when we observed someone swimming across the
> lake from where Tom made his camp—just north of Hay-
> hurst point. Shortly afterwards the swimmer turned out to
> be Tom himself. He had swum over to Winnie's cottage
> where we were from his own side of the Lake. He was an
> excellent swimmer.[36]

And so those who knew the artist best were left to ponder what
they considered to be the rather hastily reached conclusion of the
coroner's inquest; that a man who was both an excellent swimmer
and exceptional canoeist in addition to being a man of considerable
endurance fitness, could, while paddling along a familiar lake on a
calm afternoon, simply topple out of his canoe and drown.

Chapter Eight

THE BODY IS EXHUMED

If Winnifred Trainor had, as some have alleged, been expecting to marry the artist, his sudden death must have turned her world completely upside down.

Trainor was thirty-three years old when Thomson had died. Her prospects had been slim prior to meeting the artist several years previously (there is no record of her having any previous boyfriends), and Thomson must have represented a promise, a hope, of a brighter future. She had, if the old trapper Ralph Bice is to be believed, longed to move out of the family home where her father would stumble in blind drunk on a Saturday night and neither Winnifred, her sister Marie, nor her mother would see him again until Monday.[1] With Thomson's death, the one exit she had out of this environment had effectively been sealed off. She would forever after be known as Hugh and Margaret Trainor's daughter, never Tom Thomson's wife.

She had been in Huntsville when the news arrived of the artist's disappearance and had no doubt been visited by Ranger Albert Patterson when Mark Robinson had dispatched him to Huntsville to see if Thomson had visited there. We're not sure when she had received word that Thomson's body had been found, but we do know that early the very next morning she had arrived in Algonquin Park. It was Tuesday, July 17 when her train pulled into Canoe Lake Station, and all she knew at that moment was that the man she loved was going to be buried that day—right along with any future happiness she might have entertained. Even though she was

only ten years old, Rose Thomas clearly recalled the moment that
Trainor stepped from the coach at Canoe Lake Station:

> She came up after he was drowned and got off the train. I
> asked her in but she said she'd rather not, so she went and
> stood on the bridge. The bridge is still there now but the
> railings are all gone. I can always remember her standing in
> the middle of the bridge looking down into the water [of
> Potter Creek] . . . I can even remember what she had on. She
> had on a beige coat and a big beige hat. They wore big hats
> in those days. She had a lot of black hair with braids around
> her head. She was a really handsome looking girl.[2]

Winnifred had traveled to Canoe Lake with the daughter of one
of her neighbors, (referred to as "Miss Terry" in Mark Robinson's journal entry for that day). And shortly after her interlude
on the bridge that morning, the pair left for the Trainor cottage.
The cottage sat several hundred yards or so northeast of Mowat
Lodge, separated from the lodge by a massive chipyard that had
been built up and left over from when the lumber mill had been
in operation. Awaiting the girls' arrival there were Winnifred's
father and probably her mother. Her father, Hugh Trainor, had
most likely been present at the cottage since the previous Friday as he had been present shortly after the guides had towed
Thomson's body to Gillender's Point and had also been present
during the inquest. The reader will recall from an earlier chapter Charles Plewman's recollection of Winnifred suddenly arriving on the scene and demanding to view Thomson's remains. It
has been alleged by some that as soon as she arrived at her cottage she secured a watercraft and went immediately to the island
where Thomson's corpse was being embalmed. I believe this to
be highly unlikely, as her father had seen firsthand the condition

that Thomson's body was in and, consequently, no father would allow his daughter to be exposed to such a sight if he could prevent it—and Hugh Trainor was a man who could prevent it. It is far more probable that sometime after she had arrived at the family cottage she witnessed the barge containing Thomson's coffin leaving Wapomeo Island on its way to the landing point used by Mowat Lodge, which was adjacent to the Blecher cottage. As the Trainor cottage was quite close to the Blecher cottage, the barge containing the coffin would have been clearly visible to her as she looked out from her verandah. This very likely was the tipping point that caused her to briefly lose her composure and make her way over to the landing point, where she would issue her demand to see the artist's body, adamant in her belief that he must have met with foul play. At this point Mark Robinson was said to have interceded, perhaps reinforcing the objections that her father might have made to her earlier. Robinson, like Hugh Trainor, had already seen the condition of Thomson's body and he would not have been in favor of subjecting her to such a gruesome sight.

Having been turned away at the landing point, Trainor composed herself and returned to her cottage, where she then prepared to attend the artist's funeral, which would take place as soon as the mourners had been assembled. After witnessing Thomson's burial, Winnifred Trainor, in the company of her friend Miss Terry, took the next train out of Algonquin Park, first heading west to Scotia Junction, where the pair then caught another train that carried them south to their respective homes in Huntsville. Despite traveling with her girlfriend, the train ride home must have been a blur to Winnifred. But she was a person possessed of a fortitude that was as strong as it was rare, and by the next day her mind had absolved itself of any trace of self-pity and had settled sufficiently to allow her to reach out to the Thomson family to offer her condolences. According to the artist's sister Peggy:

[S]innie [?] and I were called to the telephone one night at twelve o'clock. It was Miss Trainor, a friend of Tom's, who was calling us. She told us the body had been buried and wanted to know if we would like anything done. We told her we wanted him home, so she did everything in her power and stayed up all night to help us. She called George at three o'clock that night again and in the meantime she was doing everything she could to help make arrangements.[3]

Trainor was mortified that the burial in the Park had taken place without the Thomson family's approval. Learning of their desire to have Tom Thomson's body interred in the family plot at Leith, Trainor wanted to aid the grief-stricken family of the man she cared so deeply for. And given the precariousness of the phone service within Algonquin Park, she then offered to act as a go-between for the Thomsons and the undertakers in an effort to have the artist's body exhumed and returned home.

The telephone records that have survived from July 18 indicate that on this day she had twice placed calls to the Thomson family, and also made four calls to the undertaker from Kearney, Robert Flavelle.[4] The problem, it seemed, lay in the fact that there had been a delay in Shannon Fraser receiving the telegram from the Thomson family indicating that they wanted the artist's body sent to Owen Sound. This would have required a sealable; i.e., a soldered, metal casket, which was required by law to ship a dead body by train within the province. Given the communication problems going into and out of the park, when the artist's body had first been discovered this information had not been passed along to Robert Flavelle, and he had simply brought with him a standard non-sealable casket for what he anticipated would be a local burial. Apparently, by the time Fraser was in possession of the family's telegram indicating their wishes for the body to be buried in Leith, Thomson had already been interred in the Mowat Cemetery.

Winnifred Trainor wrote to Thomson's brother-in-law Tom Harkness (who was the administrator of Tom's estate):

> And you know the tangle that now that has to be unraveled—owing to the thoughtlessness of not having a sealed casket—which anyone knows is needed in a case of that kind and also required by law [if a body is to be transported by train].[5]

Thomson's sister Peggy, in writing to her sister Minnie about the matter, blamed the original undertaker/s for the problem that ensued:

> They buried his body in the [p]ark as the undertaker said it would be impossible to ship the body. He didn't know his business at all and made a regular mess of things.[6]

Despite her ire, Trainor reached out to Flavelle, hoping that he would be willing to exhume the body and place it in a proper metal casket for transport to the family in Owen Sound. To this end, Flavelle either didn't have access to that type of casket at his furniture store, particularly on such short notice, or else he was simply not inclined to go through the ordeal that he and Roy Dixon had endured at Canoe Lake all over again.[7] To her surprise, Flavelle declined her job offer, which caused Trainor to suffer some angst—but not for long. She quickly switched to a Plan B, which had her make contact with an undertaker, Franklin W. Churchill, in her hometown of Huntsville, to see if he could be persuaded to take the job—and apparently, he could. As Churchill later recounted:

> She phoned the undertaker in Kearney, who had been in charge of the funeral near Canoe Lake, but he refused to exhume the body. Then she phoned me in Huntsville. I was not anxious to do the job, but she begged me and finally I said yes.[8]

Churchill's initial lack of enthusiasm to accept the job is worth not-ing at this juncture, as it might well serve to explain a lot of what would unfold later.

For her part, Trainor, while still angry with Flavelle, also held Shannon Fraser to blame for not following the Thomson family's wishes. She believed that Fraser had received the telegram contain-ing the Thomson family's instructions but had chosen to keep its contents to himself. According to Thomson's sister Margaret:

> She [Winnie Trainor] said the telegram, which my brother [George] sent with the directions telling what to do with the body, Mr. Fraser received and didn't let on to anyone.[9]

While there exists no direct proof for this assertion, we do know that Fraser received the Thomson family's next telegram, which informed him that a different undertaker would soon be arriving at Canoe Lake for the express purpose of undoing all of the work that he and Robinson had done in arranging and organizing Thomson's original burial. The telegram was sent without any indication of its author, for, as Mark Robinson would report in his diary for that day:

> [Wednesday] July 18, 1917— . . . S. Fraser received telegram that a steel casket was being sent in and Tom Thomson's body was to be exhumed and taken out, by whose orders I am not at present aware.[10]

Clearly Fraser had shared this news with the ranger, however nei-ther man knew whom the undertaker was, where he would be com-ing in from, or when exactly he would be arriving. As it happened, Churchill, with metal casket in tow, had made his way by train from Huntsville to Canoe Lake Station on the evening of July 18, the very evening of the same day that Fraser had received the telegram

from George Thomson.[11] Fraser would later relate to my father that
he had had no idea when the undertaker would be arriving, and
had only encountered him at the train station quite by fortuitous
circumstance, when the lodge owner had delivered a piece of lug-
gage to Canoe Lake Station that one of the guests at Mowat Lodge
had left behind.[12]

After introducing himself, Churchill was assisted by Fraser and
George Rowe (whom the lodge owner had either encountered at
Canoe Lake Station or had brought with him on the buckboard
that night for company) in loading the metal casket onto the back
of Fraser's work wagon and the three men then set off for Mowat
Lodge.[13] Both Rowe and Fraser would later recall that during that
ride back to the lodge to retrieve the necessary tools for the job,
Churchill was offered, but refused, any assistance with his impend-
ing task.[14] This caused the two local men to look at each other in
muted surprise, particularly since it was now 9:00 p.m. and darkness was rapidly descending upon them. Once at the lodge, Fraser
collected a pair of lanterns, a crowbar and at least one shovel.[15] Fraser lit one of the lanterns and hung it on the metal bracket of his
buckboard to help illuminate the roadway as the pair made their
way along the dirt road that led to the cemetery. Within a matter of
minutes the two men had arrived at their destination. Fraser helped
the undertaker unload the steel casket as well as the tools they had
picked up from Mowat Lodge. And then, in the dark of night, and
by Churchill's own request, Fraser departed from the scene, leaving
the undertaker alone to do his work.

According to Churchill's only statement on record as to what
transpired that evening, he then "opened the grave and took the
coffin and the rough-box out of the grave . . . I transferred the
remains into a metal box which I could seal. The empty coffin and
rough box were put back into the grave and the grave was filled
again."[16] The undertaker had indicated to Fraser that when he had

completed his task he would use the lantern that the lodge owner had left with him to send a signal to return and collect him. Fraser would later recall that he had not been back at the lodge very long when he saw Churchill's signal, and so he returned to the cemetery to pick up the undertaker and the newly soldered metal casket.[17] Churchill had been dropped off at the cemetery some time after 9:00 p.m. and was picked up at some point after midnight, thus the time it took him to complete his task was guesstimated by Fraser to have been approximately three hours.

And one can only imagine what a task it was that Churchill had to endure for those few hours! Algonquin Park in 1917 was a true wilderness, and according to a letter written by Tom Thomson on July 7 (the day before his death):

> The [black] flies and mosquitoes are much worse than I have seen them any year, and the fly dope doesn't have any effect on them.[18]

Given the heavy presence of these insects during that July, an oil lantern giving off light in the dead of night in the middle of a forest surrounded by swamps and lakes would only have attracted more of these creatures. The reader can well imagine that Churchill would have had a fulltime job just fighting off these ravenous pests as he attempted to dig through the better part of five feet of earth, pull out the original casket and rough box, transfer Thomson's corpse from its original casket into a new metal one, and then solder the metal casket shut, return the original casket and rough box to the grave and then refill the grave with soil. All of this accomplished, apparently, within a span of only three (maybe four?) hours.

The soldering of the casket alone would have been a lengthy process, even if the environment had been free of black flies and mosquitoes. Jack Wilkinson, whose relatives had been working at

Canoe Lake Station on the night that the Huntsville undertaker arrived (and the next evening when he departed), and who would later work at Canoe Lake station himself, had experience in soldering metal caskets for transport on trains. He laughed when told what Churchill was said to have accomplished on his own in such a short span of time:

> The train came into Canoe Lake station about eight o'clock at night from Parry Sound. I think it was around 8:00. It was after supper anyway, and was getting dark. The coffin came in on that train. It was dark when he got to the cemetery with that coffin with Shannon's rig. [The undertaker] was all alone with a coal oil lantern. He had to empty that blasted grave, put the body in that casket, seal it all around. And it takes two hours to seal a casket—I've done two of them. You seal it all around with a blowtorch. You see a body smells to high heaven, just awful. If there is any of that coming out on the train they won't even take it in the baggage compartment. So that coffin had to be sealed and be back up to Canoe Lake station by just after midnight. Now no man alone can dig down in the earth six feet, get that body out, put it in that casket, solder it all around, fill the grave back in and be back up at Canoe Lake station in just four or five hours. Now no man can do it. I don't think so, not alone he couldn't.[19]

Be that as it may, the freshly soldered metal casket was taken to the Canoe Lake Train Station platform sometime in the early morning hours of Thursday, July 19.

According to Peggy Thomson, the day after she and her brother George had spoken with Winnifred Trainor, which would have been 12:30 a.m. and 3:00 a.m., respectively, on the morning of

Wednesday July 18, George "went the next afternoon to Canoe Lake."[20] It's not clear if Peggy was referring to the afternoon of Wednesday, July 18, or Thursday, July 19. In any event, we know that George Thomson was at Canoe Lake Station, and most likely Mowat Lodge, on July 19 as he had sent a letter to Dr. MacCallum on that day written on Mowat Lodge stationary.[21] He was there to accompany the coffin home to Owen Sound and, according to an article published in the *Owen Sound Times*, was "expected in Owen Sound at noon on Friday [July 20]."[22]

When Mark Robinson had rolled out of bed at his cabin on the morning of Thursday, July 19, he had not been aware of what had transpired the previous evening at the Mowat Cemetery. He began his day as he usually did, by heading over the tracks to oversee the incoming trains at Joe Lake Station. The ranger then walked the quarter mile west along the tracks to do likewise at Canoe Lake Station. As he approached the station he was startled to see a steel casket sitting on the train platform. "Here was a steel coffin all soldered up around the edges," he recalled.

Then the ranger spied Churchill.

"What's the idea?" asked Robinson, gesturing toward the casket.

Churchill, not knowing who Robinson was, attempted to shut down the conversation before it began.

"What's it to you?"

Robinson produced his park ranger's badge, which resulted in the undertaker immediately changing his tone.

"I'm sorry. I have Tom Thomson's body in there. It's being taken to Owen Sound for burial."

"Should you not have reported to the authorities before you touched the grave?" asked Robinson. "That's an official grave."

Churchill's compliance quickly evaporated.

"No, it's not necessary; when I get instructions to remove a body, I do so."[23]

The ranger had by now reached his breaking point—first there had been the disappearance of his friend, then a fruitless search, then the discovery of his body, then the macabre task of towing it to an island and watching as the undertakers embalmed it, then having to be berated by certain parties whom he prevented from viewing the body prior to burial, then organizing a funeral, and then organizing an inquest that ended with an unsatisfactory resolution. There had been no word of appreciation from Thomson's family during any of this, and now he had to deal with an undertaker acting on their behalf who didn't believe that he needed to check in with the local authorities prior to exhuming a body in Robinson's jurisdiction—it had been an irritating week.

Robinson, barely containing his temper, turned away from Churchill and proceeded directly into the train station where he knew there was a telephone. He quickly rang Superintendant Bartlett and requested permission to interrogate the undertaker further. To Robinson's surprise, the park superintendent wouldn't back his play.

"Now Mark, we've had enough trouble over that situation. I hope that you'll let it settle, say nothing about it. If they want to take the body, let them take it."[24]

Robinson was stunned. Bewildered, he hung up the phone. He had been a soldier after all, and was not a man to disobey a superior's command. Still, rules were rules, and the rules were that park headquarters should have been contacted about the intended exhumation before it occurred. If the rules weren't going to be enforced, or if they were merely arbitrary, then what was the point of having rangers in the park at all? He could feel his anger rising; his friendship with the late artist and the work he had coordinated to see to his burial in the park notwithstanding, he had just been effectively muzzled by the park superintendent while attempting to do nothing more than his job—and it galled him. More galling still was that he now was expected to do nothing but watch helplessly as the train pulled into Canoe Lake Station and collected the undertaker and his cargo. Robinson was beginning to feel very much a paper tiger and, to add salt to the wound, the undertaker knew it. As the railway men placed the steel casket into the baggage car of the train, one of them remarked that it didn't feel heavy enough to contain a body. He turned to Churchill and asked, "Are you sure you've got Tom Thomson's body in that box?"

"Mind your own business!" snapped the undertaker.[25]

The door to the cargo car was then slammed shut and secured and Churchill made his way along the platform before climbing up and into one of the passenger cars. A blast of steam escaped from the smokestack as the locomotive lurched to life, and slowly pulled out from the station.

It is by no means clear when the train containing the metal casket left Canoe Lake Station for Owen Sound. Given the flow of Robinson's audio-recorded statements in 1953, it would suggest that it was shortly after his confrontation with Churchill; i.e., at some time that morning. According to recollections from Thomas Wilkinson and Rose Thomas, who lived at Canoe Lake Station at the time, they recalled that the undertaker had arrived on the evening train and had departed on the "weigh freight" train some time after noon the next day.[26] However, Robinson's diary entry for July 19, 1917 indicates that:

> Mr. Churchill undertaker of Huntsville, Ont. arrived last night and took up body of Thomas Thomson artist under direction of Mr. Geo. Thomson of Conn. U.S.A. The body went out on evening train to Owen Sound to be buried in the family plot.[27]

If, indeed, the body did go out on the evening train to Owen Sound on the night of Thursday, July 19, there must have been a delay somewhere, as according to Thomson's sister Peggy, George Thomson and the coffin didn't arrive in Owen Sound until Friday night (July 20).[28] It wouldn't take twenty-four hours to travel from Canoe Lake to Owen Sound by train, unless, of course, both George Thomson and the steel casket got off at some point in between and stayed the night and then caught a late morning or afternoon train to Owen Sound.

In any event, after his encounter with the undertaker Robinson returned to his cabin. The quarter-mile walk had at least allowed the ranger to burn off some steam, but he hadn't been back at his cabin long when his telephone rang. On the other end was Superintendent Bartlett with new instructions; this time for Robinson to go to the Mowat Cemetery to ensure that the undertaker had completely filled in the empty grave.[29] Once again, Robinson complied. But when he reached the cemetery that day yet another surprise awaited him. Rather than finding an open grave that would need to be refilled with soil, he found instead that only one corner of the grave had been disturbed—and the disturbance hadn't been very much at all. "Now, in one corner of the grave was a hole," he later recalled, "I wouldn't say it would be more than twenty inches across and about that depth. Now any ground hog would make a bigger hole than that—and I've often seen ground hog holes twice as large as that was."[30]

Now a new puzzle struck the ranger: how could the undertaker have exhumed a body while working within only a twenty by twenty-inch hole? Moreover, if he had dug down deep enough to remove both a casket and a rough box, why were flowers from the funeral two days before still lying untouched on top of the grave?[31] He didn't like the answer he was coming up with. "God forgive me if I'm wrong," Robinson would say many years later, while pointing in the direction of the Mowat Cemetery, "but I still think Thomson's body is over there."[32]

According to Dr. Harry Ebbs, a medical doctor who worked for the Taylor Statten camps and who had been a regular in the park since the 1920s, Shannon Fraser had also noted how little the grave appeared to have been disturbed on the evening that he had returned to the gravesite to pick up the undertaker and the metal casket:

> Shannon Fraser told me that later when he went up there, he couldn't see that the thing had been dug, and he questioned very much whether he'd [Churchill] dug.[33]

Fast forwarding to 1970, public interest in determining the location of the artist's final resting place was at an all-time high. As a result of a nationally aired television production, followed by the publication of my father's book, Mark Robinson's recollections on the matter were widely circulated, including his comment about how small the size of the hole he found in Thomson's grave was. Dr. Noble Sharpe (who will enter our narrative later) published an article in the *Canadian Society of Forensic Science Journal* in which he claimed to have spoken with Churchill and had been told that:

> He stated he had only to dig at the end of the grave, by the slope of the knoll, break open the end of the coffin and pull out the body. He did not have to expose the entire length of the coffin top.[34]

This, of course, would explain why Robinson had found only a small hole in one corner of the grave when he examined it—however it also completely contradicts the only firsthand testimony that we have from Churchill on the matter, in which he stated that he had completely removed both the rough box and the casket containing Thomson's body from the original grave.[35] Furthermore, the location of the grave was not on the slope of a knoll, but on an area that was flat and a considerable distance away from the hillside.

Not so easy to explain away, however, was the testimony of the man who had helped transport the casket to and from the Mowat Cemetery. During their one and only meeting in the 1930s, Shannon Fraser, who had assisted with the transportation of both the original oak casket brought by Flavelle and Dixon, and the steel casket brought by Churchill (the latter both to and from the Canoe Lake gravesite), told my father that "there wasn't enough weight in that [steel] casket for a body." He had also shared this suspicion with Harry Ebbs and Taylor Statten.[36]

But perhaps Fraser may have had an additional reason to suspect that the casket delivered to the Leith cemetery that day in July 1917 was empty. In a letter written to my father from Dorothy Stone, A.O.C.A., a former art student of J.W. Beatty (who had been friends with Thomson and several other Toronto artists who would later go on to form the Group of Seven), she revealed the following:

> The most fascinating of all the reminiscences took place late in September 1931 between Beatty and Shan Fraser at the hotel at Kearney, which Fraser took over after Mowat Lodge (I was told) burned down. A group of art students went to Kearney for the autumn color and Beatty turned up. It was frosty at night and we gathered after supper many times while Beatty and Fraser hoisted a few, and the warmth, inside and out, some well chosen questions and a fascinated audience was enough to set them off. . . . But the high spot of all was about the burial at Canoe Lake and the later exhumation on instructions from the family. I can see them in the glow of the firelight chuckling and exchanging knowing glances and saying something to the effect that, "we

knew where he [Thomson] wanted to stay and we saw to it that he stayed there." So since 1931 it has been my belief that the casket which went to Leith was not weighted with a human body.[37]

If this is true, then it may have been Fraser who convinced the undertaker not to exhume the body. Perhaps he made mention of the fact that Thomson had loved the park and would have wanted to be buried there; perhaps he pointed out the terrible condition that the decomposing body was in, or the fact that a lantern's light would only attract an abundance of black flies and mosquitoes to assail the undertaker over the several hours necessary to complete the task. The reader will recall that Churchill, in his own words, "was not anxious to do the job" to begin with, and this shortage of alacrity, combined with the fact that the steel casket would have to be sealed via solder and therefore was unlikely to be re-opened upon its delivery to Leith, might well have resulted in the job not being done at all. Moreover, Fraser, as we shall see, might well have had his own reasons for not wanting Thomson's body falling outside of his purview, where it might possibly be subjected to a more thorough inspection and perhaps result in the police being brought into the situation. The author is not sure how else one could interpret "we saw to it that he stayed there," short of Fraser and Churchill being complicit in shipping an empty casket back to the Thomson family.

According to Mark Robinson, Churchill had been acting "under direction" of George Thomson[38] when he had exhumed the artist's body. If so, such direction must have been provided from a considerable distance, as it is clear that George Thomson did not have a clue as to what went on during the actual exhumation, telling the *Globe and Mail* newspaper in 1956 that, "I am sure that the people who buried Tom by the lake in the first place would have made sure the undertaker got the right body."[39] This undoubtedly would have been true if, in fact, any of the original people who had been involved in the artist's initial burial had been present during the exhumation. And aside from Shannon Fraser and George Rowe, who had been summarily dismissed by the undertaker, none of the people that have been present when the artist had initially been laid to rest were anywhere near the gravesite on the night of Wednesday, July 18. Technically, the people "who buried Tom by the lake in the first place" would have been the undertakers Dixon and Flavelle, but they were back in their respective hometowns of Sprucedale and Kearney when Churchill allegedly rendered his services. George Thomson's statement is odd, particularly if he indeed was the man under whose authority Churchill was acting, for such a statement carries with it the implication that George Thomson wasn't present or even cognizant of the very exhumation he was allegedly directing. For his part, Churchill stated that:

> We placed the metal box with the body in a coffin and shipped it to Owen Sound . . . One of Mr. Thomson's brothers accompanied the coffin on the train to Owen Sound. There my instructions ended, but I heard that the undertaker from Owen Sound saw to the burial of the coffin in the cemetery in Leith.[40]

And so it came to pass that on July 21, 1917 a soldered metal casket, presumably containing the body of Tom Thomson, was buried in the Thomson family plot at the Leith Presbyterian (now United) Church cemetery in Sydenham Township. One of the attendees that day was Thomson's sister Peggy, who wrote that:

> The funeral was private, just the old Leith friends were here and a few from town who had known him and it made it so nice and peaceful not to have the crowd of curious

strangers. We all tried to be as brave as possible. Dr. Fraser opened the service by prayer and Mr. Pillser then took charge of it. Sinnie (?), Jessie, Jean, and I, Father, Tom [Harkness] and George went out to Leith. . . . There were some beautiful flowers sent from Mr. and Mrs. Fraser of Canoe Lake, but we were glad that there was not an overabundance of them. People no doubt understood his tastes and knew he would not like a display. That was one reason we wanted the funeral private. . . . Mother says she wants to remember him as he went off with the basket at Christmas time. None of us wanted to see him even if the body had been fit to see.[41]

The statement "even if the body had been fit to see" is ambiguous, and certainly suggests that none of the family had been inclined to break the solder on the casket in order to view the body when it was presumably brought to Owen Sound. This is a point that we shall revisit later. Nevertheless, there was a burial service and it was undertaken in the sincere belief that the casket the family had gathered around that morning contained the body of their late family member.

After the service had concluded, the following was then entered into the Church Burial Register:

Thomson, Thomas (artist)
Accidental drowning.
Canoe Lake, Algonquin Park
Age—39 years, born Aug. 1877
Buried at Leith, Ont—July 21st, 1917.
Talented and with many friends and no enemies, a mystery.[42]

Chapter Nine

THE SPECTER OF SUICIDE

In the hour immediately following Thomson's first burial in Algonquin Park, the Trainor and the Blecher families retired to their respective cottages, Mark Robinson and the guides to their cabins, and the Frasers, Charlie Scrim, and Charles Plewman returned to Mowat Lodge.

In order to make room for the casket, Shannon Fraser had removed a second bench seat from his buckboard, which reduced the number of people it could accommodate to three. Decorum would have dictated that preference be given to the any of the women who would be returning to the lodge with Shannon—leaving the rest of the attendees to return from the cemetery the same way that they had arrived, by foot. The walk back would probably have proven to be somewhat cathartic for the mourners, as it allowed them to talk amongst themselves about the tragedy.

Charles Plewman was twenty-seven years old and had only arrived at the lodge the day before, on Monday July 16, 1917—the very day that Thomson's body had been discovered. And almost before he knew it, he had been pressed into service as a pallbearer. Despite his youth, Plewman was in poor health, and it was his friend Taylor Statten who had made the necessary arrangements for him to stay with the Frasers at Mowat Lodge. Once he had returned to the lodge, Plewman ascended the old timber stairs to the upper level where the guests' rooms were located. He quickly entered his room and closed the door. What a strange morning it had been! He must have wondered why the hell he had ever listened to Taylor Statten and agreed to stay at such a place. He had come up north for a holiday—not to be coerced into being a pallbearer—standing among people he didn't know at a funeral for someone he had never met. Because of the morning rain his suit was soaked and so he rummaged through his valise for some dry clothes and, finding what he wanted, laid them out on the bed. Glancing out the window of his room he could see the northern portion of Canoe Lake, with its islands of Little and Big Wapomeo. Outside it was still a gray day, and a fine rain had served to keep both the tourists and guides off the lake that afternoon.

Shannon Fraser kept his horses in a barn that was situated about 100 feet east and just to the right of the lodge. The Frasers also had a small stable in which they kept cows for milk. To them, such things added a certain rural charm to their "resort," but it could be off-putting to some of their guests. And on days like this the smell of manure would occasionally waft upward to the guest rooms with such potency that it made many of the guests long for the smells they had left behind in the city. There were no screens on the windows at Mowat Lodge, with the result that one took a chance whenever a window was opened of inviting in the local wildlife. Squirrels, chipmunks, and birds were not uncommon entrants, and, of course, houseflies, horse flies, deer flies, mosquitoes, and black flies were also quick to seize the opportunity provided by an open window to fly in and pay a visit. Consequently, most guests kept their windows closed, with the result that Plewman's room would have been stale, muggy, and uninviting on such a damp and humid day. Once he had changed into the casual clothes he had picked out, Plewman then ventured downstairs to the main floor of the hotel where he quickly spied one of the lodge's plush leather chairs and promptly deposited himself in it. If there were fewer people milling about he might easily have gone to sleep.

Plewman hadn't been sitting by himself long when Shannon Fraser returned from his mail run to Canoe Lake Station. Upon entering the building, the lodge owner noted that his guest was sitting by himself and made his way over. Offering his hand, Fraser thanked Plewman for his assistance during the funeral service and then pulled up a nearby chair and sat down next to his guest. The atmosphere around the lodge had been "tense," according to Plewman, and consequently he welcomed the opportunity for some genial fellowship. Their conversation started off being somewhat stilted as is often the case when two strangers are forced to speak with one another. Small talk was made about the current weather and how it would soon clear up, the good fishing to be found in the region, and the history of the lodge. And then Plewman's curiosity got the best of him. Since he had taken such an active role in the late artist's funeral, he wanted to know something more about the man that he had just buried. And Shannon Fraser was more than willing to fill in a character sketch of his late lodge guest.

He likely informed Plewman that Thomson had been a long-standing guest of the hotel throughout the spring and summer seasons during previous years and that, when he had stayed at the lodge, Thomson's room had been the second one from the end of the upstairs hallway. Further, Plewman would have learned that Thomson had been an up and coming artist with a bright future but, like most artists, he also had to take on part time work to make ends meet. To this end, Fraser had often employed him to do menial labor and part time guide work for the lodge. Fraser then told his guest about the artist's canoe having been found floating upside down only the week before, and of the extensive search that had then occurred for several days afterward. He elaborated on the point that Thomson had been a very experienced canoeist, which left many people who had known the artist shaking their heads at how he could have come to such grief on the water. And then the lodge owner leaned in closer and told Plewman how he thought the artist had died.

Thomson, Fraser revealed, had most likely taken his own life.[1] Plewman wouldn't have been shocked by this pronouncement, as he didn't know Thomson; he was simply a tourist who was making conversation with the proprietor of an inn at which he happened to be staying. Still, such a statement would require some context, and so he asked Fraser why he believed that the man they had just buried would be moved to commit such a rash act of self-annihilation. Fraser replied that he happened to know that the artist was in a predicament; he had become engaged the previous summer to Winnifred Trainor, he said, the same woman whom Plewman had witnessed causing a scene down by the shore earlier that day when she had demanded to see Thomson's corpse.[2] Fraser then revealed that he knew that the pair "had relations more intimate than was supposed," and that the Trainor girl had become pregnant and had turned up the heat on the artist—"pressuring him to go through with the marriage." The lodge owner indicated that, while cleaning the artist's room one day, his wife had come upon a letter that Trainor had written to Thomson that indicated that she was pregnant and that they had to be married straight away. Indeed, on the very week that Thomson disappeared her letter had indicated that she would be "coming up to see Tom and have a showdown" about the matter.[3] Thomson, to Fraser's way of thinking, was "a shy and sensitive person and he just could not face the music."[4]

The lodge owner then shared with his guest what Thomson's last words were to him when he pushed off from the Mowat Lodge dock on July 8: "Don't worry if I am late getting back."[5] For some reason, Fraser considered these words to be ominous. When asked why, he replied that Thomson had said these exact same words when setting out on prior occasions. The lodge owner admitted that he had not been particularly concerned when the artist had failed to return that night or the next morning. However, upon further reflection, it struck him as odd that Thomson had said these exact same words before; perhaps, said Fraser, the artist had considered killing himself on these occasions as well, but had been unable to screw up the courage necessary to follow through with it.[6] According to Plewman:

> The impression Shannon left me with was that somehow Tom had come to the conclusion that a settled, married life was not for him, but that he just could not say so to Miss Trainor . . . Certainly from my conversations with Shannon there was little doubt in his mind as to what had actually happened. I have learned since that he expressed the same opinion to George Thomson.[7]

Now having shared what he believed happened to the artist, Fraser excused himself and set about mingling with his other guests and tending to the rest of his daily duties within the lodge. Plewman, for his part, would tuck the information away that Fraser had shared with him that day for another fifty-five years, only speaking publically about their private conversation in 1972.

While there exists no evidence for Plewman's belief that Fraser had communicated his contention that Tom Thomson had committed suicide directly to George Thomson, by late December 1917 word had somehow found its way to Tom's older brother that the Mowat Lodge proprietor had been publically stating that Tom had taken his own life. That was bad enough, but George had also come into information that suggested that Shannon Fraser had even advanced this notion at the inquest! George Thomson was furious and immediately set pen to paper to confront Fraser about it:

Dec. 25th, 1917
The Quinnipiack club
New Haven, Conn.

Dear Sir:

I am the brother of Tom Thomson who visited Canoe Lake last July. Only a few weeks ago I was informed for the first time that the coroner's conclusion at the inquest was that Tom had taken his own life based on evidence given solely by you and Mrs. Fraser.

While I was there both you and Mrs. Fraser protested over and over your great friendship for Tom, and from what I learn from various sources there was reason that you should entertain some such feeling, as a mighty good friend he had apparently been to you. . . . Now I want to say in passing that I have from various sources a pretty accurate account of what happened at the inquest and, in common with other friends and relatives of Tom's, am more firmly convinced than ever that his death was caused either by accident or foul play—and not by suicide. He had altogether too much to live for—many true friends and a remarkable success in his chosen profession.[8]

Given that the artist had been dead and buried for five months at this point, receiving a letter filled with such accusations had caught the lodge owner completely off guard. Fraser immediately fired back one of his own, disputing the allegation:

Dec. 29, 1917
Your letter of the twenty-fifth came as a great shock to both Mrs. Fraser & myself & we are grieved indeed that you should be laboring under such misapprehensions. There is not an atom of truth in your accusations & as sincere friends of Tom's, it

hurt us not a little that you, his brother, should accuse us of desecrating his memory.

We do not know who your informant is, but you might at least do us the justice of verifying such reports before wantonly accusing us, his friends, of insincerity.

You have been misinformed regarding the coroner's verdict, for at no time was there a suggestion of suicide advanced by any of those giving evidence & the verdict as given was "death due to drowning" & not as stated in your letter.

. . . . Before closing I would like to call your attention to the fact that all the debt of kindness was not confined to any one side, & I think if you would look back over the events that took place following his death, you couldn't help but admit that we gave much of our time & money to make things comfortable for all concerned. Yourself included.[9]

The more he thought about the tone of George Thomson's letter, the angrier Fraser became. He was now not content simply to reply to George Thomson; after all, some of the artists from Tom's circle had been coming up north to paint since 1914, and he didn't want any word getting out to that community that might quell their desire to continue to come to the park and rent a room or two at Mowat Lodge. To this end he decided to pen a letter to Tom's patron, Dr. James MacCallum, in the hopes of tamping out George Thomson's fiery accusation before it spread:

Mowat Lodge

Dear Dr McCallum
I am just in receipt of a letter from Geo Thomson accusing me & Mrs. Fraser of telling the coroner that poor Tom committed suicide. My wife wasn't at the inquest and never spoke to the Dr

as the inquest was held at one of the neighbors and at midnight. No one ever mentioned such a thing as suicide at the inquest. The verdict was death due to drowning. I am feeling very badly about this terrible thing as I thought so much of Tom & would be the very last to even mention such a thing. However several people have said to me it was no accident & I always assured them it was an accident. . . . You can ask Mr. McDonald [sic] or Mr. Beatty if we didn't do all we could to say Tom's death was an accident. Poor Tom how we miss him he was the nicest man I ever met & I was glad to do all I could for him . . .

Yours truly,
J. S. Fraser[10]

That Fraser, together with J.E.H. MacDonald and William Beatty, would do all they could to "say Tom's death was an accident" is suggestive that there were a number of beliefs already circulating that disputed this belief. However, despite Fraser's protests of innocence, which would be later verified by the coroner's notes from the inquest, other members of the Thomson family, such as his brother-in-law, Tom Harkness, had learned that if Fraser hadn't been spreading the rumor of suicide at the inquest, he most certainly had been spreading it to certain of Tom's artist friends, such as John William Beatty. And, to Harkness's shock, these friends had apparently been accepting of it. This prompted Harkness to write to MacCallum:

I feel rather sore at Beatty, and may have longer to talk to him the next time I see him. I cannot for the life of me understand how he, claiming to be a friend of Tom's, can so easily swallow all Fraser's talk, and knowing that Tom was one who had a high moral sense of duty to his fellow men, and he must know perfectly that he had nothing to run away from. I thought the thing over from every viewpoint and the more I think of it the more fully I am convinced that Tom had no hand in taking his life. But it makes me feel sore to think Fraser who claimed to be such a friend of Tom's could make all these suggestions and Beatty ready to take them all in. I cannot understand Fraser but he seems to have some subtle influence over people to make them believe in him.[11]

The matter had clearly been a topic of conversation amongst the Thomson siblings, as Thomson's sister Elizabeth had also been upset by the suicide allegation, feeling obliged to air her feelings in a letter to MacCallum:

I don't really know what to do about J.S. Fraser and I feel such a horror of him to think he deliberately undermined all Tom's lovely character at a blow when he was not there to defend himself. I wanted to go down to Canoe Lake as soon as I heard it, but the family did not want me to go alone, so things were just allowed to drift much against my will.[12]

It is somewhat odd that the Toronto ophthalmologist would have been the recipient of such letters decrying the suicide rumor—not only from Shannon Fraser (in pleading his innocence in spreading such a rumor) but also from the Harkness family (who were of the belief that MacCallum was sympathetic to their cause), as apparently the good doctor himself was of the opinion that the artist had, indeed, taken his own life. The famed Group of Seven artist, A.Y. Jackson, who was a close friend to both Thomson and MacCallum, wrote that:

Dr. MacCallum said they [those at the inquest] believed it was suicide and they brought in a verdict of accidental drowning to make it easier for the family.[13]

Another individual who had been present at the inquest, Martin Blecher Junior, was also said to have believed that the artist had taken his own life. Blodwen Davies (an author who wrote the first biography of Thomson), in her application for the exhumation of the body of Thomson in 1931, had mentioned that:

> Martin Blecher was believed responsible for spreading a report of suicide. He repeated this statement as late as August of 1931 when he made a trip across the Lake to Camp Ahmek on the day of the Thomson Celebration and told Dr. Harry Ebbs that Thomson's legs were bound together with a piece of rubber. This statement was untrue. He also stated that the body was cramped and rigid. This was also untrue.[14]

The Thomson family was bewildered by the emergence of such a rumor. And certainly George Thomson resolutely refused to entertain the theory that his younger brother was a candidate for suicide:

> He had too much to live for to make such a theory tenable, considering his great love for his work and the outstanding recognition he had met with. And besides he had prepared for and laid in provisions enough for a two or three week cruise when lost at the start within a mile of the lodge.[15]

Surprisingly, by the time Martin Blecher Junior was spreading the suicide rumor in 1931, neither Fraser nor Beatty were quite as certain about it as they evidently had been in 1917. The reader will recall Dorothy Stone, a member of the Ontario College of Art in Toronto, and her account of an evening spent in Kearney during September 1931 when both Beatty and Fraser held court before a group of art students. Stone recalled that, "they [Fraser and Beatty] were as mystified about his [Thomson's] death as we were, although they did not accept the explanation of suicide. Some people believed he was despondent at not joining the army."[16]

Whatever caused Fraser and Beatty to change their minds on the matter is unknown. What is known, however, is that in the summer and fall of 1917 a rumor that Tom Thomson had committed suicide was being circulated, and that the Thomson family was blaming Shannon Fraser for its dissemination. Perhaps the rumor had stung the Thomson family all the more because Tom's personality and behavior were by no means incompatible with such a notion.

GENIUS AND DESPAIR

The artistic temperament is a notoriously mercurial one. The famed Dutch Post-Impressionist painter, Vincent van Gogh, for example, was said to have "had fits of despair and hallucination during which he could not work, between long clear months in which he could and did, punctuated by extreme visionary ecstasy."[17] And the famed painter of "Starry Night" is not an isolated example.

A study published in the *Journal of Psychiatric Research* in 2012 revealed that creative professionals were eight percent more likely to be bipolar than other members of society.[18] Another study investigating a co-relation between psychopathology and creativity in 300,000 people revealed that individuals with bipolar disorder, along with the healthy siblings of people with schizophrenia or bipolar disorder, were "overrepresented in creative professions," causing the researchers to conclude that "a familial co-segregation of both schizophrenia and bipolar disorder with creativity is suggested."[19]

And while most reports of Tom Thomson's nature that have come down to us over the decades depict a man of quiet, gentle humor, there are other reports that would suggest a far less sanguine disposition. Between the years 1905 to 1909, while employed at the Legg Brothers photoengraving firm in Toronto, a colleague described him as:

> Very moody and temperamental, subject to fits of depression, which I think he played up largely. I recall once he threatened to quit and leave town, saying he [had been] "down at the yards looking over the freight trains going east last night." The joke being that freight trains did not wait [twenty-four] hours in the yard and any night would do. Another time he announced that he was going to quit all his bad habits and straightway threw his pipe, matches and plug of tobacco out the window into the street. He was smoking next day.[20]

And even his friends in Algonquin Park, such as Mark Robinson, acknowledged that:

> One day he was jovial and jolly and ready for a frolic of any kind so long as it was clean and honest in its purpose. At [other] times he appeared melancholy and defeated in manner. At such times he would suddenly, as it were, awaken and be almost angry in appearance and action. It was those times that he did his best work. He would quite often come dashing into my cabin and in an excited tone ask about certain rocks or trees or rolling hills.[21]

Robinson was recorded in the early 1950s recounting his anecdotes about the artist, which included episodes of rather erratic behavior, such as the time when the artist had burst into the ranger's cabin and paced back and forth in the center of the room without speaking to anyone, and then suddenly exclaiming to no one in particular, "Where do I get it?" When pressed about what the "it" was that he wanted to get, Thomson then described a certain old weathered pine tree (another time he barged in to ask about an old spruce tree) that he thought would in some way augment a painting he was contemplating. This behavior occurred more than once during the time that Robinson knew the artist, causing those who were present to inquire of the ranger if his friend was "demented."[22]

And while fluctuating moods and bi-polar disorders don't automatically lead to suicide, if Thomson, like van Gogh, had been inclined to seek the delicate balance between fits of despair and "visionary ecstasy," then, like the famous Dutch artist, it is possible that that the inclination might well have crossed his mind. Perhaps, assuming the existence of such a predisposition, the added stress of feeling himself being forced into a marriage that he didn't want might have been the proverbial straw that broke the camel's back.

REEXAMINING THE SUICIDE RUMOR

As we've seen, the Thomson family, in addition to those who knew Thomson well, such as Mark Robinson and Alan Ross, had certainly been aware that the artist would suffer fits of melancholy from time to time.[23] But there is certainly no evidence in any of Thomson's correspondence, nor from his demeanor on the day that he went missing, that would suggest that he had been despondent or was preparing to take his own life. Indeed, according to Blanche Packard:

> He seemed normal, cheerfully looking forward to his work and solitude. . . . If he contemplated suicide he gave no behavioural hint or intent, nor did he limp or complain of any injury to motherly Mrs. Colson.[24]

However, as we've seen, the earliest reason brought forth to support the contention of suicide was not depression, melancholy or a bipolar condition, but rather a desire to avoid matrimony. And this premise requires a closer look before it can be accepted as the *sine qua non* that would compel a man like Thomson to take his own life.

A look into Thomson's prior history of relationships with the fairer sex ought to reveal certain patterns of behavior, such as whether he tended to react with suicidal thoughts and/or actions when things weren't going the way he preferred, or whether he was more inclined to simply move on.

GOING AGAINST TYPE

Tom Thomson had been in love once before, in 1905. He had been living in Seattle at the time and, according to some accounts, the twenty-seven-year-old Thomson had been so smitten with eighteen-year-old Alice Lampert that he had proposed marriage to her. Upon receiving the artist's proposal, the young lady had responded with a nervous laugh, which the artist had interpreted as a rejection. According to the *Canadian Encyclopedia*:

> He doubtless looked forward to a career in Seattle, probably wanting to settle down, advance in his trade and marry as his brother Ralph did in 1906. That he did not was likely the result of an incident involving Alice Elinor Lambert, eight or nine years his junior, to whom he proposed. At the crucial moment the effervescent Miss Lambert nervously giggled, causing the very sensitive Thomson to abandon his matrimonial ambitions and leave for Toronto. It was on his return from Seattle that he decided to become an artist.[25]

According to the author Joan Murray, who had corresponded with Alice Lambert during the latter's autumn years, the reason for the dissolution of the relationship was the interference of a third party, Horace Rutherford, a friend and roommate of Thomson's, while the artist had been living in Seattle:

> Rutherford falsely told Thomson that he and Alice were engaged. According to Alice, Tom forced Rutherford to go with him when he left Seattle. Alice still called Rutherford a "swine," even sixty-five years later. In this version, Thomson meant to save her. Thomson's behaviour in Seattle cast a light on both his sensitivity and chivalry, a relative said later. . . . As Lampert put it later, Thomson "fled" Seattle. To leave, of course, was his typical response to incidents that made him angry.[26]

In either scenario, the artist had believed that he had been rejected; in the former directly by the lady herself, and in the latter by the lady via a rival for her affections.

The pain of the rejection of the young lady that he was in love with was sufficient enough for the artist to leave both the city and the country in which she resided and never come back. One would think that if Thomson were prone to suicidal thoughts, such a perceived rejection would have been sufficient impetus for the artist to have terminated his life in 1905. However, Thomson simply lived with the hurt a while until it faded, and by then he was well on his way to unleashing an artistic talent that few at the time knew that he possessed. That the shoe should suddenly be on the other foot; i.e., that a woman he was seeing wanted him to marry her when he did not, might have caused the artist some consternation to be sure—as few people enjoy dashing another person's hopes for the future—but if he could live with the rejection from Alice Lampert (a woman whom he truly loved) it's doubtful that he would opt to kill himself when pressured to marry by Winnifred Trainor (a woman whom he didn't love as much, if at all—as if he did there should exist no reason for her to need to apply pressure for the nuptial).

But what if Winnifred Trainor had been pregnant? That might change things. Given the morals of the time, such an occurrence would have, if word got out, most certainly brought a degree of shame to the Thomson family name, particularly in the tightly laced Ontario of 1917. And there is some evidence, or at least there was a rumor circulating at the time of his death, that Trainor was, in fact, pregnant with his child. Recall that immediately after Thomson's funeral Charles Plewman had been told by Shannon Fraser that Trainor had been pregnant. But how did Fraser come to know such intimate details of Miss Trainor's biology? According to Plewman, Fraser had shared with him a story that his wife Annie, "who cleaned Thomson's room, read letters exchanged between the artist and Miss Trainor,"[27] and happened upon one that was suggestive that this was the case. Would the artist have been so worried about preserving his image in the eyes of, say, his family and friends that the only option that lay before him was to take his own life? It's hard to know with certainty the mind of another when faced with such a circumstance. However, one would think that by this point in his life Thomson must already have been accustomed to being considered the black sheep of the Thomson family. Unlike his elder brothers Ralph and George, Tom was essentially unemployed and didn't have much in the way of prospects. Art in Canada was not yet the big business it would later become (A.J. Casson would tell me that, "you couldn't make a living painting in this country until the 1950s") and so painting would have been a pretty precarious way to support oneself. At age thirty-nine, Thomson was still single and had no career to speak of. Add to this the news that he had gotten a small-town girl pregnant out of wedlock and it's possible that he might have been wracked with concern about the news getting back to his family. Such a scenario strikes one as possible if not particularly probable. After all, if the artist had been okay with how his family had felt about his lifestyle up till that point in his life, would he, less than a month away from turning forty, really have cared whether or not his family would be disappointed in him yet again? After all, Thomson was Kerouac before Kerouac; a bohemian who, by 1917, was pretty well settled with being unsettled.

Moreover, hurting himself would run completely against type. The artist's approach to dealing with conflict in the past had typically been to walk away from it—not to attempt suicide. Plewman had indicated that the word around Mowat Lodge at the time of the artist's death was that he was a pacifist—and perhaps this extended beyond merely his attitude toward World War I.[28] In personal antagonisms he was said to prefer to walk out of a room when someone he didn't care for walked into it,[29] and he chose to walk away from a job and a life in Seattle when a relationship didn't work out. Indeed, in terms of instinctive impulses the artist displayed more flight than fight.

NOT THE MARRYING KIND

And then there is the matter of whether or not Thomson and Trainer had ever been engaged at all. When the author looked into the status of Thomson's relationship with Winnifred Trainor, he could find "zero" hard evidence of any plan for matrimony between the artist and Miss Trainor, and certainly no plan to book a cabin at Billie Bear Lodge for a honeymoon that August (as A.Y. Jackson had told my father). In a letter written by the artist nine weeks prior to his death, he clearly states what his immediate plans were—and they did not revolve around Winnifred Trainor—despite Fraser having told Plewman that the pair had been engaged since the previous summer:

I may possibly go out on the Canadian Northern this summer to paint the Rockies but have not made all the arrangements yet. If I go it will be in July and August.[30]

August, the reader will recall, was the month that Thomson had allegedly booked the honeymoon cabin at Billie Bear Lodge. It certainly would have been a disappointing honeymoon if Winnifred Trainor was at Billie Bear while her husband was out west painting the Rockies. As Thomson had written the above letter to a family member, one would suppose that the artist might have notified him if any nuptials were to be forthcoming that summer. And, if Winnifred Trainor was coming up to "have a showdown" with him about the marriage, and Thomson was planning on heading west that summer anyway, if he wanted to avoid the confrontation then one would expect the artist to revert to form; i.e., to simply leave the region where the problem was situated, just as he had done in Seattle, and the Rockies might well have proven an agreeable place to live and paint for a while.

A QUESTIONABLE ENGAGEMENT

We know that Winnifred Trainor had left the vicinity of Canoe Lake immediately after the artist's funeral and returned home to Huntsville. Afterward she had travelled to Toronto where she spent six weeks with Irene Ewing, who was perhaps her closest girlfriend. If she had been pregnant during this time one can well imagine the despair that she must have been in; to not only have lost her fiancé, but also to be carrying a child that, upon its eventual birth, she would either have to raise in shame or have torn away from her for adoption, would have been overwhelming emotionally and certainly foremost on her mind. One can also imagine that one who found oneself in such a heartrending situation would desperately need to confide in someone, an old friend perhaps, and spending six weeks with her longtime friend would certainly have afforded Winnifred Trainor such an opportunity. However, in two letters that Mrs. Ewing wrote to my father in 1969, she not only made no mention that Trainor had been pregnant, but also went so far as to state that she did not believe Trainor had ever been engaged to Thomson:

> Winnie and I were close friends then and one would imagine she would have confided in me if she and Tom were really engaged.[31]

Furthermore, according to Mrs. Ewing, she didn't think the pair had much in common:

> I heard him say once that every person must find within himself the beauty of all nature and mostly the colors. His face seemed to be transformed and was so happy when looking afar from a high mount or hill—it got him excited and he would get impatient with anyone who could not see the beauty that surrounded them. Tom would see beauty in an old shoe left on the road—that is one thing, Mr. Little, I will never understand, as Winnie could never see beauty anywhere. She and Tom were miles apart in this respect.[32]

Finally, she added:

> She liked Tom but he sure was not the marrying kind.[33]

This was a perspective that was shared by Thomson's good friend, Ranger Henry Ardagh "Bud" Callighen, who stated:

There is no doubt that Tom knew Winnie very well, and she was pretty fond of Tom. However, I think she was more interested in Tom than he was in her.[34]

So far we have seen testimony that supports the notion that Thomson was not interested in marrying Winnifred Trainor. But there was also testimony from the old trapper, Ralph Bice, who was a good friend of Trainor's, that she had no intention of marrying Thomson either:

> Miss Trainor was a very good friend of mine and she would have married him [Thomson] if he would have quit his drinking. . . . Somebody said they would have been married that summer. But she said to my sister, "I couldn't marry Tom Thomson. All my life I remember my father coming home Saturday nights so drunk that he just went into bed and we didn't see him till the next week." She said, "I wasn't going to marry him."[35]

In Roy MacGregor's book *Northern Light: The Enduring Mystery of Tom Thomson and The Woman Who Loved Him,* he reveals that Trainor's personal physician Dr. Wilfred T. Pocock, who also claimed to be Trainor's "intimate friend" for forty-three years, had no knowledge of her ever having been pregnant or of ever having had an abortion.[36] One would think that having had a child or an abortion would be something that would be known by a woman's personal physician. In addition, during an interview granted to Algonquin Park historian Ron Pittway in 1978, Dr. Pocock revealed that Winnifred Trainor had told him that she had wanted to marry the artist, but that Thomson had no money. The artist, she said, had brushed aside any talk of marriage, as he had no interest in marrying someone and being poor.[37]

If none of the close friends of either Tom Thomson or Winnifred Trainor knew anything about an engagement, if her personal physician knew nothing of her ever having been pregnant or having either a child or an abortion, and if no documents have been produced to support such allegations, then the whole idea of Thomson wanting to kill himself because of a woman who was not pregnant with his child and that he did not want to marry and who, in turn, did not want to marry him, seems as preposterous as it is convoluted.

THE LETTER

The entire belief that Winnifred Trainor was pregnant at the time of Thomson's death appears to be based upon an inference drawn allegedly by Annie Fraser regarding what she took to be cryptic content within a letter written to Thomson by Trainor. Outside of this inference there is no evidence at all that Trainor was ever pregnant. Even the existence of the "smoking gun" of a letter that Annie Fraser was said to have looked at has never been corroborated.

Shortly after Thomson's death, and in the company of Winnifred's father Hugh Trainor, Mark Robinson had read through the contents of several letters that Thomson had received that summer from Winifred Trainor. Evidently the artist had brought these letters with him to the Trainor cottage while he was staying there for a time during the Trainor family's absence. Included with these letters was one that had recently arrived that the artist had not yet opened. If Thomson had brought all of Trainor's letters over to the Trainor cottage from Mowat Lodge, then in among those letters would have been the one, presumably, that Annie Fraser had read (as it would be unimaginable that he would bring over all of the letters but the most personal one). Moreover, if there was a newly arrived letter from Trainor to the artist that had not yet been opened, one would suspect that it, above all others, would have contained the most recent evidence regarding her pregnancy and the pressing need for the pair to get married immediately. As Robinson had been tasked with investigating the case, he read through all of the letters, and even opened and read the newly arrived one. To his mind, there was nothing suggestive about the content of any of them. He most certainly did not come away from reading them with the same inference that Annie Fraser was said to have drawn regarding a pregnancy, nor with any indication of a forthcoming "showdown" regarding the matter of marriage between the two. According to the ranger:

> I was also instructed to go to the little house up here and look see what was around there . . . and there was several letters, most of them was from Miss Trainor. They were just ordinary boy and girl letters, there was nothing extraordinary about them, and there was nothing in any way to think there was anything wrong with them, so I read them. There was one still to be opened, I opened it and I handed them back to Mr. Trainor. I said, "Your daughter's letters to Tom," I said, "keep them, give them to her," and I expect he did so. We never asked for them afterwards for there was nothing in them in any way to cause any feelings of any kind, one way or another.[38]

When asked specifically about the content of the letters, Robinson replied that there was nothing of the sort within any of them that one would expect from a couple that was either head over heels in love with each other or that had been planning an imminent marriage:

> I read all the letters that was laying there belonging to him and I don't think there was anything of courtship in Tom's

mind. He was a kindly fellow with any girls that he met, he was admired a good deal by many of them, but he was always the same with everybody, especially with the ladies.[39]

It must be remembered that in 1917 Winnifred Trainor was thirty-two, soon to be thirty-three, and, in all likelihood, looking for a husband. And, if the prospects were better, she may well have found one. Thomson was unemployed, he was bouncing back and forth between Toronto (where he lived in a shack) and Canoe Lake, where he rented a small room at Mowat Lodge, stayed at the Trainor cottage or, more often in the summer months, lived in a tent. And this was the best prospect she had? Certainly her parents would have envisioned something a little better for their eldest daughter.

And while Thomson certainly enjoyed the company of women, apart from a brief interlude in 1905, there exists no indication that he was ever in love to the point of proposing marriage again. The only people who believed Thomson to have been engaged to Winnifred Trainor were evidently Trainor herself (in later years),[40] her nephew Terence McCormick (who indicated to my father that he had in his possession correspondence between the two that testified to this but which he subsequently never saw fit to produce),[41] Shannon and Annie Fraser, and A.Y. Jackson.[42]

While the evidence for Thomson being engaged to a pregnant Winnifred Trainor is flimsy at best, it doesn't change the fact that one of the earliest counter-theories to the "accidental death by drowning" verdict was that the artist had taken his own life. The fact that this rumor was believed to have been initially advanced by Shannon Fraser, a man who knew the artist well, is certainly intriguing, but, as we shall soon see, it was perhaps done for reasons quite apart from Thomson's state of mind on the day that he went missing.

Chapter Ten

A FEUD WITH A COTTAGER

Too many things about Tom Thomson's death didn't add up for it to be the result of an accidental drowning—at least, to Mark Robinson's way of thinking.

His late friend had been too good a swimmer, too good a canoeist, to just fall out of his canoe and drown. And there were other factors regarding the condition of Thomson's corpse that didn't support the coroner's conclusion of "accidental death by drowning." For example, there was blood found in his ear. This didn't sit well with the ranger—surely this was an indication that Thomson had been dead *before* his body entered the water, as dead bodies don't bleed. Had Thomson been alive when he went into the water, any blood that would be circulated to a wound would've been washed away. For blood to still be in his ear after eight days of submersion strongly suggested that the artist's heart had stopped beating sometime prior to his entering the water.

And then there was the fact that no water was found in his lungs. In which case, Thomson's death couldn't have been the result of drowning. And the bruise on Thomson's temple looked to Robinson to have been inflicted by the blade of a paddle; it was thin in width but four inches in length, and he didn't know of any rock that would match those dimensions that the artist could have fallen on. And, finally, there was the fishing line that was wrapped sixteen to seventeen times around Thomson's left ankle—now what kind of an "accident" could that be?

The more Robinson reviewed the facts of the matter, the more questions seemed to come into his mind. If the artist's death had not been the result of an accident, then that suggested foul play— but who within the Canoe Lake community harbored any ill will toward Tom Thomson? To this last question, Robinson thought he had the answer. While a fog had most certainly descended upon the ranger in the immediate weeks that followed his friend's death, when that fog eventually lifted he found himself looking squarely at Martin Blecher Junior.

When approached by Blodwen Davies in 1930 regarding which people she might interview for a biography on Thomson, the ranger had cautioned:

> You might interview Martin and Bessie Blecher, but again be careful. They possibly know more about Tom's sad end than any other person.[1]

And Robinson had evidently not been alone in his suspicions. According to Harry Ebbs, a medical doctor who cottaged at Canoe Lake and later would become the medical director for Taylor Statten's camps:

> I was there [Canoe Lake] in 1924—that's [seven] years after the event—and the person who was suspected, or whose name was whispered most often, was Martin Blecher.[2]

The Martin Blecher referred to by both of these men was known locally as Martin Blecher Junior, to distinguish him from his father Martin Blecher Senior. Martin Senior, in partnership with his half brother William Kratz, owned a successful furniture-manufacturing store in his hometown of Buffalo, New York, where Martin Senior was also a well-respected member of the Masonic community.

Martin and his wife Louisa (nee Jekel), had two children; a daughter Bessie who was born in 1886, and a son Martin, born in 1891. In 1909, Martin Senior leased what had originally been the park headquarters house on Canoe Lake. The house sat upon 1.12 acres of land and became the Blecher family cottage.

While Martin Senior had been born in the United States in 1857, his parents (Henry and Mary) were German immigrants. This fact has caused certain authors over the years to speculate that the general dislike of the Blecher family that developed within the Canoe Lake community can be attributed primarily to wartime prejudice. World War I was then being actively contested overseas, and the Blechers, being Americans of German ancestry, would not have been warmly embraced by a population that was comprised primarily of Canadians of British, Scottish, and Irish ancestry. Even the town of Berlin, Ontario had been renamed "Kitchener" in 1916 owing to the fear and enmity of anything German during that time period. Conceding this, it must also be pointed out that a lot of the ill will that the family had received from within the local community had been well earned. The women of the family, for example, had once threatened an employee of the Taylor Statten camps, Stan Murdock, with clubs, when he had inadvertently stepped onto their property.[3] Louisa Blecher, Martin Senior's better half, had even chased Mark Robinson off of their property with a broom.[4] Such erratic and violent behavior didn't particularly endear the family to the local denizens.

At the time of Thomson's death, the least popular member of the Blecher household had been the son, Martin Blecher Junior. Part of the problem might simply have been the age of the cottager; after all, Martin Junior was only twenty-five years old. Most of those who lived in his immediate vicinity were considerably older—Hugh Trainor was sixty-one, Lowrey Dickson was sixty-three, George Rowe was fifty-seven, Mark Robinson was fifty, and Thomson was almost forty. Such men thus shared a certain commonality of values that were commensurate with their age. However, in speaking with long-time Canoe Lake resident Wam Stringer in 1990, the author learned that there were other reasons for Martin Junior's lack of popularity among the locals:

> He wanted the lake for himself, as I understand. I paddled [with] him a bit. But I wouldn't put anything at all past Martin Blecher—he would pick a row with anybody. He tried to dig [information out of] me several times about this person or that person. But I was a smart duck; I wouldn't say anything.[5]

Harry Ebbs, a man who spent most of his summers at Canoe Lake starting in 1924, recalled a rather rude welcome he had once received from the cottager:

> I know on one occasion when I had a problem with our motorboat, I think it was the year we were building the new girl's camp, Big Wapomeo [1927], and my transport boat broke down and I needed a particular set of tools in order that the shaft could be repaired. I went over to the Blecher cottage and Mrs. Blecher said, "Oh, Martin's down in the boathouse, go down there." I went down and walked in the door and he was very startled and very upset and came and ushered me out, wondering what I wanted. He said, "Don't you come in here again! This is private!"[6]

On another occasion, about a year later, Blecher had believed that Ebbs had cut him off in his motorboat and confronted him before a crowd of people at the Canoe Lake Train Station:

Blecher came over to me and, in front of the rest of them, he said, "Look young fellow, if you ever try any tricks like the one yesterday, you are going to find yourself in trouble!" And then walked away. A couple of the older men there from the mill came over and said, "Don't ever cross with that fellow, you just stay out of his way."[7]

There was also evidence that Blecher had already embraced the anti-Semitism that would in many ways come to define the Germany of World War II. Ralph Bice, who had been a guide for the various lodges in and around Canoe Lake, recalled that:

I saw Blecher a year after [Thomson's death]. I guided tours in [Joe Lake?] . . . we were guiding a big party of Americans who were Jews. Blecher hated Jews. And he would always say something and I said, "Listen Martin, it's a job to me. I've even guided Germans, so don't talk to me about the Jews."[8]

And there was another reason that the Blecher family would have been unpopular. To the blue-collar Canadian workers within Algonquin Park, the Blechers were "tourists," which, while indispensable for their livelihoods, fostered resentment by virtue of the locals' dependency upon them. Without tourists, there would be no lodges and without the lodges, there would be no jobs for guides. Moreover, then like today, only those who had disposable income could afford vacations, and the guides in the park, like the lumbermen who came before them, had little disposable income to speak of, which simply underscored the social class differential that existed between the two groups. In addition, the Blecher family was American, and Canadians have long defined themselves in the negative; i.e., by that which they are not, such as "not" British or "not"

American. Such contradistinction creates stereotypes against which those of one class believe themselves to look better by comparison. Hence, the British can be held up to be snobbish and arrogant; the Americans held up to be boorish, oafish, and too self-absorbed— but since the locals were Canadians they could not possibly possess any such negative character traits. Even if inaccurate caricatures, this latter stereotype of how the locals perceived Americans was precisely how many of the locals viewed Martin Junior. Taking all of the above together, there existed a multitude of reasons for the Blecher family's lack of popularity in the area. But none of these reasons played a role in why Thomson and the Blecher family would eventually come to be at odds with each other.

It is clear that Thomson did not share in the resentment harbored by some of those in Algonquin Park toward American tourists. Not only did he enjoy guiding American tourists within the area, but he was also something of a tourist himself, spending his summers in Algonquin Park and the rest of his time in Toronto. Thomson also held no animus against Americans, per se. As we have seen, he had lived in the United States for a time, and had even fallen in love with an American girl. Moreover, one day while in the employ of the Toronto photoengraving firm Legg Brothers, one of his coworkers, Stuart L. Thompson, recalled an exclamation made by the artist that we would consider shocking coming from a man who would go on to become one of Canada's greatest icons:

> He professed a great liking for the United States, saying he had been at a band concert last night and when they played the "star-spangled banner" he stood up and took his hat off. "By God! I like the country better than Canada" he protested.[9]

And so there was nothing, initially at least, that should have set Thomson and the Blecher family at odds with one another.

However, the fact that Martin Blecher Junior was of German stock might easily have led to a belief that he stood on Germany's side during World War I. And this would have been viewed as another matter entirely.

THE FIRST WORLD WAR

There are conflicting views regarding Thomson's attitude toward World War I (and, indeed, toward the concept of war in general) that have come down to us over the years. We do know that while he was in his twenties, the young Thomson had wanted quite keenly to enlist in the military. His sister, Louise Henry, had recollected that he had attempted to enlist in the Boer War (1899-1902), but had been turned down owing to an athletic injury he had sustained playing soccer.[10] And while Thomson may have been disappointed at not being able to enlist in the army prior to the turn of the twentieth century, by 1909 his attitude toward war, per se, had evidently changed. S.H. Kemp, who was a friend and colleague of Thomson when the latter worked in Toronto, recollected that:

> Norman Angell's book *The Great Illusion* had been published [1909] and at the shop we were discussing it. It made out a clear case that in no war could the victor be any better off than the vanquished. The Great World War I had not yet cast its shadow before [us], but Norman Angell had not a few converts. Thomson had long been of the opinion that war was a snare and a delusion, and that militarism and what we now call preparedness, were quite wrong. He held that view with passion and sincerity. He was not impressed when one of our fellow artists was seen in the garrison parade in the scarlet coat and busby of a private in the 10th Royal Grenadiers, a local militia unit.[11]

By 1914, World War I had commenced and, according to Mark Robinson's daughter Ottelyn Addison:

> Friends (Dr. A.D.A. Mason, for example) believed that Thomson never tried to enlist and there seems to be little doubt that he gave that impression. He detested war; in a conversation with a sister he stated he would willingly serve as an ambulance man but could not face the prospect of killing.[12]

E.E. Godin, a man who had shared a cabin and fire ranging duties with Thomson during the summer of 1916, recollected that by this point in time Thomson was very much against Canada's involvement in World War I:

> We had many discussions on the War. As I remember it, he did not think that Canada should be involved. He was very outspoken in his opposition to Government patronage, especially in the appointment of Commissions in the Militia. I do not think that he would offer himself for service. I know up until that time he had not tried to enlist.[13]

Such statements corroborate what Charles Plewman had heard said around Mowat Lodge that Thomson had been considered a pacifist who had no interest in enlisting in World War I.[14] However, in stark contrast to the testimony cited above, Mark Robinson was convinced that Thomson had indeed attempted to enlist at some point during 1915 for the allied cause:

> Well, most of the boys with any blue blood in their veins enlisted at once. Tom endeavored to do the same thing. He was turned down, and he felt very keenly about it. He went

to Toronto and tried it there. Turned down again. Went to some outside point in the country; was again turned down. Then he came back to the park. I remember him looking around and counting the boys that had gone, a lot of them had become his friends, and . . . he came up to my place and he said, "Well, I've done my best to enlist and I cannot, but I'm going to go with the fire ranging. I've been to see them at the department and I can get on fire ranging. And if I cannot fill a place in the Army, I can fill a place here at home of a man who's gone to the Army," and he seemed pleased that he could do that.[15]

Robinson, having served in the army, would have had his radar out for any man who did not support the Canadian war effort.[16] Supporting Robinson's contention that Thomson had at least entertained the idea of enlisting for service in World War I is this recollection from Thomson's sister Minnie:

> He told us then [November 1915] that he was going to try again to enlist, and if they turned him down he might come west and paint the Rocky Mountains.[17]

Obviously, there are some serious contradictions regarding Thomson's attitude toward World War I. The only first-hand testimony that has come down to us directly from Tom Thomson regarding his view on the matter is to be found in a letter that he wrote on April 22, 1915 to J.E.H. MacDonald:

> As with yourself, I can't get used to the idea of [A.Y.] Jackson being in the machine and it is rotten that in this so-called civilized age that such things can exist. But since this War has started it will have to go on until one side wins out,

and of course there is no doubt which side it will be, and we will see Jackson back on the job once more.[18]

Whether Thomson had attempted to enlist or not, by the time that World War I was underway, a war in which sixty thousand Canadians would lose their lives and that involved friends of his such as A.Y. Jackson and Mark Robinson, there is no doubt that Thomson's loyalty and support were firmly on the side of England and her allies. Perhaps the varying viewpoints cited above speak to the fact that the artist had been conflicted between his philosophic antipathy to war in general, and the fact that other men his age were actively engaged in fighting and dying overseas in an effort to preserve the freedoms he presently enjoyed.

By contrast, there is no evidence that Martin Blecher Junior had made any attempt to enlist from 1914 to the summer of 1917, and no indication that he felt any such pangs of conscience about not having done so. We do not know his reasons; perhaps he was more akin to Thomson in his thinking about the war than either man would have cared to admit. While Mark Robinson and Shannon Fraser would tell my father that Blecher had been vociferously pro Germany in the matter of World War I, I have been unable to find any corroborating testimony in support of this contention. All we know is that Blecher-the-younger had, by the summer of 1917, successfully avoided his country's efforts to enlist him in the cause of service overseas. There evidently had been whispers among certain Canoe Lake residents that Blecher had been in Canada primarily, if not solely, to avoid being drafted into the American army.[19]

In both an interview with Audrey Saunders in 1944 and in an audio recording made in 1953, Mark Robinson indicated that he had been approached by an agent named Comiskay who had been sent to the park by the United States military to bring back Martin Blecher Junior.

"Is there a man named Martin Blecher Junior around?" the agent had asked.

"He is," Robinson replied.

"He's a deserter from the American army," Comiskay had said. "I'm going to take him back."

Robinson was somewhat startled by the news. "Well, that's up to you," the ranger had responded, "I'll have nothing to do with it. I've had my share in the game and I don't want anything more to do with it."

Comiskay appeared surprised by the ranger's attitude. "But, if I wanted him arrested I might [need to] get you."

"Well, in that case give me a warrant and I'll carry it out," Robinson had replied, "I have the full authority to do so if you produce a warrant."[20]

According to the ranger:

Well he stayed around, and he was here for a considerable time was Mr. Comiskay. He went back without Martin. He didn't take him back with him. And I know for a fact that Tom twitted him [Martin] about deserting.[21]

In notes from an interview Audrey Saunders conducted with Robinson in 1944, she stated that the ranger had suspected that the Blecher family might well have paid off the agent, as they had been wealthy enough to do so.[22] Nevertheless, if Comiskay had been looking for a "deserter," then his encounter with Robinson would had to have occurred sometime after August 24, 1918, which was when Martin Junior had been ordered to report for military duty and entrainment—and not during the summer of 1917.

After the US Congress had passed the Selective Service Act on May 18, 1917, there had been three draft registrations in the United States. The first was held on June 5, 1917, in which men were registered between the ages of twenty-one and thirty-one. The next two dates would come a year later, on June 5, 1918, which registered men who had turned twenty-one after June 5, 1917, and on September 12, 1918, to register men who had turned twenty-one since June 5, 1918. Martin Blecher Junior had been born on July 11, 1891, and so June 5, 1917 would have been the date he should have registered. Blecher, however, had failed to do so and consequently would have been considered a "draft-dodger" rather than a "deserter," which would have required him to have been both registered and enlisted to warrant such a charge.

That a charge of desertion would in time be brought against Martin Junior is a fact, however it would not have been applicable during the time that Tom Thomson was alive. At the very least, Blecher might rightly have been viewed as having been disloyal to the allied war effort by his absence, but this is a charge that could just as easily have been made of Thomson, and which, in and of itself, would have cast both men in a bad light locally.

Mark Robinson, however, having just returned from fighting against the German forces in World War I, was quick to cast a suspicious eye on Blecher ever since he had returned to his duties in Algonquin Park. And it may well have been the ranger who put the story of Blecher being a "deserter" in Tom Thomson's ear, as Robinson had written in his diary two months earlier:

> May 14, 1917—Martin Blecher Jr. left this morning for St. Louis. I am of the opinion he is a German spy . . . [23]

There was never any evidence to suggest that Blecher was a German spy, but Thomson's chirping Blecher about being a deserter was certainly nearer the mark, if but thirteen months premature. As indicated, Blecher had failed to register for the American draft on June 5, 1917, and would not register until almost six months later, on November 27, 1917. Later Blecher would run into trouble again when he failed to heed the call to report for military duty and entrainment on August 24, 1918. In 1931, Major General CH Bridges, then the Adjutant General of the War Department[24] in Washington, D.C., looked into the matter for author Blodwen Davies and reported that:

> The records show that he [Martin Blecher Junior] was ordered to report for military duty and entrainment by his Local Board on August 24, 1918, and because of his failure to report as ordered, he was certified to The Adjutant General of the Army as a deserter.[25]

However, his report to Davies also indicated that such a certification was not held long:

> Correspondence on file with his record shows that he subsequently voluntarily reported to the Local Board and upon investigation of his case the board found his desertion to be non-willful and reported the facts in the case to Selective Service Headquarters, Albany, New York. On February 13, 1919, those Headquarters recommended to the Commanding General, Camp Dix, New Jersey, that the registrant be discharged from the military service and the records show that such action was taken.[26]

By the time Blecher was discharged in February of 1919 the war had been over for three months, which means that Blecher did not report for duty until the last possible minute (sometime after the end of August and the end of the war in November 1918). It's also clear that if he had been touting the German cause in and around Canoe Lake during July 1917, he was doing so one month after failing to show up to register for the draft in his home state of New York, despite his having been of age to do so. While the US Army would later accept Blecher's reasons for his tardiness in registering and enlisting, the Canadians at Canoe Lake were not so empathetic.

A FEUD BEGINS

It is not clear when the conflict first arose between Tom Thomson and Martin Blecher Junior. Perhaps it simply began as a clash of personalities as Thomson was usually quiet and reserved,[27] whereas Blecher was known to be loud and, as evidenced by certain of the testimony above, somewhat aggressive.[28] There is evidence that the two had been adversarial toward each other for at least two years prior to the artist's death and, somewhat ironically for two men who sat on the sidelines while their respective countrymen went to war, that a certain patriotism held by both men was at the heart of their conflict.

In 1915, a group of schoolteachers from the Burton Avenue School in Barrie, Ontario had, on the recommendation of Mark Robinson, travelled north to Mowat Lodge for a brief vacation. One of the teachers, Hazel Barker, recalled being witness to the incident that was the genesis of the Blecher family/Thomson feud:

> On one occasion an American family rented a house across the chip yard (the lodge was formerly a lumber mill). Shortly after they arrived we noticed a flag flying from the flagpole. You guessed it—the Stars and Stripes. They were duly informed that they must fly the Union Jack if any flag was put up. The next night it had not been put up. Mysteriously the rope was cut. Next day the Stars and Stripes went up again—but beneath it—the Union Jack. Next night rope cutting was again indulged in. The following morning as I stepped out onto the veranda, which ran around the lodge—there was Tom with

the binoculars. He wore a satisfied smile. He said, "Take a look." There was the Union Jack—a little one, but right at the top of the pole, and beneath it the Stars and Stripes.[29]

In amongst the rules stipulated by the province of Ontario for each property leased within the Canoe Lake region was a clause that read "If any flag is at any time flown or displayed on said parcel or tract of land, it shall be the British flag."[30] As the park ranger for the area it had been Mark Robinson's job to ensure that this clause was enforced, but for mischievous reasons of his own it had been Thomson who had taken the matter into his own hands and had been cutting the Blecher's ropes, climbing their flagpole and hanging the Union Jack flag.[31] And while it may seem to us from our present day vantage point as being a harmless, almost schoolboy prank, and rather a silly thing to squabble about, the Blecher family was not amused. And rightly so; they had travelled a considerable distance from Buffalo to Algonquin Park in order to have a holiday from the goings on at Martin Senior's furniture manufacturing business and wanted nothing more than to relax and get away from the city—not engage in a pissing contest with some local yokel over which country's ensign warranted top billing on their cottage flagpole. And given that the family was fiercely protective of their private property, the knowledge that some unknown person should repeatedly creep onto it in the dead of night and cause damage to their personal property had left them seething.

With the Canoe Lake community being as small as it was, it didn't take the Blechers long to discern the true identity of the culprit, which immediately set the family against the artist. From Thomson's perspective, it would appear that he couldn't have cared less about how the Blecher family had felt about his actions and, consequently, an animus began to rise between the two parties, eventually growing to the point that whenever Martin Junior would walk into Mowat Lodge, Thomson would get up and leave.[32] Evidently the animus endured; Louisa Blecher, Martin's mother, when interviewed in 1930 by Blodwen Davies, refused to speak about the artist.[33]

ALCOHOL

Resentment will often lie dormant unless something mixes with it in order to bring it to the surface. And in the Thomson/Martin Blecher Junior feud, the mixing agent was alcohol. History reveals that periods of prohibition have seldom been successful in deterring people from obtaining and consuming alcohol. And so when the Ontario Temperance Act (OTA) was passed in 1916, booze had naturally continued to find its way into Algonquin Park. Most of the people at Canoe Lake who moved within Thomson's orbit were no strangers to the allure of distilled spirits; George Rowe and Lowery Dickson, for example, had repeatedly lost jobs at Mowat Lodge on account of this predilection. In Audrey Saunders' book *Algonquin Story*, she reported that:

> Both of these men, in spite of Park regulations, used to take a drop too much. When that happened, Shannon's [Fraser] business would suffer and he would fire them. It made things difficult for Shannon. In a written complaint to Mr. Bartlett, he asserted that someone had given George Rowe "licker," with the result that "the Missis had to take the mail." Before long, however, all would be forgiven and forgotten and George and Lowery would be back at work till it happened again.[34]

And while it's safe to say that Thomson was not averse to having a drink, there are conflicting accounts as to how much alcohol the artist drank, and how often he fell under its sway. Mark Robinson, for instance, believed that:

> Tom, while he wasn't a man that would drink, he'd take a couple of drinks of some kind of liquor and stop, and when he did stop nobody could coax him to take any more. He was just that type.[35]

In agreement with the ranger was Gordon Wattie, the son of Park Ranger Tom Wattie. Although he was only a boy of ten or eleven when Thomson used to visit the Wattie family in South River, he remembered the artist well and told the author in 1991 that from his recollection, "Thomson wasn't a heavy drinker. Not around our place anyways. He was a very friendly, fine fellow." Surprisingly, standing in stark contrast to these claims regarding the artist's drinking habits is that of Mark Robinson's daughter. In the one and only conversation I had with Ottelyn Addison in 1990, she told me point blank: "Thomson was a drunk." When I contrasted her statement with what her father had indicated above she quickly shut me down with, "My father felt sorry for him."

Over the years the statements that have come forth on this topic have tended to support Addison's notion that Thomson was, if not a drunk, at least a man who had been known to drink to excess on occasion. Granted, what was deemed by some to be "excess" during a time of government enforced temperance might not square with our modern day definition of the term, but it can be safely said that Thomson was not towing the government line on this particular matter. Consider the statement of Alan Ross, a man who had been a close friend of Thomson's since 1882:

> I have been with him on several occasions when I am now sorry to say that neither of us was very sober, but it is in such

times men exchange real confidences. . . . As for myself, I always seemed to get more secretive the drunker I became, but Tom was different. I remember one night in 1901, in Meaford, when he unbosomed himself, lamenting his lack of success in life in terms that rather astonished me.[36]

Ross would later add:

I think his [Thomson's] worst fault in the time referred to must have been his drinking, that is, if the stories told me be true. . . . But there is no use in trying to canonize a man simply because he is dead, and from stories Ross McKeen and others have told me there was absolutely no sense to the manner in which Tom set about his drinking when the humor seemed to take him. There may have been a reason, or rather a cause, for it, one can never tell.[37]

Apparently Ross was not alone in his opinion, as there is evidence that alcohol had played a problematic role in the artist's work habits while employed at Legg Brothers photoengraving firm in Toronto. According to his fellow employee Stuart Thompson:

Occasionally he drank too much when he would become morose and would go home. Once he drank enough to quit and stayed away. I understand he phoned in and said he was getting another job and requested the boss not to knock him when he asked for reference.[38]

As we saw earlier, the opinion that Thomson drank to excess is one that was also held by the former guide and trapper Ralph Bice. And while Bice never knew the artist personally, he did know most of the guides who had known and guided with Thomson, and he came away from these discussions with the opinion that:

> Tom Thomson was a drinker, a heavy drinker. As a matter of fact, such a thing today, you would just say that he was a drunken bum. But that's one part of his life that they never mention. He had a friend among the park rangers, Jim Hughes, [William James Hughes, who became a park ranger in 1912] who lived over in Brent [he was the ranger at Basin Depot at the time he knew Thomson] and his wife [Charlotte] was my father's cousin. . . . Anyway, he was an uncle to all those Hugheses in Port Sydney. And another girl lived with him, a sister of Mrs. Hughes [Alice Green], and Tom used to go over and see her. And she thought she was going to marry him—until she found out the reason he went there was so that he and Jim could go out and drink. And many was the night that they [the ladies] walked the shore of Acanthus [Lake] to see if they had upset [their canoe], but they always came home. That has never been mentioned in the histories of Tom Thomson.[39]

(As a side note, I must confess that the old trapper's testimony on this was enlightening to me, as my wife Terri is one "of those Hugheses" from Port Sydney.)

A QUARREL

Whether or not Thomson was a drunkard or merely a man who drank on occasion and knew when to stop, on the night prior to his disappearance he and several other men had gotten together to play cards at a guide's cabin—and all were said to have been drinking heavily. Whether the get-together took place at George Rowe's or Lowrey Dickson's cabin is unclear, made all the more unclear by the fact that the two guides had also shared the cabin that Dickson now had sole possession of for a number of years. Dickson's cabin was situated a little north from Mowat Lodge and several cottages. It sat on a sandy point near where Potter and Joe Creeks merged into the northern tip of Canoe Lake, which might have placed it within sight of certain cottagers and guests at Mowat Lodge. As the OTA was in effect, if a party was going on with alcohol being served, it might have not only proven to be off putting to certain of Fraser's more puritan guests, but if word got back to Mark Robinson, he would have had full authority to confiscate the alcohol and press charges if need be. No, something a little more secluded would have been required. This left George Rowe's old cabin as the logical choice for the get-together, as it was nestled in discreetly among a grove of birch trees on the northwestern shore of Canoe Lake, just south of the former hospital building and well out of the sight line of any lodge guests, and yet in close enough proximity for the party goers to be able to walk back to their respective dwellings after things wound down.

To put things into sharper perspective, there was no television to watch, no local sports team to cheer on, no radio to listen to, no movie houses, no theaters or other forms of entertainment. As a result, fishing, playing cards, and drinking alcohol were popular avenues of temporary escape from the often harsh and boring realities of day-to-day existence. Consequently, such get-togethers were welcomed distractions and this night was no exception. Not long after the men had gotten together, a deck of cards was brought out along with a bottle. Both Dickson and Thomson would have arrived early that evening, owing to the fact that both men would have long been familiar with the weekend routine of their friend (and in Dickson's case, former roommate) George Rowe. Shannon Fraser, it can be presumed, would have arrived later that night once he had finished up his duties at Mowat Lodge. He, too, would have long been familiar with such get-togethers involving his employees, and he was also known to be a person who could access alcohol despite the Temperance Act being in effect.[40]

Rowe's cabin lay a short distance south of the Blecher cottage, and the lamplight and the sound of voices resonating from within the cabin had evidently drawn the attention of Martin Blecher Junior, who had probably grown restless with the normal routine at his parents' cottage and, like the other men who had gathered at the guide's cabin that evening, was welcoming of the distraction that a get-together at Rowe's would have provided. It's safe to assume that Martin Junior would have been a late entry to the party and that his arrival would have raised some eyebrows, as it is unlikely that he would have been invited. The serving of alcohol, again, was prohibited in Ontario at this point in time, and while the guides trusted certain people to keep their drinking activities on the down low, they held forth no such trust for outsiders from their select group. Moreover, Blecher was then employed as a private detective by the William J. Burns Detective Agency, which was headquartered out of Chicago, but had a branch office located in Blecher's home city of Buffalo, New York. Private detectives were not then the heroic figures that would later become popular in the novels of Raymond Chandler and Mickey Spillane, but rather were generally considered to be unsavory characters that spied on cheating spouses and dug up dirt on people for a living. The foregoing notwithstanding, Blecher had suffered no qualms about making his way to Rowe's cabin, and evidently his presence had not been considered by those in attendance to be a sufficient impediment to warrant terminating or postponing their intentions of drinking that evening.

It is well established that alcohol has a way of loosening tongues and amplifying moods, and as the evening wore on and glasses were refilled, the tension between the artist and the cottager—now forced to be together within the restricted confines of a very small cabin—began to rise concurrently. Word of the incident that would occur later that evening traveled quickly via the guide's grapevine, and eventually found its way to the Algonquin Hotel, as Blanche Packard had overheard talk in the guide's dining room of "an argument the night before Tom left, and quarrels during a card game."[41] And, according to what my father would later learn from both George Rowe and Shannon Fraser, the principals involved in the quarrel were, to no one's surprise, Tom Thomson and Martin Blecher Junior.[42] Small talk between the friends within the cabin didn't exist, and such conversation as there was that night eventually worked its way round to the topic of the war, which would have been a particularly sensitive issue for both men. Thomson was known to have a quick temper, particularly when abused personally. His friend Alan Ross recollected that:

> He [Thomson] had strange antipathies, and the few people he did dislike he hated most cordially and he was not at all diplomatic in concealing it either. . . . I discovered how deeply sensitive he was and how he resented anything like public ridicule . . .[43]

This use of the term "cordially" is not the common useage and, in this instance, refers to a "sincerely or deeply felt" hatred.[44]

In fact, public ridicule was the only thing known to make the artist violent. Arthur Robson, who had employed Thomson at Grip Ltd. in Toronto, recalled an incident involving Thomson and a drunk during which Thomson was fine—until the drunk made it personal:

> Only once did I ever see him lose his temper and that was in 1912. A man under the influence of liquor got into the studio and made himself as objectionable as possible. Tom

tried to continue his work, *but when the visitor became personally abusive Tom's temper finally rose.* He took off his coat and
threw the visitor out of the building. The noise of overturn-
ing chairs and tables attracted my attention, but by the time I
got there Tom was brushing imaginary dust of his hands and
settling back to finishing his drawing.[45] (Emphasis added.)

And so this was the pressure cooker that had been slowly building
steam on the evening of July 7—a brash, twenty-five-year-old cottager who had thus far eluded enlistment in the American draft,
and a thirty-nine-year-old artist who likewise had not enlisted, but
was nevertheless loyal to the allied cause, and who had a hair trig-
ger response when it came to personal abuse. Thomson's younger
brother Fraser would later report:

> I know that there had been ill will between a German who
> worked at one of the lodges and my brother. Tom had been
> trying to enlist and the German had said something to him.
> There was a quarrel. Then Tom was found dead soon after-
> ward. Who knows what happened?[46]

One man who claimed to know what happened was Ralph Bice.
And while Bice was not present at the cabin on the evening in question, he was a friend of George Rowe, the man who hosted the get-
together. And the old guide shared with Bice his recollection of the
events that took place that evening, and how it all harkened back
to the silly game of "my flag flies higher than your flag" that had
taken place two years previously:

> I was out guiding with George Rowe the next summer
> [1918]. Well, from what I can piece together Thomson and
> Martin Blecher had once fought over a flag. Blecher refused

to fly anything but the Stars and Stripes, and he blamed it on Thomson for saying that he had to put up the Union Jack. And that was [brought up at] the last big meeting they had where everybody was drinking. All hearsay, I wasn't there. But Blecher said, "Oh well, if you're such a good Britisher, why aren't you in the army instead of up here painting second-class pictures and drinking yourself to death?" Which isn't a very nice thing to have said about you.[47]

Blecher had now insulted Thomson personally, which caused the hostility that the artist had long been harboring toward the cottager to rise instantly from a simmer to a boil. If in the past the artist would have chosen to leave any room that Martin Junior entered, it is clear that he had no such intention on this night. Instead, the artist locked eyes with Blecher and uttered a one-word response: "Deserter."[48]

That was the flash point. The two men suddenly went for each other and, as they grappled, the other men in the room quickly stepped in and tried to separate them. Once the two combatants were finally pulled apart, Blecher made his way to the door, suddenly feeling very much an outsider to the group. He turned and made one final threat to the artist: "Don't get in my way, if you know what's good for you!"[49]

The door slammed and Blecher was gone. The violent outbreak between the two men had dampened the spirit in which the evening had started and, however long the artist remained in the cabin afterward, the mood would have been dour. Eventually it became apparent to those remaining that the "party" was over, and Thomson, perhaps along with Shannon Fraser, eventually made his exit and walked along the small path that ran next to the shoreline back to the Trainor cottage where he had been staying that weekend. And that is all we know about the matter.

Both of the disputants had each said of the other what had likely been on the minds of many at Canoe Lake but, alcohol induced or not, now that the genie was out of the bottle, things were never going to return to the way they were ever again. Thomson's older brother George would learn about the altercation several days after it had occurred:

> I had heard that there was some ill feeling between Tom and some man in that region (Mowat). It was somewhat causally referred to by someone at Canoe Lake, possibly one of the Rangers, but as this was while we were still looking for Tom and I was still hopeful of his safe recovery, I didn't at the time attach any serious importance to the report.[50]

Mark Robinson, likewise, had not attached anything portentous to the rumors of the Blecher/Thomson quarrel—at least initially. But the timeline of events would cause him to reconsider. First of all was the fact that Thomson had disappeared within twelve hours after Blecher had threatened him. And then there was the fact that his disappearance had occurred on an afternoon when both Thomson (in his canoe) and Blecher (in his motorboat) had been on the lake at the same time. Indeed, the Blecher siblings would be the ones who would first spot Thomson's overturned canoe. No one else in the region had indicated being on the lake that day or seeing the abandoned watercraft. The Blecher siblings' reason for not investigating the upturned canoe at the time they had first spotted it had been that they were both quite certain that it was a stray canoe that had slipped its moorings and floated away from one of the local lodges. Robinson must have raised an eyebrow at this excuse straight away. The only hotel on Canoe Lake was Mowat Lodge, and Shannon Fraser had not reported that any of his canoes had gone missing. The next closest hotel was the Algonquin, and for one of its canoes to end up in Canoe Lake, it would have had to not only break free from its dock, but also to make its way from Joe Lake over the railway tracks and into the Joe Lake Narrows, down and over the Joe Lake Dam, and then finesse its way along Joe Creek and into Canoe Lake all by itself, which would have necessitated quite a preternatural feat of auto navigation. The missing canoe story represented more than simply a lame excuse for gross negligence on the part of the siblings; any time a watercraft is spotted floating upside down there is a good chance that its occupant (or occupants) is in trouble and approaching the craft to see if assistance is required is a moral imperative. As indicated earlier, Thomson had painted his canoe a distinct color, making it stand out from every other canoe in Algonquin Park. The Blechers had often witnessed Thomson paddling in his canoe for the better part of four summers and most certainly would have recognized the watercraft as being the artist's as soon as they had spotted it. That they would choose to ignore what they saw when Thomson may have been in trouble is itself deeply troubling. The next day the Blechers towed the canoe that they had seen the day before from the lake (they clearly *now* recognized it as being Thomson's) and, depending upon the source, they either put it into their boathouse or brought it to the attention of Shannon Fraser.[51] In considering all the foregoing, Martin Blecher Junior was starting to look very suspicious in Robinson's eyes.

And the speculation continued. The reader will recall that Robinson and certain guides who had worked with Thomson had puzzled over the way Thomson's paddles had been lashed onto the thwarts of his abandoned canoe when it had first been recovered, which suggested to them that they had been tied in by an amateur, rather than by someone who was an experienced canoeist such as Thomson. Consequently, the guides suspected that whomever had tied those paddles into the artist's canoe was most likely the one who had intimate knowledge of his death. This fact alone eliminated from their minds any of the guides or rangers as possible suspects, as both of these groups canoed for a living and all knew how to tie their paddles into a canoe in a professional and efficacious manner. To their minds this left only two classes of people as likely suspects—cottagers and tourists—and the person who fit into both of those categories was the man who had quarreled with the artist on the eve of his disappearance. In their eyes, as in Robinson's, this further served to fan the flames of speculation regarding Martin Blecher Junior's potential involvement in Thomson's "accident."

While Robinson and my father had held forth Blecher as being the most likely suspect in Thomson's death, the author must confess that he has always had a problem with this conclusion. Primarily owing to the fact that, despite a legitimate animosity that existed between the two men (In 1917 Winnifred Trainor had even felt compelled to make the comment to Thomson's brother George that, "Tom did not care for Martin Blecher,"[52]) they had nevertheless found a way to peacefully co-exist within the Canoe Lake community for at least three summers prior to the artist's death. At no time prior to their tussle at George Rowe's cabin had there been any indication of violence occurring between the two parties, and the day after a booze fueled argument one would presume that cooler, or at least more sober, heads would have prevailed and the relationship, such as it was, would have continued to go on as it had for years past; i.e., without incident. However, this is merely the opinion of someone many generations removed from the goings on at Canoe Lake during the summer of 1917.

But if Blecher was involved in Thomson's death, how did it occur? When Mark Robinson had examined Thomson's corpse, the wound on his temple had suggested to him that the artist might have died as a result of being struck by the edge of a paddle.[53] Could it have been possible that while Blecher and his sister were out in their motorboat on the afternoon of July 8 they happened upon Thomson paddling alone in his canoe? Or was it a case where Thomson paddled by the Blecher cottage and was spotted by the cottager? Did the artist resume his "twitting Martin about being a deserter" from the night before? Did Martin then hop in his motorboat and confront the artist in the bay south of Little Wapomeo Island, where he grabbed a paddle and swung it at the artist's head with sufficient force to kill him or render him unconscious? And would he then, in a state of panic, anchor Thomson's body to something heavy so that it would sink out of sight to the bottom of the lake? Certainly the area of the lake where the overturned canoe was first spotted and where Thomson's body eventually surfaced was not that far away from the Blecher cottage. And if such a scenario played out, Blecher would have been aware that he might have been spotted on the lake at the same time that the artist was. Being a private detective, he would have known the importance of being alibied and, given that there was no love lost between the Blecher family and the artist, securing his family's cover would not have been difficult. Perhaps it was an impulsive act that his family knew nothing about, in which case Blecher may well have simply secured his sister's participation for an afternoon cruise an hour or so later and then feigned surprise at seeing Thomson's overturned canoe in the bay area during their excursion to the Tea Lake Dam. But I must catch myself here; such scenarios may be simply the author indulging in some fanciful speculation, perhaps to better understand or buttress his own father's belief that the cottager had killed Thomson. After all, for this to even be plausible one would need to establish that the artist was killed as Robinson had suggested; i.e., as a result of someone swinging a paddle at his head. And certainly we have no proof of this, and even if we did, it does not in itself implicate Martin Blecher Junior. Such an act merely suggests a murderous action that could have been perpetrated by anyone. And yet there was only one family on the lake at that time that was said to have had both a long standing feud with the artist and a history of swinging clubs and other objects at people, and that was the Blecher family. Furthermore, and perhaps more to the point, there existed no history of anyone at Canoe Lake ever swinging a paddle at another person's head in a threatening manner with the exception of one man—Martin Blecher Junior.

Dr. Harry Ebbs was the one who was almost the recipient of such a blow from the cottager:

> I had seventy-five workmen up there and I had to bring all my food in from the train and I had to get my order out every day . . . This particular day I was late and I had a little outboard and in order to get up to the station, you had to go up through Corkscrew Creek, up through the little river to Canoe Lake Station. And I could see the train was in; I could see the smoke from the train and I was late. And I got halfway up and I could see Martin Blecher coming down the creek in his little boat, there was quite a big curve and I knew that if I didn't get there first, to the corner first, that I would have to go way out around him and I would lose quite a lot of valuable time. Well I did beat him and we could tell, both of us could tell, that I was going to get to that corner first and therefore he would have to swerve and go to the outside. And as he went by, he picked up a paddle and swung it, and if I hadn't ducked he would have crowned me right there on the spot![54]

If Blecher's reflex when angered was to take a lethal swing with a paddle at the head of a complete stranger during a random encounter on the lake, it's not unthinkable that he might have done the same thing on the same lake several years previously to a man with whom he had quarreled bitterly—but who simply didn't duck in time.

Chapter Eleven

A WIFE'S CONFESSION

I f it was true, as Dr. Harry Ebbs maintained, that Martin Blecher Junior's name had been the one whispered most frequently in discussions about the artist's death in the months that followed the tragedy at Canoe Lake, then it was also true that, 180 miles away in Owen Sound, the Thomson family was whispering the name of someone else entirely.

As little as two months after Thomson's death it was the Mowat Lodge proprietor Shannon Fraser whom certain Thomson family members were looking toward with a large measure of suspicion— and not just because they believed him to have spread the rumor of suicide. Writing to James MacCallum on September 9, 1917, Thomson's sister Margaret did not mince words about her belief in this regard:

> Sometimes I wonder if the man [Shannon Fraser] did do anything to harm Tom. I suppose it is wicked to think such a thing, but if anyone did harm him, it was for the little money they could pocket.[1]

Ah yes, money—always a reliable motive in matters of homicide. The Thomson family, for a time at least, believed that if there had been foul play involved in the death of their family member then the motive was most likely robbery. With that belief, the artist's

179

brother-in-law, Tom Harkness, penned an accusatory letter to the lodge owner:

> How do you account for Tom only having 60 cents when found? I know what he drew from the bank when he was away, and he was guiding a few weeks and no doubt was paid for it, and where do you suppose his money went to?[2]

Interestingly, based on the content from Harkness's letter above and from a brief statement within an article published in the *Owen Sound Sun* newspaper on July 13, we learn of the fact that Thomson had been away from Algonquin Park for an undisclosed period of time immediately prior to his death, and that during this absence he had withdrawn an unspecified sum of money from a bank.[3] If the newspaper report is accurate, the artist had returned to the park on Saturday, July 7, where we know that he wrote a letter to his patron Dr. MacCallum, and then attended the drinking party at George Rowe's cabin later that same evening. The next day he left for either an afternoon of fishing or a two-week canoe trip, and was never to be seen again. We further know from Molly Colson's testimony that the artist had fifty dollars on his person on the morning that he was last seen alive, while Harkness's testimony reveals that this amount had been lightened considerably by the time his body was pulled from the waters of Canoe Lake eight days later. And the only other person beyond Molly Colson who might have known about Thomson's bankroll on the day that he went missing was the man that he was with that morning, and that man was Shannon Fraser.

Certainly Fraser's statements and actions in the wake of the artist's death might be regarded as suspicious. As noted earlier, Fraser's testimony had been fraught with contradictions; almost from the day that the artist's body had been discovered Fraser had been the one who had immediately written a letter to the Thomson family patriarch indicating that the artist's death had been the result of an accident,[4] and then, in his very next breath, telling complete strangers such as Charles Plewman that Thomson had committed suicide.[5] Fraser was also the only one to indicate that the artist was heading out for an afternoon of fishing, while Thomson had told others such as Molly Colson that he was leaving for a two week canoe trip. The lodge owner had also been anything but exact in recounting the time that Thomson was said to have left his dock on the afternoon of July 8. And it was certainly true that Fraser had insinuated himself very thoroughly into the activities that followed the discovery of Thomson's body. He had been the one that claimed to have secured the services of the two undertakers for a quick burial of Thomson's body in the Mowat Cemetery,[6] and, according to one eyewitness, he had even implied his involvement in ensuring that the artist's remains never left Algonquin Park.[7] He also was the one who picked up the undertaker Franklin Churchill from the train station and delivered both he and his metal coffin to the Mowat Cemetery. It was also Fraser who picked up Churchill and the metal casket in the early morning hours of Thursday, July 19, 1917. Such a feverish commitment to the dead body of a former lodge guest was highly dubious, and certainly suggests that Fraser had not been in favor of allowing anyone—from the Huntsville undertaker, to the coroner, to the Thomson family—any opportunity to inspect Thomson's corpse in greater detail going forward if he wasn't around to oversee things.

In the same letter written by Thomson's sister Margaret to Dr. MacCallum on September 9, 1917, she reported on a meeting that she had with Winnifred Trainor in Toronto. During their conversation that day Trainor had evidently painted a damning picture of the lodge owner:

> I might say that I met Miss Trainor of Huntsville in Toronto
> . . . she said that Tom didn't like Mr. Fraser, as he hadn't a

good principle. She said that he [Thomson] was intending to leave there in a week or so, and that he didn't want them to know where he was going, as they were so curious about everything. She said that [Thomson] had warned her not to put anything in her letters that she wouldn't care to have them read, as they always seemed to know his business. He said he didn't know whether they opened his letters in the [post] office or whether they read them after he had opened them, as he used to leave them in his overcoat pocket.

She said that Mr. Fraser was the meanest man she ever saw and that her father detested him. She said he even tried to sell Tom's shoes after he was gone . . . [8]

While Winnifred Trainor's and Margaret Thomson's judgment of Fraser was harsh, their suspicion was nonetheless genuine and, when it was discovered that the lodge owner had owed the artist money at the time of his death, the Thomson family's anger and suspicion only intensified. During the period of time when George Thomson had been at Canoe Lake shortly after his brother had been reported missing, Shannon Fraser had in an unguarded moment revealed that he had been in debt to Thomson over the repayment of a loan made to him by the artist two years previously. The lodge owner had evidently paid a good portion of the loan back, but there was still some money owed. Collecting on this debt now owed to Tom Thomson's estate became the Thomson family's principal area of focus in the months immediately following the artist's burial. After some (at times) rancorous back and forth between the two parties, this matter was eventually resolved to the family's satisfaction, and their attention then was directed toward the return of all of Thomson's personal affects from Mowat Lodge. These items, in the event, turned out to be pathetically few:

- One plaid overcoat
- One worn out suit

- Two red Hudson Bay blankets
- Two canvas bags
- One pair of underwear
- Four pairs of socks
- One aluminum three-gallon pail
- Three lids
- Two plates
- Two tin cups
- Some handkerchiefs
- One ink bottle
- Two pipes[9]

And then, somewhat surprisingly, once the above items had been returned to the family, any further mention of Shannon Fraser in the matter of Tom Thomson's death seems to have ceased. Perhaps from the family's vantage point, while they admitted that there was certainly the possibility that foul play might have been a factor in causing the death of their family member,[10] there had also been an official inquest on the matter and it had returned a verdict of accidental death by drowning, which they were quite willing to accept. And so things eventually settled down, life gradually returned to normal, and Tom Thomson's death, when it was spoken of at all, was referred to as a tragic accident, or if it begat speculation, a "mystery."

None of the Thomson family or Thomson's friends from the Toronto art world returned to Mowat Lodge ever again. The lodge itself would burn to the ground three years after the artist's death in 1920. A new Mowat Lodge would be constructed much closer to the Canoe Lake shoreline a year later, and the Frasers would operate it for another several years before the Great Depression struck. With less disposable income, the tourists eventually stopped coming to the park in the numbers required to continue the operation. The

Frasers sold Mowat Lodge and left the park in 1929. The years passed and rolled into decades and Tom Thomson's star began a precipitous ascent until it was prominently affixed in the firmament of the Canadian art world. The Frasers, by contrast, were anonymous, save for their future appearance as footnotes in whatever biographical literature appeared on the artist. That is until Shannon Fraser's name would surface once again in regard to the death of the artist, but this time it wouldn't be uttered by any member of the Thomson family.

A STARTLING CONFESSION

Daphne Crombie was a newlywed in her twenties when she and her husband, Robert Lionel Crombie, first arrived at Mowat Lodge in the winter of 1917. Robert, whom she had affectionately dubbed "Robin," had been a lieutenant in the Canadian Field Artillery Reserve Brigade during World War I and had returned home from France with tuberculosis. His physician believed that the clean northern Ontario air coupled with its colder climate would prove to be a tonic for his patient, and so the Crombies travelled north from Toronto to stay at Mowat Lodge. Robert, wrapped from head to toe in warm blankets, had been instructed to sit outside on the Mowat Lodge veranda in the cold air as often as he could, and Daphne, being the attentive new bride that she was, would often sit on the veranda next to him.

During the winter of 1917 the only guests at Mowat Lodge were the Crombies. Tom Thomson arrived in early April, with the result that the Crombies came to know the artist reasonably well. However, Daphne also grew to welcome the company of the only other woman at the lodge during the winter and spring months, Annie Fraser, and the two women became friends or, at least, friendly, and would often go for walks together. It was during one of their excursions that spring that Thomson had painted "Larry Dixon's Cabin," which, despite a misspelling of the guide's first and last name, featured the two women walking along a path in front of the guide's cabin that sat upon a sandy point at the junction where Canoe Lake split into Joe and Potter Creeks. As Crombie recalled:

> Annie and I were walking along the road. And Tom used to go in different places to paint. And we heard a voice: "Will you stand there for a minute?" And we looked up and there was Tom painting. And it was cold and he said, "I won't keep you long." She had a bright red blanket coat on and I've forgotten what I had on. And he painted these two figures in the painting.[11]

The Crombies would stay at Mowat Lodge until May, returning again later that November only to learn from the Frasers that Tom Thomson had passed away in July. In 1977, Ron Pittaway, an employee for what would later become the Algonquin Park Archives, was seeking out former park visitors and residents to interview for an oral history of the park that he was then in the midst of compiling. In due course he tracked down the nonagenarian Mrs. Crombie in an effort to solicit her recollections about the park during the time that she had visited it in 1917. To Pittaway's delight Mrs. Crombie proved to be a veritable fount of information, and even provided recollections about a good many of the local people from the era in which she was there—Shannon Fraser, George Rowe, Martin Blecher Junior, and, of course, Tom Thomson. But it was what she revealed about the content of a conversation that she had with Annie Fraser in November 1917 that would stun her interviewer.

According to Crombie, when she and her husband had returned to Mowat Lodge that November, she and Annie Fraser quickly resumed their habit of taking walks in and around the vicinity of the lodge. And it was during one of these walks that Mrs. Fraser un-burdened herself of a grave secret she had been harboring—that her husband had killed Tom Thomson.[12]

Annie revealed that shortly before Thomson's death she had come upon a letter that had been left unattended on the artist's dresser at the lodge.[13] The temptation to read it had proven irresist-ible and so Annie opened it. The letter was from Winnifred Trainor, and it contained the information that she would be returning to Canoe Lake the following week and that the pair would need to be married quickly. Trainor had allegedly written the statement, "Please Tom, you must get a new suit because we'll *have to be* mar-ried."[14] This, Annie believed, was a clear indication that Trainor was pregnant, and that she was pushing to have a marriage arranged quickly in order to avoid a scandal. The content of the letter had evidently served to rattle the artist, and as the only suit he possessed was evidently worn out, he now was in dire need of money in order to purchase a new one.[15] Annie went on to confess that her husband Shannon had owed the artist money, and that Trainor's dilemma had made its collection a matter of some urgency to Thomson.

Thomson, apparently, wasn't one to pick his spots in discuss-ing such matters, as Annie related that he chose to confront Shan-non when he, George Rowe, "and another guy" had a party, which sounds suspiciously like the one where the altercation with Martin Blecher Junior had occurred. According to Crombie:

Tom and George and . . . I know his name quite well, it will come to me . . . they had a party. And they used to go and have drinks. They were all pretty good drinkers, Tom as well. They went up and they had this party. And they were tight. Tom asked Shannon Fraser for the money that he owed him because he had to go and get a new suit. Anyway, they had a fight and Shannon hit Tom, knocked him down by the grate fire, and Tom had a mark on his forehead. I don't know where it was . . . they had this fight and Tom was knocked out completely. And of course, Fraser was simply terrified—he thought he'd killed him! This is my conception, and I don't know about other people's. Although he [Fraser] was a big heavy Irishman [Fraser was actually of Scottish descent], he was timid about those kinds of things—devious, if you know what I mean. So my conception is that he took Tom's body and put it into a canoe and dropped it in the lake and that's how he died . . . I know he hit him, but I don't think he was dead. I think that Shannon Fraser was terrified. I think he [Tom] might have been unconscious but I think Shannon Fraser was terrified that he was dead. And I believe that Annie helped him pack the canoe and he went off into the lake with Tom's body, cause she always helped him pack his canoe quite often . . . But Annie [was] decent and very, very honorable. She never told me lies—ever.

. . . Now Annie told me that from her own lips, having read the letter.[16]

Crombie's information represented a startling revelation and seemed to tie together a lot of loose ends—from how the artist met his death and why his canoe was discovered before his body, to the head wound and the fishing line that was wrapped around his left ankle. It further explained why Shannon Fraser's testimony—from Thomson's destination on the day that he left the lodge, to the time of Thomson's departure, to telling one person that the artist committed suicide while telling another that he hit his head on a rock and died an accidental death by drowning—had been so contradictory. Based on what Crombie had said, the logical conclusion was that Fraser had obviously been in a panic to cover his tracks and so had fabricated these various theories to deflect attention away from himself. Crombie had even reported that at some point after she had received Annie's confession she had paid a visit to Thomson's patron, Dr. MacCallum, and that he, likewise, had known of it.[17] Crombie's testimony was certainly fascinating —but not without its problems. And as logic professors like to point out, extraordinary claims demand extraordinary evidence.

THE LETTER REVISITED

As both Annie and Shannon Fraser had made mention to Daphne Crombie and Charles Plewman respectively that Winnifred Trainor's letter to Tom Thomson contained the implication that she was pregnant, and that she was coming up that week to have a "showdown" with the artist regarding an immediate marriage, it is worth revisiting that alleged document at this time. And immediately there are problems.

As we've seen, Winnifred Trainor, in a meeting with Thomson's sister Margaret in Toronto in September 1917, had related that shortly before Thomson had died he had warned her directly to not put anything in her letters to him that she didn't want the Frasers to know about as he believed that they were reading his mail. This being the case, why would she then proceed to write a letter to the artist that included a statement that strongly suggested that she was pregnant? That she would include information about such a highly personal and sensitive matter in a letter that would likely be read by the Frasers is inconceivable. Furthermore, with regard to an imminent wedding, Trainor had told Margaret in that same meeting that, in the last communication she had received from the artist, he had revealed that he would be leaving the area in about a week—which would have put his departure at precisely the same time that Fraser indicated Trainor would be arriving at Canoe Lake for the "showdown" about their marriage:

> She said that he was intending to leave there in a week or so, and that he didn't want them [the Frasers] to know where he was going, as they were so curious about everything.[18]

And then there was the matter of Trainor's alleged desire for Thomson to purchase a "new suit," which indicates that Trainor had in mind a public wedding (were it to be a private ceremony, the artist could have worn whatever he wished; a new suit would not have been a necessity). However, as we've seen earlier, neither Thomson's nor Trainor's close friends or family knew anything about any imminent wedding between the two. The need for a new suit was advanced as being what had prompted Thomson to confront Fraser for the money that he owed the artist, and that this confrontation is what led to the fight that caused the artist's death at Fraser's hands. How much money did Thomson require to purchase a new suit in 1917? The closest the author could come to estimating the costs were prices from a men's fashion catalogue in 1918, which indicated that a "smart gray suit" of an English Worsted fabric that was "firmly well woven and well vanished," and that consisted of a single breasted coat with durable Italian lining, a five-button vest, and trousers could be had for $15.00;[19] a dress shirt could be picked up for $1.50;[20] a decent tie would set a person back .65 cents[21] (or if you wanted a fancy Swiss silk tie, you would be looking at .75 cents); a nice pair of leather shoes could be had for $2.75;[22] and if you wanted to top that off with a stylish hat, you could pick up a black soft felt hat trimmed with a wide silk band for $1.00 or, upgrading to one with a genuine leather sweat band and the best quality silk band, you could have your choice of black or gray for $1.50.[23] Keep in mind that the above represent the costs of putting together a very fine suit, not an off-the-rack special, so, for the complete wardrobe, Tom Thomson would have been looking to spend in the neighborhood of $20.90 to $21.50 for a good suit and considerably less for a new suit of lesser quality.

However, as Thomson had already earned some money from guiding and had made a recent withdrawal from a bank[24] shortly before his disappearance—indeed, he was said to have had $50 in cash on his person on the morning that he disappeared[25]—he already had ample funds on hand to cover the cost of a new suit with money to spare. This being the case, why would the artist feel compelled to press Shannon Fraser for what little money was still owing on a debt? To add to the confusion, according to Winnifred Trainor, at the time of Thomson's death, the artist didn't believe that Fraser owed him any money at all:

> Well Tom said this spring while at our house that he had loaned Fraser $250.00 for canoes, but that he had got it all back but in little bits though.[26]

And if all of this already seems confusing, it gets more so. While Thomson might have told the Trainors that Fraser had already paid his debt for the canoes in full, the lodge owner had told George Thomson that he still owed the artist money on the account.[27] We note that in a letter written to Dr. MacCallum in November 1917, some four months after Thomson's death, that Fraser mentioned that he had (just) paid off the balance owing on the canoes:

> I bought Tom's two canoes and his people said to pay the men out of the canoe money that searched for Tom's body so I am sending your $17.50 back after paying out of it $3.20 for cement and freight [this was for the memorial cairn that would be erected in Thomson's memory at Canoe Lake later that fall].[28]

So the amount that was still outstanding on the account at the time of the artist's death was just a little north of $20, and that amount would certainly have covered the cost of a new suit but, again, at the time of his death Thomson had more than enough money on hand to buy a new suit and he was of the opinion that Fraser didn't owe him any money. But then, all of these issues arise from the content of a letter from Winnifred Trainor that has never been proven to have existed at all.

Having raised these concerns, it must be conceded in fairness to Daphne Crombie that there does exist at least some support for her in terms of knowing whereof she spoke. She certainly had interactions with the principals of the drama on a personal level, which bolsters her credibility, and she also knew details about Thomson and the Frasers that were not known by anyone outside of the parties directly involved. She knew, for example, that Fraser had still owed Thomson money. This is a fact that was known to very few people (including the artist himself apparently). Revealing that her husband was in debt to the artist would seem an odd topic for Annie Fraser to randomly interject into a conversation with a temporary lodge guest, but it turned out to be true. The correspondence containing this information was kept private between the Thomson estate and the Frasers until it was released into the Canadian archives many decades later. The correspondence revealed that Thomson had in fact loaned Fraser money in 1915 for the purchase of two canoes—but this most certainly was not common knowledge to those who stayed at Mowat Lodge in 1917, perhaps known only by Shannon Fraser, Tom Thomson, and Winnifred Trainor (who, as we've seen, had indicated in correspondence with Thomson's family in 1917 that she had learned of this directly from the artist himself). But as this corroborating correspondence wouldn't be released into the public archives until many years after Crombie had been interviewed,[29] and as she was never known to have had any direct contact with either Winnifred Trainor or the immediate Thomson family, that Crombie should possess such intimate knowledge of Shannon Fraser's financial situation with regard to Thomson at least suggests that she had obtained this information from someone who would have known about such things, which lends support to her claim that she had heard it from Annie Fraser.

We have earlier examined the lack of supporting evidence with regard to Thomson and Trainor's assumed engagement and Trainor's alleged pregnancy. Nevertheless, that there was a rumor being disseminated around Mowat Lodge immediately after the artist's death indicating that Trainor was pregnant is indisputable, as Daphne Crombie had testified that she had heard it from Annie Fraser and Charles Plewman revealed that he had heard the exact same rumor while staying at Mowat Lodge directly from Shannon Fraser himself.[30] And her 1977 interview wasn't the only time that Crombie had shared her anecdote about Trainor's alleged letter to Thomson. Ottelyn Addison (or her co-author Elizabeth Harwood), had learned about the letter, as evidenced by a footnote that appeared in Addison's book, *Tom Thomson: The Algonquin Years* (published in 1969):

> It was rumored around Mowat Lodge in 1916-17 (chiefly by Annie Fraser) that Tom Thomson and Winifred Trainor were to be married. A letter left carelessly lying on a dresser gave some substance to this rumor.[31]

So this much is clear: for someone who had only visited Mowat Lodge twice in her lifetime, Daphne Crombie found herself in possession of a great deal of intimate information regarding certain individuals within the Canoe Lake community. However, unlike her testimony on the financial and personal relationship matters indicated above, Crombie's testimony implicating Shannon Fraser in the death of the artist has found "zero" corroborating evidence in any of the surviving correspondence. Consequently, as tantalizing as it is, her statement in regard to this matter has been largely dismissed as being the foggy and inaccurate speculation of a nonagenarian that may well have been brought forth for the sole purpose of garnering attention. But Crombie's story would be easier to dismiss were it not for the fact that the exact same story had apparently been known by other people from the time who had simply chosen not to make their knowledge public. And this group of people, according to one individual at least, included certain members of the Group of Seven.

A CONSPIRACY OF SILENCE

Ruth Upjohn was a well-known patron of the arts within the city of Toronto for many decades. She had first been introduced to the arts as a child when members of the Group of Seven, whose studio was located just behind her childhood home in Rosedale, would occasionally stop by her parents' home to visit. Thomson himself had known her parents briefly, having lived for several winters in a shack (that he rented for a dollar a month) that was situated directly behind her family's home. Upjohn recalled that during one particular winter when she was a little girl Thomson had come down with the flu, and that she and her mother had brought him soup.[32]

Upjohn had grown up witnessing the struggle that many artists endured in delivering their art to the world, and this served to inspire her to become a life-long patron of artists—and this was particularly true in her cottage area of Muskoka. Various members of the Group of Seven had stayed at her cottage on Lake Muskoka over the decades and quite often would leave her a painting on their exit by way of thanking her for her hospitality and support. And quite apart from the well-established artists whom she had befriended and patronized in Toronto, Upjohn also patronized lesser-known artists that lived closer to her cottage, one of which was the Bracebridge artist Doug Dunford. One day, shortly before her death, Dunford answered the phone in his home and discovered that Ruth Upjohn was on the other end of the line and had a story to tell:

> Ruth knew about my interest in Tom Thomson but she never had said much to me about him. And then one day she called me and told me what she knew. Thomson, when he was in Toronto, lived in a cabin or shack that was on Ruth's property in Toronto. And that's where he preferred to stay. And they also had a large greenhouse that was turned into a studio, where a lot of the Group of Seven members used to go and paint. Anyway, sometime after Thomson had passed away the Group of Seven members had a get together at the Green House, and she sat outside and listened in to the conversations. And what she heard the Group of Seven members say is that Thomson had been having a few drinks at Shannon Fraser's place, and Thomson needed his money back to purchase a suit and so forth—that he had to get married, married quickly, because Winnie [Trainor] was pregnant. And the owner of the lodge, an Irish guy, Shannon Fraser, and Thomson got into an argument. And they got into a pushing match. And the Irish guy pushed Tom Thomson and he went flying back and there was a steel thing beside the fireplace at the lodge and Thomson hit his head on this stake beside the fireplace. And that's what caused Tom Thomson's death . . . and they tied a stone or a brick or something to his ankle with a wire, went out in the middle of the lake, and dropped him overboard and he sank. And then of course his body showed up a week later.

I know she passed away shortly after that phone call and she wanted to tell me the story of what happened and that's what she told me.[33]

And while it may seem a bit of a stretch that certain members of the Group of Seven would find themselves in possession of knowledge of how Thomson met his end that, for reasons of their own, they opted to keep amongst themselves, the reality is that there were members within the Group who believed that certain other of its members knew more about Thomson's death than they were willing to let on. When contacted by the author Blodwen Davies to share whatever insights he might have about Thomson, Group of Seven member J.E.H. MacDonald had declined to comment on the matter, stating that:

> I feel sure that it is best for me to associate myself with the silence of an old friend.[34]

And this silence was not just confined to members of the general public, but also to members within the Group itself. When the author spoke with Alfred Joseph (A.J.) Casson at his home in 1990, the artist was then the last surviving member of the Group, and Casson revealed the reason why he believed MacDonald was so secretive:

> I have an idea that Alex Jackson and Jim MacDonald knew more about his [Thomson's] death than they let on. I was pretty young then—Jim [MacDonald] was twenty years older than me—but whenever I asked them about Thomson they just shut up. If I came into the room when they were talking about Thomson they just stopped the conversation abruptly. I think they knew something.[35]

A.Y. Jackson, in a letter written in 1966, indicated that another member of the Group had also entertained suspicions:

> I think Lawren [Harris] always had the feeling there was foul play, but there was no evidence.[36]

Jackson was quite right. There has never existed a smoking gun for any of the foul play beliefs. Perhaps a police investigation performed at the time might have uncovered some evidence of wrongdoing, but that never happened. And Shannon Fraser? By most accounts, prior to the burial and inquest, there existed no evidence at all that Thomson and the lodge owner any shared any antipathy toward one another. The bloom only came off of Fraser's rose when Winnifred Trainor (because she believed Fraser had ignored the wishes of the Thomson family when the artist had first been buried) and the Thomson family (because they believed Fraser had spread a rumor that the artist had committed suicide) began to speak ill of the lodge owner amongst themselves. But as for Thomson and Fraser, the pair spent time together, seemingly quite amicably, on the last morning that Thomson was seen alive. If such a drunken brawl took place, it would have to have been at one of two places; either Mowat Lodge (in which case the guests would surely have heard the ruckus coming from the floor below), or at the guide's cabin on the night of the party, which would have implicated George Rowe, Lowrey Dickson, and perhaps Martin Blecher Junior in an elaborate cover up and conspiracy. Crombie's version has the altercation taking place at the drinking party that Thomson and Fraser attended, which occurred on the night of July 7, 1917. And the only problem with that scenario was that Thomson was seen—very much alive and without any head wounds—on the morning of July 8.

It has been suggested by the author Roy MacGregor that Thomson may have returned on the evening of July 8 and had his altercation with Fraser then. But this would appear to be an attempt to create a scenario to fit a hypothesis, as there is no evidence at all supporting the contention that Thomson returned and confronted Fraser on the Sunday evening. Moreover, such a hypothesis is without motive. The motive advanced for Thomson confronting Fraser was for money he was owed as he was now in need of it to get married—and quickly. However, as we've seen, Thomson was of the opinion that Fraser had already paid him back all the money that he was owed, so why would he confront him about a debt that to his mind didn't exist? And the existence of the alleged letter indicating that a "showdown" was looming with Winnifred Trainor regarding Thomson's pledge to marry her has likewise never been established. Consequently, we are left without Thomson having a motive to confront Fraser at all. And if all of these issues were weighing that heavily on the artist's mind, why would he not have brought any of it up with Fraser during their time together on the morning that Thomson left? After all, they had time together by themselves during their mile and a half walk from the Algonquin Hotel to the Canoe Lake Section House and back, and perhaps a little over an hour or so during their paddle to and from the Joe Lake Dam. Instead, all that has come down to us from their final conversation that day is that Thomson was going to head out for an afternoon of fishing to play a joke on Mark Robinson and not to worry if he was late getting back. This does not seem to be the mindset one would expect of a man in dire financial straights who was worried about his ability to "face the music" with his fiancée.

Nevertheless, the rumor that Tom Thomson might have died at the hands of Shannon Fraser is one that has gained traction over the years. But, as we shall soon see, perhaps there was a different motive at play than merely the repayment of a small sum of money for the purchase of two canoes.

Chapter Twelve

THE HOOTCHIE KOOTCHIE MAN

Shortly after Thomson's body had been initially laid to rest a rumor began to circulate that he had been seeing another man's wife. Blanche Packard recalled that she had been working in the Algonquin Hotel on the evening of the coroner's arrival from North Bay. As the coroner had come to the area solely to conduct an inquest into the death of Tom Thomson, the talk amongst the guides in the guides' dining room that night was centered on this topic. While waiting tables that evening, she overheard one of the guides mention that Thomson had been "too friendly with one of the ranger's wives."[1] This evidently piqued her interest, as she reported that the guide went on to name the ranger and that he would "be glad Thomson's gone, since he was courting his wife on the sly." Packard further recalled that she heard the guides laughing and joking about Thomson taking one of his paintings down to the cabin of this particular ranger's wife.[2]

The Canadian historian Edwin C. Guillet was the author of over a hundred books on Canadian history, and in his book, *The Death of Tom Thomson, Canadian Artist: A study of the Evidence at the Coroner's Inquest, 1917*, that he published in 1944, he likewise looked into the matter of Thomson's death during his research and revealed that:

The late A. H. Robson also made some investigations. . . . From what he could learn, however, Thomson and a guide or forest ranger were in love with the same girl, possibly a half-breed; and that through jealousy Thomson was murdered by his rival.[3]

A variation on this rumor was repeated in Roy MacGregor's book *Northern Light: The Enduring Mystery of Tom Thomson And the Woman Who Loved Him* when MacGregor quoted the research of Dr. Philip Hall, a forensic specialist from the University of Manitoba who, according to the author, knew a number of longtime Canoe Lake residents, including some of Thomson's contemporaries from 1917. Hall is quoted as saying:

> The story I was told was that Thomson was having an affair with the wife of his murderer, and that he was killed by a man who was perhaps "the most respected person in the community." My sources claim that the facts were known to several people, but that everything was hushed up due to the status of and esteem for the murderer.[4]

Hall's sources, however, did not indicate that Thomson was carrying on with the wife of a guide or a park ranger. Instead, they indicated that the woman that the artist had been seeing was married to Shannon Fraser. This was a belief that would later be corroborated by one of Thomson's artist friends from Toronto. According to the author and art historian Joan Murray:

> On the evidence of an artist who knew him in the Studio Building, it was widely assumed that Thomson "had a thing" going with Annie [Fraser]. An affair seems unlikely, but nevertheless Shannon Fraser may have suspected one . . .[5]

Murray came by this information during an interview she had conducted in 1985 with William L. Drake, whose father was the

Toronto-based artist William A. Drake, a man who had known Tom Thomson well.[6] Certainly money and adultery have been very well settled motives for murder throughout human history. Consequently, if Shannon Fraser had suspected that Thomson had been having an affair with his wife, the proprietor of Mowat Lodge might well have resorted to a violent act that resulted in the death of the artist. And an attempt to avoid prosecution by getting rid of the evidence would explain why the body ended up at the bottom of Canoe Lake—after all, getting rid of his wife's paramour was one thing, hanging for it was something else entirely.

It must be remembered that capital punishment was fully in effect in Canada in 1917, having been enacted in 1859 (it would remain in effect until 1967). Consequently, if Thomson had been found to have died by Fraser's hand, the lodge owner would have faced the gallows for it unless he had an alibi or at least a means of deflecting suspicion away from himself should the authorities come calling. Consequently, the entire scenario about his wife discovering a letter indicating Trainor's pregnancy, and her forthcoming "showdown" with the artist in an attempt to bring pressure on him to marry her, may well have been made up out of whole cloth, and advanced by the Frasers in an effort to divert attention away from the infidelity issue that resided within their marriage—and from the action the lodge owner had taken to eradicate it.

To this end we've seen that Dr. Pocock, Winnifred Trainor's personal physician, knew nothing about her ever having been pregnant or having had an abortion. In addition, Trainor had told him directly that, while she and Thomson had discussed marriage, it just wasn't going to happen. According to Pocock:

> One thing she did confide in was that the big pity was she wanted to marry but there wasn't any money to make it possible. He didn't want to marry a woman and be poor.[7]

So it would appear that there was never going to be any "showdown" coming from Winnifred Trainor at all, as the artist had already effectively shut down the engagement by crying poor. Indeed, Trainor herself had told the artist's sister that Thomson had planned to leave the park the very week he went missing, which would have put it at the very time Fraser had indicated that the "showdown" was supposedly going to take place.[8] And with no "showdown" looming, there existed no "music" that Thomson would have had to face and, thus, no pressure that would have pushed the artist over the edge to either commit suicide or to confront the lodge owner for immediate repayment of a twenty-dollar debt. Besides, to a fast-talking businessman like Shannon Fraser it would have been child's play to put Thomson off for another week or two in the collection of such a debt. There existed no need for things to get violent between the two men over a situation that Fraser could have diffused quite handily. But if Fraser had discovered that the artist had been sleeping with his wife—now that might have led to a confrontation of a different kind entirely.

MacGregor's book further relates a fascinating anecdote that lends some credence to such an event occurring that was shared with him by a man named Brad McLellan. McLellan was a teenager when Shannon Fraser had passed away. The recently widowed Annie Fraser had by then moved to the town of Huntsville and onto the same street as McLellan's family. According to MacGregor:

> Brad McLellan, the young neighbor of both Winnie Trainor and the widowed Annie Fraser on Minerva Street in Huntsville during the 1950s, told me shortly before his death that he had overheard Annie tell his parents the story of Fraser teaching Tom "a lesson" only to have the lesson go tragically wrong.[9]

Both MacGregor and McLellan believed that the lesson Fraser intended to dispense was one intended to ensure that the artist kept

Grand Trunk Railway Passenger train No. 90, heading eastbound from Parry Sound to Ottawa. The train is pictured pulling into Canoe Lake station in the spring of 1915. Train and canoe were the only way one could enter Algonquin Park in Tom Thomson's day. (Photo Courtesy of the Algonquin Park Archives)

Mowat Lodge. Formerly a pair of bunkhouses for the Gilmour Lumber company, by 1916 Shannon Fraser had converted them into a tourist inn. When Thomson stayed here only the building on the right was in use year-round. His room was on the upper floor, second window in from the right. (Photo Courtesy of the Algonquin Park Archives)

One of the few photos of Lowrey Dickson and Charlie Scrim. Left to right, Dr. R.P. Little of Columbus, Ohio, (who would later recount Annie Fraser's version of Thomson's final hours), Lowrie Dixon, guide, (who along with George Rowe would recover Thomson's body from Canoe Lake), Lt. and Mrs. Crombie, (who would later report that Shannon Fraser had killed the artist), Charlie Scrim of Ottawa (who spotted Thomson's canoe in the Blecher family boathouse), and Shannon Fraser, aboard Fraser's horse drawn sleigh in front of Mowat Lodge in the winter of 1917. (Photo Courtesy of the Algonquin Park Archives)

Shannon Fraser, Tom Thomson, and Charles Robinson displaying the results of an afternoon of fishing while sitting on the steps of Mowat Lodge in May of 1917. Robinson and his wife were staying at Mowat Lodge and Thomson had been their fishing guide. (Photo Courtesy of Victoria University Archives, Toronto)

Tom Thomson, having beached his canoe and tending to a campfire, with an unidentified guide (perhaps George Rowe) in May of 1917. (Photo Courtesy of Victoria University Archives, Toronto)

In a letter written in September of 1917, Winnifred Trainor had stated, "About the overcoat I am enclosing a snap with the one he wore this spring. It was a green plaid Mackinaw. He also bought the Mackinaw trousers, socks & shoepacks he has on, here this spring." Given that this photo was taken in the Spring of 1917, it may well have been this photo that she was referring to. (Photo Courtesy of Victoria University Archives, Toronto)

Two of Algonquin's first rangers Bob (Robert) Balfour (left) and Mark Robinson (right) standing on the Joe Lake Station platform. Thomson knew both of these men but was particularly close with Robinson. The ranger would later be placed in charge of investigating the artist's death and believed to his dying day that Thomson had been murdered. (Photo Courtesy of the Algonquin Park Archives)

ALGONQUIN PROVINCIAL PARK.

100   Guide's License

Algonquin Park, Ont. *April 28* 1917

Fee $1.00

The herein named *Tom Thompson*

of *Mowat Lodge Ont* having paid the fee of $1.00

is entitled to act as Guide in conducting tourists and visitors into and through the Algonquin Provincial Park for one year from and after this date. This license may be cancelled by the Minister or Park Superintendent upon proof of a contravention of the Provincial Parks Act, or the Regulations made thereunder, by the holder hereof.

G. W. Bartlett

Superintendent, Algonquin Provincial Park.

Tom Thomson's guide license, issued in April of 1917. The license was written by Mark Robinson. Note the misspelling of Thomson. (Photo Courtesy of the Algonquin Park Archives)

Lost in the mythologizing of Thomson as a woodsman who preferred to rough it in the northern wilderness is the fact that he was also a man who spent a great deal of time in cities like Seattle and Toronto, and who liked the finer things in life. Thomson was also a cigarette and pipe smoker throughout most of his adult life. (Photo Courtesy of the Algonquin Park Archives)

The Algonquin Hotel, owned by Edwin and Molly Colson, viewed from across Joe Lake. The Joe Lake store is to the left, the Algonquin Hotel in the middle up on the hill, and Joe Lake station on the right. Thomson visited the hotel on the morning of his disappearance. (Photo Courtesy of the Algonquin Park Archives)

Rangers Cabin, Ranger's Point, Smoke Lake. Left to right, Tom Hayhurst, Kaye Dickson (sitting on rail), Do Dickson (left, standing), Mrs. Dickson (sitting with broad hat), Charles Plewman (holding loonskin, the man that Shannon Fraser told that Thomson committed suicide), George Rowe (one of the two guides that retrieved Thomson's body from Canoe Lake). It may have been the fireplace within this cabin in which Thomson burned several of his paintings. (Photo Courtesy of the Algonquin Park Archives)

The Joe Lake Dam. According to Mark Robinson it was here that he last saw the artist on the morning of Tom Thomson's disappearance. Pictured here on this day are (Sitting L. to R.), Mrs. Edwin Thomas (who saw the artist walk past Canoe Lake station on the morning that he was last seen alive), Miss Annie Colson (Edwin's sister); and standing L. to R., Helen Colson (Edwin and Molly Colson's niece), Molly Colson and Edwin Colson (both of whom met with Thomson on the morning of July 8, 1917 when Thomson had visited their Algonquin Hotel). Note: The body of water above the dam is the Joe Lake Narrows and cabin in the background is the Joe Lake Shelter House, which was used by Park Ranger Mark Robinson as his cabin. Thomson used to visit the ranger there quite often. (Photo Courtesy of the Algonquin Park Archives)

Mark Robinson's cabin can be seen in the background, with the Grand Trunk Railway tracks running along next to it. Robinson's cabin was near Joe Lake Station (which is the location where this photo was taken). When Dr. Ranney came to Algonquin Park to conduct the inquest into Thomson's death he stayed at this cabin and walked with Robinson across these tracks to both the Algonquin Hotel and the Joe Lake train station (the southern tip of Joe Lake is visible in the left of the photograph). (Photo Courtesy of the Algonquin Park Archives)

The Blecher family boathouse. One of the theories advanced regarding the death of the artist was that he was shot from this boathouse. (Photo Courtesy of the Algonquin Park Archives)

A photo taken from Hayhurst Point, one of Thomson's favorite camping sites on Canoe Lake. Mowat Lodge can be seen across the lake on the opposite shore. (Photo Courtesy of the Algonquin Park Archives)

Superintendent G.W. Bartlett, left, with Mark Robinson, park ranger, Jim Bartlett (background), park ranger, and an unknown man, right, cooking over a fire in the winter. Bartlett would issue the death certificate stating "accidental death by drowning" without ever seeing Thomson's body. (Photo Courtesy of the Algonquin Park Archives)

The 1956 dig. The four men who discovered what many people believe to this day is Tom Thomson's body. From left to right: Leonard Gibson, Bill Little, Jack Eastaugh, and Frank Braught. (Photo Courtesy of the Judge William T. Little Archives)

The skull found within Tom Thomson's original grave at the Canoe Lake Cemetery. The hole in the left temple corresponds with the location of the head wound that Thomson had suffered. The hole was believed upon initial examination to have been caused by a .22 caliber bullet. (Photo Courtesy of the Algonquin Park Archives)

Dr. Harry Ebbs during the exhumation of the complete skeleton in October of 1956. Ebbs would be told by the attorney general that the Thomson family wanted the investigation shut down. He believed that the skeleton he helped to exhume that day was that of Tom Thomson. (Photo Courtesy of the Algonquin Park Archives)

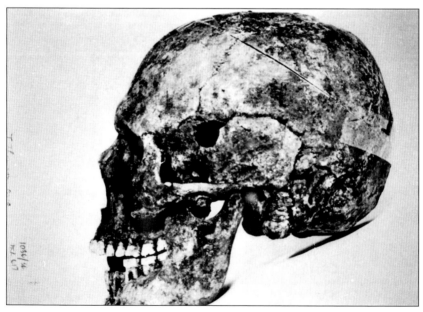

Once the skull had been cleaned up at the Crime Lab, the hole in its temple was said to be a result of trephining; an ancient and exceedingly rare surgical procedure. (Photo Courtesy of the Algonquin Park Archives)

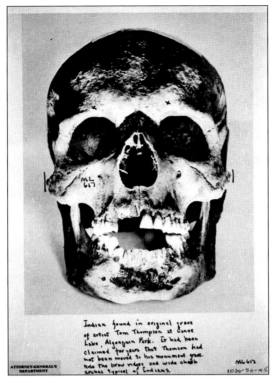

Indian found in original grave of artist Tom Thompson at Canoe Lake, Algonquin Park. It had been claimed for years that Thomson had not been moved to his monument grave. Note the brow ridges and wide cheek arches typical of Indians.

A frontal view of the Canoe Lake skull. The Crime Lab concluded that the skull was that of an indigenous person owing to its high cheekbones. Thomson had high cheekbones but no photographs of the artist were looked at for purposes of comparison when the skull was examined in Toronto in 1956. (Photo Courtesy of the Algonquin Park Archives)

The Trainor cottage had originally been a ranger cabin on Canoe Lake. This photo, taken circa 1910, reveals how it would have looked in Thomson's day. (Photo Courtesy of the Algonquin Park Archives)

The view from the Trainor Cottage porch looking out across Canoe Lake. Tom Thomson had been staying here on the last day of his life and it was also here that Mark Robinson read the letters that Winnifred Trainor had written to the artist that summer. An interesting side note; Thomson was said to have swam to this cottage from the far shore on occasion. (Photo Courtesy of the Algonquin Park Archives)

Lowrey Dickson's cabin on Potter Creek. It may well have been this shack where the infamous drinking party was held that some contend ended in the artist's death. Thomson was said to have painted the northern lights from this cabin in 1917. (Photo Courtesy of the Algonquin Park Archives)

A.E. RANNEY

Dr. A.E. Ranney, the coroner from North Bay who never saw Thomson's body prior to the inquest. It was his verdict of "accidental death by drowning" that has endured to this day. (Photo Courtesy of the William T. Little Archives)

Dr. Goldwyn Howland was the University of Toronto neurology professor who first saw Thomson's body rise in the water off of the island he had been vacationing at. (Photo Courtesy of the William T. Little Archives)

Annie (left) and Shannon (right) Fraser, the proprietors of Mowat Lodge, where the artist often stayed while in Algonquin Park. Annie was alleged to have confessed that her husband had killed Thomson and that she and Shannon had dumped his body in Canoe Lake under cover of darkness. (Photo Courtesy of the Algonquin Park Archives)

Tom Thomson near the shore of Mowat Lodge with a catch of fish. The artist was prouder of his fishing skills than his painting skills. Almost every photograph of Thomson or taken by him in Algonquin Park involve fishing. None depict him painting. (Photograph taken by H. A. (Henry Ardagh) Callighen, Courtesy of Richard Callighen)

Shannon Fraser (nearest to fireplace at left) and Annie Fraser (far right) with guests of the lodge next to the fireplace at Mowat Lodge. It may have been the fire grate from this fireplace that Thomson was said to have hit his head on during a fight with Shannon Fraser. (Photo Courtesy of the Algonquin Park Archives.)

Bill Little kneeling next to what he believed was Tom Thomson's grave at Canoe Lake in 1990. It was this grave that he and his friends discovered thirty-four years earlier. (Photo Courtesy of John Little)

The author and his father still looking for clues during a trip to Canoe Lake in 1990. My father's interest in the Tom Thomson mystery continued unabated right into the final five years of his life. (Photo Courtesy of John Little)

his pledge to marry Winnifred Trainor. He had been solicited for the task, so the theory goes, by Hugh Trainor, Winnifred's father. MacGregor's theory is that it had been decided that some "frontier justice" was required to bring about a change in Thomson's thinking on the matter. We have earlier noted the problems inherent in the pregnancy theory and, indeed, in the belief that Thomson and Trainor were engaged to be married. But it is also problematic to believe that Hugh Trainor, who by all accounts made a living as a tough lumberman whose job required him keeping other tough lumbermen in line, would feel the need to solicit the services of Shannon Fraser to do a job that Hugh Trainor could have done quite easily (and with far more enthusiasm). Fraser was a lodge owner after all, not an enforcer, and what did Shannon Fraser have to do with the situation anyway? He would have had a lot to lose if word got out about his performing such a service, as it would not have looked good to any prospective tourists to Mowat Lodge to learn that its proprietor was going around pummeling his lodge guests. Even more bizarre is that Hugh Trainor would opt to share with the owner of Mowat Lodge the Trainor family's shameful secret that their daughter had become pregnant outside of wedlock; as this would not be information one would want getting out in the community, especially in 1917. Moreover, there is no indication that the Trainors and Frasers were close enough to have shared such a confidence. Indeed, according to Thomson's sister Margaret, Winnifred Trainor had told her that her father "detested" the lodge owner.[10] It simply makes no sense that an outsider to the family would be informed of (and brought in to handle) something that was a (very) private family matter, let alone that the patriarch of the family would share such personal information with a man whom he intensely disliked.

For Shannon Fraser to perform such a violent act would have required the occurrence of something that impacted him personally.

The pregnancy of the daughter of a cottager wouldn't qualify; that he discovered that the artist was sleeping with his wife most certainly would. And while both McLellan and MacGregor had assumed that Fraser had been selected (or volunteered) to deliver a beating to Thomson (a beating that went too far) in order to teach the artist to respect his pledge to marry Winnifred Trainor, perhaps the lesson that Fraser had intended to mete out was more one in learning to respect the pledge to a marriage that already existed between Annie and Shannon Fraser.

Interestingly, Dr. Pocock, who first arrived in Algonquin Park in 1919, a mere two years after the artist's death, had likewise been aware of the rumor that had been circulating of Thomson sleeping with another man's wife, but he had heard it wasn't Annie Fraser who had succumbed to the artist's charms, but rather the wife of Martin Blecher Junior:

> Blecher was blaming Tom Thomson for being with his wife. While he was suspicious of him, some say that he got back at Tom Thomson by killing him on the side, quietly.[11]

It's possible that Pocock was confusing Blecher with Shannon Fraser, although this is unlikely as he knew the people in and around Canoe Lake quite well. Moreover, Martin Blecher Junior would not be married until September of 1918, over a year after Thomson's death, so Thomson could not have been with his "wife." It is possible (though remotely) that the artist may have been seeing the lady who eventually would become Martin Blecher Junior's wife, Patricia Bahmer. However, for this to have occurred, Miss Bahmer would have had to have visited Canoe Lake during the summer of 1917. The author has encountered no evidence to support her being at Canoe Lake during that summer, but if Blecher was married in September 1918, he may well have been engaged by July

1917 and quite possibly could have brought his fiancée up to the family cottage that summer. If this in fact happened, it would explain a rumor that has endured over the decades that both Martin Blecher Junior and Tom Thomson had been involved in a love triangle with a woman (who was mistakenly presumed to be Winnifred Trainor) that resulted in the artist being killed by his rival.[12]

It would also speak to the fact that Miss Bahmer wasn't that committed to the man who would later become her husband. While I grant that this is quite an aspersion to cast on someone who is no longer around to defend herself from such an allegation, there does exist evidence to support the fact that this was indeed the case. While Mark Robinson had entered a notation in his journal for September 19, 1918 indicating that he had shared lunch with the newlyweds,[13] by May of 1922 Robinson had made a journal entry of a different sort, indicating that Mildred Fraser, the eighteen-year-old daughter of Shannon and Annie Fraser, had (for some reason) accompanied Martin Blecher Junior to Mark Robinson's cabin regarding a matter of "domestic trouble in the Blecher home."[14] And a few days after this meeting, according to author Mary Garland in her book *Mowat: Little Town of Big Dreams*:

> Martin and Patricia went to Park headquarters to "settle domestic affair," leaving on the evening train. Whatever happened between Martin and Patricia, it seems to have affected their marriage. By 1925 she was living on her own in Buffalo . . . [15]

The "whatever happened" that precipitated the collapse of the Blecher marriage, according to Ralph Bice, was that Martin had discovered that his wife had been having an affair (perhaps yet again), but this time it was with the genial host of Mowat Lodge— Shannon Fraser:

You know, he [Blecher] and his first wife were divorced—and the third party was Shannon Fraser. Shannon Fraser had a nice wife, she was an awfully good cook, but apparently he had a little affair with Mrs. Blecher.[16]

Affairs are certainly not uncommon, whether in small towns or big cities, and it must be pointed out that Tom Thomson was single, young (not yet forty), and healthy. Further, he had proven himself to be a man who had no interest at all in marching in step with societal norms. We've seen that he believed that the standards for men and women should be the same (this was said two years prior to women being allowed to vote in the province of Ontario), that he rejected the prohibition ruling on alcohol that was in effect in the province, that he didn't believe in war (including the one that was being waged internationally in 1917), and essentially lived life on his own terms. Should a woman—married or not—indicate that she was available to him in an environment where his only other distraction would have been fishing and painting, it's not likely that he would have thought twice about it.

THE ARTIST'S WILD SIDE

The passage of time served to loosen not only Canada's moral strictures about sex, but also more tongues that were now willing to share what they knew about Thomson's interaction with women. On December 27, 2012, the *Toronto Star* newspaper published a story about the artist that added additional insights into the artist's sexual promiscuity. It was falsely entitled "Rare Letters Reveal Rowdy Side of Tom Thomson, Group of Seven Painter" (false in the fact that Thomson was never a member of the Group of Seven) and was written by Peter Goddard, a freelance writer for the *Star*. It began:

He could be an ornery cuss. Unkempt, he didn't have much time for kids. He did like a stiff belt of hooch now and then, which would send him off into the bush looking for "hootchie kootchie."[17]

Goddard based his statement upon two letters that had been written by a former hunting lodge (Kish-Kaduck Lodge) proprietor by the name of Jack Wilkinson. Wilkinson, the reader will recall, had grown up in and around Canoe Lake, where both of his parents, together with his aunt and uncle, had overseen the operations at Canoe Lake Station. Wilkinson had been five years old when Thomson died, but claimed to remember the artist vividly:

> I can see him to this day, as clear as though I saw him yesterday. He was always grubby looking, wore a felt hat at all times, his shirt with the sleeves down around his wrists on the hottest day, an old pair of pants and shoepacks . . . high moccasins but oiled, tanned and waterproof (sic) but had no soles or heels on them.[18]

The article cited a letter written by Wilkinson on August 17, 1976, in which he states:

> [When Thomson] wanted to do the 'rain dance' he used to beat it up to the old Indian Farm where Ignace and Mabel Dufond had a cute little niece of 'dancing age' and that is where he danced the hootchie kootchie (sic) . . . Old Pete Ranger, the park ranger of those days, used to tell me that after the joy juice had gone, and all heads were back to normal, they used to kick him out until he would arrive back for another party. Hell of a way to write about a celebrated Canadian.[19]

The Dufond farm was located on the northwest shore of Manitou Lake, which, if Thomson were to "beat it up" there from Canoe Lake, would have seen him paddling and portaging the better part of 174 miles to attend one of the Dufond brothers' parties. The Dufonds were of native descent, and were first mentioned in Audrey Saunders's book *Algonquin Story* as being one of Algonquin Park's original pioneer families. They apparently reflected "the spirit of the times," according to Saunders, which included the distribution and consumption of alcohol. Saunders, like Wilkinson, had acquired her information about the Dufonds from Pete Ranger:

> When Peter called around at the Manitou farm he was always greeted warmly and invited to share the next meal. The Dufonds were clean as well as hospitable, and Peter was usually glad to accept their invitation . . . the guests sat around in a circle and passed a dipper of the alcohol mixed with a little water around the ring. Each person took a drink before passing it on to the next.[20]

While there exists no record of the Dufonds having had a niece living with them on their farm, they did, according to Saunders, have an adopted daughter named Pinonique, who was said to be very attractive and rather free spirited, which certainly would have appealed to Thomson. Pinonique would later elope with a man named Alex Baptiste who had worked on the Dufond farm. The pair eventually settled in Mattawa.[21]

As the Dufonds had closed down their farm (lot 25, concession 12, in Wilkes Township) on the north end of Manitou Lake in 1916,[22] Wilkinson's tale of Thomson's partying days on the Dufond farm could only have taken place during a period of time that fell between 1912 (when he first arrived in the park) and 1916 (when the farm closed down); that is to say, within a period of four years. The reader is free to make of this what they will.

To add to the drama, Roy MacGregor's book includes the statement that:

> Toronto researcher Iris Nowell travelled to Owen Sound to interview the McKeen sisters for David Silcox and Harold Town's book *Tom Thomson: The Silence and the Storm*. Margaret, known as "Etta" to the family, was then ninety-four. . . . Etta even offered the perplexing nugget that a small child was also buried in the family grave at Leith, along with Tom Thomson's casket, which was said by some to be "Tom's by some Indian woman—but who would bury it with Tom?"[23]

Perhaps the only take away from the various testimony cited above is that at the time of Thomson's death it was rumored that the artist had been sleeping with multiple women—the unnamed wife of a park ranger, Annie Fraser, Martin Blecher Junior's (future) wife, the Dufond's niece (or adopted daughter), Winnifred Trainor and, according to Ralph Bice, a young lady from Depot Bay named Alice Green. Both Miss Green and Miss Trainor, we're told, believed that Thomson had intended to marry them.

If the above is true, then what starts to form is a picture of quite a different sort concerning the character of the artist. And while Queen Victoria had been dead for sixteen years, the highly moralistic, straight-laced culture that her monarchy had inspired was still very much evident in the Ontario of 1917. When viewed through this lens, a bohemian who didn't fight in the war, who had no fixed job to speak of, and who was acting Lothario in his relationships with women in small communities and perhaps fathering children out of wedlock, would not have been well thought of. Indeed, there may well have been family or friends of the many women with whom the artist interacted who had decided that Canoe Lake would be well rid of Tom Thomson and who decided to take matters into their own hands when the opportunity presented itself.

Chapter Thirteen

BLOOD MONEY

The Tom Thomson depicted in the previous chapters is directly at odds with the image of the artist that I (and millions of other Canadians) grew up with. We were taught that he was a trailblazing artist who kept to himself, and was respected by all who were fortunate enough to know him; we were never taught that he was a man who drank heavily, periodically sank into bouts of depression, engaged in fist fights, and slept with other men's wives. And why would this aspect of his humanity be suppressed? There's a simple one-word answer: money.

While there had unquestionably been interest in Tom Thomson's paintings while he was alive, it paled in comparison to the interest that blossomed after his mysterious death. Indeed, by 1924 Thomson's paintings were being exhibited overseas in the British Empire Exhibitions at Wembley, heralding "a new spirit in Canadian art."[1] By extension, even those artists who knew and had painted alongside him, such as various members of what would become the Group of Seven, acquired a cache after his death that they never quite enjoyed during his life, resulting in a rise in public interest in their art as well. If in fact Thomson had been murdered, then his killer might well be said to have inadvertently launched the Canadian art movement.

Prior to his death, an original Tom Thomson painting could be had for peanuts (quite literally, as Thomson was known to exchange his paintings for food on occasion). In a letter written in 1914, Thomson had priced his art thusly:

> About the sketch; if it could get $10 or $15 for it I should be greatly pleased but if they don't care to put in so much, let it go for what they will give. The same applies to all the others . . .[2]

Fast forwarding to 2009, the final bid on an 8½ x 10½ oil on panel of the artist's, entitled "Early Spring, Canoe Lake," at Heffel's Fine Art Auction House went for a cool $2,749,500.00.[3] Even if one adjusts for the inflation that has occurred over the decades, Thomson's own estimate of the value of his paintings would have put his $10 asking price in 1914 up to only a modest $181.23 in 2009 (the year that Heffel's made the sale). Death, indeed, can be a boon to commerce.

Upon his passing Thomson had left behind approximately three hundred small panels, such as the one sold at the Heffel auction, in addition to fifty larger canvases.[4] However, as we've seen, the artist had never been particularly aggressive about marketing his work, often giving away his paintings to people who commented positively on them or, if pressed for a price, selling them for as little as two or three dollars a piece to guests at the various lodges throughout Algonquin Park.[5] He had also been known to throw many of his paintings away. I once spoke with Richard Callighen, the son of Thomson's good friend, Park Ranger Henry A. ("Bud") Callighen, and he recollected witnessing Thomson paddle up to the family cabin on Smoke Lake with the bow of his canoe loaded up with 8 x 10" paintings that he had spent the previous week creating:

> He paddled up to the dock and grabbed an armful of these paintings and came into our cabin and then he threw them into the fireplace. He then took us outside so that we could look at

the different colors of smoke that came out of the chimney as
the various colored oil paints on his boards were burning.[6]

As a result of Thomson's seeming apathy to the value of his paintings (he referred to his "Northern River" canvas as "the swamp
picture"[7]) he was virtually penniless when he died. Indeed, we've
already seen the accusatory statement that the artist's brother-in-
law Tom Harkness had penned to Shannon Fraser two months after
Thomson's death, when he had asked pointedly, "how do you account for Tom only having 60 cents when found?"[8]

However, after word of his mysterious death got out, the Thomson family found themselves, to their surprise, to be in a rather
serendipitous position; their black sheep, the little-known itinerant
handyman and landscape artist, was becoming quite popular, and
they, by virtue of their relationship to him, were now the benefi-
ciaries of this rapidly growing goodwill. In addition, in their legal
capacity as heirs to his estate, they had inherited all of his unsold
artwork, which was considerable, and the price of these surviving
paintings was beginning to rise. Tom Thomson may have had little
interest in making money from his art apart from what was required
to grant him the freedom to fish, paint, and live a simple life in and
around Algonquin Park, but his family, by contrast, were not ones
to let sleeping dollars lie. They may have lost a brother, but as was
becoming readily apparent, they had gained a business.

In 1931, the author Blodwen Davies had reached out to the
family of the artist to inquire into the details surrounding his death.
George Thomson, in his reply, explained that, "I have always favored
the accident theory, though I realize the possibility of foul play."[9]
Having stated this, however, he closed off his missive by advising
Miss Davies that, "speaking for the family, we would very much
deplore any discussion of the matter before the public. Such a discussion would do no good, and would likely result in much harm to

Tom's name."[10] This is a curious statement, as how Davies's attempt to investigate the truth of Thomson's death would result not just in harm, but in "much harm" being done to the late artist's name is unclear. An innocent victim of either an accident or foul play does not typically come away from such an investigation with his name besmirched. However, if looking closely into the matter would have revealed that Thomson was not an innocent victim at all; i.e., that alcohol problems, suicide, fighting, having affairs with other men's wives, and/or getting a woman pregnant out of wedlock had played a role in his demise, George Thomson may well have had a point.

In any event, apart from a day or so worth of inquiries at Canoe Lake in July 1917 by George Thomson, there exists no evidence at all that the Thomson family expended any additional effort in investigating the matter of their family member's death. The artist's sister, Margaret, who was clearly pained by her brother's passing, wrote to Dr. MacCallum on August 2, 1917 that:

> Our hearts are still almost broken and I don't know whether our sorrow will ever wear away or not. His death was the first break in our large grown up family. Tom seemed to have a place in each of our hearts that could not be filled by anyone else. He was so good and so kind and he seemed almost perfect in every way. He was so much alone that we seemed to think more about him than any of the others of the family. Poor boy, he worked so hard, denied himself so much and now to think he is gone.[11]

However, Margaret then got to the point of why she was writing to an art broker such as MacCallum:

> We wouldn't like to see any of his work sold at a sacrifice and we trust everything will turn out rightly.[12]

And while speculation as to how Tom Thomson met his death continued to spread, such speculation was only given voice by people who lived outside of Owen Sound, and who were, in terms of influence, few and far between. The Canoe Lake community in 1917 was small. There were no local newspapers in the area, and the provincial and national newspapers that did carry the story of the artist's death had obtained their information about Thomson directly from either the Thomson family or the Ontario art community, personified in 1917 by Thomson's patron Dr. James MacCallum. And both of these parties had now become united in the interest of commerce, as both had paintings to sell. And from their perspective in wanting to broaden their market in straight-laced and moralistic 1917 Ontario, an intriguing, mysterious death was far better for business than an accidental homicide resulting from, say, a drunken brawl. In a letter written by Dr. MacCallum to Thomson's older brother George on September 1, 1917—less than two months after Thomson's death—one finds no trace of any condolences or lamenting about the passing of Tom Thomson. The focus is squarely on the money:

September 1, 1917

Dear Sir,

. . . I saw Mr. Harkness [Tom Thomson's brother-in-law who was entrusted with settling Tom's estate] on Saturday last and arranged so that he got [Tom's] money out of the bank. . . . I want to buy some of these last sketches of Tom's, especially the little ones—you set the price and I will pay it. I want you also to give me your ideas as to prices to be asked the National Gallery. I broached the idea to the Curator that they should buy 40 or 50 of the sketches and keep them as an Encyclopedia of the North Country. He seemed to be impressed with the idea but said his trustees had to go cautiously during war time—I see by the papers that their appropriation for buying pictures was cut off, but they can always get credit from the Bank of Commerce of which one trustee is President. He thought he ought to have some at least tentative amount which could be discussed between him and me before any official presentation to his board.

There of course he had me, because I hesitated to name any price. I was offered $200.00 the other day for the picture with those two pine trees in deep blue (after sunset) but as I was prepared to pay more than that myself I said nothing. I have traced up some sketches to a magazine editor—he was given 7 or 8 to choose from—he told Tom he could not pay more than ten dollars a piece and was to take 4—now he wants to give me a cheque for $40.00 and return the balance—His story is corroborated by Williamson who was present during the transaction— One good thing is that in my judgment he had rotten taste in selecting them. Another factor is that we shall want to make use of his magazine—What do you advise? Cummings wants to be allowed to meet any offer made for that moonlight picture in his studio—which you saw. The Insurance agent returned the sketch through Mr. Davidson and Mr. Harkness—It was standing on my desk after Harkness left and a patient said I will give you $25.00 for that now, so we will not lose on it—What am I to do in such an event—I hate to let money get away, for this war is going to make money very tight here—yet I cannot say yes until I have your consent—This man has money and I can probably talk $30.00 or more out of him if you say so. I am rushing off for my train for Georgian Bay and will write if anything further occurs to me on my return on Monday 3rd Sept.

Yours,
James MacCallum[13]

George Thomson, in his reply, had his eyes fixed squarely on the money as well:

Dear Doctor,

Your letter came today. In regard to some of the more important questions brought up I shall give a provisional answer, merely, subject to Harkness's ratification, since as you know he is acting administrator of Tom's estate. It is possible that he will defer somewhat to my judgment in respect to valuation and sale of the pictures in view of my experience in such matters, but the final decision rests with him. I shall write him tonight enclosing first, a copy of your letter, and second, a copy of my reply to you and ask him to let you know his wishes by return mail if possible.

In regard to the sale of the four sketches to the magazine editor, it seems to me that this would be nothing more than fulfilling a contract already entered into by Tom himself, therefore, I would close up the deal.

As to your tentative offer to the curator of the National Gallery, the idea is a good one and worth making special terms as an inducement to the government to buy so many as 40 or 50, at one time. Aside from the desirability of selling so many paintings at one time, it is a fitting thing that as many of them as possible should be accessible to the public permanently as they would be in the national gallery.

I had thought that Tom's price of $25.00 on the larger size of sketch—8 ½ x 10 ½" if I remember correctly—was perhaps a little lower than we should fix for that size of sketch. It would perhaps be best not to go too high, however, especially now when there are so many unusual outlets for money. I think perhaps $30.00 for that size would be equitable.

In the case of the offer of 40 or 50 of that size to the government, however, I would suggest making the price $20.00 framed. A decent frame could be secured for $1.00 or less, I imagine. As an inducement for purchase of the larger number—50, how would it be to sell subject to a 10% discount from the whole bill?

I cannot recall accurately the size of the smaller sized sketch but it may possibly be roughly ½ the size of the other. In that case I should make the price $15.00 with a corresponding 33 1/3 % discount to the government in case they should select some of these among the lot.

As to the sketch returned by the insurance agent—I had got the impression loosely, that the agent had accepted the sketch in payment of the premium but this apparently was not the arrangement. I should say that it would be good policy to sell the sketches of more than average merit, such as might be selected for the memorial exhibition.

Now in regard to the larger paintings, I hardly know what price to fix. I understand that the government paid Tom $500 each for perhaps two of his paintings. I have never seen these paintings and as my experience goes the size of the artist's paintings largely determines the price. For instance, I should say that judging from the price Tom held his sketches and the price received for his larger and outstanding work, a painting the size and quality of the moonlight in Cummings studio should bring $250.00 to $300.00. However, not knowing the size of this various paintings I hesitate to fix any exact sum.

It seems to me that fixing of the prices on various larger sized paintings could be done most intelligently under the circumstances by yourself and perhaps one or two of the artists who were not familiar with Tom's prices, such as MacDonald and

Williamson, say. It might be a good plan to select some appropriate title, size and price and send the list to me or Harkness, saving a copy for yourselves. This would get the matter on more of a working basis.

I do not know about the trunk and so will ask Harknesss to write you about it.

Thank you for your kindly interest in Tom's affairs.

I am, Sincerely Yours,
Geo Thomson[14]

Right off the bat the Estate and MacCallum had jacked up the price of Thomson's art by 100 percent, and any input from people who had been familiar with "Tom's prices" was no longer welcome. Indeed, Tom's prices were now as dead as the artist himself. The focus of the Thomson family and Dr. MacCallum in the immediate months following the artist's death was obviously not on investigating what had happened at Canoe Lake that resulted in the death of a friend, son, and brother in the prime of his life, but rather on where and how the most money could be made from selling what paintings he had left behind. The juxtaposition of Thomson dying with 60 cents in his pocket while MacCallum and the Thomson family were setting up deals to cash in on hundreds if not thousands of dollars from the sales of his surviving artwork, is striking to say the least. George Thomson's letter above runs over two pages; it's doubtful that he ever wrote a letter that long to Tom in his entire life.[15] "Poor boy," indeed.

Eight months later, in May 1918, Dr. MacCallum wrote a letter to Tom Harkness, who, as George Thomson pointed out above, was the acting administrator of Tom Thomson's estate. It is evident at this point that all concerns over rumors of suicide and foul play were no longer an issue. Once again the focus was on selling Thomson's remaining paintings:

Mr. T.J. Harkness,
Owen Sound, Ont.
May 6th 1918

Dear Sir,

I am enclosing the letter from the National Gallery, of which I wrote you. The sketches, of which they propose to take 25, include only about eight that are really good. I cannot lay my hands on George's [Thomson's] letter just now, but his idea was that if they took fifty, to let them have at $20.00 a piece. His idea about the large pictures was $500.00. The one called "The Woodland Garland" is one which we would have great difficulty in getting rid of, both on account of its subject and because of its size. I had thought that if we got $500 for it, we would be very lucky indeed. The other one—The Jack Pine—I asked them one thousand dollars for, and I asked them for the Woodland Garland, $750.00.

The Government is now making a very poor mouth. Under ordinary circumstances I think I would have succeeded in getting what I asked. You may have noticed that in the May Exhibition here, that $300.00 was the highest price paid for any picture, so that we have no reason to complain. The difficulty is that the Parliament has not made any allowance as yet for this year to the National Gallery, so that there is some doubt as to the time when payment will be made. I have left it in such a way that I can back out of the proposition, but it seems to me that it is wise to accept it, because I believe the War will last for some years yet. I wish you would consult with George about it, and see what he thinks. His idea, was, as I understand, that we would have got about $500.00 for each of the big pictures. It must not be overlooked that the fact of their being sold to the National Gallery will help us in the sale of the small sketches. I think it well, too, because of the retaining the goodwill of Sir Edmund Walker. I think he will make special effort to have two of the large pictures and some 20 or 30 of the small sketches bought for the Art Museum of Toronto. He has said to me privately that he wished to keep the best of Tom's work for the Museum here and he has already picked out, if I remember rightly, 20 sketches for the museum here . . .

Truly Yours,
James MacCallum[16]

It was now evident to the parties above that if they could increase the volume of sales of Thomson's larger paintings into the National Gallery, then sales of the more plentiful smaller panels the artist had left behind would be smooth sailing. And that became their focus. And by August of 1918 they had their hooks set deep into Eric Brown, the then Chairman of the National Gallery of Canada, who wrote to MacCallum:

National Gallery Of Canada Office Of The Director Ottawa
Dear Dr. MacCallum:
The Trustees of the National Gallery of Canada beg to inform you that they desire to purchase the following pictures and sketches by the late Tom Thomson: "The Jack Pine" Seven Hundred and Fifty Dollars ($750.00), "Autumn's Garland" Seven Hundred and Fifty Dollars ($750.00, twenty-five (25) oil sketches previously chosen and set aside, Twenty-five Dollars ($25.00) each, total Two Thousand One Hundred and Twenty-five Dollars ($2,125.00).

In view of the fact that owing to the war the National Gallery of Canada has no funds available for the purchase of works of art, the Trustees agree to pay for the pictures and sketches as early as possible during the fiscal year of 1919-20 provided the Government makes appropriation for the purchase of works of art, and failing any appropriation for 1919-20 that they will be paid as soon as such appropriation be made for this purpose.

Yours faithfully,
B. E. Brown, Chairman
Eric Brown, Director.[17]

Over the next five years their plan had proven to be working out beautifully, and the consortium had grown in confidence that galleries would be quite willing to part with (what for the time were) exorbitant sums for the late artist's works. In a letter from Thomson's brother-in-law to MacCallum, we learn that the family was now seeking a 300 percent increase over the previous maximum price that Thomson had received for one of his larger paintings:[18]

What price do you think we should we put on "The West Wind"? . . . Do you think $1,500.00 too much to ask for "West Wind"?[19]

From the correspondence that has survived, it is clear that while George Thomson had entertained suspicions about his brother's death, over the six years that had elapsed since his passing he had apparently grown content to let these go. Tom's sister Elizabeth Harkness had been ready to travel to Canoe Lake in 1918 to confront Shannon Fraser about his spreading the rumor that Thomson had committed suicide, but the family had shut her down.[20] And Dr. MacCallum, for his part, had also been privy to information that Thomson's death may not have been the result of an innocent accident. He had, for example, stated his belief that Thomson had committed suicide to Group of Seven member A.Y. Jackson,[21] and had also been aware of Annie Fraser's confession that her husband had killed Thomson.[22] But neither the Estate nor Dr. MacCallum had chosen to pursue any of these leads into Tom Thomson's death. While thoroughly investigating the matter might have resulted in bringing certain family members and friends of the artist some peace of mind, what bills could you pay with that currency?

It must be remembered that if Thomson had indeed been murdered, then by the time MacCallum and the Thomson Estate were strategizing on how to get top dollar for his canvas *The West Wind* in 1923, his killer would still have been alive. And if people such as George Thomson were willing to concede the possibility that his younger brother may have been the victim of foul play (which he clearly did based upon his surviving correspondence), his turning a blind eye toward investigating the matter meant that he was okay with the idea that his brother's killer would never be brought to justice. In addition, while MacCallum may have believed that Thomson had taken his own life, he made certain not to share this belief with the Canadian public. In an article he penned about the artist that appeared in *The Canadian Magazine* on March 31, 1918, there is no mention of his belief that the artist had committed suicide, or of any contextual matters that might have led to his death, such as heavy drinking, promiscuity, and fistfights. The Thomson family and the Toronto ophthalmologist were by this time reading off the same song sheet in implementing certain strategies regarding Tom Thomson's image and legacy that would provide them a far greater return on their time investment.

A PHOENIX RISES

In an effort to commemorate Thomson and, thus, raise the late artist's profile in the eyes of Canadians and prospective art buyers, plans had been set in place to erect a cairn to Thomson's memory as early as the end of July 1917. On Thursday, July 19, 1917, Mark Robinson made the following entry in his daily journal:

> The Arts Association of Toronto propose having a memorial exhibit of Mr. Tom Thomson's paintings and to place a memorial in the Park near where he loved to work, [and] sketch so well. Thus ends a career of unselfishness, of a gentleman, sportsman, artist and friend of all.[23]

Within two months of this entry, Thomson's Toronto-based artist friends, William Beatty and future Group of Seven member J.E.H. MacDonald, with the financial backing of MacCallum, had constructed a cairn on Hayhurst Point in Canoe Lake that was topped off with a brass plaque designed and inscribed by MacDonald, who had written to Thomson's father on October 13, 1917 that:

> I have just returned from Canoe Lake where I spent the weekend helping Mr. Beatty to put on the plate and give the cairn a few finishing touches. The cairn is a fine piece of work and with the brass plate in position it looks quite imposing. It stands on a prominent point in Canoe Lake right at the head of the lake facing north [facing south actually] and can be seen from all directions. It is situated near an old favorite camping spot of Tom's. . . . The result goes a long way to beautifying the tragedy of his death.[24]

The cairn was indeed a touching and tasteful tribute to the artist, but it also accomplished something else. It served to fashion an image of Thomson that both MacCallum and the Thomson family wanted put forth to the Canadian public, and it is an image that has endured to this day. The image was that of the solitary, visionary artist, at one with nature, heroically exploring the northland on his own and who gave his life in an attempt to capture its secret treasures on canvas so that he could share them with the rest of the world. This was not Thomson the handyman and part time fishing guide who liked chasing skirts and a few drinks in a musty cabin; this was Canada's Prometheus. Such an image was inspirational, and it further served the function of protecting the Thomson family name from any scandals, such as the aforementioned theories that were then in their infancy, such as the artist being a heavy drinker and womanizer, or that he had been (as suicide was viewed at the time) a mental deficient who had taken his own life.

The brass plate read:

To the memory of Tom Thomson

Artist, woodsman and guide who was drowned in Canoe Lake July 8, 1917.

He lived humbly but passionately with the wild. It made him brother to all untamed things of nature. It drew him apart and revealed itself wonderfully to him. It sent him out from the woods only to show these revelations through his art. And it took him to itself at last.

His fellow artists and other friends and admirers join gladly in this tribute to his character and genius.

His body is buried at Owen Sound Ontario near where he was born August, 1877.[25]

Despite the error regarding his burial place (the casket was buried in Leith, not Owen Sound), Thomson's image was now set in place. And the image of Thomson the heroic artist who gave his life in the task of revealing to the world the truth of the Canadian north began to catch fire, and the value of his paintings, sure enough, began to rise. MacCallum did his part to fan these flames by writing in the same *The Canadian Magazine* article cited above (you will recall his statement to George Thomson that "we shall want to make use of his magazine") that:

> Motionless he studied the night skies and the chang-
> ing outline of the shores while beaver and otter played
> around his canoe. Puffing slowly at his pipe, he watched
> the smoke of his campfire slowly curling up amongst the
> pines, through which peeped here and there a star, or
> wondered at the amazing northern lights flashing across
> the sky, his reverie broken by the howling of wolves or the
> whistling of a buck attracted by the fire. In his nocturnes,
> whether of the moonlight playing across the lake, or
> touching the brook through the gloom of the forest, or of
> the tent shown up in the darkness by the dim light of the
> candle within, or of the driving rain suddenly illuminated
> by the flash of lightning, or of the bare birch tops forming
> beautiful peacock fans against the cold wind-driven blue
> skies, one feels that it is nature far apart, unsullied by the
> intruder man.[26]

And then, after playing up Thomson's affinity with howling wolves, whistling bucks, and beavers and otters that playfully frolicked alongside his canoe, came an approving stroke from the hand of the good doctor to the "intelligent" buyers of art and the larger galleries:

The intelligent public rather liked his work. . . . It is to the credit of the Ontario Government and the trustees of the National Gallery of Ottawa that they recognized his value. He never exhibited at the Ontario Society of Artists without having one of his pictures bought for the Province of the Dominion.[27]

As to what really happened to cause the death of the artist, well, it was "nature" that "took him to itself at last"—not suicide, or an alcohol induced brawl resulting from Thomson's philandering ways. Now that he was dead, a newer, nobler (and far more marketable) image of Thomson was being presented—one that was rather at odds with the real Thomson. Certainly Thomson's bohemian lifestyle had proven to be a source of irritation within his staunchly Scottish family when he had been alive. Even Thomson's sister Peggy had indicated that they had argued during their last get together:

> I feel disappointed when I think of his last visit as we had a few little arguments, which I wish we had never had. It was just after my operation and I suppose that accounted for it. I wasn't able to enjoy his visit as [I] had done every time before. . . . I often think now that he was many times lonely when all by himself and none of us did anything when he was away to cheer him up. We might have written him letters even though he didn't answer them.[28]

Who knows what the arguments had been about; brothers and sisters are known to bicker even into their later years. However, the fact that none of the family members, by their own account, "did anything" to cheer him up while he was up north being "brother to all untamed things in nature," and refrained from even writing letters to him as the artist "didn't answer them," does speak to the fact that there existed some degree of friction between the artist and his siblings. Ralph Bice had his opinion on the matter, and it was one that those responsible for recasting Thomson's image would have been sure to avoid:

> One of his family told my sister that they were always glad when Thomson left for Algonquin . . . because he was just drinking so much.[29]

Be that as it may, the Canadian public was now not only intrigued but also reverential in its conception of not only Thomson, but of the family that had raised such an iconic figure. This meant that the Thomson family was now starting to enjoy a prestige and an income from their late family member's legacy that prior to his death had not existed. Tom Thomson the artist had become Tom Thomson the product, and Tom Thomson the potential homicide victim was now of little concern. There simply was no return on the latter.

And so it went through the 1920s, with questions regarding the artist's death receding into the background like the wake behind a ship. Tom Thomson the visionary artist had taken center stage, and Tom Thomson the human being was fading slowly from memory.

Chapter Fourteen

THE SKELETON IN THOMSON'S CASKET

While Dr. McCallum and the Thomson family had been generating money from the sale of Tom Thomson's surviving paintings, there was one man back at Canoe Lake who was still troubled over the manner of the artist's death—and that man was Thomson's friend, Park Ranger Mark Robinson.

From his investigation into the matter, Robinson had come away convinced that Thomson had met with foul play—but he was not one to mount a challenge to the verdict of a regional coroner or a park superintendent on such matters—and so he only shared his thoughts on the subject when asked about it. And, in the years immediately following the artist's death, the ranger wasn't asked about it at all.

But as the efforts of the Thomson family and Dr. MacCallum in promoting the late artist began to bear fruit, interest in Tom Thomson's life and mysterious death grew at a much quicker rate than anyone could have anticipated, and such interest only continued to expand over the passing decades. And once the Taylor Statten camps opened on Canoe Lake (Camp Ahmek in 1921 and Camp Wapomeo in 1924) there then proceeded into the park a torrential flood of young men and women from Toronto and other major cities that were interested in learning more about the artist who had died under such mysterious circumstances. Given that Mark Robinson was one of the few people still at Canoe Lake who had known the artist well and had also been the one placed in charge of investigating the matter of his death, he quickly became one of the more frequently sought out sources of information on the artist.

And counted in among the many people with whom the old ranger shared his insights was a young student from McMaster University, Bill Little (my father) who would be impacted by the saga like few before or since. For while my dad certainly appreciated Thomson's talent as a landscape artist, he had been far more intrigued by Robinson's emphasis on the human being behind the paintbrush than he was with the art world's more recent construct of a new St. Thomas.

In 1930, the year that Robinson and my father first met, my dad was an energetic twenty-year old. The old ranger, by contrast, had just turned sixty-three. This was also the year that Robinson first began his correspondence with the author Blodwen Davies, with whom he would likewise share his belief that Thomson had met with foul play and that his body had never left its original grave in the little cemetery next to Canoe Lake. Both Davies and my father would in time play significant roles in bringing public attention to the mystery of how Thomson had met his end and where his final resting place might be. Of course, the trio's area of interest in Thomson put them immediately at odds with both the Thomson family and the Canadian art world, who were by this time well invested in the mythological image of Thomson that they had created. An unspoken battle line gradually became drawn in the sand; on one side of it stood the newly minted Thomson image and painting sales, on the other a desire to find out the truth.

A LITTLE BACKGROUND

My father had been born in Toronto, where his father had been a builder and, during the years of the Great Depression, I've been told that the Little family, consisting of my grandfather, grandmother, and father, found itself on the move quite often in an effort to go where jobs might be found. The family lived in British Columbia, Montana, Alberta, and even in a tent during one winter in Winnipeg while my grandfather was building homes in Manitoba. The family next relocated to Buffalo, New York, where my father lived until he was in his late teens. He returned to Canada to attend McMaster University, which was then located in Toronto, and having just completed his first year at university, he decided that he wanted to spend that forthcoming summer in Ontario.

An offer was extended and accepted for summer employment as a counselor and guide at Camp Ahmek, a boys' camp that was then in its ninth year of operation on the northeastern shore of Canoe Lake. The owner of the camp was Taylor Statten, a man who had known Tom Thomson personally, albeit briefly, when he had hired the artist to do odd jobs for him on the little island he had leased and upon which he had built his cottage.[1]

My father was quite athletic; he had been on the track and field team at McMaster University, where he would befriend future Toronto Maple Leafs captain Syl Apps (indeed, Apps would later be the best man at my father's wedding), and Camp Ahmek with its prospect of canoeing all summer held great appeal. The next summer allowed my father the opportunity to study boxing under Cosmos Canzano, who had been a silver medalist in the lightweight division at the 1930 Commonwealth Games, and saw my father win a boxing competition hosted by Camp Ahmek. The Statten camps would draw many luminaries to Canoe Lake over the ensuing decades, including future Canadian Prime Minister Pierre Trudeau. Long after he had left Statten's employ, my father retained a strong affection for Camp Ahmek and the Statten family (indeed, he met the woman who would eventually become his wife, Corinne Johnson, at Canoe Lake while he was working as a guide at Camp Ahmek and she was teaching horseback riding at Camp Wapomeo). In return, the camp taught him much about living out of doors and made him into quite an accomplished canoeist in his own right. He learned a great deal of his paddling skill (and particularly the famed "J-Stroke") from Bill Stoqua, a member of the First Nations Algonquin Band from Golden Lake, who had worked for Statten as a paddling instructor when he was not employed as a guide by the Algonquin Hotel. My father and Stoqua actually were credited for co-creating what has been dubbed "the Brent Run."[2] The Brent Run is a non-stop canoe trip that puts two people in a cedar-strip canoe starting from the middle of Canoe Lake and has them paddle all the way to Brent (a community on Cedar Lake on the Petawawa River in the northern portion of Algonquin Park) and back to Canoe Lake nonstop (a distance of just over one hundred miles, which includes twenty-seven portages, the longest being the better part of a mile and a half in length). My father and Mr. Stoqua, despite getting lost when fog descended upon them, accomplished this feat in thirty-two hours—a record that stood from 1932 until 1948, when their time was broken by Hank and Carl Laurier, who did it in twenty-seven hours. I further recall being on a canoe trip with my dad and another father and son duo in the park when the hull of the other party's cedar strip canoe scraped against a rock and began taking in water. My father immediately headed off into the woods and returned a few minutes later with a wad of pine pitch, which he then spread over the hole in our friends' canoe and it made a perfect seal. As a result we were able to continue for another three days of canoeing and our friends' canoe never again took in another drop of water.

THE GENESIS OF A PASSION

How my father came to learn of Tom Thomson happened quite by chance. One day during a lull at camp, my dad and several other counselors had paddled over to the Portage Store (which by this time had moved from the shores of the Joe Lake Narrows to the southern end of Canoe Lake) to await the delivery of some supplies. When the supplies arrived, the counselors packed them into their canoes, and quickly discovered that they had more supplies than they had space to accommodate them. A guide named Jim Rowe happened to be at the Portage Store at the time and said that one of the counselors could paddle back to the camp with him. Dad took him up on his offer and the two-headed north in Rowe's canoe toward Camp Ahmek. As they were en route, however, Rowe, who was paddling stern, suddenly steered the craft directly towards Hayhurst Point, a large rocky promontory that cut into the northeast portion of Canoe Lake. Rowe offered no explanation for the abrupt departure from the normal route to their destination, but just continued paddling toward the shoreline. As they approached, my father noticed that they were heading toward a large pine stump that was partially submerged near the shore. As Dad remembered it:

> We came up right beside the stump and Rowe motioned toward it. "See those paint marks up there?" I looked and it did seem like somebody had been cleaning their paintbrushes on the stump, for there were all different colored marks on it. "Yeah," I replied. Then he said, "You know who put them there?" "No," I replied. He said, "Tom Thomson." And without another word he turned the canoe around and started back to camp. I didn't know Thomson from Adam, but I didn't want to say it. I was in university but it was the first time I'd been in Canada, really, to know much of what was going on. So that left me with kind of a problem in my mind: who was Tom Thomson?[3]

When he returned to camp, my father began to ask questions about this Tom Thomson person who apparently was in the habit of cleaning his paint brushes on old stumps. Apart from learning that Thomson was a landscape artist who was believed to have drowned in the waters of the very lake that my father had just paddled on, he quickly discovered that there were a lot of people in and around the camp that summer who had known Thomson personally. As indicated, his employer, Taylor Statten, had known the artist, as did people such as George Chubb, Shannon Fraser (who had dropped by the camp for a visit, his original Mowat Lodge having burned down in November 1920, but having since been rebuilt a little closer to the water in 1921), Pete Sauvé (who was employed as a cook for the Taylor Statten camps), George Rowe (who by this point had a year-round cabin on Joe Creek) and, of course, there was Mark Robinson, who often would drop in to visit with Statten during the summer months.

My father made it a point to speak with each of these people about Thomson, and kept notes on what he had learned—"just college notes" as he referred to them. At the end of each summer that he worked at Ahmek thereafter, he would bring these notes home and, over time, he began collating and reviewing them, trying to construct a timeline of what happened to the artist. Over the ensuing years my father would meet other people who had known the artist well, including various members of the Thomson family (particularly Thomson's older brother George), but without question he garnered the bulk of his information about Thomson directly from those who orbited around Camp Ahmek, and from those who knew the artist best, such as Mark Robinson. According to my father:

Mark Robinson was Tom's close friend. This incident of Thomson going missing and then finding his body was a surprise and a disappointment and a sad affair to Mark. But nothing more was thought of it because there was no real evidence of foul play, except that it worried Mark when he got to thinking about the fishing line being wrapped around Tom's leg—and it wasn't Tom's fishing line! Even the guides said that. They also said that he always lashed two paddles into the canoe. Well, one paddle was missing and never was found, even though they searched high and low from there to Tea Lake, and all around Canoe Lake with a fine-toothed comb. And the paddle that was in the canoe was never lashed by Thomson, so they said. What that really meant I could never piece together. Who in hell would bother lashing that paddle in the canoe other than Thomson, unless it was to make it look as though he had been portaging and fell? But he didn't have an opportunity to portage. The portage was down at least a mile and a half. There was nothing that he could have struck his head on. That shoreline is gravel, that's all. It's typical. I daresay there'd be a million people paddle up and down that way never have a mishap.[4]

Dad recalled that he was always waiting for Mark Robinson to show him exactly where Thomson's original grave was located in the Mowat Cemetery:

I talked to Mark many times out on the trail on various trips, and very often we'd wind up talking about Thomson. He had said that Thomson's grave was on the north side of, and adjacent to, the old Mowat cemetery. That was the only information I had. He'd said that sometime when he was over at camp, we'd go over there together, but when he'd come to camp, I wouldn't be there or if I was there, he wouldn't be. I'd seen him three or four times in the summers, but he was busy and I was busy. The opportunity just never presented itself.[5]

And while the old ranger never made it up to the old cemetery with my father, he still went up there on occasion as evidenced by notes from an interview conducted with Robinson in 1944 by author Audrey Saunders, wherein he shared the news that a small balsam tree had started to grow atop the very location of Thomson's original grave.[6] Mark Robinson would pass away in 1955, believing to his final day that the artist had met with foul play, and that Thomson's body had never been removed from its original grave.

DIGGING FOR CLUES

Several months after Robinson's passing, in September 1956, my father and his good friend (and fellow Camp Ahmek alumni) Jack Eastaugh found themselves back at Canoe Lake on a sketching expedition. The two men had often discussed the Thomson story over the years whenever they had guided together or, more frequently, during canoe trips that they would take on various weekends. However, on this particular weekend my father and Estaugh had only made it as far as the northwestern shore of Canoe Lake. Beaching their canoe, the pair hiked up the hillock behind where the original Mowat Lodge had once stood, and eventually found themselves alone at the little cemetery.

In Tom Thomson's time, the lumber industry had cleared away most of the trees in and around this area. By the 1950s the trees had started to return, but were small and, thus, an excellent view of Canoe Lake could still be had from the top of the hill where the cemetery is situated. Owing to the view afforded from this area Thomson often used to come to the cemetery to paint, and tourists would likewise venture up to this location to take still pictures of the lake. This weekend my father and Eastaugh were also looking to take advantage of the view afforded by the cemetery area to do a little painting of their own. My father dabbled in painting, but Eastaugh was a very accomplished landscape artist in his own right. As my father recollected:

> The site of the cemetery is a very picturesque spot with a nice view of the lake. I have the painting that Jack did from the sketches made that day. He included some birch trees that aren't far from the grave. I'm not really an artist, and I became disinterested in my sketching. In a while I began to think about Mark Robinson. Finally, I mentioned to Jack that we should try to find the grave while we were there. It was unmarked and well grown over by that time but I said I'd like to investigate.[7]

The pair agreed to return the next day to try and locate Tom Thomson's original gravesite. But for the moment it had been a long day and both men were hungry. And given the fact that they also happened to be longtime alumni of Camp Ahmek, they decided to head east across the lake to the camp where they knew Pete Sauvé, who was then the chief chef for Ahmek, would probably be preparing food for whatever staff were still present (the campers having departed at the end of August). The two men entered the large dining hall at the camp and sat down at one of the tables. Over dinner they were joined by some of their friends on staff, and, after catching up with the goings on at camp, the topic eventually worked its way round to the subject of Tom Thomson. Seated nearby was Frank Braught, another friend of the men from the old days, who pulled up a chair and joined in the conversation. One of the men was heard to comment that, "It seemed too bad that we couldn't establish some definite understanding as to what had really occurred at the time Tom's body was buried at Canoe Lake." This set off a chain of recollections from the men at the table about what they had heard about the situation of Thomson's supposed exhumation from those who had been there at the time it was said to have occurred.

Mark Robinson, who had been known by most of the men seated around the table that evening, was remembered, as were his views on the matter. Shannon Fraser's name was then brought up, along with his expressed opinion that the undertaker that he dropped off and picked up at the Mowat Cemetery that night in 1917 hadn't been there long enough to do the job. Another man brought up the memory of speaking with one of the railway men who had told him that the casket he had helped to load into the baggage car in 1917 hadn't been heavy enough to contain a body. Finally, Jack Eastaugh addressed the elephant in the room.

"It seems to me that some of us ought to do something definite and try to establish the fact as to whether Tom's body is actually buried here or whether it was removed to Owen Sound," he said. "You know I'd like to go over there and investigate and see if we can't find something."

One of the men at the table wondered aloud about potential legal ramifications if they actually found Thomson's body within the grave. Eastaugh, however, shot it down.

"Now we wouldn't be committing anything illegal because we have public evidence that the body was removed and taken to Owen Sound. So, if we go over there, all we'll be doing is to investigate for our own selves and find out if this is true or not."

The exact same thought had percolated through Frank Braught's mind quite frequently over the years, but entertaining the notion was as far as he had been willing to go—until now.[8] Wanting to strike while the iron was still hot, he moved his chair in closer to Eastaugh and my father.

"Listen," he began, "if you two fellas are of the same opinion as I am, I'll go with you tomorrow morning."

"What time?" my father asked.

"Nine o'clock."[9]

Braught also indicated that he could secure some extra help for the task in the person of Leonard "Gibby" Gibson, a local friend who also would be keen to help solve the mystery. Pete Sauvé, the only one of the group at Camp Ahmek that evening who had actually known Tom Thomson personally, had by now caught wind of what was being discussed and made his way out of the kitchen and pulled up a chair to sit at the table. He, likewise, had decided that it was time to get an answer to the question as to whether or not Thomson's body had ever left the Park.

"We'll have breakfast at nine o'clock," Sauvé said, "and you fellows can go right after that."[10]

With the next day's plan now in place, the men then retired for the evening.

When morning arrived, Gibson, Braught, Eastaugh, and my father met back at the Ahmek dining room to discuss their plans for the dig over breakfast. By 1956, the Mowat Cemetery was still accessible by car and Gibson quickly volunteered the use of his Jeep, which would prove useful to the enterprise. Gibson had already loaded three shovels and an ax into the vehicle. By 9:45 a.m. the four men were in Gibson's Jeep and on their way to the little cemetery. The sky that morning was a dull gray and a fine rain had started to fall, perfectly matching how it had been on the day that Thomson's body had originally been laid to rest there thirty-nine years previously. The digging was not going to be easy or pleasant, particularly when there was no guarantee that there would be anything there to be found. All the men had to guide them on their quest was the testimony of those who had been directly involved in the Thomson saga but who had now passed on to graves of their own, chiefly Mark Robinson and Shannon Fraser.

According to the author Roy MacGregor, my father and his three companions "admitted to having had a few drinks"[11] before commencing their dig that morning. This is a puzzling bit of news, however, given that my old man was a teetotaler. And as MacGregor has never listed his source for this information, I'm at something of a loss as to whom they would have admitted this to—or why. For the record, Jack Eastaugh wasn't a drinker either; in fact, I don't ever recall him having a drink over the many years that he and his wife Elizabeth visited our house. I know that neither my father nor Jack Eastaugh ever made any reference to consuming alcohol beforehand in anything they wrote about the dig afterwards and, in checking the testimony of another man who was present that day, Frank Braught, I further note the absence of any statement indicating that the men needed alcohol to accomplish the task they had set for themselves that morning.

Perhaps MacGregor made this statement to imply that what the men were up to that dreary morning in 1956 was simply the result of a drunken lark—rather than an attempt to solve a long-standing mystery. If so, then nothing could have been further from the truth.

But while the men had no need of alcohol to fortify them in their quest that day, they certainly could have used Mark Robinson's help in determining where Thomson's original grave site lay, as none of them knew exactly where it was. Robinson had mentioned that a balsam tree marked the site of the grave, however he had evidently only mentioned this to Audrey Saunders in 1944. And while she had jotted this bit of information down in her notes for her book *Algonquin Story*, it was not included in her final manuscript.

Robinson had said that Thomson's grave lay just to the north of the two marked graves that resided within the cemetery proper, and so the men selected a spot that was just outside of the fenced in area of the cemetery as the most probable location. Their shovels bit into the earth at 10:00 a.m.[12] The digging was easy to start, that is until they hit some tree roots at about the three-foot level. Undeterred, they continued digging until they were six feet down—but found nothing. A flicker of doubt now began to flit through my father's mind; this location had been their best bet, as it had been the closest to the marked graves, and yet they had come up empty. Perhaps Robinson had been mistaken in his assumption that the undertaker had not removed the body. But still, Churchill was said to have reburied Thomson's empty oak casket and rough box, and the men had found no evidence of such thus far. The men decided that they would move another three feet or so further north and try their luck again. Once more they dug down six feet and once more they found nothing. At this point, the men had been hard at it for several hours and decided it was time to take a break from their labors and reassess if they were inclined to continue with the enterprise.

During the respite Braught mentioned to the group that he had been at the cemetery several years previously and had noted a distinct depression in the surface of the ground not far from where they were digging. Perhaps that was suggestive of the original gravesite? This triggered a recollection from Gibson that a friend of his had also gone over to the cemetery several years back after he had learned that some people had planted trees atop Thomson's original grave. He added that he had heard that when Winnifred Trainor had caught wind of this she immediately went up to the cemetery and pulled out all of the newly planted trees. This anecdote triggered a recollection from Braught—when he had last been to the cemetery he had seen a small balsam tree growing next to the depression in the earth that was believed to have been Thomson's original grave site.[13] Upon hearing this bit of news, Jack Estaugh put down his pipe and pointed to a location about twenty-five feet north from the fenced in area of the cemetery.

"There's a depression over there," he said. "I wonder if that could be it?"

Braught walked over to inspect the area that Eastaugh had indicated and immediately spied a balsam tree at the edge of the depression. The tree was almost ten feet high, far taller than the small one he had recalled seeing several years previously.[14] Braught was soon joined by the other three men and, collectively, they surveyed the area. It seemed like this spot might be their best bet. All the men agreed that if they dug here and again came up empty, they would call a halt to the enterprise.

They began digging on the west side of the balsam tree. Its roots were proving to be much bigger and more unwieldy than the men had anticipated, requiring them to use their axe almost as often as they used their shovels. Only one person could dig (and chop) at a time and each of the men took their turn, every now and then pausing briefly to employ the axe and to remove the roots from the balsam as they went along. After an hour or so of this the men were running out of strength, as they had now been working for several hours. As they continued to dig deeper, their increasing level of fatigue prevented them from widening the hole, making the diameter narrower and narrower the further down they dug. My father was the slightest built person in the group and, noting the palpable fatigue in the others, he volunteered to hop in the hole and continue on.

As he was digging at a depth of approximately four and a half feet his shovel suddenly struck something hard. Placing his shovel aside, he bent down to explore the object with his hands and quickly realized that it wasn't a rock. He began to work the object free with his hands and finally brought up a small piece of wood. He looked it over and handed it up to Jack Eastaugh, who, in turn, passed it along to Leonard Gibson for inspection. Gibson looked at it and shook his head. He pointed toward a white pine stump that was nearby.

"I think it's a piece of root from that old stump," he explained. "They stay in the ground a long time before they disintegrate."[15]

Dad nodded, picked up his shovel, and resumed digging. Almost immediately his shovel again struck something solid. He again worked the object free with his hands and once again came up with a piece of wood, but this one was different than the previous piece; a tool of some sort had clearly rounded the edge of it.

"You hit another root?" asked Gibson.

"If so, this is the first root I've seen with a beveled edge," my dad replied.[16]

The piece of wood was brought out and quickly passed around. By the time it reached Eastaugh's hand he was pretty confident that he knew what it was.

"It's a mortise from the corner of a box—likely a casket or rough box you've found!"[17]

Any fatigue the men had been feeling quickly evaporated at this point. Putting his shovel aside, Dad began digging with his hands until he felt a smooth piece of board. He pried it free from the soil and quickly realized he had just exposed the end of a coffin. And reaching his hand into the aperture of the casket he quickly discovered that it wasn't empty. He felt something hard but of a different texture than what he had pulled up previously. He wrapped his hand around the object and pulled it out where he could take a look at it. To his shock, he realized that what he was now holding in his hands was a human shin (tibia) bone. That was enough to satisfy his curiosity and he quickly returned the bone from where it came and climbed out of the hole and told the others what he had discovered.

At this point, according to Braught, Leonard Gibson opted for a unique method of excavation:

Gibby looked down into the hole and says, "Hold on a minute there, I see something!" And he went head first down into the hole and Jack Eastaugh or Bill grabbed a hold of both his feet and was hanging onto his feet while he was headfirst down in the hole, digging with both hands like a badger. And then he brought out some pieces of wood and when he threw those up onto the bank we examined them and realized right away that it was a part of either the box that contained the coffin or the coffin itself. Then he says, "Wait a minute!" While he was still head down there we were hanging on to him . . . he said, "What do you think of that?" And he reached into the hole in the ground and he grabbed a hold of a couple of bones and he said, "Look there's a couple of bones right there" and he threw them out and from then on the excitement began to pile up.[18]

While the men were most definitely excited by their discovery, they were also exhausted. They also understood that anything further would have to be done by the proper authorities. The phalanges that had been brought out of the grave by Gibson were placed into a small box, and then the men returned to Camp Ahmek. Once back at camp it was decided that the one man who would know what to do going forward would be the camp's medical director, Dr. Harry Ebbs. Moreover, it was discovered that Dr. Ebbs happened to be at Canoe Lake that weekend staying at Taylor Statten's cottage (the same one that Dr. Goldwyn Howland had occupied when he had first spotted Thomson's body floating on the surface of Canoe Lake in 1917). As Little Wapomeo Island was only accessible by water, both my father and Jack Eastaugh volunteered to take one of the camp's canoes and paddle over to the Statten cottage to pay Dr. Ebbs a visit.

THE AUTHORITIES ARE NOTIFIED

Harry Ebbs was eating dinner with his family when Jack Eastaugh and my father arrived at the Statten cottage and knocked on the door. Both men were filthy due to the rain and dirt they had exposed themselves to that morning, and so they declined the doctor's invitation to come inside. They instead requested that Ebbs join them outside, whereupon they produced a little box and opened it up to reveal its contents.

"We'd like you to tell us what this is," my father said.[19]

Ebbs examined the contents of the box with his full attention.

"You know very well what this is,"[20] he began. "You've got the bones of a human foot—where did you get them from?"[21]

Eastaugh then got right to the point. "Well, would you like to come over to the cemetery and see whether you think it is Tom Thomson's grave?"[22]

Having been a regular at Canoe Lake for thirty-two years, Dr. Ebbs was very conversant with the Tom Thomson story. Consequently, his interest in the matter had long ago been piqued and he didn't require a formal invitation to take part in attempting to solve the mystery of the artist's final resting place. The three men quickly made their way back to the Mowat Cemetery. Upon arriving, Ebbs recalled that:

> There was a rectangular depression in the ground and there was a balsam tree in the middle of it and I think the balsam tree would be about fifteen years old, judging by the branches on it. And in one corner there was a hole and they said, "That's where we got the bones."[23]

Ebbs inspected the hole and then informed the men that he would require something a little more substantial than some loose phalanges to take back with him to present to the authorities. It's unclear who volunteered to step back down into the hole to retrieve more osseous artifacts, but evidently someone did and came back up with a fibula (one of two lower leg bones that reside on the outer or lateral portion of the shin) from within the remains of the rotted casket, which Ebbs then placed into a box.

Ebbs explained to the men that he would be heading back to Toronto that Tuesday morning (October 2) and that once there he would bring the bones to the attention of the attorney general's office, which at that time was headed by Archibald Kelso Roberts. This he did and Ebbs further brought the discovery to the attention of Frank MacDougall, who was then the deputy minister of the Department of Lands and Forests. As a matter of course, the Ontario Provincial Police (O.P.P.) were then brought into the matter. The commissioner of the O.P.P. was Edwin McNiell, and gauging from the content of the police files, it was McNiell's Assistant Commissioner Jas Bartlett who directed this matter going forward on behalf of the O.P.P. Shortly after he dropped off the bones, Ebbs received a phone call from Assistant Commissioner Bartlett inquiring if he would be willing to return to the gravesite and lend his assistance to a Corporal A.M. Rodger from the Burk's Falls detachment of the O.P.P., who had received instructions to investigate the situation on behalf of the Province.[24]

It is unclear how Dr. Noble Sharpe from the crime laboratory in Toronto came to be involved, as his report from October 30, 1956 indicates that he was contacted by Assistant Commissioner Bartlett about the matter, while in a memorandum written on February 20, 1967, he indicated that his involvement was purely accidental. According to this later report, the sequence was that Dr. Ebbs had reported the discovery of the bones to the assistant commissioner, who then ordered Corporal Rodger to investigate, and it was Rodger who was the one who had decided to exhume the grave. Sharpe had been with Corporal Rodger earlier in the day to attend an inquest at Ahmic Harbour, a small village located near Corporal Rodger's detachment in Burks Falls. According to Sharpe, it was at this point that Corporal Rodger asked him to accompany him to the gravesite at Canoe Lake. To Sharpe's surprise, he later learned that no order for exhumation had come from the commissioner's office, but that both he and Rodger had simply assumed that it was a necessary step in determining the cause of death of the deceased.

In any event, there had to be some planning for an exhumation prior to that morning, as when Corporal Rodger and Dr. Sharpe pulled into the parking lot of the Portage Store on the morning of October 5, 1956, waiting there to meet them was Dr. Harry Ebbs, along with Frank Braught and Leonard Gibson, two of the four men from the original dig, who were now ready to do it all over again. Given that they would have to travel to the graveyard on dirt roads that could wreck havoc on the undercarriage of a police issue automobile, it is likely that the men opted to head to the gravesite in Gibson's Jeep.

Upon arriving at the cemetery, the four men climbed out of the vehicle and surveyed the gravesite. Spotting the balsam tree, it was decided that in order for the grave to be opened fully, the tree would have to be removed from the site. Leonard Gibson then secured a chain around the tree and pulled it out with his Jeep.[25] With the obstacle now removed, the four men began to dig. They also sieved the earth that was removed from the grave, looking for any artifacts that might have been buried with the body. They were specifically looking for remnants of clothing, such as buttons or rings, which might help to date the time of burial or to identify the remains. To the men's surprise they found no items at all, save for the remains of one woolen sock on the right foot of the skeleton. Frank Braught was certain that he also saw "part of a cloth shoe, evidently a canvas shoe."[26] If so, then the canvas shoe never made the trip to Toronto, as the crime lab would make no mention of it. If there was a canvas shoe in the grave, then this would indeed be significant as Charlie Scrim had reported to Mark Robinson in 1917 that when Thomson was last seen paddling away from the

Mowat Lodge dock he had been wearing canvas shoes. This was further corroborated by Dr. Howland, who had noted in his report for Dr. Ranney that canvas shoes were still on the body when it had been pulled from the water. Intriguing as Braught's statement is, however, it bears repeating that only Braught made mention of a canvas shoe being present in the grave. Neither Dr. Sharpe nor Corporal Rodger in their reports made reference to the presence of any remnants of clothing apart from the existence of a woolen sock on the right foot of the skeleton.

For the men the importance of a shoe or sock being on the skeleton's foot paled in significance to what was discovered next. Corporal Rodger had stopped using a shovel once they were down approximately four feet and began pulling away earth with his hands. When he removed his next handful of dirt he was startled to find himself looking directly into the empty eye sockets of a skull. He cleared some more dirt away from the skull and pried it from the earth. After examining it in his hands, he handed it up to Drs. Sharpe and Ebbs, who then placed the skull upon some leaves and began to lightly brush away some of the dirt that remained in order to get a better look at it. As they were doing so, a section of earth fell from the left temple region of the skull, revealing a hole that measured three-quarters of an inch in diameter.

Ebbs immediately turned to Corporal Rodger.

"What do you do you think that is?" he asked.[27]

"That's a .22 caliber bullet," replied Rodgers, "nothing else could do that."[28]

Sharpe knew that if what he was looking at was the entrance wound of a bullet, there either had to be an exit wound on the opposite side of the skull or that there was a bullet still within it.

"Do not disturb anything within the skull!" Sharpe declared. "Take it as it is and we'll have an x-ray taken of it immediately"[29]

Over the next hour, all of the skeletal remains were exhumed and these, along with the remnants of the casket and rough box, were placed into a large cardboard Sunkist Oranges box, which was then placed in Gibson's Jeep. The men filled the grave back in and then headed back to the Portage Store parking lot, where the box containing the bones was then transferred into the trunk of Corporal Rodger's car. Corporal Roger and Dr. Sharpe then said their goodbyes, and Ebbs, Braught, and Gibson watched as the two men drove away.[30]

My father had not been present for the exhumation but he told me something many years later that made me kind of glad he wasn't. He had brought me to Canoe Lake one weekend some years after the dig, and as it happened we had dropped in to visit Leonard Gibson at his cabin on the lake. I recall that Gibson looked old and frail then, even to my young and inexperienced eyes. He had been hobbling around his cabin all weekend with the aid of a cane. When the weekend concluded and Dad and I were heading home, I felt comfortable in asking my father what had happened to his friend that had resulted in his injury.

"It wasn't an injury," my father explained. "Gibby lost his foot as a result of diabetes." He could tell by the look in my eyes that at my age I didn't have a clue what diabetes was. I was probably looking out the window at the scenery zipping past our vehicle as he attempted to explain the metabolic disorder that make up the disease that Mr. Gibson was suffering from. But then he said something that grabbed my attention immediately.

"It's odd," he said. "I heard from Frank [Braught] that when he and Gibby went back to exhume the grave with the police that Gibby had kept one of the foot bones from the skeleton."

"Why would he do that?" I asked.

Dad shook his head in bewilderment. "I don't know. But I do find it strange that Gibby was the only one involved who took one of the skeleton's foot bones, and he was the only one who ended up losing a foot."

Nothing more was said on the matter, but I will admit that my Dad's comments served to unnerve me a little bit.

Chapter Fifteen

WORD GETS OUT

Approximately five days after Dr. Sharpe had returned to Toronto with his box of bones from the Mowat Cemetery, the phone rang on the secretary's desk at the Ontario Reformatory in Brampton.

The man on the other end of the line asked to speak with Bill Little, the superintendent of the institution. The secretary patched him through and, when my father picked up the phone, he was surprised to learn that he was speaking with a reporter from the *Toronto Star*. The reporter stated that he wanted to know the details of the dig at the Mowat Cemetery, and whether or not my father believed that the body that he and his friends had discovered was indeed that of Tom Thomson. Less than twenty-four hours after my father hung up the phone that day, the rest of Canada would learn the news of the recent discovery at Canoe Lake, as the story made headlines across the nation:

Toronto Star
October 10, 1956
ALGONQUIN GRAVE REVIVES THOMSON LEGEND
Algonquin Park, Oct. 10—A skeleton dug up from an unmarked Algonquin Park grave has added another chapter to the legend of Tom Thomson, famed Canadian painter who, according to official reports, drowned accidentally in Canoe Lake 39 years ago. William Little, amateur artist and superintendent of

the Ontario reformatory at Brampton, said today he is almost certain the bones he and three friends found 10 days ago on a hillside grave overlooking Canoe Lake are those of Thomson.

Official records say the painter was buried at Leith, near Owen Sound, where he spent his early childhood. However, legends prevalent in this area for many years say the body was never moved from its Algonquin Park burial place. . . . Mr. Little said he had been told 25 years ago by Mark Robinson, a Forest Ranger who investigated Thomson's death . . . the body was never moved to the church cemetery at Leith; that the undertaker hired to look after the reburial took an empty coffin to the new grave. . . . After police were called in and the attorney general's department informed of the discovery, the bones were turned over to Dr. Noble Sharpe, of Toronto, medical director of the provincial crime laboratory. Dr. Sharpe said last night he is still examining the bones and the investigation may last another two weeks. "I will be very surprised if these are Thomson's bones," Dr. Sharpe said. "That story is only a local legend."

The doctor confirmed a report by the four men that there was a small round hole in the skull but added he did not think it was caused by a blunt instrument or a bullet. "It is probably nothing more than the result of normal erosion," he said.

For years mystery and bizarre legends have surrounded Thomson's death. . . . To this day, old-time park residents think Thomson's death was not accidental and point to the fact that he had two known enemies in the area.

The foul play theory was given added impetus in 1937 when Blodwen Davies of Markham published her book, "A Study of Tom Thomson". . . . "The undertaker arrived after dark," declared the author. "The ranger who examined the grave after the undertaker's visit told me only a one-third area of the mound had been disturbed. A body could not possibly have been taken up through that small hole, he said." Davies proposed that the undertaker had been in a hurry and had simply filled his casket with gravel and stones. "The body was badly decomposed. Nobody who knew Thomson ever saw a body in the undertaker's casket. The family never opened it," she said.[1]

AN UNANXIOUS UNDERTAKER

Almost immediately after the story broke, reporters set about tracking down F.W. Churchill, the undertaker who had been tasked with exhuming Thomson's body from its original resting place at the Mowat Cemetery in 1917. When they approached the elderly gentleman for comment at his home in Kirkland Lake, the then seventy-three-year-old man was understandably caught completely by surprise and, quite naturally, struggled somewhat to recollect the events that occurred some thirty-nine years before. His thoughts on the matter were recorded as follows:

> Mr. Thomson's relatives and friends were not happy with the burial spot. Miss Blodwen Davies, a friend, wanted him buried at Leith. She phoned the undertaker in Kearney, who had been in charge of the funeral near Canoe Lake, but he refused to exhume the body. Then she phoned me in Huntsville. I was not anxious to do the job, but she begged me and finally I said yes. By that time the body had lain in the water for 10 days and been buried seven days. Mark Robinson, the park ranger, gave me four men to help me with the job. We opened the grave and took the coffin and the rough-box out of the grave. The body was badly decomposed but still recognizable as Tom Thomson. I transferred the remains into a metal box, which I could seal. The empty

coffin and rough box were put back into the grave and the grave was filled again. We placed the metal box with the body in a coffin and shipped it to Owen Sound, as Miss Davies had requested. One of Mr. Thomson's brothers accompanied the coffin on the train to Owen Sound. There my instructions ended, but I heard that the undertaker from Owen Sound saw to the burial of the coffin in the cemetery in Leith.[2]

A certain amount of the undertaker's confusion was understandable; after all, the event he had been asked to comment on had happened almost forty years previously. That Thomson had been in the water eight days rather than ten, had been buried a little over twenty-four hours—not seven days—before Churchill arrived to exhume it, are errors of detail that one might likely be unclear about after the passage of so much time. Less understandable, however, were his claims regarding under whose instructions he was acting, and the parties he believed to have been present with him during the exhumation. With regard to the person who secured his services for the task, it most certainly was not the author Blodwen Davies, who had never corresponded with Churchill in her life. We know from the evidence that has survived that Winnifred Trainor (who was, indeed, "a friend" of the artist) had been the one who had contacted him on behalf of the Thomson family to secure Churchill's services to perform the job. However, as the undertaker had indicated that the person under whose instructions he had been acting for the exhumation was Miss Davies, the press went to her for a reply:

AUTHOR DID NOT KNOW ARTIST
Miss Blodwen Davies, Saskatchewan Arts Board executive secretary, added fresh fuel Tuesday to the 40-year controversy on the death and burial of woodsman artist Tom Thomson,

officially reported drowned in 1917. Author of the only book-length biography of Thomson, believed by many to be Canada's foremost painter, she emphatically denied she ever knew the artist.

A Friday news report from Kirkland Lake, Ont. quoted F.W. Churchill, 73-year-old former undertaker, who claims to have removed the painter's body from its original grave . . . was reported as saying: "Mr. Thomson's relatives and friends were not happy with the burial spot. Miss Blodwen Davies, a friend, wanted him buried at Leith . . . she phoned me at Huntsville. I was not anxious to do the job, but she begged me and finally I said yes."

"That is utterly ridiculous," declared Miss Davies, who had been away at a handicraft festival at Sheho over the weekend and had not seen the Kirkland Lake news report until Monday. "At the time of the artist's death I was living with my parents in Fort William and going to school. I had never heard of the name of Tom Thomson." . . . Mr. Churchill was quoted as stating he had removed the body from the original grave with the help of four men given to him by Park Ranger Mark Robinson. Miss Davies said the Ranger told her in 1930 he had not provided any help to disinter the body[3]

Churchill's comments to the press had served to dig a deeper hole for the undertaker to extricate himself from. His statement, "The body was badly decomposed but still recognizable as Tom Thomson",[4] was in itself an odd statement to make, as Churchill had never seen Tom Thomson before in his life and, thus, would have had no idea what the artist looked like for purposes of comparison. And given that Thomson's body, by Churchill's own admission, was badly decomposed and that the alleged exhumation took place in the dark of night, a positive identification would have been challenging even to those who had known the artist, let alone someone who had never laid eyes on him. Churchill also seemed to have been ignorant of the fact that Dixon and Flavelle had wrapped the artist's body in a shroud prior to its original burial, which would not only have covered any facial features necessary to making a positive identification, but also, one would think, would have been a detail of fact that the undertaker might have recalled—if he had actually exhumed the body.

Having read the newspaper stories and perhaps feeling the need to respond to his colleague Churchill's public comments about how badly decomposed Thomson's body was when it was removed from its original casket, Roy Dixon, one of the two undertakers who had been tasked with Thomson's original burial, and the one who had been responsible for embalming the artist's body, wrote a letter to the *Toronto Star* in defense of his embalming skills:

> Sir:
>
> I was the undertaker who embalmed and interred the remains of Tom Thomson at Canoe Lake in 1917, and have a very distinct recollection of all the official proceedings at that time. I beg to take issue with reports that appeared last week suggesting death by foul play. . . . There was certainly no blood on the face or any indication of foul play, just the usual post mortem staining that is on the body of any person that is in the water of a small lake for 10 days in the heat of the summer.
>
> No one else assisted us. . . . I cannot believe Mark Robinson said, as reported by Mr. Little, that the body was never removed. He told me they removed the body some time later and that it was in a remarkable state of preservation and must have been well embalmed. If these people wanted to make sure of these "old wives tales" why didn't they get an exhumation order and examine the casket that was alleged to be empty instead

of desecrating the cemetery at Canoe Lake? In British Columbia they put them in jail for that kind of thing.
M.R. Dixon
Parry Sound[5]

Mark Robinson, having passed away in 1955, was of course no longer available to refute his cousin's assertions that the ranger had "removed the body sometime later." Nor was he available to refute Dixon's claim that the ranger had been present when Churchill allegedly exhumed Thomson's body and had been particularly impressed by the result of Dixon's embalming skills. After all, Thomson had been embalmed and buried on Tuesday, July 17 and presumably exhumed on Wednesday, July 18—a need to mention how well preserved the body had remained over a twenty-four hour period seems a rather superfluous comment to make. One wouldn't expect that in such a short passage of time that that there would be much change at all in an embalmed body to cause one to comment on its "remarkable state of preservation." Obviously unbeknownst to Dixon at the time that he wrote his letter to the paper was the fact that three years prior to his death Mark Robinson had recorded an interview detailing his recollections on the matter, which stood in distinct contrast to his cousin's claims.

As to Mr. Dixon's final comment, regarding desecrating a grave within the Mowat Cemetery, it must be remembered that the cemetery, per se, was enclosed by a picket fence and contained two headstones—and no digging took place there. Where the men dug was outside the confines of the fenced in cemetery area and, more to the point, by Churchill's own testimony, he had exhumed whatever body had been buried there four decades previously, leaving behind only an empty casket and rough box. Consequently, there was not supposed to be a grave in that location for anyone to desecrate. And it would be unprecedented, even in British Columbia, for anyone to be put in jail simply for digging up earth in a location that wasn't supposed to contain a grave.

And while the crime lab had not yet made an official identification of the skeletal remains that they now had in their possession, the circumstantial evidence was strongly suggestive that they were those of the late artist. And if this was true, then apart from deliberate negligence on the part of the Huntsville undertaker, there existed no reason why Thomson's body should still have been in its original grave in the Mowat Cemetery. That is, unless action had been taken to ensure that Thomson's body had never left Algonquin Park. And there is some hearsay testimony that would support this contention, which came in the form of a statement from art patron Ruth Upjohn to artist Doug Dunford:

> Ruth told me that she had heard certain members of the Group of Seven say that Tom Thomson had said that he wanted to be buried in Algonquin Park if anything ever happened to him. And she heard the members take an oath that no one would ever find out that they knew he was buried in the park. And she felt they had something to do with it; that when the undertaker went to dig up the remains they made sure that his body stayed there and it had to be kept a big secret. Plus they were concerned about the Irish guy [Shannon Fraser] being charged with murder, or whatever. That they felt it was better to keep everything hushed, private.[6]

If this is true, the Group may have learned that Thomson's body had never been removed from its resting place in the park from one of their contemporaries, William Beatty. The reader will recall the statement presented earlier by Dorothy Stone, who had been an art student of Beatty's, and who had witnessed both Beatty and Fraser essentially testifying that they ensured that Thomson's body never left Algonquin Park:

> I can see them [Beatty and Shannon Fraser] in the glow of the firelight chuckling and exchanging knowing glances and saying something to the effect that, "we knew where he wanted to stay and we saw to it that he stayed there."[7]

That Beatty had knowledge that Fraser might have had a hand in keeping Thomson's body in its grave at Canoe Lake isn't as far-fetched as it might seem at first blush. After all, certain members of the Thomson family had considered Beatty as being a little too easily led by Shannon Fraser. Thomson's brother-in-law, Tom Harkness, as we've seen, had been particularly displeased with how easily Beatty had seemed to fall under Fraser's sway in accepting his belief that the artist had committed suicide.[8] And, if Beatty had been receptive to that, perhaps he had also been accepting of the lodge owner's reasons for wanting to keep Thomson's body buried in the Mowat cemetery.

Less understandable was the apparent apathy of the Thomson family regarding the whole affair. One would presume that the surviving members of the family would have been shocked to learn that there was still a skeleton residing in their family member's original grave and, indeed, in his original casket. One would also presume that they would have been mystified by the news that an undertaker whom they had entrusted and paid to transfer their family member's body to the family plot thirty-nine years previously was now making nonsensical statements to the Canadian press about under who's orders he was acting when he allegedly performed the exhumation. Such news should at least have been cause for concern for the family and perhaps even served as impetus for them to check the contents of the grave at Leith in order to ensure that their family member's body had, in fact, been returned home. But one would be wrong in making such presumptions.

Certainly the circumstantial evidence in support of the skeleton in the Canoe Lake gravesite being that of Tom Thomson was strong, and three points in particular served to underscore the belief:

1. When Thomson had been buried in 1917 there had been no time to have the artist's name inscribed on the nameplate that was affixed to the coffin. The casket that was exhumed in 1956 also had a nameplate without a name inscribed upon it; the only inscription being a generic "At Rest."[9]

2. In order for Dr. Howland to perform his medical inspection on Thomson's body, the clothing had been removed from the corpse. The body was then embalmed and wrapped in a canvas shroud that had been brought to the island by the undertakers Flavelle and Dixon.[10] When the grave was opened in 1956, there was no evidence that the body in the grave had been clothed when buried—there were no rings found, no belt buckle, no buttons, etc. But there were found fragments of a canvas shroud, and portions of a woolen sock attached to the foot bones of the right leg.[11]

3. Dr. Howland and Mark Robinson had both noted a four-inch bruise on Thomson's temple when they had pulled the artist's body from the water (Robinson had noted that it was on the left temple,[12] and two conflicting reports by Howland, one in the possession of the Thomson family, had indicated that it was on the left temple;[13] the other based upon the notes of Dr. Ranney, the coroner from North Bay who never saw the body, indicated it was on the right temple).[14] When the skeleton was unearthed in 1956,

the skull was found to have a hole in the left temple region that measured three-quarters of an inch in diameter.[15]

According to my father:

> This absolutely proved to our satisfaction that the grave, which was for almost forty years considered to be empty, contained the body of Tom Thomson.[16]

But the belief of my father along with his three companions, in addition to Dr. Ebbs, Blodwen Davies, Mark Robinson, William Beatty, and Shannon Fraser, would need verification via a scientific analysis of the bones that were retrieved from what was supposed to have been an empty grave. And while the bones were in the process of being inspected by the Ontario crime lab, and as the national newspapers churned out their speculative columns in 1956, the conclusion that the attorney general's office was about to release to the Canadian public was going to leave everyone mystified.

Chapter Sixteen

THE CRIME LAB DECISION

O nce the bones had arrived at the crime laboratory in Toronto, Dr. Sharpe was in a bit of a quandary. To begin, the crime lab did not own an x-ray machine at this point in its history, and Sharpe, by his own admission, "did not then feel competent to pass on skeletal remains (it is a subject pathologists do not usually know much about)."[1]

However, he did know that he would need to have the skull x-rayed in order to determine if it contained any evidence that the hole in the temple region had been caused by a bullet. According to Dr. Sharpe:

> I was busy with court appearances at the time and it was October 11th, 1956 before I was able to commence a detailed examination. Dr. A. Singleton, a well-known Toronto specialist, co-operated with me in the initial x-ray examination of the skull and contents. Finding no evidence of the presence of a projectile we cleaned out the skull to facilitate examination of both inner and outer surfaces. There were no radiating fractures around the hole and there was no beveling—a condition generally associated with passage of a bullet.[2]

With the gunshot theory now effectively disproved, Sharpe still needed to find out what had caused the hole in the skull. He thought for a time that the wound might have been the result of a blow to the head by an object such as a pick, a narrow hammer-head, or an arrow. Given that Canoe Lake had also been a logging locale, he had even considered whether the hole had been caused by a peevee (a pole with a spike on the end of it for turning logs in the water), but ultimately dismissed each of these as being unlikely.[3] He sought out another professional opinion on the matter, this time from Professor Eric Linnel from the University of Toronto's Department of Neuropathology. After examining the skull, it was Professor Linnel's professional opinion that "this opening is in the classical position for the operation of trephining of the skull for hemmorrage following a head injury."[4] This conclusion was agree-able to Dr. Sharpe.

With the issue of the head wound now settled to his satisfac-tion, Dr. Sharpe still required some further forensic information about the bones in order to put a sharper point on the age of their owner at the time of death, the sex of the person, his or her prob-able height, and ethnicity. For an opinion on this he then delivered the bones to the British-Canadian anatomist John Charles Boileau Grant, who was then in his final year of serving as chair of Anatomy at the University of Toronto's Faculty of Medicine, a position he had held since 1930. Grant's work in anatomy was not only lauded during his lifetime but is renowned to this day, owing largely to the textbook on the subject that bears his name—*Grant's Atlas of Anatomy*—which has had thirteen printings and is still used by medical students from all over the world.

Professor Grant took possession of the bones, but was told nothing about their presumed identity, nor was he provided with any photographs of Tom Thomson for purposes of comparison, as such could possibly prejudice his conclusions. After analyzing the bones and making certain measurements, Grant turned in a report of his analysis to Dr. Sharpe.[5] Once Sharpe had time to review Professor

Grant's report, he, in turn, advised Attorney General Kelso Roberts of its conclusions, chiefly that the bones from the Mowat Cemetery were not those of Tom Thomson, but of an indigenous person who had died while in his mid twenties. As Sharpe had not yet finished his final report, the cause of the hole in the skull was not addressed at this time. It was decided that Attorney General Roberts should release a statement to the Canadian press to quell the growing speculation that the skeleton belonged to Tom Thomson and, on October 19, the story broke nation wide:

KELSO ROBERTS, ALGONQUIN PARK BONES NOT THOSE OF THOMSON
Toronto Daily Star, October 19, 1956
A mysterious skeleton dug from an unmarked grave on a lonely hill in Algonquin Park three weeks ago is not that of Canadian painter Tom Thomson, Attorney-General Kelso Roberts said yesterday.

Mr. Roberts said it has been determined the bones are those of a male Indian or half-breed of about 20 years of age. He said officials are continuing their investigation of a hole in the skull.[6]

By October 30, 1956, Dr. Sharpe had completed his official report on the matter. He later made some revisions and crafted a final report on December 12, 1956. The contents of both reports were fascinating.

1. The bones found were those of an Indigenous person or nearly full breed Indigenous person.
2. The sex of the skeleton was male.
3. The estimated height of the deceased was 5'8" (give or take two inches).

4. The person had been muscular and robust in stature.
5. The age of the person at the time of death would have been twenty to thirty years.
6. The indigenous person, in Sharpe's opinion, "was buried in Mr. Thomson's original grave, either in or on top of his empty coffin."[7]

It was evident that, at least in 1956, forensic anthropology was still an inexact science as there was some confusion as to the length of time that the experts thought the body had been buried. Indeed, Dr. Sharpe presented conflicting conclusions on this topic, sometimes even within the same report. Professor Grant had gone on record in his report indicating that the body had been buried "Over ten or fifteen years, but how much longer I cannot say."[8] Dr. Sharpe, however, stated in his report from October 30, 1956 that, "It is impossible to be definite about this. The bones are so light (from loss of calcium) that burial could be 20 to 40 years and even longer."[9] However, by the time he got to the Conclusions section of this same report, he was of the opinion that the body had been "buried for twenty years at least, more likely 20 than longer."[10] His basis for this belief was the absence of flesh on the bones, particularly after learning that Thomson's body had been embalmed.

In his final report on the matter dated December 12, 1956, Dr. Sharpe reiterated his opinion that that the body had "been buried for 20 years at least, more likely 30 to 40." But then added "From recent tests not then available, I place the time of burial up to 20 years before 1956, not longer."[11] While these were educated guesses, the reality is that neither Grant nor Sharpe knew conclusively how long the body had been buried and, indeed, Sharpe had indicated that it was "impossible to be definite" about this fact. However, he felt comfortable that twenty years (give or take) was a good estimate.

There are, of course, some problems with some of these conclusions, chiefly that if the body had been buried in the Mowat Cemetery in Tom Thomson's original casket in 1936, why would nobody from the area have known of such a burial having taken place? Secondly, the belief that flesh should still have been on the body after a forty-year interment is an opinion contrary to fact. When the author spoke with Paul Faris, retired professor, Funeral Service Education, at Humber College in Toronto, the facts that Thomson's body was already decomposed to some extent prior to being embalmed, that there was water (seepage) in the grave (according to Sharpe's report),[12] that the oak casket would not have been air tight as it had rotted out and pretty much disappeared by 1956, and that undertakers during the era that Thomson was buried routinely made their own embalming fluid (thus its potency varied), he believed that forty years was more than enough time for all of the flesh to have disappeared.

And finally, the "tests" that Sharpe refers to that allowed him to pinpoint the time of burial as being no later than twenty years are not specified. More importantly, if these tests were not available to the department in October, when the department had the bones in hand and when he filed his first report with the attorney general's office, that means that they must have come into existence sometime in November or early December (by the time Dr. Sharpe filed his final report). Dr. Sharpe's earlier conclusion was based on the fact that there had been a loss of calcium indicative that the bones had been buried for thirty to forty years or longer, so the new tests must have established that the bones had somehow acquired additional calcium since their original inspection in October to suggest a shorter time of burial.

There would be other problems with Dr. Sharpe's report/s that we shall consider later, but even prior to Dr. Sharpe's first report having been submitted to the attorney general's office, the news that the bones were not those of Tom Thomson had left the four men who had first discovered them incredulous. In my father's conversations with people in the Canoe Lake area, many of whom had been living in the region since before the turn of the twentieth century, none had ever heard of any other bodies being buried in the little cemetery other than James Watson, Alexander Hayhurst, and (for a time at least) Tom Thomson. What made the matter even more bizarre was that the provincial police had advised that the rotted remains of both the casket and outbox were, in fact, those in which the artist had originally been buried.[13] This, in turn, posed a very intriguing question: how would another body—belonging to an indigenous person—find its way into a casket that had been occupied by Tom Thomson at (depending upon which statement of Dr. Sharpe's you were looking at) approximately the same date that the artist had been buried in it?

In defending his department's conclusion on the matter during an interview with the CBC in 1969, Dr. Sharpe advanced a theory about how this might have occurred, indicating that the area where the grave was located had been a common place for native people to "roam" and was in fact a portage that they had used. To his way of thinking, "If an accident occurred, or maybe foul play or a fight, and a death resulted, they would naturally want to get rid of the body quickly. They wouldn't waste clothing on it. And they would dig in a place where digging was easy. And this hill where these graves were would be an easy place to dig."[14]

When the CBC approached my father for comment on Dr. Sharpe's hypothesis, he was happy to oblige:

I can't subscribe to it on either count; first of all, there is no portage by the little cemetery, the closest portage is a matter of a mile and a half and doesn't go by that section whatsoever. As far as an Indian being slipped surreptitiously in a casket, when, indeed, nobody knew there was any casket there, is rather difficult to believe. And roving bands of Indians have not been noted to have been in Algonquin Park since long before the turn of the century.[15]

One man who would later come out in support of Dr. Sharpe's conclusion, however, was Charles Plewman, who had been present on the day that Thomson had been buried. According to Plewman:

> As to the skeleton that was recently unearthed at Canoe Lake and which some people firmly believe was Tom Thomson's, I am strongly of the opinion that it was that of an Indian. This was the verdict of the experts in this field. Apart from all of this, I am told that an Indian was buried in this cemetery around 1894 and probably other persons too. Fifty-five years is a long time in which to recall with accuracy what happened at that time, but to the best of my knowledge, I would have to say that we buried Thomson inside the area enclosed by a small fence. The skeleton that was unearthed was found outside, not inside, the railing. In any event it is hard to imagine what ulterior motive would cause the undertaker not to follow the family's instructions of sending the body to Owen Sound for interment in the family plot at Leith. After all he did make the trip to Canoe Lake for that purpose.[16]

If we are to grant legitimacy to statements that Plewman made on other topics, such as his hearing the suicide rumor from Shannon Fraser, and his details regarding the burial of Tom Thomson, we cannot simply discount his testimony on this matter. As with his other statements, however, we can examine it critically. There exists, for example, corroborating evidence for Plewman's belief that

Shannon Fraser had spread the rumor of Thomson's suicide, as well as for the circumstances he described regarding the day of the artist's funeral. However, there exists no such corroborating evidence for Plewman's belief that an indigenous person was buried in the same cemetery that Thomson was shortly before the turn of the previous century, as he does not name a source from whom he might have obtained this information.

Additionally, the alleged date of burial as suggested by Plewman is at odds with the analysis from the crime lab on how long the bones they examined had been buried (Grant and Sharpe were of the opinion that the bones had been buried for a period of twenty to forty years prior to being exhumed in 1956; i.e., they were interred sometime between 1916-1935, while Plewman stated that the indigenous person that he had heard about had been buried in 1894; i.e., twenty years earlier than the oldest time allotted by the forensics laboratory in analyzing the bones).

Given that Plewman made his statement on this matter some sixteen years after the attorney general had made the crime lab's findings public, it is likely that he was simply repeating the Attorney General's conclusion, which of course had been published in the newspapers (indeed, his statement, "the verdict was made by experts in the field," refers to this very point). His recollection that others had been buried in the Mowat Cemetery is certainly true, as the headstones of James Watson and Alexander Hayhurst bear witness to this. His contention that Thomson had been buried within the fenced in area of the cemetery, however, is directly at odds with the recollection of Mark Robinson, who also had been present at the funeral and, indeed, had been the one who had organized it. The ranger had related that the original burial spot for Thomson was outside of the enclosed area.

FIRST NATIONS PEOPLE WEIGH IN

So far the only opinions on the matter that have been considered are those of Caucasians, who do not share the same burial customs as our indigenous peoples. Consequently, if in fact the person that had been buried in the Mowat gravesite that was exhumed in 1956 had been native, then one would presume that someone within the indigenous community in Algonquin Park might have some information on the deceased. To this end, the author contacted the Algonquins of Ontario Consultation Office and was informed that they knew of no such member of their band having been buried in the Mowat Cemetery. Moreover, Aimee Bailey, the Heritage and Cultural Planner of the Consultation Office of the Algonquins, informed me that the burial of an indigenous person would have included the interment of specific items with the deceased:

> Our people would have been carrying a bundle, containing personal items that they would use on a day-to-day basis that had a spiritual basis. I find it hard to believe that in all of Algonquin Park they would happen upon a location and find an empty casket in it. Moreover, when we bury our dead we typically re-clothe them in their ceremonial regalia. Now if the indigenous person had been converted to Christianity he might not have been dressed in the ceremonial regalia, but he would have been dressed, and so buttons should have been found in the grave. He would also have been buried with a tobacco pouch, which was typically made of deerskin, that would be used as a prayer offering, and that should have survived. If done in the community, especially if the death was expected, the people would have made things to include in with the burial, embroideries, etc., but if the death occurred suddenly out in the woods, they most certainly

would have buried him with a tobacco pouch and medicine bag, which might have contained sacred items such as bear claws, roots, and perhaps a pipe.[17]

As no such items were found within the grave at Canoe Lake when exhumed, it argues against the body that was unearthed being that of a native.

But if the body was not indigenous (according to the Algonquins) and not Thomson's (according to Professor Grant and Dr. Sharpe), then it had to belong to a Caucasian that just happened to be buried in an unmarked grave at a time that predated the existing marked graves or that otherwise went unrecorded. This belief first surfaced in 1956, shortly after news of the discovery of the skeleton had gotten out, when the *Globe and Mail* newspaper ran a story by Don Delaplante, in which he indicated that there were in fact other bodies buried in the Mowat Cemetery beyond the three previously indicated:

> Some residents think the body may be that of an unidentified lumberjack who worked for the Gilmour firm many years ago. Mrs. Jean Chittendon said she had been told there are several unmarked graves adjacent to those of Hayhurst and Watson.[18]

The fact that my father and his three companions dug in two spots adjacent to the graves of Hayhurst and Watson and found nothing negates the validity of what Mrs. Chittendon had been told about the location of even one additional grave being in that location. However, the belief that there was an "unidentified lumberjack" buried in the Mowat cemetery gained traction many years later when Thomson researcher and author Neil Lehto discovered what he believed was the identity of this individual. His sleuthing had turned up a name—Antoine Chouinard—and this looked promising. Chouinard was a Roman Catholic French Canadian who had been born in Trenton, Ontario but resided at Canoe Lake, and was employed by the Gilmour Lumber Company. Lehto's research indicated that Mr. Chouinard had been killed in an accident, presumably while working at the sawmill at Canoe Lake, and his death was recorded as having occurred on September 25, 1897. He was forty-two-years old.[19] Unfortunately, as Lehto admits, the Ontario government registrar, J. A. Diversey, in his annual report of deaths for the Division of Murchison, District Nippissing, while indicating the death of Chouinard on September 25, 1897, did not make mention of Chouinard's place of burial. While one can infer that, like James Watson the Gilmour Lumber employee who died four months before Chouinard, that Mr. Chouinard would likewise be buried in the same cemetery as his colleague, the absence of a headstone (as was put up for Watson), and no record of his being buried there, does give one pause. Moreover, the grave that was opened in 1956 was twenty-one feet north of the fenced in area of the cemetery that contained Mr. Watson's grave. As Chouinard's would have been the second Gilmour lumber company employee to be buried in the Mowat Cemetery, his burial area would have constituted the cemetery proper, so why would he be buried in an unmarked grave so far away from where Watson was buried? This is not to suggest that it couldn't have happened, but rather to advance the proposition that there is no hard evidence that it did.

But there are other problems to consider with regard to another Caucasian body having been buried in the Mowat Cemetery besides Watson and Thomson (as the Hayhurst grave contained the body of a young boy, and is clearly marked, I shall omit it from this consideration of the matter). To begin, if Chouinard, a Roman Catholic lumberman, was in fact the body found within the grave that was opened in 1956, there should have been evidence that would be supportive of a burial of someone of French Canadian ancestry. Thomson, the reader will recall, had been buried nude, save for the shroud that he had been wrapped in, as his clothing had to be removed to allow for a full medical inspection and embalming immediately prior to burial. This, one would have to admit, would have been atypical. Unless Antoine Chouinard had died under the exact same circumstances as the artist, such a procedure as the one indicated above would not have been necessary. That is to say, there would not have existed a need to remove the deceased's clothing in order to determine a cause of death, nor would there have been a need to wrap the body in a shroud, but rather the deceased would have been buried in the manner that most people are who are of European or French Canadian ancestry; i.e., dressed in whatever clothing his family (or friends or colleagues if the family wasn't available) considered appropriate. And if this was the case then evidence of such clothing—buttons from a shirt, a buckle from a belt, a ring from a finger, a neck chain (and, being a practicing Roman Catholic, a cross or other Christian artifact), nails from a boot, eyelets from footwear, rivets from jeans, etc.—should have been present in the grave when it was opened. And despite being told to search for such items, the men who opened the Mowat Cemetery grave found no such materials even after specifically sieving for them.

And then there exist the same problems that faced people such as my father when he believed that the skeletal remains belonged to Tom Thomson. To begin, the fact that the skeletal remains that were exhumed from the Mowat cemetery were determined to have been buried no longer than fifteen to twenty years (Sharpe/Grant) to forty years (Sharpe). A burial in 1897 would have put the remains in the ground for sixty years prior to their exhumation, which is some twenty years beyond the longest time allotted as being possible by the crime lab. Moreover, the forensics of the time deemed the bones to be indigenous, while Chouinard was Caucasian, and the sutures in the skull suggested to Professor Grant an age of between twenty and thirty years; Chouinard was forty-two.

Adding further intrigue to the matter, within Dr. Noble Sharpe's official report on the Canoe Lake skeleton, is the statement:

> The coffin appears to be too expensive for an Indian or casual worker such as a lumberjack. Sifting the contents showed up no rings or buttons. Only fragments of the canvas covering were found. Part of a sock remained on one foot. . . . So the body was buried naked, except for one sock, or in a shroud without buttons.[20]

This statement is telling for a number of reasons, particularly Sharpe's reference to the existence of the remains of a single sock (which was corroborated by Corporal Rodgers in his report) and it speaks strongly against the skeletal remains from the Mowat Cemetery as belonging to either Chouinard or an indigenous person. If the corpse had been clothed when buried then surely remnants of clothing over and above a single sock should have been found. It would be a very odd burial custom indeed—whether we are talking about indigenous or non-indigenous people—to bury someone "naked, except for one sock." In researching indigenous burial traditions the author could find no evidence of such a practice amongst our First Nations population (nor, for what it's worth, among non-indigenous peoples). And if a Caucasian family or group wished to bury one of their own in what Sharpe insultingly believed was a coffin thought "to be too expensive for an Indian or casual worker such as a lumberjack," why hadn't the nameplate been inscribed with the name of the deceased? The nameplate on Thomson's casket had not been inscribed because of the haste with which the burial took place; a normal burial would not have required such haste, and, thus, such a standard formality should have been observed. Moreover, if those who buried the deceased had time to order such an "expensive" casket for the occasion, then its safe to assume that they would also have had time to have a name-plate inscribed and to fully dress the corpse. Again, there exists no known European/Caucasian burial tradition that requires that the deceased be wrapped in a canvas shroud completely naked except for a single sock.

The existence of this solitary article of clothing suggests one of two things—either a heretofore-unprecedented burial custom was observed, or that in their haste to remove Thomson's clothing for the medical inspection a single sock had remained on the corpse and was either overlooked or ignored when Thomson's body was stripped for examination by Dr. Howland. I'll leave it to the reader to decide which of these scenarios is the most probable.

Still, the professionals in such matters had now spoken—the bones that had been exhumed from the Mowat Cemetery had been professionally analyzed and deemed not to have been Caucasian at all, but rather those of an indigenous person. And despite my father's incredulity at the attorney general's official conclusion, the reality was that my father was not a forensic anthropologist and, thus, his opinion on the matter held a degree of significance that fell somewhere between "zero" and "very little," particularly when contrasted with that of those whose business was the forensic knowledge of bones.

After the crime lab's analysis, Corporal Rodger placed the bones back into the same cardboard Sunkist Oranges box that they had been transported to the crime lab in, and then reinterred the box of bones within the same grave at the Mowat Cemetery from which they had been removed. A small white cross was then erected atop the grave, indicating to all amateur sleuths of the future that this was now an official grave, and that if anyone should choose to disturb it, they would now be proceeding at their legal peril. The cross that the government erected bore no inscription—and so it remains to this day—for the simple reason that nobody knows to whom the bones belong.

Chapter Seventeen

AFTERMATH

Dr. Sharpe had relied solely on Professor Grant's interpretation of the bones in determining the race, age, sex, and estimated height of the skeleton. The professor had written in his notes that, "The skull could hardly be that of a white man. Some of the facial features are strongly mongoloid—and under the circumstances of location—presumably having North American Blood."[1]

The "circumstances of location" would be in reference to the fact that the bones were found in Algonquin Park, rather than, say, Toronto and, thus, in the professor's estimation, they were far more likely to be indigenous than Caucasian. In addition, the facial features that struck Professor Grant as being "strongly Mongoloid" were most notably the high cheekbones of the skull, a trait common to our indigenous peoples. However, "common" does mean "exclusive to," and upon examining photographs of Thomson we note that the artist did in fact possess very high cheekbones. Indeed, this was noted by certain of those who knew the artist, such as Blanche Packard, who recollected that the artist was "high cheek-boned in the Indian way."[2] And given that Professor Grant had not been given any photographs of Thomson to compare with the skull when he made his analysis, he would not have been aware of this fact of Thomson's physiognomy.

Another factor that had led Professor Grant to the conclusion that the skeletal remains he examined had belonged to an indigenous person were the teeth, in particular the shovel-shaped upper incisors. While there have been people of European ancestry that have displayed shovel-shaped upper incisors, the belief (particularly in 1956) was that this was a predominantly Asian (Mongoloid) trait that was quite common in indigenous peoples, and considerably less so in Caucasoids. This fact, together with the high cheekbones and the locale where the body was found, had convinced the professor that the bones were undoubtably those of an indigenous person.

Dr. Harry Ebbs had been surprised by the crime lab's conclusion regarding the ethnicity of the skeleton that he had helped to exhume and, unlike Professor Grant, Ebbs had a long-standing knowledge of Tom Thomson. Looking to correct what he perceived as an innocent oversight, he collected some photographs of the artist and travelled to Toronto to share them with Professor Grant. However, Grant remained undeterred. According to Ebbs:

> I asked him if he even looked at the photograph of Tom Thomson, the one of him standing with his canoe, in which I pointed out the cheekbones were high and that I didn't know of any Indian ancestry in the Thomson family. On the other hand, there was certainly a resemblance in that regard but as far as I was concerned, the facial contour in the photograph would certainly fit that particular skull . . . he stuck to it [his report] . . . He was a person you didn't argue with.[3]

A QUESTION OF HEIGHT

The only skeletal remains that Professor Grant had received for purposes of analysis were the skull and lower jaw, the first three cervical vertebrae, the sacrum and hipbones, along with the right and left femur and tibia, the right and left humerus and radius, and left ulna.[4] Most of the spinal bones were absent as were the bones comprising the rib cage. While the missing torso bones would have been helpful in more accurately determining the height of the deceased, absent that, most calculations of stature are based upon the length of the femur and/or tibia, and so Professor Grant felt comfortable in measuring these for the purpose of estimating the stature of the skeleton. Based upon the calculus he was using in 1956, he made the following projection:

> The femora were 47.2 cm. long and the tibiae 38.2 cm. Accordingly, the stature in life should have been 5 feet 8 inches (five feet, eight inches) +/- 2 inches.[5]

Professor Grant's calculus indicated that the person to whom the skeleton once belonged would have stood somewhere between five feet, six inches and five feet, ten inches in height. Upon reading the professor's report, Dr. Sharpe concluded that since he had read in books that Thomson was reported to be six feet tall, this clearly could not have been his skeleton.[6] However, the various calculi for determining height based upon the measurement of the femur and tibia bones has proven to be anything but exact over the years. When the author typed "femur measurement to determine height" into an internet search engine, he was given the formula of "length of bone in centimeters, x 2.6 + 65." As the femur from the Mowat Cemetery measured 47.2 centimeters, applying this formula resulted in the final number being 187.72 centimeters or an estimated height of six feet, 1.906 inches. When I contacted the University of Toronto's Department of Anthropology, Professor Tracey Rogers, via Ashley Smith, provided me with a formula that they use to estimate height from femur and tibia measurement that is based upon research performed by forensic anthropologists Mildred Trotter and Goldine Gleser in 1952.[7] When this formula is applied, the projected height of the skeleton from the

Mowat Cemetery comes out at five feet, 9.758 inches.[8] When the plus/minus calculation of 3.58 centimeters is factored in we get an estimated stature of 173.606 centimeters or five feet, 8.349 inches on the low side of the projection, and 180.766 centimeters or five feet, 11.168 inches on the high side. These last two calculi (the search engine and Trotter and Gleser) put the projected height of the skeleton very close to (or in the case of the search engine, slightly higher than) the six-foot stature that Dr. Sharpe had read regarding Thomson's height.

However, while the general image of Thomson is that of a man who stood approximately six feet tall, the author has not come across any evidence in the surviving literature that establishes categorically what the artist's height actually was. It is certainly true that Thomson had been considered by some to be "tall," however according to an article published by the CBC, the height of the average Canadian male in 1914 was five feet, seven inches (it is presently five feet, ten inches).[9] Consequently, in Thomson's era one didn't have to be six feet in height in order to be considered tall. Indeed, any man who was taller than five feet, seven inches would be considered taller than average, and any man below this height would have been considered shorter than average. The only person that the author ever met who had once stood next to Thomson was Ralph Bice, who claimed to have walked past the artist at a Regatta in 1915. When I asked him how tall Thomson was, Bice replied that he was roughly the same height as the author (i.e., five feet, ten inches). If the trapper's recollection is accurate, then Professor Grant's projected height of the Canoe Lake skeleton as being five feet, eight inches with a plus/minus of two-inches, would place the high end of the skeleton's estimated height at five feet, ten inches—the same height that Bice had estimated the artist to be. However, in Audrey Saunders's notes from her interview with Molly Colson in 1944, when she asked about Thomson's appearance Colson had replied,

"Round face, not tall."[10] Consequently, in the final analysis, the attempt to pin down an exact height for Thomson (or the skeleton that some believed to have been Thomson's) is speculative at best.

TREPHINING

And then there was the issue of what had caused the hole in the temple region of the Canoe Lake skull. Quite apart from Dr. Ebbs and Corporal Rodger believing that a bullet had caused the hole, Dr. Sharpe himself had originally shared the same conclusion. But then, as his report from December 12, 1956 indicated, he later suspected that it might have been the result of blunt force trauma from a pick, a small hammer, an arrowhead, or possibly a peevee.[11] He later changed his mind again and, based upon his conversations with Professor Linnell from the University of Toronto, came to an entirely different conclusion regarding what caused the hole in the skull:

> Prof. Eric Linnel of the Dept. of Neuropathology agrees this opening is in the classical position for the operation of trephining of the skull for haemorrhage following a head injury.[12]

Trephination is an ancient (some authorities say the oldest in human history) surgical procedure. It consists of boring a hole in the skull, and the reasons for having such a procedure performed have ranged from releasing evil spirits to relieving pressure on the brain. It is obviously a very delicate surgical procedure and, by 1917, if performed at all, was only undertaken in a hospital that was equipped for such an operation. Dr. Ebbs considered this a highly unusual operation both in itself and particularly for that time period. He decided to go to the attorney general's office and confront Dr. Noble Sharpe about it:

The hole in the skull he said could have been due to a trephining operation to probe the inside of the brain. I countered that by saying I didn't think that in 1917 there was very much of that operating being done, and that it was hard to believe that an Indian would have had an operation like that and go up to Algonquin Park without anybody knowing anything about it. However, he stuck to his guns and we argued about it but he stuck to it.[13]

In Dr. Sharpe's report he had indicated that he had discussed the hole in the Canoe Lake skull with Professor Eric Linnel from the Department of Neuropathology at the University of Toronto and that Linnel had agreed that, "this opening is in the classical position for the operation of trephining of the skull for hemorrhage following a head injury." Such a statement doesn't really resolve anything, however, as the only "head injury" that was noted on the skull was the hole itself. By Dr. Sharpe's own statement, "No radiating fractures were seen in x-ray,"[14] so there was no indication of the head being damaged in any way save for the three-quarter inch hole that he believed had apparently been bored into its left temple. Moreover, it's very hard to determine exactly what the "classical position" is for a trephining surgical procedure. If "classical" can be likened to "most common" then there is a problem with Professor Linnel and Dr. Sharpe's conclusion, as most photographs of skulls that have undergone this procedure depict a hole that is drilled (or in older times scraped) most frequently into the parietal (top) section of the skull, and less frequently in the occipital (rear) and frontal sections—but not the temple area, which is where the hole was located on the skull.

It is indisputable that Tom Thomson had suffered a wound to his head just prior to his death and that the skull of the man that was found in the grave at the Mowat cemetery had likewise suffered a wound in the same location shortly before his death—an interesting coincidence, perhaps, but still far from conclusive. One thing known about the wound in the Mowat cemetery skull, however, was that the person to whom the skull belonged died almost immediately after suffering it. Indeed, one of the medical directors at the crime lab, Dr. Frederick Jaffe, in examining photos of the wound on the skull, indicated that:

> I can see on the photograph [of the skull] that there is no evidence of healing of these wound edges. And this would indicate that whatever caused this hole caused it shortly before the death of this individual.[15]

In other words, contrary to Dr. Sharpe's belief that the trephining operation had been performed "following" a head injury, there was no indication of any head injury that would have required a trephining operation to be performed. Indeed, the hole itself was the only wound found on the skull. So we are left with the fact that a trephining operation was performed for no apparent reason and that it was the surgical procedure itself that led to the almost immediate death of the person who received it. The deceased was then transported to the Mowat cemetery where he was buried in Tom Thomson's original grave and inside what was left of the artist's original casket. As to whether or not the remains found in that grave were those of Tom Thomson, my father believed until his dying day that this was a mystery that could be settled easily. He held that:

> The question of where Thomson is buried could be very easily established if we had an opportunity to know what was in the grave at Leith. We would then be sure that, indeed, the body had been transferred there. Until that happens, I think we have to speculate, and on very firm ground, that the body was never taken from Canoe Lake and is still there.[16]

The suggestion that the casket at Leith be exhumed was surprisingly (given his certitude regarding the ethnicity of the Mowat cemetery skeleton) a position that was supported by Dr. Noble Sharpe:

> I would like to see this solved. I think that a lot of people don't accept our findings entirely and I would like to see them satisfied. And the only way to do it that I can see is to open the grave at Leith and see if Tom Thomson actually is there.[17]

This was also the thought shared by a subsequent head of the Ontario Crime Lab, Mr. Doug Lucas:

> I feel, as I'm sure anyone who has read this story feels, that there's only one way of actually proving where Tom Thomson is buried and that is by examining the grave at Leith.[18]

But this was never going to happen for reasons that will be explored later. The identity of the skeleton from the Mowat Cemetery had been established categorically by the attorney general's department, and was the official and final word on the matter; the bones were those of an indigenous person, not Tom Thomson. And who, apart from hubris intoxicated amateur sleuths (like authors of books about the late artist) would dare to dispute the learned conclusions of people who were specialists in matters of forensic anthropology?

Perhaps indeed the bones were those of an indigenous person who had died as a result of an obscure medical operation that had been performed behind Mowat Lodge in and around the time that the artist was buried and who ended up being buried in Thomson's empty casket. Perhaps. But according to Dr. Harry Ebbs, other factors might have been at play during this time as well. If the skeleton had turned out to be that of Tom Thomson, an investigation of sorts would then have followed to determine the cause of death, and this was not an enterprise that the attorney general's office was interested in.

Shortly after the crime lab had released their report on the Canoe Lake skeleton, Dr. Ebbs found himself called into a meeting with Attorney General Kelso Roberts and Frank MacDougall, the deputy minister of the Department of Lands and Forests. During this meeting it was put to the good doctor that nothing more was going to come of things:

> And so then we had a meeting with the attorney general and Frank MacDougall and agreed that because of the family, the Thomson family, did not wish to have the thing opened up and anymore fuss. They were satisfied with the verdict of accidental drowning and they would like it just left alone.[19]

The Thomson family's wishes, then, appeared to have played a roll in staving off any further investigation into the matter. The Thomson family wanted the matter dropped. And so it was.

Since their reburial in the Mowat Cemetery in 1956, the skeletal remains have continued to decompose inside a cardboard box under four feet of earth within the same grave from which they had originally been removed. As to the bones in the grave, no one has stepped forth to claim them—be they native or Caucasian—and all efforts to more precisely identify these remains have been blocked.

But if these are indeed the bones of the Canadian icon Tom Thomson, a less dignified send off would be hard to imagine.

Chapter Eighteen

DAMAGE CONTROL

If nothing else, the news of the 1956 dig had served to bring to the nation's attention the fact that the death and burial of one of their most beloved historical figures was not as well settled as had once generally been believed. Still, after the attorney general had ruled on the matter, the issue eventually receded from the public's consciousness, as more current affairs assumed center stage.

But in 1968, the Canadian Broadcasting Corporation (CBC) decided to produce a documentary that would thoroughly explore the evidence surrounding Tom Thomson's death and burial. Their researchers, in addition to conducting their own investigation into the matter, reached out to my father to provide details not only of the dig that he was a party to, but also to share some of the information he had picked up over the years from having interviewed individuals who had known the artist personally such as Shannon Fraser, the ranger Bud Callighan, and Mark Robinson. Dr. Noble Sharpe was also interviewed before the cameras to reiterate his conclusions regarding the skeleton that he had exhumed and examined in 1956.

The documentary would air in 1969, and came down firmly on the side that the artist had likely been the victim of foul play and that it was probable that his body had never left its original grave at the Mowat Cemetery. The broadcast of the documentary was seen by millions of Canadians and soon there was a growing wave of public support for opening the grave at Leith in order to find out if, in fact, the artist's body had ever been interred there.

While the documentary had enjoyed high ratings, it had not been well received within the city of Owen Sound, where the majority of the surviving members of the Thomson family resided. While the community was certainly proud of their native son, they had no interest in shining a brighter light on the matter of how he met his end. And sometime after the CBC documentary had aired, persons within Gray County had decided that something had to be done to make the matter go away.

Tom Thomson's older brother George, along with the Owen Sound Junior Board of Trade, even as early as 1956, had been attempting to solicit funds publically to build a memorial Art Center to the memory of the fallen artist and part of their pitch had indicated that Owen Sound was not only Thomson's home during his formative years but was also the region in which his body was buried.[1] Consequently, local interest in the creation of an art gallery that would honor the artist's memory and bring government funding into the area rose rapidly within Owen Sound. Two years prior to the release of the CBC documentary, the Tom Thomson Art Gallery (TOM) had been established, opening its doors on May 27, 1967. As Tom Thomson was the drawing card that led to its creation and that kept the donations flowing in, preserving his image as that of the heroic artist who drowned accidently in Canoe Lake and was buried near his old childhood home in Leith was a high priority. And thus far their efforts had been well rewarded; Thomson's name and works of art would bring the gallery in ten short years from being but a small room to a magnificent building of its own that showcased works not only of Tom Thomson, but also other regional artists. In 2017, its website described its vision as being "recognized as the guardian of Tom Thomson's story, his work and his legacy. The TOM will be his foremost authoritative interpreter."[2]

The Thomson family had been major contributors to the gallery since its inception and their largess had been, as the TOM freely admitted in 2017, largely responsible for its "stability and credibility."[3] And so the gallery readily adopted the vision of the artist that the Thomson family and art people such as Dr. MacCallum wished to have put forth, particularly in regard to sensitive matters such as how he died and (particularly) where he was buried. Consequently, when the CBC aired its program indicating that there were grounds for believing that the artist had been murdered (not drowned accidentally) and that his body had never left its original grave in the Mowat Cemetery (let alone been buried in the family plot in Leith), this was totally opposed to the beliefs advanced by the gallery and was viewed as a direct assault upon its authority in such matters. Consequently, it was decided that there was too much at stake to let such allegations go unchecked.

The result was an article published in the *Owen Sound Sun-Times* on February 8, 1969, which made it clear that the Thomson family, along with the good folks of Gray County, were not welcoming of any further inquiries into the matter:

TOM THOMSON FAMILY WILL BAR EXHUMATION OF BODY
A CBC TV producer's demands that the grave at Leith [be opened], where most accept lie the remains of the world famed Canadian artist, Tom Thomson, pioneer of the Group of Seven school of Canadian art, have aroused considerable revulsion in Owen Sound.

Not only do people, many of them long time friends of members of the Thomson family, feel that opening the grave 50 years after the painter's death would be in very bad taste and would cause surviving members of his direct family great anguish, but they can see no point, even should the unlikely suggestion he was murdered be indicated to be true . . . The final decision must rest with the surviving members of the family, two sisters and a nephew. The latter, Geo. Thomson [the son of Tom's elder brother George], of the Brantford Art Gallery, stated that his aunts, himself, and other members of the family will not give permission to open the grave neither now nor at any time.[4]

The author or authors of the article had created a straw man of sorts, as the producer of the CBC documentary, Peter Kelly, had at no time issued a "demand" to anyone to have the grave at Leith opened. However, the article's statement that, "they can see no point, even should the unlikely suggestion he was murdered be indicated to be true" was particularly telling, as it revealed that the truth of how Tom Thomson had met his death was of no matter at all to the Thomson family and their friends that the article was representing. The article then made the following claim:

There has never been question in the minds of any members of the family but that Thomson died accidently, as stated officially following the inquest which found death by drowning.[5]

The record shows that the above claim is simply not true. Tom's older brother George Thomson, for example, had gone on the record twice, indicating his belief that foul play might have been involved.[6] Fraser Thomson, Tom's younger brother, had likewise spoken publically that he had no idea how his brother had died, but had indicated a feud with a German as being a possibility.[7] Thomson's sister Margaret had written a letter to Dr. MacCallum indicating that Shannon Fraser might have had something to do with the death of her brother and believed the motive might have been robbery.[8] So, quite clearly there had been considerable question in the minds of the Thomson siblings regarding the official verdict of accidental death by drowning. Still, to show that it wasn't simply the Thomson family that would object to any further probing into the matter, and to show strength in numbers, the paper presented the names of eight citizens, along with their statements, that largely condemned any attempt to solve the mystery by opening the grave at Leith.

The first person quoted was Mrs. S. H. Pearce, who had been active in establishing the Tom Thomson Memorial Art Gallery in Owen Sound for the artist. She expressed her belief that the 1956 dig wasn't a step to resolve the mystery of Thomson's resting place but rather the work of "a group of ghouls."[9] Next up was Ald. Clifford Waugh, who was then a city council representative on the civic gallery committee. He chastised the CBC, who, "in their stupidity, have deliberately tried to destroy the image of this revered artist."[10] Then came Mrs. John Harrison, the president of the women's gallery committee, who actually broke rank when she said she thought the mystery should be cleared up,[11] but her voice was countered by William Parrott, the head of the art department at the Owen Sound Collegiate and Vocational Institute (OSCVI), who drew an odd parallel with his statement that, "Christians do not feel they need to know beyond doubt where Christ is buried before they can honor him, so why should we feel we need to know the location of Tom Thomson's grave in order to honor him?"[12] (The reader will note that my earlier "St. Thomas" reference wasn't so far off the mark at this point.) Then W. M. Prudham, a former principal of the OSCVI, opined that he thought that opening the grave would remove all doubt, but this was quickly shot down by Mrs. John Rowe, a member of the gallery committee, who opposed the plan, stating "I think the idea of digging up graves is horrible."[13] Mrs. K.C. Quirk, another member of the gallery committee, weighed in with her opinion that an "exhumation would be pointless"; which, given that the thesis of the article was not the pursuit of truth in the matter of how the artist met his death, was perfectly in keeping.[14]

And finally there was the opinion of Stan Latham, from CFOS radio, who attempted to wax poetic by stating, "I would say we do him dishonor to wrangle over his bones. Let the mystery remain with him and the good earth he loved so well and held as sacred."[15]

It's telling that six of the eight people that the *Owen Sound Sun-Times* elected to poll were members of their local art community, which of course benefitted from the prestige of the Thomson Gallery and the Thomson image that been crafted long before by MacCallum and the Thomson family. Their unanimity in protest was supposed to serve as a shot over the bow, a warning, from the Thomson family and the people of Owen Sound to leave well enough alone, and that any attempt to determine the true location of Thomson's final resting place would be vigorously opposed.

MUCH ADO ABOUT NOTHING

And the Gray County pushback didn't stop there. Two days after the above article appeared, the same paper had, in a very timely fashion, come into a scoop of sorts; some fascinating information that would clearly prove—without having to disturb the grave at Leith at all—that all of this speculation about Thomson's body never having left Algonquin Park was but a tempest in a teacup. The paper broke the story that not only had the body been viewed prior to its interment at Leith, but that Tom Thomson's father had insisted upon viewing it prior to burial:

> Two elderly ladies who were childhood neighbors of Tom Thomson and his family, Misses Agnes and Margaret McKeen, R.R. 1, Owen Sound, recall clearly the burial of Tom Thomson in the Leith Cemetery, following his tragic drowning at Canoe Lake, Algonquin Park. Their comments were

aroused by the present revived controversy as to whether or not the famous Canadian artist is actually buried at Leith and whether or not his death was accidental. Those who are pressing for reopening the grave insist that Mr. Thomson was murdered, did not die as the result of accidental drowning, and that his remains are still near Canoe Lake.

The two ladies' niece, Miss Catherine McKeen, an Owen Sound nurse, reports her aunts have a clear memory of the evening. They recall that their cousin, the late John McKeen, called at the home of his former neighbor, Tom's father John Thomson who, at the time of Tom's death, was living on 4th ave. east in Owen Sound.

An Owen Sound undertaker was at the home as well as the coffin containing the body of Tom Thomson. John Thomson insisted that the coffin should be opened, although the undertaker was reluctant to do so because of the advanced decomposition of the body after being in the water for eight days.[16]

So there it was. QED.

This would explain the family's apparent apathy at the time of the skeleton's discovery. However, if true, it also suggested that Thomson's father had his suspicions about Mr. Churchill having done the job that the Thomson family had paid him to do right from the get go. Now why would this be? That he would be so suspicious thirty-nine years before it was established that he would have any reason to be is of a prescience level that is off the charts. It further suggests that John Thomson (for some reason) was also suspicious of his son George having done his job of overseeing that the body of their beloved family member had indeed been exhumed and brought back to Leith, and was not content in simply taking his son's word that he had done so.

Nevertheless, what a helpful bit of news this testimony was for those looking for evidence that the artist had been buried in Leith in 1917. And how much more helpful it would have been to the crime lab had the ladies remembered this anecdote back in 1956 when speculation about the body that was discovered in Tom Thomson's original grave was front page news all across Canada. That they only remembered it in 1969, when the local art community within Owen Sound and the Thomson family were looking to aggressively counter the allegation that the artist's body was still buried in Algonquin Park was certainly convenient, if not highly suspect.

The newspaper article served to satisfy most of the people within the art world that there had never been any mystery at all regarding where the artist's final resting place was. Not surprisingly, their representatives also downplayed the implication of the skeleton found in the artist's original grave. Robert McMichael, from the McMichael Gallery in Kleinburg, Ontario, in his book entitled *One Man's Obsession* (1986), devoted several pages to the question of Thomson's final burial place but accepted the anecdotia that Thomson's father had asked that the casket be opened prior to its interment in Leith.[17]

The newspaper article had served its purpose and, in the minds of many, effectively countered my father and Blodwen Davies's earlier attempts to suggest that the artist's body had never left Algonquin Park. And that article might well have been the end of the matter, but for a couple of niggling details. The first being the contention that the coffin containing Thomson's body had actually been brought into the Thomson family home, and the second being that it had been opened—both of which are at odds with firsthand testimony from Thomson family members who had actually been present when the second burial took place.

An article published in the *Owen Sound Times* had indicated that the body was expected to arrive in Owen Sound at noon on Friday July 20, 1917. The plan had evidently been to bring it immediately to the Thomson family home (then situated at 528 Fourth Ave East) and then to have a private funeral later that afternoon, followed by the casket being interred in the Leith cemetery.[18]

However, this plan evidently got changed when George Thomson and the casket did not arrive in Owen Sound until Friday evening. In a letter written by Thomson's sister Peggy to her sister Minnie in 1917 she related that:

> George went the next afternoon to Canoe Lake and brought Tom's body on the Friday night train to Owen Sound. The body was left at the undertakers Friday night and the funeral was Saturday morning at ten o'clock.[19]

Peggy Thomson's statement makes it clear that the casket was taken from the Owen Sound train station directly to the undertakers (and not to the Thomson family home) on the night of Friday July 20, 1917, where it remained until the next morning when it was transported to the Leith Presbyterian Church for the funeral at 10:00 a.m. Had the body been brought into the Thomson home, that would have been indicated in Peggy Thomson's letter—rather than the phrase "the body was left at the undertakers." There is absolutely no indication that the casket was ever brought into the Thomson family home.

That the casket was never opened after it arrived in Owen Sound is evidenced by two statements made by Tom Thomson's siblings; the first, again, found within Peggy Thomson's letter to her sister Minnie Thomson (who had been unable to make the trip home to attend her brother's funeral), who indicated that: "None of us wanted to see him even if the body had been fit to see."[20]

There is no mention in Peggy's letter to her sister of their father insisting upon taking a blow torch to melt the soldered seal on the steel casket and opening up the coffin in the family home, which would have made seeing the body unavoidable to the family members that had gathered there. One would think that had such an event occurred, it might have been worthy of inclusion in her letter to her sister about the goings on in the family home preceding the burial. The fact that "none" of the Thomson family even knew "if the body had been fit to see" clearly is an indication that they never saw it. Had the casket been opened there would have been no "if" about the matter; they would have known conclusively whether the corpse had been fit to view or not.

George Thomson, Tom's elder sibling who had been in charge of overseeing the return of his brother's body to Leith, had also been quite specific in telling my father that no one within the Thomson family had ever seen the body upon its alleged return to Owen Sound:

> George Thomson, the older brother, told me that none of the family had ever seen the body upon its return to Leith —and I asked him specifically. George was the one who had ordered the exhumation and looked after all the funeral arrangements in Leith. He said that the body had not been viewed before burial. After all, why would anyone open a casket with a body in a state of decomposition in a house! George Thomson also told me that he had read the interview with Churchill in the newspaper in which Churchill stated Blodwen Davies had asked that Tom Thomson's body be exhumed. He told me that he wrote to Churchill, questioning him on this very point, but that he never received a reply. Thomson also told me that he would help me in attempting to solve the mystery of where Thomson was buried, but that I would have to get permission from every other member of the family to open the grave in Leith. It

just wasn't possible to do that as some had strong feelings about it.[21]

And George Thomson hadn't just shared the fact that none of the family had seen the body prior to burial with my father. He also had gone on record as saying the same thing to the *Globe and Mail* newspaper in 1956, shortly after the skeleton in the Mowat Cemetery had been discovered:

> George Thomson, 89-year-old brother of painter Tom Thomson, said tonight he is sure his brother is buried at Leith near Owen Sound, but that no family members saw the artist's body after death.[22]

As Thomson's father was most certainly a "family member," the statement that "no family members saw the artist's body after death" speaks for itself. That a former neighbor would be granted access to such a highly personal and macabre event that none of the artist's siblings knew anything about, despite allegedly occurring within the living room of the Thomson family home, is beyond belief.

Nonetheless, firmly believing that the 1969 newspaper stories had sufficiently squelched the notion that Tom Thomson's body was still residing within the Mowat Cemetry, the next problem that needed to be dealt with was the suggestion of foul play. One of the hardest things for the family and art community to square with their preferred belief that the artist had suffered an accidental death by drowning had been the testimony from Mark Robinson regarding the fishing line that he had observed wrapped sixteen times around Thomson's left ankle. To most people this suggested an anchor line, which, in itself, suggested foul play. But four years after the Owen Sound newspaper had broken their story about John Thomson insisting on viewing his son's corpse in the family home, Elva Henry, who had been married to Thomson's nephew George, decided to share with the author Harold Town the news that, "Tom had sprained his ankle a few days prior to the time of his death"[23] and that Tom's elder brother George had felt obliged to inform his son "on a number of occasions that he figured Tom had probably tried to bind it up somehow with the fishing line— which would account for the neatness with which it was wrapped around his ankle. There seems to be no dispute about the fact that it was wrapped about sixteen or seventeen times around and very neatly done."[24]

As this information came from the family it carried with it the air of authority. After all, the family didn't speak publicly very often about the death of their famous relative, with the result that when they did serve up an offering like this, people listened—and accepted it as being true. Indeed, this theory would be advanced as fact by Town and his co-author David Silcox in their book *Tom Thomson: The Silence and the Storm*, and yet there exists no evidence at all in support of such a contention outside of the Elva Henry quote above.[25] In the author's humble opinion, the statement lacks credibility on two counts. First, neither the speaker, Elva Henry, nor the man from whom she allegedly learned of the theory, her husband George Thomson Junior, had ever met Tom Thomson and, thus, were not witness to the artist's alleged injury; and secondly, the alleged source of the theory, Tom's elder brother George, likewise had had no contact with his younger brother in the immediate days and weeks prior to his death to learn of the occurrence of such an injury to his younger brother's ankle, nor how he chose to treat it.

Thomson's body had not yet been discovered when George Thomson first went to Canoe Lake to investigate his brother's disappearance, and so the news of a fishing line being found wrapped around his ankle had not yet been observed. And if news of Thomson having sprained his ankle and then wrapping it with fishing line had been mentioned during the time that Mark Robinson had taken George Thomson around Canoe Lake to speak with various people who had been in contact with his brother in the days prior to his disappearance, then Robinson would have learned about Thomson's makeshift splint at the same time that George Thomson did, and there would exist no need for the ranger to later come to view the existence of the fishing line around the artist's ankle as anything suspicious. Clearly the ranger's testimony indicates otherwise.

Moreover, Robinson testified that he wasn't certain that the fishing line that had been wrapped around the artist's ankle was one that belonged to Thomson.[26] And, if it did, it certainly was not one that the artist had regularly used. If this was true, then why would the artist treat his sprained ankle by wrapping it with somebody else's fishing line? More to the point, why would he wrap a sprained ankle with fishing line at all? Molly Colson, the woman with whom the artist met to obtain his supplies on the morning of his disappearance, was a nurse and would have noticed such an infirmity immediately. She also could have treated any such injury properly and quickly as she had been no stranger to making splints for injured legs.[27] However, not only did she not do this in Thomson's case, but neither did she comment to anyone afterward that the artist had been suffering from a limp or any other physical infirmity on that day. For that matter, neither did anyone else who came into contact with the artist on the morning of his disappearance. By contrast, there does exist testimony from those who did interact with Thomson on that morning that indicates that, for a man allegedly suffering from the effects of a badly sprained ankle, the artist had been inordinately mobile; both Shannon Fraser and Winnifred Trainor had said that the artist had helped the Mowat Lodge proprietor lift a boat over the Joe Lake Dam—certainly a risky endeavor for someone who's stability had been severely compromised;

Edwin and Emily Thomas, who ran the Canoe Lake Train Station, along with their young daughter Rose, testified that they had witnessed him walk along the railroad tracks for a half mile to the Canoe Lake section house (and back); Mark Robinson testified that he had witnessed the artist walking along a path that ran beside the Joe Lake Narrows; Thomson would also have had to climb the stairs that lead up to the Algonquin Hotel. Robinson also testified that he later saw the artist climb the bank on the far side of the Joe Lake Dam with no apparent difficulty. Edwin and Molly Colson, along with their staff member Blanche Packard, had been with Thomson when he walked into the kitchen of the Algonquin Hotel, apparently with no discernable limp. Indeed, not one of these people noticed so much as a hitch in the artist's stride on the morning of his disappearance, and none indicated that they had observed his ankle bound with fishing line in some makeshift splint. From whom George Thomson received this information has never been indicated, nor was this anecdote related in any of his surviving correspondence. Indeed, it would appear that the only person George Thomson is alleged to have shared it with in the many decades that passed since his younger brother's death was George Junior.

Consequently, as Christopher Hitchens once pointed out, "what can be asserted without evidence can also be dismissed without evidence." And when this allegation is dismissed we are left with a not-so-innocent alternative explanation as to why a fishing line had been found wrapped around the artist's left ankle when his lifeless body was pulled from the waters of Canoe Lake on July 16, 1917.

Chapter Nineteen

A NEW THEORY EMERGES

For a time after the airing of the CBC documentary, there had been considerable public pressure put on the attorney general's office to exhume the grave at Leith. However, this would have required the agreement of the Thomson family, and by 1969, the surviving senior members of the family were clearly disinterested in lending their support to anything that might upset the status quo. The theory of accidental death by drowning had worked out okay for them so far; their brother had become famous, his paintings were selling for record sums, and the Tom Thomson Gallery was even displaying paintings that had been created by Tom's siblings. It was certainly okay by them to leave well enough alone.

Outside of the art world, however, the rumblings continued. And, interestingly enough, a new theory regarding how Tom Thomson had met his fate had begun to percolate within the mind of one of the men who had exhumed the skeleton from the Mowat Cemetery, Dr. Harry Ebbs.

Ebbs had been born in England but had moved to Peterborough, Ontario with his family when he was six years old. By 1924, the eighteen-year-old Ebbs was working for Taylor Statten as a counselor at Camp Ahmek on Canoe Lake. He continued to work for Statten while pursuing his medical degree, which he earned in 1931 from the University of Toronto. Ebbs would practice medicine in northern Canada as well as at hospitals in India and Malaysia, later becoming the senior staff physician at the Hospital for Sick

Children in Toronto and eventually a professor of pediatrics and a director of the school of physical and health education at the University of Toronto. Through all of this—from 1938 to 1975—he continued to be a counselor (and eventually the medical director) for the Taylor Statten camps of Ahmek and Wapomeo. As an accomplished medical man, Dr. Ebbs knew whereof he spoke in terms of pathology, anatomy, and physiology. And, apart from Dr. Nobel Sharpe, Ebbs was the only other medical doctor who had been given the opportunity to inspect the bones that had been removed from the Mowat Cemetery. Officially, Ebbs had been unwilling to fight City Hall over their conclusion regarding the identity of the bones that he had helped to disinter from the Canoe Lake grave, but unofficially he was convinced that the bones that he had held in his hands that October day back in 1956 were those of Tom Thomson. "All the circumstances fit," he said, "the timing, the place, the circumstances, everything fits perfectly."[1]

Ebbs had known from his conversation with Attorney General Kelso Roberts that the Thomson family had exerted some degree of influence to have the crime lab abandon any plans they might have entertained for conducting an investigation. After all, if the bones were found to be those of Tom Thomson, an investigation into the cause of the artist's death would follow as a matter of course. And, apart from trephining, which was a theory that would only be floated much later, the earliest belief shared by all of the parties who had exhumed the Canoe Lake skeleton was that they were looking at the victim of a gunshot wound. Even Corporal Rodger had stated that only a .22-caliber bullet could have produced a hole such as the one that was present in the skull that they had removed from the grave. Ebbs futher noted a peculiarity with the skull's dentition:

> I cleared off the front of the face and found that the right incisor, eyetooth, upper, was missing and that was the only

tooth that was missing. There were no fillings and no other [missing] teeth and otherwise there was a complete set of 32 adult sized teeth.[2]

The hole in the temple of the skull, along with the missing tooth, strongly suggested to Dr. Ebbs that the person had been shot. And as Ebbs was already of the opinion that this was the body of Tom Thomson, his mind turned to how such a scenario could have played out. He knew, for example, that Martin Blecher Junior had quarreled with the artist on the night before Thomson went missing. He also knew that on the day that Thomson set off on what was supposed to be an afternoon fishing trip that he would have had to paddle right past the Blecher family cottage, and that both Thomson's canoe and body had first been spotted just a little south of this location. The pieces of the puzzle suddenly seemed to snap into place:

> [Thomson] would be paddling south [when he left the Mowat Lodge dock], and within 300 yards he would be passing Martin Blecher's boathouse, which is right on the shore where the present one is, and so it would be quite easy for [Blecher] then to shoot from the crack in the boathouse door at Thomson as he went past. I've had other people paddle for me, and the angle from the floor of the boathouse, a person standing there with a gun and shooting someone, that person with the wind blowing from the west would undoubtedly be paddling on the left and therefore the head would be slanted slightly to the left and that would account for it [the bullet] going in the right upper jaw and coming out above the temple on the left side—the angle is perfect for it. Also the canoe would continue to float down and pass the front of Little Wap [Little Wapomeo Island],

and it ended up behind Little Wap; that is, to the southwest in amongst the stumps.[3]

Moreover, Ebbs reported, Blecher was an individual who had access to a firearm:

Blecher was suspected of doing all kinds of things up there that were illegal, one of them having rifles.[4]

Things were finally starting to make sense now from Dr. Ebb's perspective. It made no sense at all for Thomson to have been bushwhacked at the Gill Lake Portage (as my father had speculated), as that portage was located on the southwestern shore of Canoe Lake, and there was no way that both his body and canoe could then work their way north for the better part of a mile against the current to end up where they ultimately did. The event that cost the artist his life had to have occurred in the immediate vicinity of where both the canoe and the body were found. Given the presumption that the skeleton in the Canoe Lake grave was indeed that of the artist, and that a bullet coming from a .22-caliber rifle had caused the hole in the skull, Ebbs' theory was most certainly a plausible one.

But there were problems with the theory. Certainly a bullet hole on Thomson's temple would have been obvious to a trained medical doctor such as Goldwyn Howland, and when he had examined the artist's body he noted nothing more than a four-inch bruise across the artist's temple. Surely the eye of a well-trained medical man could distinguish the difference between the exit wound of a bullet and a mere bruise! Ebbs disagreed:

[The body] being in the water for 8 days, it would be in pretty bad shape and you wouldn't see a hole anyway. Where it [the bullet] came out, it came through his scalp and there was hair on it and so there would be clotted blood or evidence of bleeding and swelling in that particular area. That's what he saw. Obviously, he didn't probe it and find a hole . . . It went right through the bony part of the gum of the upper, of the maxilla. But that would not be seen because the whole thing was bloated, was badly swollen, in very bad condition. And unless they pried the mouth open and looked, and even then it probably was in such condition that they wouldn't have suspected anything of the kind. As a matter of fact, I didn't find that until I had completed my questioning of the inspector with regard to the hole in the left side. It wasn't until I cleaned the skull off . . . that I noted that there was a hole above where that tooth had been. So then I went back and sieved and tried to see if by any chance there was a tooth in the sand or button or anything—and we couldn't find anything.[5]

Even Dr. Noble Sharpe offered some support for Ebb's theory:

It was stated that on the night before Tom Thomson disappeared that a man threatened him. Still later it was rumored a shot had been heard coming from the direction Tom had taken when he was last seen.[6]

However, it is likely that Dr. Sharpe received this bit of news from Dr. Ebbs, as there is no record of anyone other than Ebbs making mention of it and Ebbs had been in contact with Sharpe right from the beginning of the investigation. But there was a bigger problem with Dr. Ebbs's belief; namely, that the skull he examined was not missing the upper right incisor that he had indicated. While Corporal Roger had supported his contention that only one tooth was missing from the skull when it was exhumed,[7] by the time it was examined at the crime lab, it was evident that the missing tooth was from the jaw—not the skull—and a lower molar, not an upper incisor.[8] Indeed, in photos taken of the skull on the day it was exhumed from its grave, the upper incisors (both right and left) are clearly present. Even his nomenclature is incorrect, as the upper incisor is not what is referred to as an "eye tooth," which is a term used to describe a canine tooth, not a lateral incisor. It is hard to imagine such a well-trained medical man as Dr. Ebbs making a mistake of this magnitude on so simple a matter, and yet, if his observation was correct, then the only way a missing tooth could change its location would be if either the skull was switched or Dr. Sharpe deliberately falsified his report, both of which are speculations that are highly improbable.

And so, dear reader, after pouring through all of the evidence we are left with few facts and a jumble of speculative questions. Did Thomson commit suicide or was he killed? If he was killed, who was the perpetrator? Was he shot, or was he on the receiving end of a punch that saw him hit his head on a fire grate—or was he struck on the temple by the blade of a paddle? Was his body anchored to something heavy by cotton fishing line and dumped into the waters of Canoe Lake or did he simply sprain his ankle and use the fishing line as a makeshift splint? Was his death a simple matter of his falling out of his canoe and drowning? Did the undertaker from Huntsville exhume Thomson's body all alone on the night of July 18, 1917, or did he shirk his duties and solder shut an empty casket that he knew would never be opened and then pack it onto a train that was headed for Owen Sound? And if he did perform the exhumation, then whose body was laid to rest in Thomson's original grave? Unfortunately, I have no answers to these questions, and having now presented the facts and problems inherent in the Tom Thomson story, it is now time to do what should have been done in 1917—to turn the matter over to the police.

Chapter Twenty

THE DETECTIVES WEIGH IN

Having now fully reviewed the facts and various testimonials regarding the Tom Thomson case, what are we to conclude? What really happened to Tom Thomson? The beliefs that have been advanced over the past century on the matter are so disparate that no firm consensus has ever been reached in the matter.

If you are someone like Mark Robinson, the official version of accidental death by drowning is preposterous, particularly given how adept Thomson was at swimming and canoeing. And the four-inch bruise across his temple and the fishing line tied around one of his legs is certainly suspicious. However, if you're someone like Charles Plewman, and a lodge owner who was a friend of the late artist told you immediately after Thomson's funeral that the artist had committed suicide, who are you to question it? But if you are someone like the author Harold Town, the mythology of Thomson being a saintly painter of the north is ridiculous, and if in your research you come to suspect that the artist may have been a heavy drinker, then it's reasonable to assume that alcohol, combined with an ignorance of what one should and shouldn't do in a canoe, seems a rational explanation to support the coroner's original conclusion. If you're a medical man, such as Harry Ebbs, who examined a skull that you believed belonged to the artist and noted a hole that could only have been caused by a .22-caliber bullet, then you will be satisfied that the artist was shot. But then someone comes along like Daphne Crombie, who was told by a woman who owned the lodge

that the artist roomed at that she had read a letter from Winnifred Trainor to Thomson that indicated that Trainor was pregnant
with the artist's child and that this was the flash point that led to
a drunken Thomson's death at the hands of Shannon Fraser. And,
finally, if you were the coroner from North Bay, you would believe
the opinion of the medical man who examined the body, and that,
along with what evidence you could amass from those who were
there at the time, would lead you to conclude that the artist suffered an accidental death by drowning. Obviously not all of these
beliefs can be true as they all contradict each other. But which one
is accurate? Are any of them accurate? And how would you know?

Given that most of us, including the aforementioned individuals
(save for Dr. Ranney, who never saw the body), were never trained
in matters of forensic science or criminal investigation of any kind,
the simple truth of the matter is that none of us are qualified to say.
And this is why it is (well past) time that the facts of the Thomson
case were put before individuals who are qualified to render a professional opinion on such matters. To this end I approached two
veteran detectives from the Ontario Provincial Police (OPP) and
asked them to examine the facts of the case.

Detective Scott Thomson was a member of the OPP for over
thirty-three years, and a detective for over twenty-five of those
years. He worked in the capacity of detective constable, detective
sergeant, detective staff sergeant, and detective inspector. It is difficult to provide an exact number of death investigations that he was
involved in but, according to Thomson's own admission, it would
be in the hundreds. He served as detective inspector for Major Case
Manager Criminal Investigations from January 2008 to December 2012, where he case managed the most serious of criminal investigations (i.e., homicide, suspicious death) providing leadership,
investigative excellence and case management services to the OPP,
municipal police services, government agencies and others to ensure

the efficient and effective resolution and enforcement of major cases in accordance with federal and provincial laws. He was the case manager to no less than twenty homicide or suspicious death investigations over a five-year period, during which 100 percent of the assigned cases were solved.

Detective Dan Mulligan is a thirty-four-year veteran of the Ontario Provincial Police who has amassed considerable experience specializing in criminal investigation. During this time, he has been involved as the primary investigator in dozens of suicide and sudden death investigations, and was the assisting investigator on more than a dozen homicides, and the lead investigator on two homicide investigations. His contribution to these cases included writing information to obtain search warrants (where necessary) and also interviewing relevant witnesses. As a result, Mulligan is particularly adept at critically evaluating witness testimony in an attempt to determine truth from falsehood. Mulligan's experience ultimately led to a position as detective sergeant within the Ontario Provincial Police's Electronic Interception Section (aka "wiretaps") where he would make applications to superior court justices for Authorization to Intercept Private Communications, which is the most intrusive search and seizure authority within Canada's Criminal Code.

I was delighted to discover that Detectives Thomson and Mulligan were willing to invest the time necessary to examine the statements and testimonials that the reader has thus far been presented, in order to offer their own independent and professionally considered opinions on the Tom Thomson case—and specifically on how they believe the artist met his end and where his body is buried.

Gentlemen, what stands out about the Thomson case to you?
Thomson: There are several things that stand out to me in relation to Thomson's death, as well as the subsequent investigation conducted and the burial. I have to keep in mind that the citizens

of Ontario in 1917 didn't enjoy the services that we enjoy today and, consequently, when tragedy struck these small communities they were put in a position where they had to be the ones to resolve issues—as opposed to relying on professionals. I have been involved in numerous drowning and recovery cases, and pulling a body from the water that was in the condition that Thomson's body would have been in is extremely difficult—especially for his friends and acquaintances that were involved in the recovery. They would have to contend with the bloated look of the body as well as the smells of the body's gasses that would be released when the body was moved. Consequently, I imagine that they would have wanted to get the task of examining the body over with as quickly as possible.

Are you suggesting that Dr. Howland's examination of the body was performed too hastily?

Thomson: I realize that Dr. Howland was a medical doctor who specialized in neurology, however he was not a pathologist or a coroner. This may explain the lack of detail he provided when he examined Thomson's body.

Mulligan: What stands out about this case to me is primarily the complete absence of any police involvement from an investigative review perspective whatsoever. Had this incident been profession-ally investigated from the outset—which is certainly standard oper-ating procedure/protocol in relation to any sudden and unexpected death scenario—I would suggest that the truth would have ulti-mately been determined.

Thomson: I would also like to add that the following points stood out to me about this case, and I will address each of these points in more detail:

1. Large bruise found on the temple
2. Fishing line wrapped around Thomson's ankle

3. No water found in the lungs.
4. Overall condition of the body
5. Thomson's canoe
6. Thomson's property
7. Thomson's Exhumation

Would you please elaborate on these points?

Thomson: Certainly. First, the large bruise found on the temple. I note that there are discrepancies as to whether it was on the left or right temple, however Robinson and one of Dr. Howland's reports described it as being on the left temple. Robinson further describes the injury as looking like Thomson was struck with a paddle. Second, the fishing line wrapped around one ankle; Robinson says that the line was wrapped around the ankle sixteen or seventeen times. It was also a fishing line that Thomson did not use. I cannot understand how this line would end up on his ankle or how Thomson would accidently have it wrapped around so many times. What interests me also about the fishing line is that once Robinson removes the line there is no mention of any cuts or marks caused by the line. I would assume that if the fishing line played a part in his death that Thomson would have struggled with the fishing line, causing some sort of marks on his skin. By the lack of any marks it appears to me that this line was wrapped around his ankle after his death.

No water found in his lungs; Dr. Howland also discovered that there was no water in the lungs and that blood was observed coming out of Thomson's ear. My experience with drowning victims is that they will enter the water and attempt to breath in oxygen, which, in turn, causes them to fill their lungs with water. Also, the blood coming from the ear would indicate that Thomson was alive after he received the injury to the temple and the heart was still pumping, causing the blood to continue to flow.

The next issue that stands out to me is the condition of the body. It seems that those involved created a scenario to match the evidence they found on Thomson's body; that is, that he fell, struck his head, and drowned. If we go with that scenario and contend that he did fall causing the trauma to his head, why then were there no marks, bruises, or cuts to any other part of his body such as his hands, legs, arms, or torso? The injuries to the skull appeared to be significant and should have been caused by a very large fall. This should have caused other injuries to the body.

And then there is the matter of Thomson's overturned canoe; Canoe Lake was a very small community where all the residents were familiar with each other. The means of transportation was either by boat or train. I assume that people who lived on the lake would be able to identify the fellow residents on the lake by their boats. Thomson owned his canoe. He had painted the canoe a distinctive color of gray, which would have made his canoe stand out from all of the other canoes on the lake as being Thomson's. However, Martin Blecher Junior sees the canoe floating upside down, leaves it in the lake, then twenty-four hours later returns and tows it to his or Shannon Fraser's boathouse—but didn't say anything. This seems to be odd behavior considering that Thomson would have paddled by his cottage only hours earlier in that same canoe. And the manner in which the paddles were lashed into the canoe when recovered was not consistent with Thomson's lashing style. It appears another person had placed them in the canoe.

With regard to Thomson's property, he had packed his canoe with enough supplies to last him a few weeks in the bush. These supplies and his backpack were never located. If he fell in the water and drowned I would have assumed that some of these items would have been located.

And finally, the matter of his supposed exhumation from the Mowat Cemetery; the manner in which Mr. Churchill retrieved

Thomson's body seems suspicious. I am of the understanding that he required three hours to dig up Thomson's body and place it in the metal casket that he brought with him. Now I spoke with an individual who was employed as a gravedigger and he provided me with the following information. In his opinion it would not be difficult to dig up a body under these circumstances. The individual would have to dig down only four feet or so to the casket and then break it open and retrieve the body. However, Mr. Robinson states that only twenty inches of earth was disturbed and the entire grave remained intact. It appears the body was not removed. One could speculate that Churchill placed this earth into the new casket to add some weight.

Having now examined all of the testimony underlying the various death theories that have been advanced over the decades and running them through your investigating detectives' filter, I would like to ask you both some direct questions about these theories. To begin, based upon the evidence, do you believe that Tom Thomson committed suicide?
Mulligan: I do not believe Mr. Thomson was responsible for his own death by suicide. What limited evidence derived from his body's cursory—and only—examination by Dr. Goldwyn Howland strongly suggests that his death was a direct result of foul play. I should also add, with respect to the suicide rumor, that Thomson's current life circumstances were sufficiently optimistic to negate any rumor/innuendo of suicidal ideations.

Detective Thomson, what is your conclusion regarding the suicide theory?
Thomson: I do not believe that Thomson committed suicide. There are absolutely no indications of any suicidal behavior. Experts advise that there are warning signs that people exhibit who may be suicidal. These signs include:

1. Always talking about death
2. Clinical depression
3. Participating in risky behavior
4. Losing interest in things they used to care about
5. Low self esteem
6. Putting affairs in order
7. Mood swings
8. Visiting people and saying good-bye

Thomson did not exhibit any of these signs at the time of his death. His artistic career was starting to take off, he may have been engaged to Miss Trainor, and he appeared to be in a good place according to his friends and family. The evidence cannot support suicide.

Do either of you believe that the evidence supports that his death was the result of falling out of his canoe and drowning?
Mulligan: No. The evidence supports the notion that Thomson was both an accomplished canoeist and a strong swimmer, and these facts do not support any theory(ies) that he possibly fell out of his canoe and drowned. The complete absence of any/all of his numerous supplies, as well as the standard, canoe trip-related articles such as his paddle, packs, etc., which should have been found floating in the lake if his canoe tipped over, negate any such theory as well.

And yet three men—Dr. Howland, Park Superintendent Bartlett and the coroner Dr. Ranney—were all of the opinion that Thomson suffered an "accidental death by drowning." Why do you think that they came to this conclusion?
Mulligan: To begin with, Mr. Bartlett never saw the body, and neither did Dr. Ranney. According to Dr. Howland's daughter, who went on record in 1970, her father also believed that foul play was a possibility. That aside, drowning does not result in bleeding from

an ear—bleeding from an ear is an indication of some form of blunt force trauma to the head. Sixteen or seventeen strands of fishing line tightly bound around one ankle amounts to an anchor line in my experience; an anchor line that failed miserably after only eight days following Thomson's alleged "disappearance."

So you are suggesting that Dr. Ranney was negligent in his duties as coroner presiding over the case?
Mulligan: I would simply state that, in my experience, this evidently wasn't Dr. Ranney's finest hour. Dr. Ranney arrived on-scene late on the second day following the body's recovery, with no post-mortem examination conducted as a result of a premature burial. The attending coroner should have made an Order for Exhumation, and an appropriately experienced pathologist should have professionally examined Thomson's body.

Thomson: I do not believe Thomson's death was the result of falling out of a canoe and drowning. The evidence cannot support this theory. It appears that the Coroner Dr. R.A. Ranney was in a rush to get the inquest over with and move on. In addition, there was no opportunity for the witnesses to prepare for the inquest. It was held at midnight at Blechers' cottage and some key witnesses did not testify. But let's for the moment assume that the cause of Thomson's death was actually falling out of his canoe and drowning. It would have to occur as follows: Thomson is canoeing on Canoe Lake with all of his supplies stowed in the bow of the canoe, including his backpack, as when his body was recovered he was not wearing it. He then lashes his paddles into the canoe in a manner that was not consistent with his canoeing practices. He then falls from his canoe with such force as to cause major trauma to the left temple from a distance of approximately three feet—this kills him instantly and he stops breathing (as there was no water found in his lungs). Because of water conditions or current, Thomson's body rotates sixteen or seventeen times, causing fishing line to wrap around only his left ankle—but it is fishing line that does not belong to Thomson. His body then sinks into the lake and resurfaces eight days later. It has been my experience that bodies will typically surface quicker in warmer water, which, given that it was July, the water would have been warmer in a small body of water such as Canoe Lake. No, in my opinion Dr. Ranney may have been influenced by those he shared dinner with on the manner in which Thomson died.

Do you suspect foul play?

Mulligan: I most certainly do suspect foul play was involved in Thomson's death. As I indicated earlier, the most compelling evidence to support this perspective would include the bleeding from the ear, which is an indicator of blunt force trauma, the ankle wrapped sixteen or seventeen times with strong fishing line, and the evidence of a gaping hole found on the left temple of the skull exhumed by Judge Little, et al, in October, 1956.

Thomson: I believe that Thomson was the victim of foul play. The evidence that has been presented leaves no other conclusion.

PERSONS OF INTEREST

Given that both of you are of the opinion that Thomson met with foul play, do either of the two people held forth as likely candidates over the years—Martin Blecher Junior and Shannon Fraser—strike you as likely suspects?

Mulligan: It's hard to say after one hundred years, but I would say that both of these individuals would be "Persons of Interest" if I were investigating the case. If Shannon Fraser was the man who killed Thomson, it was probably not so much a murder as a "manslaughter" scenario that took place; that is, an unintentional homicide resulting from a drunken brawl that resulted in death. What little evidence is available is consistent with Daphne Crombie's statement to Ron Pittaway as well as Ruth Upjohn's disclosure to Muskoka artist Doug Dunford. Upjohn's statement is intriguing; that is, the conversation that she allegedly overheard within her family's Rosedale residence that was carried on amongst Thomson's closest comrades (subsequently comprising the Group of Seven). The details of the conversation amount to a "conspiracy of silence" amongst this small group for reasons unknown. Whatever specifically happened involved sufficient trauma to Thomson's head that it killed him. And it was at this point that the perpetrator went into panic mode, which precipitated an ill-conceived dumping of Thomson's body into the depths of Canoe Lake. The head wound on the skull that was discovered in Thomson's original grave suggests blunt force trauma. The blow rendered him unconscious and he died shortly thereafter. It would have occurred to the man who struck the blow that he could dispose of Thomson's body most assuredly by anchoring it down via sixteen to seventeen strands of braided fishing line wrapped around an ankle, however that evidently proved to be insufficient in securing down a decomposing body of Thomson's physique eight days later. The lack of relevant articles which would normally be located floating in the location of an overturned canoe speaks to the fact that the murder occurred on shore and the cover up was a rushed job, which speaks to minimal premeditation having been involved in the killing.

Thomson: While Shannon Fraser would certainly be a person of interest, so would Martin Blecher Junior. He had motive as well as opportunity. In my opinion he would be the stronger of the two suspects in Thomson's death. Assuming that Thomson's death occurred shortly after leaving Mowat Lodge, I would have to say that Blecher's post offence behavior is very suspect—especially hiding Thomson's canoe. Was this done to delay the discovery that Thomson was missing and to delay a search? Did he only mention that he located the canoe because he was seen placing it in his boathouse? And although Shannon Fraser would have to be a person of interest in this matter, as far as his motives are concerned there was never a confrontation between the two men as far as I know. If their issues were posing a problem in Thomson and Fraser's relationship I'm sure it would have been well known in the community. There is no evidence of that, but there is evidence of Thomson and Blecher's issues posing a problem as indicated in the family correspondence that has survived, as well as Blodwen Davies's statement about one of the Group of Seven members, Arthur Lismer, knowing about the Blecher/Thomson feud via a letter from Thomson himself—this in addition to their row at the guide's cabin. Fraser appeared to me to be a guy who wanted to know everyone's business and appear that he was in the loop and always had the answers. If, in fact, he did kill Thomson and dispose of his body in the lake there are a few things that I think stand out as being questionable. When it was learned that Thomson was missing, it is Fraser who suggests to Robinson to drag the lake for the body. Now why would he take the time to ensure that the body was tied down and hidden beneath the water only to turn around and attempt to have it found? Fraser was also on the Mowat Lodge dock when Thomson left the dock on the last day of his life and Mark Robinson spoke with other independent witnesses who substantiated that this was the last anyone saw of Tom Thomson. Tom Thomson left the dock at Mowat Lodge on July 8, 1917 at approximately 1:00 p.m. He had packed enough supplies for a two-week stay in the bush. He canoed south on the lake past both the Trainors' and Blechers' cottages toward the Gill Lake Portage. Thomson was observed, according to Mrs. Fraser's testimony (via R.P. Little), letting out his fishing line while paddling the narrows by the Twin Islands. This is a ten-minute canoe paddle south from Mowat Lodge. This would place the time around 1:10 or 1:15 p.m. At 3:05 p.m., Martin and Bessie Blecher locate Thomson's canoe floating upside down in the lake near the area he was last seen. Martin Blecher and his sister Bessie continue on their way and leave the canoe. Upon their return, or sometime the next day, they again see the canoe and tow it to Mowat Lodge and/or store the canoe in the Blecher boathouse, not telling anyone about their discovery. The Blechers were of the opinion that the canoe was the property of one of the lodges. In my opinion, Thomson made it to a landing point somewhere in the south end of Canoe Lake. There he encountered his killer and was struck on the left temple with a large object and died as a result of this head trauma. This attack would have occurred prior to Thomson preparing his canoe and equipment to be portaged. His pack that he always wore, as well as other supplies, were never located. These items were discarded or hidden by the suspect and never found. Thomson's paddles were lashed into the canoe in a manner not consistent with Thomson's techniques. The suspect then loaded Thomson's body into his boat or into Thomson's canoe, and wrapped fishing line around Thomson's left ankle and attached the line to a heavy object. Thomson was then dumped into the lake. Thomson's canoe was then overturned and left in the lake. I assume that if it was Blecher who killed Thomson, he wanted to conceal the body quickly to avoid discovery. The area where he was dumped was most likely out from the shore area where he was murdered.

What do you make of Dr. Harry Ebbs's theory that the artist had been shot?

Thomson: Dr. Ebbs's theory is possible. The only thing I'm not sure of is if a .22 caliber bullet would be powerful enough to make an exit wound. I think that a full forensic testing of the skull would be the only way to substantiate the doctor's beliefs. I would talk to someone who is a firearms expert to see what they think of this theory. Dr. Ebbs is certainly qualified to provide an opinion and we can't discount that he actually examined the skull. It would be interesting to know how proficient Blecher was with a firearm. To hit his target from the distance Dr. Ebbs states is very impressive. Also firing from this distance would drastically drop the velocity of the bullet. An expert could also comment about the power of a .22 at that distance, and what damage it would do under these circumstances.

Mulligan: Given the discrepancy of opinions amongst Doctors Ebbs and Sharpe, with primary consideration to their respective medical backgrounds/expertise/credentials, I would be inclined to endorse the position of Dr. Sharpe, who makes specific reference to the "small, round hole in the skull" and concluding that "it is probably nothing more than normal erosion." Sharpe was obviously a well-seasoned, forensic pathologist at this time. Blunt force trauma alone could additionally be responsible for the deterioration of the skull over such a time frame, in my opinion.

THOMSON'S TRUE GRAVE

Since you both have mentioned the head wound found on the skull that was unearthed, what is your professional opinion on the skeleton found in the Canoe Lake grave in 1956? Do you believe it was that of Tom Thomson?

Mulligan: My professional opinion as to the body discovered by Judge Little, et al, within the Canoe Lake gravesite in 1956 is that it is undoubtedly Tom Thomson.

Thomson: I am of the opinion that the body found in 1956 was the remains of Tom Thomson. I don't believe that Mr. Churchill ever exhumed his body in 1917. As Mr. Robinson said upon his inspection of the grave the next day after Churchill was finished, only a twenty-inch area of the grave was disturbed. This would make it impossible to remove a body six feet down through a twenty-inch hole.

Would you then favor exhuming it to perform DNA testing?
Thomson: I believe that the remains in this grave should be exhumed and tested for DNA as well as a full forensic autopsy should be conducted on the remains.
Mulligan: I would most certainly favor an exhumation of this body for the purposes of conducting a DNA comparison.

Why do you think the crime lab concluded that it was native (or half-native)?
Mulligan: I am of the opinion that this body was determined to be either full or [half-native] First Nations origin simply by virtue of the fact that the remaining skull displayed evidence of "high cheek bones." Any/all photographs of Tom Thomson would suggest he, in fact, shared that physiological trait, which is obviously not exclusively the characteristic of First Nations peoples!
Thomson: As far as the crime lab is concerned I don't know why they arrived at their conclusion that the remains were native or half-native. I recall early in my career that there was a belief that the shape of the rear molars from First Nations people were different than those from Europeans. The tooth was described as concave. However, these same similarities have been found in people of Scottish ancestry. This is where they may have based their opinion.

Do you accept the crime lab's conclusion that the hole in the skull was caused by triphining?
Mulligan: Absolutely not. In this scenario, trephining would only have occurred during the course of a post mortem examination—which was never conducted. The crime lab's conclusion on this issue

is not at all consistent with all the evidence gathered subsequently by Judge Little.

Thomson: I cannot accept the cause of the trauma on this skull was the result of triphining. My understanding of this process is that an individual who is experiencing pressure will have a hole drilled in their skull. This process has been in use for thousands of years and practiced all over the world. However, the First Nations people of the Algonquin Nation did not practice this procedure. A full forensic examination should determine how the skull was damaged.

So you believe that the undertaker from Huntsville did not do his job and simply left Thomson's body in its original grave? Why would he do that?

Mulligan: It is my personal opinion that the undertaker from Huntsville was probably simply convinced by Thomson's friends that Canoe Lake was his appropriate final resting place. Given Thomson's love for this locale, he had undoubtedly previously expressed that personal desire within his small circle of friends. And while the sealing of this casket would be reasonable under these circumstances, it further solidified the fact that his coffin would never be opened by Thomson's family in Leith.

Thomson: That is a very difficult question to answer. From the information I have reviewed we can't determine exactly what or whose instructions he was acting on. Was Mr. Churchill instructed to attend Canoe Lake and make it look like he was taking the body, so Thomson could be left in his original grave in order to fulfill this person's [Winnifred Trainor's] wishes—as well as looking after the needs of Thomson's family to have them believe he was buried in the family plot? In later years Churchill contended that he did ship Thomson's body to Owen Sound. However, the evidence for him doing so is highly suspicious.

Some people have opined that the mystery of Tom Thomson's death and burial location should remain a mystery. Why should resolving the matter of Tom Thomson's death and final resting place be significant to Canadians?

Thomson: Tom Thomson is one of the most famous artists this country has ever produced. He influenced the Group of Seven, as well as generations of Canadian artists. I don't know if the cause of Thomson's death can ever be fully resolved because of the passage of time. However, we do have a responsibility to ensure that the body that currently occupies the unmarked grave near Canoe Lake is exhumed and examined to determine its origin. If this body is a First Nations' person, it should be buried in the manner that respects their religious beliefs. But if this body is determined to be Tom Thomson's, it, too, should be buried in a manner that reflects the Thomson family's religious beliefs. Tom Thomson should be buried in a grave that is fully marked and that pays respect to this great Canadian artist. It's the fair thing to do and that's what Canadians know is important.

Mulligan: I believe that resolving the matter of Tom Thomson's death and final resting place is, in fact, quite significant to Canadians for a number of reasons. To begin with, Thomson's artistic talents were undoubtedly responsible for contributing to Canada's economic growth by demonstrating this country's incredible beauty to people from around the world, many of whom then chose to make Canada their home. Additionally, the Algonquins of Pikwakanagan are deserving of a positive identification of the remains identified as probable First Nations origin by the Centre of Forensic Sciences in 1956. Thomson's current status as an iconic Canadian artist remains somewhat tainted in mystery, rumors, and innuendo, and these will continue so long as these questions remain unanswered. Thomson's legacy of artistic truth given of himself to Canadians is well deserving of the same in return.

So now the detectives have weighed in and the takeaways from their analysis are significant. To begin, neither man accepts the official conclusion of "accidental death by drowning." Nor does either man subscribe to the rumor of suicide. They both believe that the skeleton that was unearthed in the Mowat Cemetery in 1956 was that of Tom Thomson and that an empty casket was sent to the family plot for burial in Leith, Ontario. Moreover, both detectives would very much like to see that same skeleton exhumed and subjected to modern DNA testing. And, perhaps most importantly, both detectives believe that the evidence of the Thomson case clearly points to homicide.

EPILOGUE

My interest in the Tom Thomson mystery was riding high in 1991 when I secured the services of two divers to see if they could discover any evidence of foul play from the region of Canoe Lake where the artist's body was said to have been discovered. I had hoped that we might find something, some objects that had fallen out of his canoe when it capsized perhaps, but, alas, it was like looking for the proverbial needle in a haystack. And, to no one's surprise except my own, the divers came up empty.

By 1992 my family and I had moved to the United States where we remained until 2001. At this point my wife Terri and I decided to return home to the town of Bracebridge in the Muskoka region of Ontario in order that our children might be closer to family, and learn something of their heritage. And, wouldn't you know it, Bracebridge is only a scant sixty-one miles from Canoe Lake. Being in such close proximity, the Tom Thomson saga started creeping back into my consciousness.

As often is the case when a new family moves into a neighborhood, neighborly get togethers are often initiated to welcome the new arrivals. Among the first people I met upon returning home was a detective and chopper pilot for the Ontario Provincial Police by the name of Daniel Mulligan (the same Detective Mulligan whose opinion on the Thomson case the reader encountered in Chapter Twenty). We hit it off right away, owing largely to Mulligan's sense of humor and keen mind, which was noticeable right off the bat. One evening the subject of Tom Thomson was brought up and I mentioned my family's connection to the saga.

"Are you Judge Little's son?" Dan asked me.

As my father had passed away in 1995, the question had caught me by surprise, as Dan looked too young to have been a contemporary of my father's.

"Yeah," I replied. "Did you know him?"

"No, but I read his book. I think he raised some valid points in the Tom Thomson case and that they should be followed up on."

And that, to borrow from Bogey, was the beginning of a beautiful friendship.

For the next several months we talked about the contradictions in the Thomson case whenever we got together and eventually decided that there might be some steps that could still be taken that might just lead to solving the mystery. We were in agreement that the (by now) many generations removed members of the Thomson family would have no interest in solving the mystery based upon the family's prior position on the matter and the fact that they had gone on record as believing that the artist's body resided in the family plot within the cemetery at Leith. However, as the attorney general's office had been categorical in its conclusion that the bones that were exhumed from the Mowat Cemetery in 1956 were definitely those of an indigenous person, and given that this was (and remains) the government's official position on the matter, it struck us both as highly inappropriate that once the government had reached this decision and had concluded with their examination of the bones, that they then made no attempt to contact any native body when it came time to return them. If the bones were indisputably those of an indigenous person, then the Algonquins of Pikwakanagan on Golden Lake, which is the nearest First Nations band, should have been notified and given the skeletal remains to be disposed of in the fashion of their people.

The mystery of the occupant of Thomson's first grave, and the government's apparent apathy as to the identity of the man, was certainly troubling. Who could he be? Was the crime lab wrong in their conclusion in 1956? After all, there was no DNA testing available at the time when Professor Grant had first examined the bones. Perhaps if the bones (or even a bone) could be retrieved from the Mowat cemetery grave, a DNA test could then be performed which would go some distance in determining the true identity of the man who was presently interred within the confines of a cardboard box beneath four and a half feet of Algonquin soil. Indeed, DNA testing would reveal beyond any doubt whether or not the bones were those of an indigenous or a Caucasian person, and if they were determined to be Caucasian, then further DNA testing could categorically rule out—or confirm—if in fact they were the bones of Tom Thomson. And the fact that doing so would resolve this part of the mystery, while not having to disturb the grave at Leith at all, seemed to us like a win-win for all parties concerned.

It seemed to us a solid idea, but a great many obstacles barred the path to the idea becoming reality, not the least of which was that the bones were now interred within a grave that had been marked, which meant that any attempt to remove them for analysis would be against the law, and neither of us were keen to risk a fine or jail time in an effort to solve the mystery. But then it was put to me that perhaps there was a way in which we could obtain the answers we sought legally, if we proceeded through the appropriate legal channels and chain of command.

In an effort to find out if this would be possible, Detective Mulligan contacted the regional supervising coroner at the Office of the Chief Coroner in Peterborough, Ontario, who at the time was Peter A. Clark, M.D. To my surprise, Dr. Clark was intrigued by the idea of resolving this long-standing mystery and he and Detective Mulligan then corresponded about how best to proceed. The upshot of their correspondence was that there were several boxes that required a check mark before such an investigation could commence; first, we would need to secure the participation from the appropriate First Nations people; then we would need to get the Thomson family's blessing; and finally, if possible, we would need to obtain statements from high ranking members of the Canadian art world who could speak to the importance to Canada and to Thomson's legacy by the solving of this long-standing mystery. It was a tall mountain that we had to climb, but it represented the only shot we had at bringing some sort of resolution to the matter of where Tom Thomson was buried and, perhaps, even provide some insight into how he might have died. And so, we proceeded.

Since the bones had been judged to be those of an indigenous person when they had been examined in 1956, we first attempted to reach out to the First Nations people in an effort to secure their participation in attempting to determine the full identity of the Canoe Lake skeleton. Consequently, on a summer's afternoon in 2003, Dan and I found ourselves heading north on Highway 11 for a meeting that he had arranged with Kirby Whiteduck, who was (and remains) the chief of the Algonquins of Pikwakanagan.

It was our intention to meet with Chief Whiteduck and solicit his opinion on Dr. Sharpe's report from 1956 and to see if he thought the matter was significant enough to his people to warrant any further action. Chief Whiteduck proved to be most cordial and was very interested in the matter. And, more importantly, he had not been impressed with the crime lab's original conclusion. Detective Mulligan then asked him if he would be willing to write a letter to Dr. Clark in support of an exhumation of the Canoe Lake grave and the chief said that he would. Detective Mulligan said he would write a draft of the letter for the chief to review, and that he would forward it to him sometime over the following week. We had obtained the first check mark.

Next it was decided to test the waters of the art world to see if we could garner support for our enterprise from one of its brightest stars. We reached out to Canadian art icon Robert Bateman to see if he would support our venture. Given that Bateman was by now one of the alpha lions of the Canadian art world, if we could get him to lend his support it would help the cause, and perhaps even bridge the gap that existed between those that cared about the artist's death and those that heretofore had seemed only to care about the sale of his paintings. To our delight and my surprise, Bateman readily agreed with the idea. Bateman said he would write a letter in support of our venture to Mr. Stuart Reid, who was then the director/curator of the Tom Thomson Memorial Gallery in Owen Sound. It was hoped that, given the close connection of the Thomson family with the Tom Thomson Memorial Gallery, that he might be instrumental in bringing the gallery on board and perhaps even the Thomson family.

Bateman's letter was amazing and revealed, among other things, that Tom Thomson had been his "hero" for over fifty years. He further stated that, "I am convinced that the overwhelming evidence, as well as the fact that his body is not in the coffin at Owen Sound, points to foul play. I have visited the Canoe Lake grave many times and talked to some of the locals (decades ago) who were involved at the time of the death and burial." Bateman then went on to add:

> I was astonished and pleased when Judge Little came out with his book and the [CBC] television program. I thought that, at last, we will bring Tom Thomson the truth he deserves. But unfortunately it seemed that the Thomson family was reluctant to re-open the case and reach the truth of the story. I was afraid that might actually be the end of the line until (also out of the blue) I was contacted by Dan Mulligan of the OPP. Actually, he is the stimulus for my writing this letter. He is working with Judge Little's son, carrying on the quest. We hope that you might be able to help us.

Dan would like to contact you and receive some information on the Thomson family tree. New techniques using DNA could help to identify the body still in the ground above Canoe Lake. And it would be wonderful if the family would agree to disinterment of the coffin at the official gravesite. My informants who helped load it on the wagon to take it from Algonquin Park to Owen Sound said that at the time "it felt like it was full of rocks" . . . If things do reach the stage of action, I think that the story would be a wonderful addition to the legends of Canadian heroes. It will bring a surge of interest in Tom Thomson. Even though the "scandalous" aspect may be the initial titillation for the media, his work, his life and his reputation will receive a boost in much-deserved attention for thousands of people who have never heard of him. We owe it to him.[1]

Securing Robert Bateman's support was huge for us. And, true to his word, Detective Mulligan had outlined a letter for Chief Kirby Whiteduck's review. Chief Whiteduck reviewed it, made some amendments, and then sent it off to Dr. Clark at the Coroner's Office. Chief Whiteduck indicated that he believed that it would be in the best interests of both the Algonquins of Golden Lake First Nations—as well as all other Canadians in general—that the matter be investigated utilizing the full forensic capacities of the Coroner's Office of Ontario and the Centre of Forensic Sciences. He further indicated that he was providing the Office of the Chief Coroner of Ontario with both the Algonquins' request and full authority to conduct the investigation/disinterment of the unidentified remains that the government had long ago determined to belong to an indigenous (or half indigenous) person. He went on to state that if DNA testing revealed the bones to be Caucasian, then the Algonquins of Pikwakanagan would relinquish any and all proprietary claims upon the remains in consideration of the potential interest of the Tom Thomson family/descendants. He concluded his letter by stating that the Algonquins' prime consideration at this point in time was to identify the bodily remains, and that their mutual co-operation with the Coroner's Office in re-investigating this (then) 87- year old mystery represented an opportunity to, the Chief's words, "right some wrongs of the past."[2]

Now that the chief of the Algonquins of Pikwakanagan had formally requested the bones in the Canoe Lake grave be ex-humed and a DNA test conducted to confirm their identity, all that now stood between us and the answers to this one hundred-year old mystery was a nod in the affirmative from the Ontario Coroner's Office and we were fairly confident it was going to come.

Two months passed and then came a response that none of us had anticipated—the Ontario Coroner's Office officially denied Chief Whiteduck's request, believing that there was "insufficient grounds to either initiate or reopen a coroner's investigation."[3]

We were shocked. Neither Chief Whiteduck nor Detective Mulligan could understand the Ontario Coroner's refusal. Once again, the government had been uninterested to even make an attempt to determine the identity of the man whose skeleton had somehow appeared in Tom Thomson's original grave. If the bones were, indeed, those of an indigenous male, not giving them to the Band that the man was most likely a member of, and simply reburying them (as the government did) in a cardboard box within the same grave from which they were removed, and then erecting a white cross (indicating that its occupant was of the Christian faith) atop it, was a slap in the face to the indigenous people.

In speaking with Chief Whiteduck, Sergeant Mulligan and I learned that nobody from the Council of the Algonquins of Pikwakanagan had ever heard from the attorney general's office regarding the matter of the Canoe Lake skeleton from the time my father, Jack Eastaugh, Frank Braught, and Leonard Gibson first discovered it, until present day. Most telling of all was when the chief answered the question about whether he believed the bones found in Thomson's original casket were those of an indigenous person—"It's not the way we bury our dead," he had replied.

We had reached an impasse. If the government had denied an official request from the Algonquins, it wasn't very likely that they would accommodate a similar request from Detective Mulligan and I. But then a thought out of left field came to us. What if the Thomson family could be brought on board? The Coroner's Office would have to respect their wishes in the matter, and certainly enough years had gone by that the elder Thomson siblings, the ones who had been so rattled by the theory of suicide, had passed on by now. Tom Thomson was now so firmly entrenched in his role of Canadian icon that determining where his body was truly buried couldn't in any way represent a threat to his status, and might just be viewed as something that was long overdue. Indeed, Robert Bateman had said as much.

In going over the various files I had amassed since the 1990s, I discovered in among them an article that had been published in the *Toronto Star* by columnist Ellie Tesher in which she quoted Tom Thomson's grandniece, Tracy Thomson, as saying the following:

> I'm as curious as anyone else about finding out the truth . . .
> I agree with treating the bones already dug up once.[4]

And then the article went on to state that another grandniece of the artist was also okay with the idea:

> Thomson's grandniece Helen Young has said that it would be acceptable to do DNA testing to see if these Canoe Lake bones are Thomson's.[5]

The article made it clear that neither grandniece was in favor of disturbing the grave at Leith, which was not our intention and so was fine by us. We believed that the bones within the Mowat Cemetery would be sufficient to yield the answer as to whether their owner had been native or Caucasian. And, if the latter, a simple DNA test would reveal if they belonged to Tom Thomson. The cemetery at Leith would not need to be disturbed at all.

Intrigued, I shared the above article with Detective Mulligan. He held out hope that perhaps the Thomson family might well be ready to come on board. Tracy Thomson had, after all, expressed her desire to find out the truth, and Helen Young had gone on the record as being okay with DNA testing the skeleton in the Canoe Lake grave. As Robert Bateman was already on board, perhaps if we could secure the support of an additional icon from within the Canadian art world, we would then be in a position to reach out to the Thomson family and, by demonstrating that not only regular folks but also those within the art world wanted to see this matter resolved, we could secure their blessing to find out the truth. And so Detective Mulligan reached out to another Canadian art icon, Ken Danby, and, to our delight, the artist agreed to come on board.

Both Ken Danby and Detective Mulligan then met with Tracy Thomson to discuss the matter and Detective Mulligan had reported back that she had seemed if not receptive, at least willing to entertain the idea. She would need to discuss it with her family members, she said, which seemed to us to be progress of a sort. As a follow-up, Ken Danby sent her a letter indicating that he had hoped that their meeting had encouraged her interest in resolving the mystery of Tom Thomson's burial location, and that doing so would be both respectful to his being and a tribute to his legacy. He further indicated that solving this mystery would only reinforce Thomson's legacy and reputation (not diminish it), which from

Danby's perspective was Thomson's art and its "profound" contribution to our Canadian consciousness. He closed by stating that he believed it was our collective duty to Tom Thomson's memory to find out the truth of his final resting place.[6]

However, Danby wanted a stipulation put in that may well have rubbed the Thomson family the wrong way; he believed that if the remains were DNA tested and determined to be Thomson's, then they should remain buried in the grave at Canoe Lake.[7] I viewed this as being a potential deal breaker; after all, the Thomson family had clearly gone to great effort to have what they believed were his remains returned to the family plot at Leith. That a DNA test should prove that the bones in the Canoe Lake grave were those of the artist—and then deny these to the Thomson family—was, in my opinion at least, wrong. I didn't have a good feeling about where this was headed, and that feeling was confirmed when Tracy Thomson eventually replied to Mr. Danby. She replied via letter, stating that neither she nor the Thomson family could support such a venture for the simple fact that as far as the Thomson family was concerned there was no mystery to solve— Tom Thomson was buried in Leith. And not only would the family not allow any DNA testing of the contents of that grave, but they would also oppose any attempt to perform DNA testing or any other other forensic examination of the skeleton in the grave in Algonquin Park.[8]

While the Thomson family couldn't have it both ways; i.e., they couldn't contend that the artist's body is buried in Leith and that all outside parties would also require the family's sanction to test the bones in the Mowat Cemetery, Tracy Thomson's conclusion that the family would not support our quest to find out the truth of where Tom Thomson was buried was final, thus proving how prophetic Robert Bateman's statement had been from several years previously:

Unfortunately it seemed that the Thomson family was re-luctant to re-open the case and reach the truth of the story.[9]

I should not have been surprised. For if I had bothered to read fur-ther in the 1999 *Toronto Star* article that quoted Tracy Thomson I would have seen the real reason why the Thomson family wanted to leave well enough alone. The young artist had stated:

> I fear that once people know the truth, that's the end of the intrigue and the chatter about it.[10]

The reader will recall from the prologue that I had made mention of the fact that there are those "who think it's a good thing that the matter never be looked into in any meaningful way for fear of spoiling a good mystery." Once again, Thomson the human being had been denied. The mythmakers had won the battle. But only the future will determine if they will win the war.

2017. Canoe Lake. My daughter Taylor and I are standing atop what we believe is Tom Thomson's grave in Algonquin Park. I share with my daughter my belief that Tom Thomson lies buried beneath our feet under four and a half feet of soil. It's an irony seldom noted that Thomson had himself often frequented the cemetery that my daughter and I now find ourselves standing within. He not only painted from this location but even took a photograph of James Watson's headstone with its foreboding epitaph:

> Remember Comrades (when passing by)
> As you are now so once was I
> As I am now so you shall be
> Prepare thyself to follow me.

Thomson could not then have comprehended when he snapped the shutter for that photograph just how prophetic those words etched into that headstone would prove to be.

It's frustrating for me being in this cemetery; the answers to many of the questions I've grown up with my entire life are but four and a half feet below me and yet they may as well be a million miles away. The wind picks up and the leaves rustle. Given how many trees surround the cemetery now it's spooky here—even in the afternoon. You never quite feel that you are totally alone. It dawns on me that all the principals in the Thomson drama had once stood where Taylor and I are standing now—Tom Thomson, Mark Robinson, Winnifred Trainor, Shannon Fraser, Martin Blecher Junior, George Rowe, Lowrey Dickson, Dr. Howland, Ed and Molly Colson, my father, Jack Eastaugh, Frank Braught, Leonard Gibson, Roy Dixon, Robert Flavelle, Dr. Noble Sharp, and F.W. Churchill (although he may never have been closer to Thomson's body than we are on this day). Being here with Taylor this afternoon feels as though the ghosts of these people surround us. All of them had to prepare themselves to follow Mr. Watson into the great unknown.

Each of the individuals indicated above played a part in the Thomson drama as it has come down to us and, according to our detectives, it is probable that at least one of them knew exactly how the artist died. I look down at the grave. If only the skull that lies beneath our feet could talk, what a story it could tell!

I feel a tug on my arm. Taylor has a question.

"How did he die, Dad?" she asks. I tell her the story. Who knows, I think, maybe she will pass it on to her kids one day.

ACKNOWLEDGEMENTS

The author is indebted to many people in the creation of this book. Particularly those who sought to preserve testimony from those who were in and around Canoe Lake at the time that Thomson lost his life, as well as those who struggled to bring the truth of the artist's death and burial before the public. People such as Mark Robinson, Taylor Statten, Ron Pittaway, Rory MacKay, Library and Archives Canada, the Algonquin Park Archives (and particularly Trina Chatelain who was amazingly helpful in my research), the family of Dr. Harry Ebbs, Ralph Bice, A.J. Casson, Wam Stringer, the Callighen boys: Richard, Harry, and Jack. My appreciation is also extended to Muskoka artist Doug Dunford, Detective Dan Mulligan, Detective Scott Thomson, Detective Troy Martin, Nick and Saundra Turnbull, Bruce Turner, Paul Faris, Sue Morris, Rod and Anne Mundy, and all who listened to me as I grappled to weave together the many threads of the tapestry that is the Tom Thomson story. The author is also beholden to Edward Britton for his humor and insights during the writing, and to James Loftus and Ashley Dunn for their support and high professionalism in helping to get the word out about this book's existence. A special acknowledgment is reserved for my siblings, Tom, Sally, and Jane, who grew up with the Thomson story as much (if not more) than I did. I am also grateful to Skyhorse Publishing for taking a chance on what many would consider to be a story of interest only to a portion of nostalgic Canadians, and to my editor Caroline Russomanno, for her keen eye and very helpful suggestions. A particular acknowledgment is due the website, "Death on a Painted

Lake," which was created in 2008, via funding by the Canadian Heritage ministry. It contains many transcripted documents that were invaluable in the author's research. I am also beholding to those researchers who went before me such as Blodwen Davies and my father, William Little, who were willing to take a stand based upon the facts they had amassed rather than on the myths that had predominated. The authors who came after my father should also be acknowledged for their research and contributions to the story; people such as Joan Murray, Harold Town, David Silcox, Roy MacGregor, Gregory Klages, and Neil Lehto, have all ferreted out pieces of the puzzle that is the Tom Thomson mystery and their passion for the subject matter has allowed not only myself but future generations a far more complete and accurate picture of the late artist. Anything that I might have added to the research and data of the Tom Thomson story is but a footnote compared to the work of all those who came before me.

I am particularly indebted for the support that I have received over the years from my wife Terri (who often accompanied me during numerous interviews with people connected with the story), and our children Riley, Taylor (who accompanied me to Algonquin Park on numerous research trips), Brandon and Ben. They are and will always be my greatest inspiration for everything I do.

ABOUT THE AUTHOR

John Little is uniquely qualified to write about Tom Thomson as his father, Judge William T. Little, was the one who discovered the skeleton in Thomson's original grave and who first broke the story nationally about the mysterious death and burial of the artist. John has continued in his father's footsteps and brings startling new data to light in *Who Killed Tom Thomson?* The author of multiple titles ranging from fitness to philosophy, Little has also authored feature articles in the Arts & Entertainment community, including the *Toronto Star* (Canada's largest daily newspaper) and has been interviewed on shows ranging from Canada AM and NPR, to CNN and *Entertainment Weekly.*

NOTES

Chapter One

1. Mark Robinson audio recording, circa 1953 with Alex Edminson. In 1977, an article was published in the *Toronto Star* newspaper that quoted two letters written by a former fishing lodge proprietor in the Park named Jack Wilkinson. The first of these letters contained the statement that:

    [Doctor Howland] . . . wrapped his daughter's fishing line around the body, towed it to shore, and fastened it to a stump so it could not float away, and then went up to the house and got a piece of canvas and threw (it) over the body.

    (Source: https://www.thestar.com/entertainment/2011/03/21 /rare_letters_reveal_rowdy_side_of_tom_thomson_group_of_seven _painter.html)

    However, Wilkinson's assertion is not supported by the testimony from either Dr. Howland or Mark Robinson, who indicated that Howland had called out to the two guides (Rowe and Dickson) who, in turn, were the ones who towed the body to shore. As to Howland being the one who covered the body with a canvas tarpaulin, this is contradicted by Robinson's diary entry from this day, which indicates that it was a blanket placed over the body by Hugh Trainor and Martin Blecher Junior. (See endnote 11).

2. The only photograph that the author has ever seen of Rowe and/or Thomson in a canoe featured both men paddling stern. However, guides could typically paddle either bow or stern but as Rowe was the only one of the two who would be called to testify at the inquest, and was said by Robinson to have been the man who discovered Thomson's body, it was likely that he was paddling bow that day.

3. According to Paul Faris, former professor of Funeral Education at Humber School of Health Sciences in Toronto, and from the embalming textbook used at Humber, "Dead bodies float or rest head downward in the water . . . with the result that the head discolors and decomposes with increased rapidity." (L.G. Frederick, *The Principles and Practice of Embalming*, 4th Ed, (Lawrence G. "Darko" Frederick Publisher, 1976), 517.)

4. Library and Archives Canada/Bibliotheque et Archives, Canada, MG30 D284 "Tom Thomson Collection," Vol. 1, File 3., J. S. Fraser, Letter to John Thomson, July 18, 1917.

5. Letter from George Thomson to Blodwen Davies, June 8, 1931 in which Dr. Howland's report of the condition of the body, as given at the inquest, was presented. Library and Archives Canada/Bibliotheque et Archives, Canada, MG30 D38 Blodwen Davies fonds, Vol. 11, George Thomson, Letter to Blodwen Davies, June 8, 1931. Notes: Original document withdrawn from circulation. Copy available on microfilm C-4579.

6. Tape recording of Mark Robinson, circa 1953, in conversation with Alex Edminson.

7. It has long been held that the body was, upon its discovery, towed directly to Big Wapomeo Island. However, testimony from both the undertaker Roy Dixon and from Mark Robinson indicate that the body was not moved to the island until the next day. In notes taken from an interview with Mark Robinson in 1944 by Audrey Saunders for her book *Algonquin Story*, in addition to notes left by Robinson himself that Saunders had mimeographed copies of, as well as an audio interview Robinson conducted in 1953, he clearly states that the body was taken initially to Gillender's Point. This makes sense, as it would have been the closest point of land next to Little Wapomeo Island.

8. Tape recording of Mark Robinson, circa 1953, in conversation with Alex Edminson.

9. Ralph Bice in conversation with the author, July 25, 1990.

10. Tape recording of Mark Robinson, circa 1953, in conversation with Alex Edminson.

11. Mark Robinson's diary for Monday, July 16, 1917: . . . "Martin Blecher Jr. and Mr. Hugh Trainor put blanket over body and it remained there all day." Trent University Archives, Addison Family fonds, 97–011, Mark Robinson, Daily Journal, July 16, 1917.

12. Ibid; "Charles Scrim reported that Tom Thomson's body was found in Canoe Lake by George Rowe this morning about 9 a.m." Trent University Archives, Addison Family fonds, 97–011, Mark Robinson, Daily Journal, July 16, 1917.

13. In a letter from George Thomson to Blodwen Davies, June 8, 1931, Thomson presents a statement from Dr. Howland in which the following testimony appears: "Certified to be the person named by Mark Robinson, Park Ranger." Library and Archives Canada/Bibliotheque et Archives Canada, MG30 D38 Blodwen Davies fonds, Vol. 11, George Thomson, letter to Blodwen Davies, June 8, 1931. Notes: Original document withdrawn from circulation. Copy available on microfilm C-4579.

14. Mark Robinson diary entry for Tuesday, July 10, 1917: "Mr. Shannon Fraser came to house about 9:15 a.m. and reported that Martin Blecher had found Tom Thomson's canoe floating upside down in Canoe Lake and wanted us to drag for Mr. Thomson's body." Trent University Archives, Addison family fonds, 97–011, Mark Robinson Daily Journal July 10, 1917.

15. Tape recording of Mark Robinson, circa 1953, in conversation with Alex Edminson.

16. Ibid.
17. Library and Archives, National Gallery of Canada, Dr. James M. MacCallum Papers, Tom Thomson, Letter to Dr. James MacCallum, ca. October 4, 1916.
18. Tape recording of Mark Robinson, circa 1953 in conversation with Alex Edminson:

> "Tom returned, was returning that fall and one day there were two or three, several of the old guides, were in the house, the ranger's house at Joe Lake, when [Park Ranger] Belfour turned to me and he said, "Thomson should be home today." He'd been over looking at the calendar. And some of the guides made a kind of slighting remark about Thomson—nothing serious, you know, just sort of a slighting remark. I suppose he had taken some of the jobs that they had counted on the year before. However, they sort of smiled over it and not many minutes afterward Belfour looked out the window and said, "I think Mark that's Thomson paddling down the lake." Now Thomson, it was Thomson all right, and up he came, paddled down to my wharf, jumped out, brought his kit bags up to the house and I met him out the door. "I'm stopping with you tonight." "Good Tom. Come on in." So, he came in and Belfour assured him that there was a nice roast in the oven and we'd have dinner. The other fellows vanished out the front door as Tom come in the back door."

19. Hazel Barker, "Artist Says Tom Thomson Was Kind, Helpful Man," *Barrie Examiner*, March 30, 1967.
20. Ibid.
21. Mary I. Garland, *Algonquin Park's Mowat: Little Town of Big Dreams* (Whitney, Ontario: Friends of Algonquin Park, 2015), 76.
22. Library and Archives Canada/Biblioteque et Archives Canada, MG30 D284 "Tom Thomson Collection," Vol. 1 File 3, J.S. Fraser, Telegram to John Thomson, July 16, 1917.
23. Ralph Bice in conversation with the author, July 25, 1990.
24. M.R. Dixon, "I Buried Tom Thomson, No Foul Play," *Toronto Daily Star*, October 12, 1956.
25. Entry from Mark Robinson's diary for Tuesday, July 17, 1917: "Undertakers Dixon and Flavell came in last night. Roy Dixon staying with me." Trent University Archives, Addison family fonds, 97–011, Mark Robinson Daily Journal, July 17, 1917.

Chapter Two

1. Saunders, Audrey, notes from 1944 interview with Mark Robinson, courtesy of Algonquin Park Archives. Also, the recollections of Rose Thomas and her cousin Jack Wilkinson:

Question: Why was it in this case that Thomson's body was taken out before the coroner got there?

JACK: Well, he was stinking so bad, and the coroner was in North Bay. It would take about four days for him to get there.

ROSE: It was two or three days before he came up.

JACK: Yeah, Lord Almighty, with the body up and exposed to the air, the maggots would be on it.

ROSE: Of course, he raised Cain about it. He was so decomposed that the three doctors, they just had to do something about it. He had a lot of black hair, and they said there was just a little black tuft [was] on it because he was so badly decomposed.

JACK: Oh yeah, all the hair would fall off. You get those big blue blowflies working on a body, well you know what happens in the sunshine, eh?

Question: Yeah.

JACK: Boy, all those maggots.

(Rose Thomas and Jack Wilkinson, Interviewed at Kish-Kaduk Lodge, Algonquin Park, February 11, 1976, by Rory MacKay, courtesy of the Algonquin Park Archives).

2. Rose Thomas and Jack Wilkinson, Interviewed at Kish-Kaduk Lodge, Algonquin Park, February 11, 1976, by Rory MacKay, courtesy of the Algonquin Park Archives.

3. Library and Archives Canada/Bibliotheque et Archives Canada, MG30 D284 "Tom Thomson Collection," Vol. 1 File 3, J.S. Fraser, Telegram to T.J. Harkness, July 17, 1917.

4. Library and Archives Canada/Bibliotheque et Archives Canada, MG30 D284 "Tom Thomson Collection," Vol. 1 File 3, A.E. Needham, Telegram to George Thomson, July 17, 1917.

5. Tape recording of Mark Robinson, circa 1953, in conversation with Alex Edminson.

6. M.R. Dixon, "I Buried Tom Thomson, No Foul Play," *Toronto Daily Star*, October 12, 1956.

7. Dr. Howland was employed by the Toronto General Hospital as its Chief Neurologist, an association that would continue on until his retirement.

8. Tape recording of Mark Robinson, circa 1953, in conversation with Alex Edminson. Regarding the location being the northwest corner of Wapomeo Island, this was the information Robinson had passed along to author Audrey Saunders during her interview with the ranger in 1944 and that she had copied into her notes. Courtesy of the Algonquin Park Archives.

9. M.R. Dixon, "I Buried Tom Thomson, No Foul Play," *Toronto Daily Star*, October 12, 1956.

10. Tape recording of Mark Robinson, circa 1953, in conversation with Alex Edminson.

11. All statements regarding embalming and the removal of the body from the water by undertakers have been the conclusions shared with the author by Paul Faris, professor of Funeral Service Education at Humber School of Health Sciences, Toronto.

12. Library and Archives Canada/Biblioteque et Archives Canada, MG30 D38, "Blodwen Davies fond," Vol. 11, copy of Dr. G.W. Howland's affidavit, July 17, 1917. Notes: Originals withdrawn from circulation. Copies available on microfilm C-4579.

13. Entry from Mark Robinson's diary for Tuesday, July 17, 1917: "Undertakers Dixon and Flavell came in last night. Roy Dixon staying with me." Trent University Archives, Addison family fonds, 97–011, Mark Robinson Daily Journal, July 17, 1917.

14. Tape recording of Mark Robinson, circa 1953, in conversation with Alex Edminson.

15. Ibid.

16. Audrey Saunders, notes from 1944 interview with Mark Robinson, courtesy of Algonquin Park Archives.

17. "Artist 'Mystery' Angers Mortician," unknown newspaper at Algonquin Park Archives, references the dig "early this month" which would place it in October of 1956.

18. Tape recording of Mark Robinson, circa 1953, in conversation with Alex Edminson.

19. "Types of Fishing Lines—What fishing line should I use?" http://www.seafishinghowto.com/fishing/articles/types-of-fishing-lines-what-fishing-line-should-i-use.html#braided

20. Audrey Saunders, notes from 1944 interview with Mark Robinson, courtesy of Algonquin Park Archives.

21. Tape recording of Mark Robinson, circa 1953, in conversation with Alex Edminson:
    "[The undertakers] washed the body and they made a nice clean job of it. They reduced the swelling so that we could put him into the coffin quite natural . . ."

22. The author is taking a liberty here, as nowhere is it indicated how the men transported the casket from Wapomeo Island to the mainland. However, a canoe would not have sufficed, nor would the Blecher's small motorboat. Moreover, there is evidence that a barge or scow was available to transport materials to and from the various islands on the lake and, indeed, was employed by Tom Thomson himself when he was delivering sand and materials to Statten's Island to assist in building the chimney for Statten's cabin. Please see C.A.M. Edwards, *Taylor Statten: A Biography*, (Toronto, Ontario: Ryerson Press, 1960), 66.

23. Charles F. Plewman, "Reflections on the Passing of Tom Thomson," *Canadian Camping Magazine*, 24, No. 2 (Winter 1972), 6–9.

24. Tape recording of Mark Robinson, circa 1953, in conversation with Alex Edminson, wherein Robinson says: "And the grave was dug good and deep by the two old guides—about 6'4" I think it was dug in depth."

25. Ibid. "There was a funeral service read. I had taken my little Anglican Prayer Book that was given when I was a boy—I generally carried it with me—and he, Mr. Blecher Senior, read the service from it, and a very nice funeral was held. There was several from the Hotel in attendance and around about."

26. Charles F. Plewman, "Reflections on the Passing of Tom Thomson," *Canadian Camping Magazine* 24, No. 2 (Winter 1972), 6–9.

27. Ibid.

28. Ibid.

Chapter Three

1. Tape recording of Mark Robinson, circa 1953, in conversation with Alex Edminson.

2. Interview with Jack Wilkinson and Rose Mary Thomas by Rory MacKay. APMA Oral History Series. Algonquin Park Museum and Archives, February 11, 1976.

3. Ibid.

4. Library and Archives Canada/Bibliotheque et Archives Canada, MG30 D284 "Tom Thomson Collection," Vol. 1 File 3, J.S. Fraser, Letter to John Thomson, July 18, 1917.

5. Tape recording of Mark Robinson, circa 1953, in conversation with Alex Edminson. "About two hours after we'd laid [Thomson] to rest, I received a message that the coroner would arrive at my place. The train was stopped to let him off there and I was to have the witnesses summoned. Well, I got a hustle on—bustled around. About 10:30 that evening the train pulled up in front of the old—there at the Ranger's house and Dr. Ranney got off."

6. Archives of Ontario, RG 4–32 'Attorney General Central Registry Criminal and Civil Files,' File #2225, Blodwen Davies, "Application for the exhumation of the body of one Thos. Thomson drowned in Canoe Lake in 1917," July 27, 1931.

7. Trent University Archives, Addison family fonds, 97–011, Mark Robinson Daily Journal, July 17, 1917: "About 8:00 p.m. Dr. Ranney arrived and took the evidence of Mr. Edwin Colson at Joe Lake."

8. "Tuesday night on the 9:12 train Dr. Ranney arrived. He said he had wired his intention to arrive Tuesday. Those in charge of the case at Canoe Lake were unable to find any trace of such a message being filed. The telegraph files for that year have since been destroyed." Archives of Ontario, RG 4–32 'Attorney General Central Registry Criminal and Civil Files,' File #2225,

Blodwen Davies, "Application for the exhumation of the body of one Thos. Thomson drowned in Canoe Lake in 1917," July 27, 1931.

9. Ibid.

10. Tape recording of Mark Robinson, circa 1953, in conversation with Alex Edminson.

11. Trent University Archives, Addison family fonds, 97–011, Mark Robinson Daily Journal, July 17, 1917: "We then went to Canoe Lake and met at Martin Blecher's home where I had assembled Dr. Howland, Mr. and Miss Blecher, Hugh Trainor, George Rowe and self. Evidence was taken, etc." Also, Dr. Ranney's letter to Blodwen Davies on May 7, 1931 indicates: "Those who were present at the inquest were as follows: Dr. G. W. Howland, Miss Bessie Blecher, Mr. J.E. Colson, (Ed Colson was not present at the inquest proper; he had already been interviewed along with his wife at Joe Lake shortly after the coroner's arrival. Already having his statement in hand, the remaining individuals were then summoned to the inquest at the Blecher cottage), Prop Algonquin Hotel, Mr. J.S. Fraser, Prop Mowat Lodge, Canoe Lake, Mr. Mark Robinson, Park Ranger, Mr. Martin Blecher, Tourists and Mr. G. Rowe, Resident guide." Library and Archives Canada/Bibliotheque et Archives Canada, MG30 D38 "Blodwen Davies fonds," May 7, 1931. Notes: Original document withdrawn from circulation. Copy available on microfilm C-4579. The statement about George Rowe's initial absence from the inquest and Robinson having to collect him is found in Blodwen Davies "Application for the exhumation of the body of one Thos. Thomson drowned in Canoe Lake in 1917," July 27, 1931. Archives of Ontario, RG-4-32, "Attorney general Central Registry Criminal and Civil Files," File # 2225.

12. Blodwen Davies, "Application for the exhumation of the body of one Thos. Thomson drowned in Canoe Lake in 1917," July 27, 1931. Archives of Ontario, RG-4-32, "Attorney general Central Registry Criminal and Civil Files", File # 2225. "The inquest was held in the Blecher home instead of in the hotel nearby. The Blechers, who were not popular with the community, served beer and cigars to those who attended."

13. Shannon Fraser writing to Dr. James MacCallum indicates that, "My wife wasn't at the inquest and never spoke to the Dr as the inquest was held at one of the neighbors and at midnight." Source: Library and Archives, National Gallery of Canada, Dr. James M. MacCallum Papers, J.S. Fraser, Letter to Dr. James MacCallum, December 29, 1917.

14. Tape recording of Mark Robinson, circa 1953, in conversation with Alex Edminson. According to Robinson:

"Dr. Ranney never saw [Thomson's] body, he didn't arrive until after he was buried, and all he had to go by was the evidence given at the inquest. Dr. Howland was there and gave his evidence, among others."

15. Copy of Dr. Howland's sworn statement provided to Blodwen Davies by T. E. McKee, the Crown Attorney and Clerk of the Peace, District of Nippissing, North Bay on June 5, 1931. Library and Archives Canada, MG30 D38 "Blodwen Davies fond", Vol. 11. T.E. McKee, Letter to Blodwen Davies, June 5, 1931 and Copy of Dr. G.W. Howland's affidavit, July 17, 1917. Notes: Original document withdrawn from circulation. Copy available on microfilm C-4579.

16. Library and Archives Canada, MG30 D38 "Blodwen Davies fonds," Vol. 11. Dr. A.E. Ranney, "Letter to Blodwen Davies," May 7, 1931. Notes: Original document withdrawn from circulation. Copy available on microfilm C-4579.

17. Library and Archives Canada, MG30 D38 "Blodwen Davies fonds," Vol. 11. George Thomson letter to Blodwen Davies, June 8, 1931. Notes: Original document withdrawn from circulation. Copy available on microfilm C-4579.

18. Trent University Archives, Addison family fonds, 97–011, Mark Robinson Daily Journal, July 17, 1917.

19. The first document cited is said to be Howland's original sworn testimony; the other two variants came from both the Thomson family (said to be in the coroner's handwriting; i.e., Dr. Ranney's, but quoting Dr. Howland from the date of the inquest itself) and from Dr. Ranney (which was based upon his notes from the inquest that he had retained). The sworn testimony can be found in: Library and Archives Canada, MG30 D38 "Blodwen Davies fonds", Vol. 11. Copy of Dr. G.W. Howland's affidavit, July 17, 1917. Notes: Originals withdrawn from circulation. Copies available on microfilm C-4579.

20. Library and Archives Canada, MG30 D38 "Blodwen Davies fonds," Vol. 11. Mark Robinson and Blodwen Davies, Response to Blodwen Davies' questions, September 4, 1930. Notes: Originals withdrawn from circulation. Copies available on microfilm C-4579.

21. Tape recording of Mark Robinson, circa 1953, in conversation with Alex Edminson. Courtesy of the Algonquin Park Archives.

22. Ibid.

23. Trent University Archives, Addison family fonds, 97–011, Mark Robinson Daily Journal, July 17, 1917: [Wednesday] July 18, 1917 – About 1:30 a.m. Martin Blecher Junior brought Dr. Ranney and self up Joe Creek in yacht to portage from where we walked to Joe Lake Shelter House, arriving there about 2:30 a.m. Up at 6 a.m. and Dr. Ranney took train to North Bay. I met trains as usual. Also, tape recording of Mark Robinson, circa 1953 in conversation with Alex Edminson: "Well, I took Dr. Ranney up to my place and put him to bed and in the morning after breakfast the train was coming through. He went on it and went away and still assured me, 'It's a case of accidental drowning,' he said."

24. Tape recording of Mark Robinson, circa 1953, in conversation with Alex Edminson.

Chapter Four

1. Tape recording of Mark Robinson, circa 1953, in conversation with Alex Edminson. Also, Mark Robinson's mimeographed notes given to Audrey Saunders in 1944: "The morning was dull. There was a raw east wind driving rains and clouds across the sky. Towards noon when the weather cleared . . .", courtesy of the Algonquin Park Archives.

2. Archives of Ontario, RG 4–32 'Attorney General Central Registry Criminal and Civil Files,' File #2225, Blodwen Davies, "Application for the exhumation of the body of one Thos. Thomson drowned in Canoe Lake in 1917," July 27, 1931.

3. Mark Robinson's mimeographed notes given to author Audrey Saunders in 1944, courtesy of Algonquin Park Archives. While R.P. Little had indicated that Annie Fraser told him that Thomson had been living at Mowat Lodge when the tragedy occurred (Dr. R.P. Little, "Some Recollections Of Tom Thomson And Canoe Lake", Culture 16 (1955): 210–222), Mark Robinson, who was tasked with investigating the facts surrounding Thomson's disappearance and death, had mentioned the Trainor cottage as being Thomson's "home" on the day that he went missing: "And he [Thomson] went home, from the evidence that was given at the inquest he had gone to his home, to this little cottage up here that used to be known as "the manse," now Mr. Trainor's." According to Robinson, "In that year [1917] he came up early and stayed at Trainor's little house during the Spring." Robinson further noted that the artist had moved a great deal of his personal affects to the Trainor cottage and that when the ranger had been instructed to go there to investigate after the artist's death these items were still there: "I was also instructed to go to the little house up here and look see what was around there and Mr. Trainor and I found—I forget—it was 40 I guess, or somewhere, maybe less of the 62 pictures, or sketches that were laying around there and there was several letters, most of them was from Miss Trainor." Tape recording of Mark Robinson, circa 1953, in conversation with Alex Edminson. Supporting this is the fact that Thomson had grown irritated with the Frasers, believing that they were going through his mail. His sister Margaret wrote on September 9th, 1917 that: "I might say that I met Miss Trainor of Huntsville in Toronto. She said that Tom didn't like Mr. Fraser, as he hadn't a good principle. She said that he was intending to leave there in a week or so, and that he didn't want them to know where he was going, as they were so curious about everything. She said that he had warned her not to put anything in her letters that she wouldn't care to have them read, as they always seemed to know his business. He said he didn't know whether they opened his letters in the office or whether they read them after he had opened them, as he used to leave them in his overcoat pocket." Library and Archives, National Gallery of Canada,

Dr. James M. MacCallum papers, Margaret Thomson, Letter to Dr. James MacCallum, September 9, 1917. And finally, according to testimony from Mark Robinson, he had been told that on the last morning he was seen alive Thomson had gone to pick up his fishing tackle from the Trainor cottage. Being an avid fisherman, it is unlikely that Thomson would not have left his tackle at the Trainor cottage if he had been dwelling at Mowat Lodge that summer as walking well over a hundred yards every day to pick up his fishing rod, tackle box, landing net, etc., would not have been practical.

4.   Thomson was said to have come into Mowat Lodge that morning "freshly shaved, hair brushed and shining." Archives of Ontario, RG 4–32 'Attorney General Central Registry Criminal and Civil Files', File #2225, Blodwen Davies, "Application for the exhumation of the body of one Thos. Thomson drowned in Canoe Lake in 1917," July 27, 1931. The clothes he wore that day were reported on by Charlie Scrim who saw him leave the Mowat Lodge dock in a statement he gave to Mark Robinson. Trent University Archives, Addison family fonds, 97–011, Mark Robinson, Note re: Tom Thomson artist, July 1917.

5.   According to Blodwen Davies' research in 1930, "On the morning of Thomson's death he rose rather late and breakfasted with Mrs. Fraser at Mowatt Lodge. He sat long at table, eating and talking in a leisurely way." Archives of Ontario, RG 4–32 'Attorney General Central Registry Criminal and Civil Files', File #2225, Blodwen Davies, "Application for the exhumation of the body of one Thos. Thomson drowned in Canoe Lake in 1917," July 27, 1931.

6.   Ibid. ". . . [he] then lit a cigarette and wandered out."

7.   According to Jack Wilkinson, his aunt [Emily Thomas] recollected that, "it was a drizzly morning. Then he [Thomson], I don't know, it was something about he was dissatisfied with something. He was going to go out on a trip but then the weather wasn't very nice. He waited till the afternoon or something. Jack Wilkinson and Rose Thomas, Interviewed at Kish-Kaduk Lodge, Algonquin Park, February 11, 1976, by Rory MacKay. Courtesy of the Algonquin Park Archives.

8.   According to Margaret Thomson, Winnifred Trainor had told her that, "Tom didn't like Mr. Fraser, as he hadn't a good principle. She said that he was intending to leave there in a week or so, and that he didn't want them to know where he was going, as they were so curious about everything." Thomson had also been peeved as a result of his belief that the Frasers had, for reasons of their own, been reading his mail: "She [Winnifred Trainor] said that he had warned her not to put anything in her letters that she wouldn't care to have them read, as they always seemed to know his business. He said he didn't know whether they opened his letters in the office or whether they read them after he had opened them, as he used to leave them in his overcoat pocket." Library and Archives, National Gallery of Canada,

Dr. James M. MacCallum papers, Margaret Thomson, Letter to Dr. James MacCallum, September 9, 1917.

9. Library and Archives Canada/Bibliotheque et Archives Canada, MG30 D284 'Tom Thomson collection', Vol. 1 File 3, J. S. Fraser, Letter to Dr. J. MacCallum, July 24, 1917. Winnifred Trainor corroborated this when she wrote in September 1917 that, "Tom, the day he was drowned, helped to cadge a boat for Shannon to rent." Library and Archives Canada/Bibliotheque et Archives Canada, MG30 D284, "Tom Thomson Collection," Vol. 1, File 5, Winnifred Trainor, Letter to [George] Thomson, September 17, 1917.

10. Ibid. See also Blodwen Davies' report: "He [Thomson] joined Shannon Fraser and together they went across to Joe Lake Portage. . . . It was nearly noon."Archives of Ontario, RG 4–32 'Attorney General Central Registry Criminal and Civil Files,' File #2225, Blodwen Davies, "Application for the exhumation of the body of one Thos. Thomson drowned in Canoe Lake in 1917," July 27, 1931.

11. Thomson had written to his patron James MacCallum and to his brother-in-law Tom Harkness that April complaining that the black flies would soon be arriving; writing to MacCallum on April 21, 1917 that they should go out on their fishing trip "sometime around the tenth of May as the flies are not going properly until the 24th;" Library and Archives, National Gallery of Canada, Dr. James M. MacCallum papers, Tom Thomson, Letter to Dr. James MacCallum, ca. April 21, 1917. Two days later, in a letter to his brother-in-law Tom Harkness, the artist had commented, "we have nearly another month before my friends the black flies are here;" Library and Archives Canada/Bibliotheque et Archives Canada, MG30 D284 'Tom Thomson collection,' Vol. 1 File 2, Tom Thomson, Letter to Tom [T. J. Harkness], April 23, 1917. In a letter written to his patron, Dr. James MacCallum, on July 7, the day before his disappearance, the artist mentioned that, "I am still around Frasers and have not done any sketching since the flies started. The weather has been wet and cold all spring and the flies and mosquitoes much worse than I have seen them any year and the fly dope doesn't have any effect on them. This however is the second warm day we have had this year and another day or so like this will finish them. Will send my winter sketches down in a day or two and have every intention of making some more but it has been almost impossible lately." Library and Archives, National Gallery of Canada, Dr. James M. MacCallum papers, Tom Thomson, Letter to Dr. James Mac-Callum, July 7, 1917.

12. Ibid. "Have done a great deal of paddling this spring and the fishing has been fine. Have done some guiding for fishing parties this spring and will have some other trips this month and next with probably sketching in between."

13. Doug Mackey, "Tom Thomson in our Neck of the Woods," Past Forward Heritage Limited, August 9, 2002, http://www.pastforward.ca/perspectives /august_92002.htm."See also Winifred Trainor's letter to George Thomson, which states: ". . . in July 1915 Tom bought a new chestnut canoe silk tent etc. and went from Canoe Lake on a long trip coming out at South River about Labor Day." Library and Archives Canada/Bibliotheque et Archives Canada, MG30 D284 'Tom Thomson collection,' Vol. 1 File 5, Winifred Trainor, Letter to [George?] Thomson, September 17, 1917."

14. The Raven, July 1, 2004 (a newsletter printed by the Friends of Algonquin Park) printed excerpts from an article that had appeared in the Toronto Tele-gram newspaper: "Some years ago, another friend of ours, Mrs. Newton Pincock, had a summer cottage beside North Tea Lake. . . . There she became acquainted with a park ranger named Tom Wattie. . . . Tom Wattie told Mrs. Pincock that it was while Thomson was about to start on his annual pilgrimage to the northern corner of Algonquin Park in 1917 that he was drowned in Canoe Lake. Wattie was expecting him and had made plans to give his friend a cordial reception. It was many days later when he learned of the tragedy." When the author spoke with Tom Wattie's son, Gordon, on March 20, 1991 he related that he believed that his father was waiting for Thomson at (North) Tea Lake: "He was waiting . . . for Thomson to come up for a fishing trip when he received news that Thomson had died and was quite upset by it. He also believed that Thomson's death wasn't accidental."

15. These items now reside at the Algonquin Park Archives. The list of items was confirmed to the author by Trina Chatelain on March 25, 2017 via e-mail and viewed by the author and Detective Mulligan on May 19, 2017. This had previously been reported by Doug Mackey in his online article entitled, "Tom Thomson in Our Neck of The Woods," http://www .past forward.ca/perspectives/august_92002.htm. See also Addison, Ottelyn, in collaboration with Elizabeth Harwood; Tom Thomson: The Algonquin Years, McGraw-Hill, Ryerson: 1969, 66. Addison/Harwood write: "Tom Wattie looked forward to seeing him again at the north end of the Park." Thomson would be dead, however, by the time the camping supplies arrived in South River.

16. Library and Archives Canada/Bibliotheque et Archives Canada, MG30 D284 'Tom Thomson collection,' Vol. 1 File 2, Tom Thomson, Letter to Tom [T. J. Harkness], April 23, 1917.

17. Tape recording of Mark Robinson, circa 1953, in conversation with Alex Edminson. Courtesy of the Algonquin Park Archives.

18. Ibid.

19. Addison, Ottelyn, in collaboration with Elizabeth Harwood; Tom Thomson: The Algonquin Years, McGraw-Hill, Ryerson, 1969, 66. Addison/ Harwood write: "Thomson put in gardens for Frasers and the Trainors." With regard to Lowrey Dickson's garden, Winnifred Trainor wrote: "Tom

ploughed and planted their [the Frasers'] garden & ploughed Larry Dixon's garden too." Library and Archives Canada/Bibliotheque et Archives Canada, MG30 D284 'Tom Thomson collection,' Vol. 1 File 5, Winifred Trainor, Letter to George Thomson, September 17, 1917.

20. Library and Archives Canada/Bibliotheque et Archives Canada, MG30 D284 "Tom Thomson Collection," Vol. 1 File 21, Algonquin Provincial Park, Tom Thomson's Algonquin Park Guide License, April 28, 1917. Thomson's guide license read as follows:

   Guide's License
   Algonquin Park, Ont. April 28, 1917
   Fee: $1.00
   The herein named Tom Thompson [sic; obviously not written by Thomson himself] of Mowat Lodge Ont, having paid the fee of $1.00 is entitled to act as Guide in conducting tourists and visitors into and through the Algonquin Provincial Park for one year from and after this date. This license may be cancelled by the Minister or Park Superintendent upon proof of a contravention of the Provincial Parks Act, or the Regulations made thereunder, by the holder hereof.
   G. W. Bartlett
   Superintendent, Algonquin Provincial Park

21. Reynolds, Nila, "Blanche Linton Remembers Tom Thomson," Early Canadian Life, February 1979 edition, Page 18. Also, Blanche Linton quoted in letter, circa 1970, Judge William T. Little archive.

22. Blanche Linton quoted in letter, June 5 1971, Judge William T. Little archive.

23. Ibid.

24. Library and Archives Canada/Bibliotheque et Archives Canada, MG30 D38 Blodwen Davies fonds, Vol. 11, George Thomson, Letter to Blodwen Davies, June 8, 1931. Notes: Original document withdrawn from circulation. Copy available on microfilm C-4579.

25. Library and Archives, National Gallery of Canada, Dr. James M. MacCallum papers, Tom Thomson, Letter to Dr. James MacCallum, July 7, 1917.

26. Blanche Linton quoted in letter, June 5, 1917, Judge William T. Little archive.

27. Reynolds, Nila, "Blanche Linton Remembers Tom Thomson", Early Canadian Life, February 1979 edition, Page 18.

28. Ibid. "At quitting time he gathered up the larger pieces while Mrs. Colson joked about 'Tom and his chips' and explained that he must prepare many sketch boards for painting trips, then reproduce the best on canvas." See also Blanche Linton quoted in letter, June 5, 1971, Judge William T. Little archive.

29. This document was first brought to light by the author/researcher Neil Lehto in his book Algonquin Elegy: Tom Thomson's Last Spring (http://

www.algonquinelegy.com). A copy of it resides in the Library and Archives, National Gallery of Canada, Dr. James M. MacCallum papers, George Thomson, Letter to Dr. James MacCallum, July 19, 1917. On Mowat Lodge stationary George Thomson writes:

> Dear Doctor,
> Just another little note in addition to the letter already sealed up to say that I'm also shipping to you a crate of Tom's unused sketching boards. It may be that some of Tom's artist friends may be able to use them. If so, just give them to whoever can use them.
> Very Sincerely,
> George Thomson

30. Blanche Linton quoted in letter, June 5, 1971, Judge William T. Little archive.

31. Ibid.Also, according to the writer Nila Reynolds: "Blanche made the pot of tea and snack he [Thomson] shared with the Colsons and she accompanied Mrs. Colson and Thomson to the walk-in cold storage where she measured off a slab of bacon and cut the amount he suggested. She also assembled freshly-baked bread, butter and other food which Thomson stowed in his brown knapsack. If he contemplated suicide he gave no behavioural hint or intent, nor did he limp or complain of any injury to motherly Mrs. Colson;" Reynolds, Nila, Early Canadian Life, February 1979 edition; "Blanche Linton Remembers Tom Thomson," Page 19.

32. Saunders, Audrey, handwritten notes from interview with Molly Colson during the summer of 1944. Courtesy of the Algonquin Park Archives.

33. Ibid.

34. Ibid.

35. Ibid.

36. Library and Archives Canada/Bibliotheque et Archives Canada, MG30 D284, "Tom Thomson Collection," Vol. 1, File 5, T. J. Harkness, Letter to J.S. Fraser, September 12, 1917.

37. Letter to Ottelyn Addison from Mrs. Edwin Thomas, Kish-Kaduk Lodge, Algonquin Park, February 16, 1956 and excerpted in the book Tom Thomson: The Algonquin Years, by Addison, Ottelyn, in collaboration with Elizabeth Harwood; McGraw-Hill, Ryerson, 1969, 95.

38. "I saw Tom and Fraser crossing the Joe Lake portage. They waved howdies and went down to there to try for a big trout," Mark Robinson's mimeographed notes that were given to Audrey Saunders in 1944, courtesy of the Algonquin Park Archives. In her notes from her interview with Robinson, Saunders recorded that "J.S. Fraser who ran Mowat Lodge was seen by Mark walking down the portage with Tom . . . As Tom was going towards Joe Creek he shouted across to Mark saying no, he wouldn't be over, he was going to the lodge with Shannon in the canoe;" Audrey Saunders typed notes entitled, "Mark Robinson's information Connected

With Tom Thomson, Given in Conversation at Algonquin Park During The Summer of 1944."

39. Tape recording of Mark Robinson, circa 1953, in conversation with Alex Edminson. Courtesy of the Algonquin Park Archives.

40. Ibid.

41. Ibid. See also Audrey Saunders notes from her interview with Mark Robinson entitled "Mark Robinson's Information Connected with Tom Thomson, Given in Conversation AT Algonquin Park During the Summer of 1944 to A.H.S.," indicated that, "Tom said to Fraser that he would catch a big fish at Gill's Lake and would leave it for Mark as a joke, pretending that it was the big fish that they had both been trying to catch below the falls," courtesy of the Algonquin Park Archives. Also, in Mark Robinson's mimeographed notes given to Audrey Saunders by Mark Robinson in 1944 the ranger states: "When they failed in this attempt Tom decided to go to Gill Lake to try for a few speckled beauties. If there should be a big one, he planned to return and leave it on our doorstep. His idea was that he would think it was the big fellow from the pool close by"; see also Mark Robinson's letter to Blodwen Davies in which he states: "on the morning of his death he almost got the old trout and, as he missed it, he said I am going to one of the little lakes and get a trout and put it on Mark's doorstep early in the morning and he will think it's the old fish from the dam;" Source: Library and Archives Canada/Bibliotheque et Archives Canada, MG30 D38 'Blodwen Davies fond,' Vol. 11, Mark Robinson, Letter to Blodwen Davies, March 23, 1930. Notes: Original document withdrawn from circulation. Copy available on microfilm C-4579.

42. Tape recording of Mark Robinson, circa 1953, in conversation with Alex Edminson. Courtesy of the Algonquin Park Archives.

43. Mark Robinson's mimeographed notes containing his memories of Tom Thomson, given to author Audrey Saunders in 1944, courtesy of Algonquin Park Archives.

44. Ibid. "Together they paddled to Canoe Lake (Mowat Lodge)." Also, Audrey Saunder's typed notes from 1944 entitled: "Conversation With Mark Robinson, Information Re The Day Of The Drowning, Page 4: "As Tom was going towards Joe Creek he shouted across to Mark saying no, he wouldn't be over; he was going to the Lodge with Shannon in the canoe."

45. Audrey Saunder's typed notes from 1944 entitled: "Conversation With Mark Robinson, Information Re The Day Of The Drowning, Page 5: "Charlie Scrim and Shannon Fraser had taken out the supplies that Tom wanted for his fishing trip amongst them was a tightly fastened syrup can. This can was found behind Little Wapomeo [Island]." See also, Mark Robinson's note regarding contents found in Thomson's canoe:
Found in boat [canoe?] floating in lake by Martin and Bessie Bletcher:

       1 gal can maple syrup
       1.5 lbs of jam
       1 rubber sheet
Trent University Archives, Addison family fonds, 97–011, Mark Robinson, Note re: Tom Thomson artist, July 1917.

46. Trent University Archives, Addison family fonds, 97–011, Mark Robinson, Note re: Tom Thomson artist, July 1917.

47. Audrey Saunders notes from interview with Mark Robinson conducted for her book Algonquin Story. Courtesy of the Algonquin Park Archives.

48. Library and Archives, National Gallery of Canada, Dr. James M. MacCallum papers, Tom Thomson, Letter to Dr. James MacCallum, May 8, 1917.

49. Tape recording of Mark Robinson, circa 1953, in conversation with Alex Edminson. Courtesy of the Algonquin Park Archives. Bread is also mentioned in Audrey Saunders typed notes entitled, "Mark Robinson's information Connected with Tom Thomson, Given in Conversation at Algonquin Park During The Summer of 1944": "At the Lodge he got some syrup for the Gill Lake trip and someone gave him a package of bread at the landing," courtesy of the Algonquin Park Archives. However, according to the writer Nila Reynolds, when she had interviewed Blanche Linton (nee Packard), Thomson had received his loaf of bread from Molly Colson at the Algonquin Hotel that morning: "She [Blanche] also assembled freshly-baked bread, butter and other food which Thomson stowed in his brown knapsack." Reynolds, Nila, Early Canadian Life, February 1979 edition; "Blanche Linton Remembers Tom Thomson", Page 19.

50. Library and Archives, National Gallery of Canada, J.S. Fraser letter to Dr. James M. MacCallum, July 12, 1917.; Charles F. Plewman, "Reflections on the passing of Tom Thomson," Canadian Camping Magazine, 1972.

51. Dr. R. P. Little, "Some Recollections of Tom Thomson and Canoe Lake," Culture 16 (1955): 210–222.

52. Tape recording of Mark Robinson, circa 1953, in conversation with Alex Edminson. Courtesy of the Algonquin Park Archives.

53. Trent University Archives, Addison family fonds, 97–011, Mark Robinson, Note re: Tom Thomson artist, July 1917.

54. Library and Archives Canada, MG30 D38 "Blodwen Davies fonds," Vol. 11. George Thomson letter to Blodwen Davies, June 8, 1931. Notes: Original document withdrawn from circulation. Copy available on microfilm C-4579.

Chapter Five

1. Jack Wilkinson and Rose Thomas, Interviewed at Kish-Kaduk Lodge, Algonquin Park, February 11, 1976, by Rory MacKay. Courtesy of the Algonquin Park Archives:

Can you tell me what you recollect about the year 1917 when Thomson died, and the circumstances surrounding the finding of his body?

ROSE: Well, in the morning it was very muggy and a fine warm drizzle rain. Then in the afternoon the sun came out. Oh, it was so hot.

JACK: Well, you and Auntie [Emily Thomas] were talking to him [Tom Thomson] in the morning weren't you? He came up with Shannon Fraser in the morning before he got drowned in the afternoon. He came up . . . didn't he walk up and walk to the section house?

ROSE: No, we weren't talking to him. Him and Mr. Fraser walked up the track.

JACK: But that day he got drowned. He was up at the station.

ROSE: That's right.

JACK: And they took a walk up to the section house, which was about a half a mile. The section house was right where the Arowhon Pines road goes in now. The section house was right there.

ROSE: And another old building which is gone now.

JACK: And another old house across the road, across the track from it. It was right there where the Arowhon Pines road [note: the Arowhon Pines is a resort that was built in the 1930s on the shore of Little Joe Lake] turns in and goes across the creek. That's where the section house was. There's a big patch of grass there now. They were up there and they came back again, so Rose and Auntie used to tell me. I don't remember. And it was a drizzly morning. Then he, I don't know, it was something about he was dissatisfied with something. He was going to go out on a trip but then the weather wasn't very nice. He waited till the afternoon or something.

2.   Dr. R. P. Little, "Some Recollections of Tom Thomson and Canoe Lake," *Culture* 16 (1955): 210–222.

3.   Charles F. Plewman, "Reflections on the passing of Tom Thomson," *Canadian Camping Magazine*, 1972.

4.   Dr. R. P. Little, "Some Recollections of Tom Thomson and Canoe Lake," *Culture* 16 (1955): 210–222.

5.   Library and Archives, National Gallery of Canada, J.S. Fraser letter to Dr. James M. MacCallum, July 24, 1917.

6.   Library and Archives Canada/Bibliotheque et Archives Canada, MG30 D38 Blodwen Davies fonds, Vol. 11, George Thomson, Letter to Blodwen Davies, June 8, 1931. Notes: Original document withdrawn from circulation. Copy available on microfilm C-4579.

7.   Library and Archives, National Gallery of Canada, Dr. James M. MacCallum Papers, Elizabeth Harkness, Letter to Dr. James MacCallum, February 19, 1918.

8.   Ibid.

9. Library and Archives, National Gallery of Canada, Dr. James M. MacCallum papers. J.S. Fraser, Telegram to Dr. James MacCallum, July 10, 1917.
10. Library and Archives, National Gallery of Canada, J.S. Fraser letter to Dr. James M. MacCallum, July 12, 1917.
11. Trent University Archives, Addison family fonds, 97–011, Mark Robinson, Note re: Tom Thomson artist, July 1917.
12. Dr. R. P. Little, "Some Recollections of Tom Thomson and Canoe Lake," *Culture* 16 (1955): 210–222.
13. Tape recording of Mark Robinson, circa 1953, in conversation with Alex Edminson.
14. Trent University Archives, Addison Family fonds, 97–011, Mark Robinson, Daily Journal, July 10, 1917.
15. Tape recording of Mark Robinson, circa 1953, in conversation with Alex Edminson, in which Robinson states: "I'm the man that took that canoe and turned it over and examined what was in the canoe; there was none of his equipment in it—his little axe even was gone—and the paddles were tied in for carrying."
16. Tape recording of Mark Robinson, circa 1953, in conversation with Alex Edminson, in which Robinson states: "And where was Tom Thomson from half past one to something after three, which would be another hour and a half, in travelling about, well, hardly half a mile? There was something fishy."
17. Ibid.
18. Library and Archives Canada/Bibliotheque et Archives Canada, MG30 D38, Blodwen Davis Fond, Vol. 11, Mark Robinson, Letter to Blodwen Davies, March 23, 1930. Notes Original document withdrawn from circulation. Copy available on microfilm C-4579.
19. Library and Archives, National Gallery of Canada, Dr. James M. MacCallum Papers, J.S. Fraser, Letter to Dr. James MacCallum, July 12, 1917.
20. Trent University Archives, Addison family fonds, 97–011, Mark Robinson, Note re.: Tom Thomson, artist, July 31, 1917.
21. Library and Archives Canada, MG30 D38 "Blodwen Davies fonds," Vol. 11. Mark Robinson and Blodwen Davies, Response to Blodwen Davies' questions, September 4, 1930. Notes: Originals withdrawn from circulation. Copies available on microfilm C-4579.
22. Tape recording of Mark Robinson, circa 1953, in conversation with Alex Edminson.
23. Ibid.
24. Dr. R. P. Little, "Some Recollections of Tom Thomson and Canoe Lake," *Culture* 16 (1955): 210–222.
25. Library and Archives Canada/Bibliotheque et Archives Canada, MG30 D284, "Tom Thomson Collection", Vol. 1 File 3. J.S. Fraser, Letter to Dr. J. MacCallum, July 24, 1917.

26. Dr. R. P. Little, "Some Recollections of Tom Thomson and Canoe Lake," *Culture* 16 (1955): 210–222.

27. Trent University Archives, Addison family fonds, 97–011, Mark Robinson, Note re: Tom Thomson artist, July 1917.

28. Saunders, Audrey, Notes from her interview with Mark Robinson in 1944, courtesy of Algonquin Provincial Park Archives & Collections.

29. Trent University Archives, Addison family fonds, 97–011, Mark Robinson, "Daily Journal, July 10, 1917."

30. Library and Archives, National Gallery of Canada. Dr. James M. MacCallum papers, J.S. Fraser, Letter to Dr. James MacCallum, July 12, 1917.

31. Saunders, Audrey, typed pages entitled "Mark Robinson's Information Connected with Tom Thomson, Given in Conversation at Algonquin Park During the Summer of 1944 to A.H.S." Courtesy of Algonquin Provincial Park Archives & Collections.

32. Dr. R. P. Little, "Some Recollections of Tom Thomson and Canoe Lake," *Culture* 16 (1955): 210–222.

33. Trent University Archives, Addison family fonds, 97–011, Mark Robinson, "Daily Journal, July 10, 1917."

34. Tape recording of Mark Robinson, circa 1953, in conversation with Alex Edminson.

35. Dr. R. P. Little, "Some Recollections of Tom Thomson and Canoe Lake," *Culture* 16 (1955): 210–222.

36. Saunders, Audrey, notes from her interview with Mark Robinson in 1944, plus typed notes indicating Mark Robinson's own writings on the matter in among pages entitled "Mark Robinson's Information Connected with Tom Thomson, Given in Conversation at Algonquin Park During the Summer of 1944 to A.H.S." These same typed statements of Robinson's would be read onto tape by Frank Braught in 1956, who was interviewed by Taylor Statten. Courtesy of Algonquin Provincial Park Archives & Collections.

37. Tape recording of Mark Robinson, circa 1953, in conversation with Alex Edminson.

38. Letter to Ottelyn Addison from Mrs. Edwin Thomas, Kish-Kaduk Lodge, Algonquin Park, February 16, 1956 and excerpted in the book *Tom Thomson: The Algonquin Years*, by Addison, Ottelyn, in collaboration with Elizabeth Harwood; McGraw-Hill, Ryerson, 1969, 95.

39. Dr. R. P. Little, "Some Recollections of Tom Thomson and Canoe Lake," *Culture* 16 (1955): 210–222.

40. Trent University Archives, Addison family fonds, 97–011, Mark Robinson, "Daily Journal, July 10, 1917."

41. Fraser wrote:
    Dear Sir.
    Tom left here on sunday about one o'clock for a fishing trip down the lake and at three oclock his Canoe was found floating a short distance from my place with both paddles tied tight in the canoe . . .

(Library and Archives, National Gallery of Canada, Dr. James M. MacCallum papers, J. S. Fraser, Letter to Dr. James MacCallum, July 12, 1917).

42. "Tom Thomson's Canoe Found On Canoe Lake," *Owen Sound Sun*, July 13, 1917.

43. "Toronto Artist Missing in North," *The Globe*, July 17, 1917.

44. Tape recording of Mark Robinson, circa 1953, in conversation with Alex Edminson. Courtesy of the Algonquin Park Archives.

45. Ibid.

46. Library and Archives Canada, MG30 D38 "Blodwen Davies fonds," Vol. 11. Mark Robinson and Blodwen Davies, Response to Blodwen Davies' questions, September 4, 1930. Notes: Originals withdrawn from circulation. Copies available on microfilm C-4579.

47. Reynolds, Nila, Early Canadian Life, February 1979 edition; "Blanche Linton Remembers Tom Thomson," Page 19.

48. Robinson noted that the rubber sheet that had wrapped Thomson's bread and bacon was present, but not the bread and bacon. There was also a 1½-pound tin of jam and a one-gallon can of maple syrup present. Trent University Archives, Addison family fonds, 97–011, Mark Robinson, Note re: Tom Thomson artist, July 1917.

Chapter Six

1. Trent University Archives, Addison family fonds, 97–011, Mark Robinson, "Daily Journal, July 11, 1917. See also Mary I. Garland, *Algonquin Park's Mowat: Little Town of Big Dreams* (Whitney, Ontario: Friends of Algonquin Park, 2015), 115.

2. A letter from George Thomson states: "As I probably explained to you when here I was then living in New Haven, Conn. And happened to be home on a short vacation when word came of the finding of Tom's canoe." Library and Archives Canada/Bibliotheque et Archives Canada, MG30 D38, Blodwen Davies fonds, Vol. 11, George Thomson, Letter to Blodwen Davies, June 8, 1931. Notes: Original document withdrawn from circulation. Copy available on microfilm C-4579.

3. Trent University Archives, Addison family fonds, 97–011, Mark Robinson, "Daily Journal, July 12, 1917."

4. Ibid.

5. Library and Archives, National Gallery of Canada. Dr. James M. MacCallum papers, J.S. Fraser, Letter to Dr. James MacCallum, July 12, 1917.

6. Trent University Archives, Addison family fonds, 97–011, Mark Robinson, "Daily Journal, July 13, 1917."

7. Ibid.

8. Ibid.

9. Ibid.

10. Ibid.

11. Trent University Archives, Addison family fonds, 97–011, Mark Robinson, "Daily Journal, July 14, 1917."

12. Library and Archives Canada/Bibliotheque et Archives Canada, MG30 D38, Blodwen Davies fonds, Vol. 11, George Thomson, Letter to Blodwen Davies, June 8, 1931. Notes: Original document withdrawn from circulation. Copy available on microfilm C-4579.

13. Library and Archives, National Gallery of Canada, Dr. James M. MacCallum papers, J.S. Fraser, Letter to Dr. James MacCallum, December 29, 1917.

14. Library and Archives, National Gallery of Canada, Dr. James M. MacCallum Papers, Elizabeth Harkness, Letter to Dr. James MacCallum, February 19, 1918.

15. "Tom Thomson's Canoe Found On Canoe Lake," *The Owen Sound Sun*, July 13, 1917; Pg. 1.

16. Tape recording of Mark Robinson, circa 1953, in conversation with Alex Edminson.

17. Ibid.

18. Library and Archives Canada/Bibliotheque et Archives Canada, MG30 D284, "Tom Thomson Collection", Vol. 1 File 3, J.S. Fraser Letter to Dr. J. MacCallum, July 24, 1917.

19. Tape recording of Mark Robinson, circa 1953, in conversation with Alex Edminson.

20. Trent University Archives, Addison family fonds, 97–011, Mark Robinson, Daily Journal, July 15, 1917.

21. Tape recording of Mark Robinson, circa 1953, in conversation with Alex Edminson.

Chapter Seven

1. Charles F. Plewman, "Reflections on the passing of Tom Thomson," Canadian Camping Magazine 24, No. 2 (Winter 1972) 9.

2. Trent University Archives, Addison family fonds, 97–011, Mark Robinson Daily Journal, July 18, 1917.

3. Blodwen Davies had reported that "The inquest was held in the Blecher home instead of in the hotel nearby. The Blechers, who were not popular with the community, served beer and cigars to those who attended." Archives of Ontario, RG 4-32 'Attorney General Central Registry Criminal and Civil Files,' File #2225, Blodwen Davies, "Application for the exhumation of the body of one Thos. Thomson drowned in Canoe Lake in 1917," July 27, 1931.

4. "I visited trains at Canoe Lake and looked over 3 Barrells of Beer 2 1/2 per cent for Marten Bleacher Passed it as OK it being for personal use."

Trent University Archives, Addison Family fonds, 97-011, Mark Robinson, "Daily journal," June 30, 1917.

5. Trent University Archives, Blodwen Davies fonds, 91-001/1/16, Alex [Y. Jackson], Letter to Yvonne, September 15, 1966.

6. Ibid.

7. In correspondence between the author Blodwen Davies and Mark Robinson in 1930 the following Q&A is relevant:

    Q: Was there anything wrong with his [Thomson's] heart?
    A: There may have been but I scarcely think so as he could throw up his canoe and go uphill over portages without any trouble.

    Library and Archives Canada/Bibliotheque et Archives Canada, MG30 D38 'Blodwen Davies fonds,' Vol. 11, Mark Robinson and Blodwen Davies, Response to Blodwen Davies' questions, September 4, 1930. Notes: Originals withdrawn from circulation. Copies available on microfilm C-4579

8. The reader will recall Robinson's statement quoted earlier that, "Almost before we had time Dr. Ranney had declared that it was 'clearly a case of accidental drowning—accidental drowning is the verdict!'" Tape recording of Mark Robinson, circa 1953, in conversation with Alex Edminson. Courtesy of the Algonquin Park Archives.

9. "Blanche [Linton] recalls Edwin Colson's reaction when another guide brought that story [of Thomson's body being found]. He was helping dry dishes but he paused to remark, "Some of them think there's been foul play with Tom—he was too sure footed, too good a woodsman." Reynods, Nila, "Blanche Linton Remembers Tom Thomson", Early Canadian Life, February 1979 edition. Page 19.

10. Robinson testified that "And I may state right here and I think Thomson was struck on the head with a paddle by some person that afternoon. I don't think Thomson died a natural death from drowning." Tape recording of Mark Robinson, circa 1953, in conversation with Alex Edminson. Courtesy of the Algonquin Park Archives.

11. According to Blodwen Davies and Dr. Harry Ebbs: "Martin Blecher was believed responsible for spreading a report of suicide. He repeated this statement as late as August of 1931 when he made a trip across the Lake to Camp Ahmek on the day of the Thomson Celebration and told Dr. Harry Ebbs that Thomson's legs were bound together with a piece of rubber." Archives of Ontario, RG 4-32 'Attorney General Central Registry Criminal and Civil Files,' File #2225, Blodwen Davies, "Application for the exhumation of the body of one Thos. Thomson drowned in Canoe Lake in 1917," July 27, 1931.

12. Shannon Fraser—although he would deny it in letters to the Thomson family—was said to have believed that the artist committed suicide; "Shannon Fraser, operator of the lodge, confided to Mr. Plewman that he thought Thomson committed suicide because of a predicament with his fiancée." Charles Plewman quoted in "Predicament with Fiancé: Thomson May

Have Taken Life In Algonquin Park," Pembroke Observer, February 14, 1972. See also "Artist Tom Thomson May Have Killed Self, Pallbearer, 82, says, Toronto Star, February 1972; and Charles F. Plewman, "Reflections on the Passing of Tom Thomson," Canadian Camping Magazine, 1972.

13. George Thomson in a letter written to Blodwen Davies had included Dr. Howland's testimony as submitted to Dr. Ranney. Within this testimony was the statement: " There are no signs of any external force having caused death, and there is no doubt but that death occurred from drowning." Library and Archives Canada/Bibliotheque et Archives Canada, MG30 D38 Blodwen Davies fonds, Vol. 11, George Thomson, Letter to Blodwen Davies, June 8, 1931. Note: Original document withdrawn from circulation. Copy available on microfilm C-4579.

14. Rowe had attempted to object to the coroner's conclusion but was shouted down by Dr. Ranney: "Dr. Howland was there and gave his evidence among others and almost before we had time Dr. Ranney [said] 'Clearly a case of accidental drowning; accidental drowning is the verdict.' One of the old guides [George Rowe] started to remonstrate a little, but [Dr. Ranney announced], 'The case is closed.' So there's the way it went." Tape recording of Mark Robinson, circa 1953, in conversation with Alex Edminson. Courtesy of the Algonquin Park Archives.

15. Charles F. Plewman, "Reflections on the Passing of Tom Thomson," Canadian Camping Magazine, 1972. Also, Ralph Bice in conversation with the author, July 25, 1990 stated that Winnifred Trainor "always thought that there was some foul play."

16. Margaret Howland, letter to the author's father, dated May 2, 1969. William T. Little Archives.

17. Library and Archives Canada, MG30 D38 "Blodwen Davies fonds," Vol. 11. George Thomson, Letter to Blodwen Davies, June 8, 1931. Note: Originals withdrawn from circulation. Copies available on microfilm C-4579.

18. Library and Archives, National Gallery of Canada, Dr. James M. MacCallum papers, J.S. Fraser, Letter to Dr. James MacCallum, December 29, 1917.

19. Charles F. Plewman, "Reflections on the passing of Tom Thomson," *Canadian Camping Magazine* 24, no 2 (Winter, 1972) 6–9.

20. Ralph Bice in conversation with the author, July 25, 1990:
    Question: Was Winnie Trainor in touch with a lot of people [regarding Thomson's death]?
    Bice: She always thought that there was some foul play.

21. Library and Archives, National Gallery of Canada, Dr. James M. MacCallum papers, Margaret Thomson, Letter to Dr. James MacCallum, September 9, 1917.

22. Blanche Linton quoted in letter, June 5, 1971, Judge William T. Little archive.

23. Ibid.

24. Ibid.

25. Ibid.
26. Ibid.
27. Saunders, Audrey, handwritten notes from interview with Molly Colson during the summer of 1944. Courtesy of the Algonquin Park Archives.
28. Tape recording of Mark Robinson, circa 1953, in conversation with Alex Edminson. Robinson had also mentioned this incident to the author Audrey Saunders nine years previously during research for her book Algonquin Story.
29. Blanche Linton quoted in letter, June 5, 1971, Judge William T. Little archive.
30. Library and Archives Canada/Bibliotheque et Archives Canada, MG30 D38 "Blodwen Davies fonds," Vol. 11, Louise Henry, Letter to Blodwen Davies, March 11, 1931.
31. Ibid.
32. Library and Archives Canada, MG30 D38 "Blodwen Davies fonds," Vol. 11. Mark Robinson and Blodwen Davies, Response to Blodwen Davies' questions, September 4, 1930. Notes: Originals withdrawn from circulation. Copies available on microfilm C-4579.
33. Library and Archives Canada, MG30 D38 "Blodwen Davies fonds," Vol. 11. Alan H. Ross, Letter to Blodwen Davies, June 11, 1930. Notes: Original document withdrawn from circulation. Copy available on microfilm C-4579.
34. Library and Archives Canada, MG30 D38 "Blodwen Davies fonds," Vol. 11. Ed Godin, Letter to Blodwen Davies, November 17, 1930. Notes: Original document withdrawn from circulation. Copy available on microfilm C-4579.
35. Tape recording of Mark Robinson, circa 1953, in conversation with Alex Edminson.
36. Letter from Irene Ewing, to Judge William T. Little, 1969, William T. Little Archive.

Chapter Eight

1. Bice, Ralph, interview with the author in 1990. John Little archives.
2. Rose Thomas and Jack Wilkinson, Interviewed at Kish-Kaduk Lodge, Algonquin Park, February 11, 1976, by Rory MacKay, courtesy of the Algonquin Park Archives.
3. Letter from Peg Thomson to Minnie Thomson, July 22, 1917. Source: https://web.archive.org/web/20170328194615/http://tomthomsonart .com/letters/peg-thomson-minnie-thomson-july-22-1917.
4. Library and Archives Canada/Bibliotheque et Archives Canada, MG30 D284 "Tom Thomson Collection," Vol 1 File 23. The Bell Telephone Company of Canada, Winnifred Trainor's phone bill for July 18, 1917.

5. Library and Archives Canada/Bibliotheque et Archives Canada, MG30 D284 "Tom Thomson Collection," Vol. 1 Files 3–6, Winnifred Trainor, letter to T.J. Harkness, August 11, 1917.

6. Letter from Peg Thomson to Minnie Thomson, July 22, 1917. Source: https://web.archive.org/web/20170328194615/http://tomthomsonart. com/letters/peg-thomson-minnie-thomson-july-22-1917.

7. "Ex-Undertaker Says He Exhumed Tom Thomson's Body," *Regina Leader-Post*, October 12, 1956, in which the Undertaker Churchill says, "She phoned the undertaker in Kearney, who had been in charge of the funeral near Canoe Lake, but he refused to exhume the body."

8. Ibid.

9. Library and Archives, National Gallery of Canada, Dr. James M. MacCallum papers, Margaret Thomson, Letter to Dr. James MacCallum, September 9, 1917.

10. Trent University Archives, Addison family fonds, 97–011, Mark Robinson Daily Journal, July 18, 1917.

11. Trent University Archives, Addison family fonds, 97–011, Mark Robinson Daily Journal, July 19, 1917. Robinson writes of the previous evening's activities: "Mr. Churchill undertaker of Huntsville, Ontario arrived last night . . ." Also, Blodwen Davies, "Application for the exhumation of the body of one Thos. Thomson drowned in Canoe Lake in 1917," July 27, 1931. Archives of Ontario, RG-4-32, "Attorney general Central Registry Criminal and Civil Files," File # 2225: "The undertaker arrived on the 9:12 p.m. train which may have been late, as the persons concerned have a recollection of him arriving "near midnight."

12. Shannon Fraser in conversation with Judge William T. Little, recollected in the book *The Tom Thomson Mystery* (McGraw-Hill, 1970).

13. Archives of Ontario, RG 4–32, Attorney general Central Registry Criminal and Civil Files, File #2225, Blodwen Davies, "Application for the exhumation of the body of one Thos. Thomson drowned in Canoe Lake in 1917," July 27, 1931. Miss Davies, who interviewed a good many of the principals in the Thomson drama, reports that, "George Rowe was with the undertaker on his way in to Mowat Lodge. Rowe recalls that the man was anxious to be alone and refused offers of help."

14. Ibid.

15. What information regarding the tools that were picked up from Mowat Lodge was related to my father by Shannon Fraser in 1930. According to my father Fraser related that, "The plan was that the casket was to go out on the next morning's train. After an 8:00 p.m. pickup, about an hour to pick up shovels, lantern, crow bar, etc., from the Mowat Lodge tool shed, and riding up the hill to the cemetery, the undertaker said he would do the job himself and for me to return around midnight."

16. Franklin W. Churchill, quoted in the newspaper article published in the *Regina Leader Post*, October 13, 1956, pg. 13.
17. Archives of Ontario, RG 4–32, Attorney general Central Registry Criminal and Civil Files, File #2225, Blodwen Davies, "Application for the exhumation of the body of one Thos. Thomson drowned in Canoe Lake in 1917," July 27, 1931. This was confirmed to my father by Shannon Fraser in 1930 and by Mark Robinson.
18. Library and Archives, National Gallery of Canada, Dr. James M. MacCallum papers, Tom Thomson, Letter to Dr. James MacCallum, July 7, 1917.
19. Jack Wilkinson, quoted from an interview with by Rory MacKay. APMA Oral History Series. Algonquin Park Museum and Archives, February 11, 1976. Courtesy of Algonquin Park Archives.
20. Letter from Peg Thomson to Minnie Thomson, July 22, 1917. Source: https://web.archive.org/web/20170328194615/http://tomthomsonart .com/letters/peg-thomson-minnie-thomson-july-22-1917.
21. Library and Archives, National Gallery of Canada, Dr. James M. MacCallum papers, George Thomson, Letter to Dr. James MacCallum, July 19, 1917.
22. *Owen Sound Times*, July 20, 1917: "The body, accompanied by Mr. George Thomson, is expected in Owen Sound at noon on Friday, and in this case, the funeral, which is to be private, will leave his father's residence Friday afternoon. The remains will be interred in Leith cemetery."
23. Tape recording of Mark Robinson, circa 1953, in conversation with Alex Edminson.
24. Ibid.
25. Harry Ebbs, M.D., interviewed at his home in Toronto, Ontario on November 26, 1975 by Rory Mackay. Courtesy of the Algonquin Park Archives and the Ebbs family.
26. Jack Wilkinson and Rose Thomas, Interviewed at Kish-Kaduk Lodge, Algonquin Park, February 11, 1976, by Rory MacKay. Courtesy of the Algonquin Park Archives.

    Wilkinson: Well, anyway the train came into Canoe Lake Station about eight o'clock at night from Parry Sound. I think it was around 8:00. It was after supper anyway, and was getting dark. The coffin came in on that train. Shannon Fraser met them with the buggy.
    Thomas: The noon train, the "Buffalo Train" we called it, got in around noon. Then it was the weigh freight running. If I remember right, the coffin went out on the weigh freight.
27. Trent University Archives, Addison family fonds, 97–011, Mark Robinson Daily Journal, July 19, 1917.
28. Letter from Peggy Thomson to Minnie Thomson, July 22, 1917. Source: https://web.archive.org/web/20170328194615/http://tomthomsonart .com/letters/peg-thomson-minnie-thomson-july-22-1917

29. Tape recording of Mark Robinson, circa 1953, in conversation with Alex Edminson. Robinson recollected: "After [the undertaker] had gone, the Superintendent called me up and he said, 'Go down to the cemetery and if they haven't filled the grave in, fill it in. Close it up.'"

30. Ibid.

31. Archives of Ontario, RG 4–32, Attorney general Central Registry Criminal and Civil Files, File #2225, Blodwen Davies, "Application for the exhumation of the body of one Thos. Thomson drowned in Canoe Lake in 1917," July 27, 1931. Davies states: "Robinson does not believe that the body was ever disturbed. The flowers that had been laid on the grave at the funeral were not moved."

32. Tape recording of Mark Robinson, circa 1953, in conversation with Alex Edminson.

33. Harry Ebbs, M.D., Interviewed at his home in Toronto, Ontario on November 26, 1975 by Rory Mackay. Courtesy of the Algonquin Park Archives and the Ebbs family.

34. Dr. Noble Sharpe, "The Canoe Lake Mystery," *Canadian Society of Forensic Science Journal*, 3 (June 31, 1970): 34–40.

35. "We opened the grave and took the coffin and the rough-box out of the grave . . . I transferred the remains into a metal box which I could seal. The empty coffin and rough box were put back into the grave and the grave was filled again." Franklin W. Churchill, quoted in a newspaper article published in the *Regina Leader Post*, October 13, 1956, pg. 13.

36. Gregory Klages, *The Many Deaths of Tom Thomson* (Toronto, Ontario: Dundurn Press, 2016), 108. He states: "Taylor Statten recorded a response on October 17, 1956. He prefaces his recording by noting that he was not in Canoe Lake at the time of Tom Thomson's death. However, he relates what he claims Shannon Fraser told him about the 1917 exhumation.

    According to Statten, Fraser took the undertaker to the cemetery to drop off the coffin. As darkness started to fall, Fraser suggested the undertaker come down to the Lodge for something to eat. He could spend the night there and get to his work in the morning. The undertaker declined, telling Fraser that he would get to work. He asked Fraser to return the next morning [Note: not sure if this is anytime after 12:00 a.m. or later in the morning] and pick him up, when he'd have the coffin ready to go to the train station. Fraser did as requested, but concluded that there was not a body in the coffin. . . . During his reflection, Statten notes that Ed Colson, proprietor of the Algonquin Hotel, had also confided that he was sure there was no body in the coffin. Similarly, Mark Robinson, after looking at the original gravesite the day after the exhumation, concluded that the body had not been removed."

37. William T. Little, *The Tom Thomson Mystery*, "Dorothy Stone's Recollections," (Toronto, Ontario: McGraw-Hill, Toronto, 1970), 106–109.

38. Trent University Archives, Addison family fonds, 97–011, Mark Robinson Daily Journal, July 19, 1917.
39. *Globe and Mail*, "Brother Believes Thomson's Body Buried At Leith," October 11, 1956.
40. Franklin W. Churchill, quoted in a newspaper article published in the *Regina Leader Post*, October 13, 1956, pg. 13.
41. Letter from Peggy Thomson to Minnie Thomson, July 22, 1917. Source: https://web.archive.org/web/20170328194615/http://tomthomsonart .com/letters/peg-thomson-minnie-thomson-july-22-1917
42. Library and Archives Canada/Bibliotheque et Archives Canada, MG30 D38, "Blodwen Davies Fold," Vol. 11, Copy of Entry for Tom Thomson in Burial Register of Knox United Church, Owen Sound, July 20, 1931.

Chapter Nine

1. Charles Plewman quoted in "Predicament with Fiancé: Thomson May Have Taken Life In Algonquin Park," *Pembroke Observer*, February 14, 1972.
2. Ibid.
3. Ibid.
4. Charles F. Plewman, "Reflections on the Passing of Tom Thomson," *Canadian Camping Magazine*, 1972.
5. Charles Plewman quoted in "Predicament with Fiancé: Thomson May Have Taken Life In Algonquin Park," *Pembroke Observer*, February 14, 1972.
6. Charles F. Plewman, "Reflections on the Passing of Tom Thomson," *Canadian Camping Magazine*, 1972.
7. Ibid.
8. Library and Archives, National Gallery of Canada, Dr. James. M. MacCallum Papers, George Thomson, Letter to J.S. Fraser, December 25, 1917.
9. Library and Archives Canada/Bibliotheque et Archives Canada, MG30 D284, "Tom Thomson Collection," Vol. 1, File 6, J.S. Fraser, Letter to George Thomson, December 29, 1917.
10. Library and Archives, National Gallery of Canada, Dr. James M. MacCallum Papers, J.S. Fraser, Letter to Dr. James MacCallum, December 29, 1917.
11. Library and Archives, National Gallery of Canada, Dr. James M. MacCallum Papers, T.J. Harkness, Letter to Dr. James MacCallum, November 3, 1917.
12. Library and Archives, National Gallery of Canada, Dr. James M. MacCallum Papers, Elizabeth Harkness, Letter to Dr. James MacCallum, February 19, 1918.
13. Trent University Archives, Blodwen Davies fonds, 91–001/1/16, Alex [Y. Jackson], Letter to Yvonne, September 15, 1966.
14. Archives of Ontario, RG 4–32 "Attorney general Central Registry Criminal and Civil Files," File #2225, Blodwen Davies, "Application for the

exhumation of the body of one Thos. Thomson drowned in Canoe Lake in 1917," July 27, 1931.

15. Library and Archives Canada/Bibliotheque et Archives Canada, MG30 D38, Blodwen Davies Fonds, Vol. 11, George Thomson, Letter to Blodwen Davies, June 8, 1931. Note: Original document withdrawn from circulation. Copy available on microfilm C-4579.

16. William T. Little, *The Tom Thomson Mystery*, "Dorothy Stone's Recollections," (Toronto, Ontario: McGraw-Hill, Toronto, 1970), 106–109.

17. Robert Hughes, *The Portable van Gogh*, (Universe, 2002), 8.

18. Simon Kyaga, Mikael Landén, Marcus Boman, Christina M. Hultman, Niklas Långström, and Paul Lichtenstein. "Mental illness, suicide and creativity: 40-Year prospective total population study." *Journal of Psychiatric Research*, 2012, https://www.ncbi.nlm.nih.gov/pubmed/23063328.

19. Simon Kyaga, Paul Lichtenstein, Marcus Boman, Christina M. Hultman, Niklas Långström, and Mikael Landén, "Creativity and mental disorder: family study of 300,000 people with severe mental disorder," *British Journal of Psychiatry*, November 2011, https://www.ncbi.nlm.nih.gov /pubmed/21653945

20. Letter from Stuart L. Thompson to Alan Jarvis, Director of the National Gallery of Canada, Ottawa, February 4, 1956 (presently unlocated by the Library and Archives of the National Gallery of Canada), republished at: http://tomthomsoncatalogue.org/page/?name=missing _documents_1970s

21. Library and Archives Canada/Bibliotheque et Archives Canada, MG30 D38, Blodwen Davies Fond, Vol. 11, Mark Robinson, Letter to Blodwen Davies, March 23, 1930. Note: Original document withdrawn from circulation. Copy available on microfilm C-4579.

22. Tape recording of Mark Robinson, circa 1953, in conversation with Alex Edminson.

23. Minnie Henry (Thomson's sister) wrote in 1931 that, "In 1915 . . . I noticed a great change in Tom. He seemed engrossed with his work and much quieter. He told us then that he was going to try again to enlist, and if they turned him down he might come west and paint the Rocky Mountains. He was worried that no one was buying pictures." (Library and Archives Canada/Bibliotheque et Archives Canada, MG30 D38, Blodwen Davies Fond, Vol. 11, Mark Robinson, Letter to Blodwen Davies, March 23, 1930. Note: Original document withdrawn from circulation. Copy available on microfilm C-4579.) Also, Alan H. Ross, Thomson's longtime friend from childhood, got together with Thomson when the latter was twenty-three years old. During their get together Ross related that Thomson "embosomed himself, lamenting his lack of success in life in terms that rather astonished me." (Library and Archives Canada/Bibliotheque et Archives Canada, MG30 D38, Blodwen Davies Fond, Vol. 11, Alan H. Ross, Letter to Blodwen Davies, June 1, 1930.

Note: Original document withdrawn from circulation. Copy available on microfilm C-4579.)

24. Reynolds, Nila, "Blanche Linton Remembers Tom Thomson," *Early Canadian Life*, February 1979 edition, pages 18-19.

25. Joan Murray, "Tom Thomson," *The Canadian Encyclopedia*, August 27, 2013, http://www .thecanadianencyclopedia.ca/en/m/article/tom-thomson/.

26. Joan Murray, *Tom Thomson: Design For A Canadian Hero* (Dundurn Publishing, 1998) 33.

27. This quote is from an article that appeared in the *Toronto Star* entitled "Artist Tom Thomson May Have Killed Self Pallbearer, 82, Says." There is no date on the newspaper clipping for the *Star* article, but another article, appearing in the *Pembroke Observer*, entitled "Predicament with Fiancé, Thomson May Have Taken Life in Algonquin Park," contains a lot of the same information and was published on Monday, February 14, 1972, which may be the approximate date of the article from the *Toronto Star*.

28. Charles Plewman stated, "I did get the impression from someone that Tom Thomson was somewhat of a pacifist and not interested in enlisting in World War One. Incidentally, he had given up hunting." Charles F. Plewman, "Reflections on the passing of Tom Thomson," *Canadian Camping Magazine*, 1972.

29. Elva Henry stated, "She said that if he didn't like someone he'd walk out of the room, which is what he did up north whenever Martin Blecher came into the room." Library and Archives Canada/Bibliotheque et Archives Canada, MG30 D404, "Harold Town Fond," Vol. 30, File 15, Elva Henry, Interview with Elva Henry, Harold Town, November 15, 1973.

30. Library and Archives Canada/Bibliotheque et Archives Canada, MG30 D284 'Tom Thomson Collection', Vol. 1 File 2, Tom Thomson, Letter to Tom (T.J. Harkness), April 31, 1917.

31. Ewing, Irene, Letter to Judge William T. Little, July 1969; William T. Little Archives.

32. Ewing, Irene, Letter to Judge William T. Little, February 7, 1969; William T. Little Archives.

33. Ibid.

34. William T. Little, *The Tom Thomson Mystery* (Toronto, Ontario: McGraw-Hill, Toronto, 1970), 64.

35. Ralph Bice in conversation with the author, July 25, 1990.

36. According to MacGregor, "He [Dr. Pocock] told me his patient and friend 'never complained to me of any pregnancies or abortions or anything' and did not even care to imagine that any such thing could have taken place." Roy MacGregor, *Northern Light: The Enduring Mystery of Tom Thomson And the Woman Who Loved Him*, (Canada: Random House, 2010), 220.

37. Interview with Wilfred Pocock, M.D., by Ron Pittaway, November 8, 1978, Courtesy of the Algonquin Park Archives. Ibid.

38. Tape recording of Mark Robinson, circa 1953, in conversation with Alex Edminson.

39. Ibid.

40. Dr. Noble Sharpe stated, "Tom was socially inclined, and he was said to be interested in a local lady. (I had a telephone conversation with this charming person in 1956, and she told me she was engaged to him.)" Dr. Noble Sharpe, "The Canoe Lake Mystery," *Canadian Society of Forensic Science Journal* 3 (June 31, 1970): 34–40.

41. Terence Trainor McCormick in communication with my father from December 1968 and February 1969: ". . . the correspondence gave undisputable evidence that Tom and my aunt were engaged to be married." Quoted in *The Tom Thomson Mystery* (Toronto, Ontario: McGraw-Hill, Toronto, 1970), 66.

42. A.Y. Jackson, in conversation with my father at Kleinberg, July 1969 and quoted in *The Tom Thomson Mystery* (Toronto, Ontario: McGraw-Hill, Toronto, 1970), 67: "Early in the Spring of 1917, Tom Thomson wrote a letter to Mrs. Brooks, a lady proprietor of a small lodge on Bella Lake, called Billie Bear today. In his letter he asked for reservations for two in the late summer. Dr. A.Y. Jackson recalls that Mrs. Brooks was very concerned to learn from the newspaper of Tom's tragic death in mid-July and spoke of his wedding plans and the reservations to a number of friends known to Dr. Jackson."

Chapter Ten

1. Library and Archives Canada/Bibliotheque et Archives Canada, MG30 D38, Blodwen Davies Fond, Vol. 11, Mark Robinson, Letter to Blodwen Davies, March 23, 1930.

2. Harry Ebbs, Interviewed on November 26, 1975 by Rory MacKay. Courtesy of the Algonquin Park Archives.

3. William T. Little Archives, Letter from Kay Bridge, Editor, Trade Department McGraw-Hill, May 15, 1969. Kay Bridge was an editor in the Trade Department of McGraw-Hill back in 1969 when she oversaw the publication of my father's book. She was also an avid canoeist and had purchased a canoe from Stan Murdock, who at that time was sixty-nine years old. Murdock had been an apprentice with the Peterborough Canoe Company in the 1920s, and it was during this time when Taylor Statten put out the word that he required a canoe maintenance man to look after the canoes at his two camps on Canoe Lake. Murdock took the job and stayed with Statten's camps for many decades. According to Bridge, Murdock evidently had some concerns about the Blecher women:

   > He has some things to say about the women of the house—they evidently threatened him with clubs or some such when [he] once went on their property. Then, he says, they once threw some of

their furniture into the lake, among it, some tiger maple chairs, which were recovered by someone who still lives at the lake.

4. Ottelyn Addison, *Early Days in Algonquin Park* (McGraw-Hill Ryerson Limited, 1974), 126.

5. Wam Stringer, interview with the author on July 8, 1990.

6. Harry Ebbs, Interviewed on November 26, 1975 by Rory MacKay. Courtesy of the Algonquin Park Archives.

7. Ibid.

8. Ralph Bice in conversation with the author, July 25, 1990.

9. Letter from Stuart L. Thompson to Alan Jarvis, Director of the National Gallery of Canada, February 4, 1956 (presently unlocated by the Library and Archives of the National Gallery of Canada), republished at: http://tomthomsoncatalogue.org/page/?name=missing_documents_1970s.

10. Library and Archives Canada/Bibliotheque et Archives Canada, MG30 D38, Blodwen Davies Fonds, Vol. 11, Louise Henry, Letter to Blodwen Davies, March 11, 1931:

> He was very fond of sports and was an ardent football [soccer] player before he left home, and in one game he had one great toe broken, but stayed with the game till the finish, kicking with the left foot. . . . Tom tried to enlist at the time of the South African war but was turned down on account of fallen arches and the condition of the toe he had broken playing football. He was provoked about this as he could walk twenty miles without feeling it.

11. William T. Little, *The Tom Thomson Mystery,* "A Recollection of Tom Thomson," (Toronto, Ontario: McGraw-Hill, Toronto, 1970), 173–178.

12. Ottelyn Addison, in collaboration with Elizabeth Harwood, *Tom Thomson: The Algonquin Years,* (McGraw-Hill, Ryerson, 1969), 37. See also, "Margaret Thomson Reminiscences of Tom Thomson," *New Frontiers* 5, no. 1 (spring 1956): 21–24. In the article, Thomson's sister Margaret says: "He hated war and said simply in 1914 that he never would kill anyone but would like to help in a hospital, if accepted."

13. Library and Archives Canada/Bibliothequè et Archives Canada, MG30 D38, "Blodwen Davies Fonds," Vol. 11, E.E. Godin, Letter to Blodwen Davies, June 15, 1931. Note: Original document withdrawn from circulation. Copy available on microfilm C-4579.

14. Charles F. Plewman, "Reflections on the passing of Tom Thomson," *Canadian Camping Magazine,* 1972.

15. Tape recording of Mark Robinson, circa 1953, in conversation with Alex Edminson.

16. Ottelyn Addison, in collaboration with Elizabeth Harwood, *Tom Thomson: The Algonquin Years,* (McGraw-Hill, Ryerson, 1969), 37. According to Addison:

> [My father] spent long hours in conversation with Thomson and knew him very well. Given the temper of the times, it is inconceiv-

able that Robinson could have retained the respect and admiration that he always showed for the artist if he had had any doubt whatever about his attempts at enlistment.

17. Library and Archives Canada/Bibliotheque et Archives Canada, MG30 D38, "Blodwen Davies Fonds," Vol. 11, Minnie Henry, Letter to Blodwen Davies, February 2, 1931.

18. Archives of Ontario, MU583/F1066, William Colgate Collection, Files on Tom Thomson 1915–1958. File 11A—"Tom Thomson Correspondence, 1915–1943," Tom Thomson, Letter to J.E.H. MacDonald, July 22, 1915.

19. William T. Little, *The Tom Thomson Mystery*, (Toronto, Ontario: McGraw-Hill, Toronto, 1970). As my Dad recalled:

Martin Blecher was alleged to have been staying long periods of time in Canada to avoid involvement in the American war effort, which had assumed virtually active participation by early 1917, awaiting only the formality of a declaration of war to send troops to Europe. Mark [Robinson] recalled a U.S. agent looking for Blecher in the Park because he "was going to take him back," but the agent left without Martin.

20. Tape recording of Mark Robinson, circa 1953, in conversation with Alex Edminson. Courtesy of the Algonquin Park Archives. This incident was also told to Audrey Saunders; and is found in her typed research notes entitled "Mark Robinson's Information Connected With Tom Thomson, Given In Conversation At Algonquin Park During The Summer Of 1944 To A.H.S.," for her book *Algonquin Story*. She writes: "In answer to the question, "Did Tom Thomson have enemies?" Mark pointed out that he had ragged Martin Blecher (Jr.) for not being in the American army." Courtesy of Algonquin Park Archives.

21. Tape recording of Mark Robinson, circa 1953, in conversation with Alex Edminson.

22. Audrey Saunders, in interviewing Mark Robinson in 1944 for her book *Algonquin Story*, had written in her notes entitled "Mark Robinson's Information Connected With Tom Thomson, Given In Conversation At Algonquin Park During The Summer Of 1944 To A.H.S.": "A man by the name of Comiskay came to Canoe Lake, perhaps to take M.B. back for the American army. He may have been bought off because Blecher was wealthy enough to do so." Courtesy of the Algonquin Park Archives.

23. Trent University Archives, Addison Family fonds, 97–011, Mark Robinson, Daily Journal, May 14, 1917.

24. The War Department of the United States was in existence from August 7, 1789 until September 18, 1947, when it was split into the Department of the Army and Department of the Air Force and later joined the Department of the Navy as part of the new joint National Military Establishment and renamed the United States Department of Defense in 1949.

25. Library and Archives Canada/Bibliotheque et Archives Canada, MG30 D38, "Blodwen Davies Fond," Vol. 11, Major General Bridges, Letter to

Blodwen Davies, June 27, 1931. Note: Original document withdrawn from circulation. Copy Available on microfilm C-4579.

26. Ibid.

27. "Tom, as I knew him, was also a quiet, retiring, fellow. Tall, like [J.E.H.] MacDonald, they had much in common. Indeed, they exercised a steadying influence on some of the too vivacious, lively spirits who worked in the same room. Tom was generous almost to a fault and possessed a quiet sense of humor." Library and Archives Canada/Bibliotheque et Archives Canada, MG30 D284 Tom Thomson Collection, NO. T485.R82, Leonard Rossell, Reminiscences of Grip, members of the Group of Seven and Tom Thomson, Before 1953, 1–6.

28. "Well he [Blecher] used to come over to Mowat Lodge and we used to sit around in the sitting room and he was of German extraction and he had a sister living there. Whenever he had nothing to do he would come over and sit down and we would all talk. Of course Tom would go over to the farthest corner of the room where there was no light, you know, and start [to read] the book. He didn't join in so much. But Blecher was there. I don't think Blecher had anything to do with it. That was simply a myth. Just a myth to me. They never saw one another during the day and they didn't seem to have any antagonism towards him. And I'm damned sure that Winnifred never went with Blecher. He was an unattractive sort of a blowzy individual and quite German—slightly, his accent. And they had a cottage—why he was living up there I don't know. But he was." Daphne Crombie, interviewed by Ron Pittaway, Toronto, 1977. Courtesy of the Algonquin Park Archives. Also, Ralph Bice, who had known Martin Blecher Junior personally, had told the author "he was an arrogant, over-bearing German." Ralph Bice in conversation with the author, July 25, 1990.

29. "Artist Says Tom Thomson Was A Kind, Helpful Man," *Barrie Examiner*, March 30, 1967.

30. Archives of Ontario, RG 53 'Dept. of the Provincial Secretary, Recording Office', RG 53–11 Vol. 1. Algonquin Provincial Park crown leases. Container D311503 5/53/5/4/3., Ontario. Dept. of the Provincial Secretary, Recording Office, "Algonquin Park Lease #1889 (J. S. Fraser), 1913," September 18, 1913, Folio 18.

31. Ottelyn Addison, *Early Days in Algonquin Park* (McGraw-Hill Ryerson Limited, 1974), 126.

32. Elva Henry (the wife of Thomson's nephew George) learned from the family that: "If [Tom] didn't like someone he'd walk out of the room, which is what he did up north whenever Martin Blecher [Junior] came into the room." Library and Archives Canada/Bibliotheque et Archives Canada, MG30 D404, "Harold Town Fond," Vol. 30, File 15, Elva Henry, Interview with Elva Henry, Harold Town, November 15, 1973.

33. According to Blodwen Davies: "Blecher's mother, when interviewed in the summer of 1930 refused to discuss Thomson." Archives of Ontario, RG

4–32 'Attorney General Central Registry Criminal and Civil Files', File #2225, Blodwen Davies, "Application for the exhumation of the body of one Thos. Thomson drowned in Canoe Lake in 1917," July 27, 1931.

34. Audrey Saunders, *Algonquin Story* (Ontario Department of Lands and Forests, 1946), 25–26.

35. Tape recording of Mark Robinson, circa 1953, in conversation with Alex Edminson.

36. Library and Archives Canada/Bibliotheque et Archives Canada, MG30 D38, "Blodwen Davies Fond," Vol. 11, Alan. H. Ross, Letter to Blodwen Davies, June 1, 1930. Note: Original document withdrawn from circulation. Copy available on microfilm C-4579.

37. Library and Archives Canada/Bibliotheque et Archives Canada, MG30 D38, "Blodwen Davies Fond," Alan H. Ross, Letter to Blodwen Davies, June 11, 1930. Note: Original document withdrawn from circulation. Copy available on microfilm C-4579.

38. Letter from Stuart L. Thompson to Alan Jarvis, Director of the National Gallery of Canada, February 4, 1956 (presently unlocated by the Library and Archives of the National Gallery of Canada), republished at: http://tomthomsoncatalogue.org/page/?name=missing_documents_1970s.

39. Ralph Bice in conversation with the author, July 25, 1990.

40. There is some evidence that Mark Robinson was aware of Fraser's ability to bring alcohol into the park, as evidenced by the ranger's diary entry for July 19, 1917: "Morning wet. Heavy rain clearing off about 8:30 a.m. I have received instructions this morning to have Mr. J.S. Fraser have no more booze come in . . ." Trent University Archives, Addison Family fonds, 97–011, Mark Robinson, Daily Journal, July 19, 1917.

41. Blanche Linton quoted in letter, June 5, 1971, Judge William T. Little archive.

42. My father learned of the quarrel from speaking with George Rowe and Shannon Fraser. Mark Robinson would also share with my father what he had learned about it. In his book, my father referred to the altercation thusly: "Neither man had any regard for the other for a long time before this incident occurred but this had been the most open hostility anyone at Canoe Lake had seen take place between them. Mark Robinson maintained that although he had not been present on this particular evening, he had at different times noted that 'bad blood' existed between the two men from almost their first meeting." William T. Little, *The Tom Thomson Mystery*, (Toronto, Ontario: McGraw-Hill, Toronto, 1970), 40.

43. Library and Archives Canada/Bibliotheque et Archives Canada, MG30 D38, "Blodwen Davies Fonds," Vol. 11, Alan. H. Ross, Letter to Blodwen Davies, June 1, 1930. Note: Original document withdrawn from circulation. Copy available on microfilm C-4579.

44. https://www.merriam-webster.com/dictionary/cordially.

45. Albert H. Robson, *Canadian Landscape Painters* (Ryerson Press, 1932).

46. *Toronto Telegram* newspaper interview with Thomson's younger brother, Fraser Thomson; "Unearthing of Skeleton Revives Artist Mystery," October 10, 1956. Also, Davies, Blodwen, "Application for the exhumation of the body of one Thos. Thomson drowned in Canoe Lake in 1917," July 27, 1931. Archives of Ontario, RG-4-32, "Attorney general Central Registry Criminal and Civil Files," File # 2225. When Blodwen Davies was preparing her book on Thomson in the 1930s she discovered that The Group of Seven member Arthur Lismer had also known about Thomson's feud with Blecher, having learned first-hand about it from Thomson himself:

> Nothing came out at the trial [inquest – Ed] of the quarrels between Martin Blecher, who was then about 25 years of age, and Thomson. The quarrels are said to have been violent. Thomson wrote Lismer, then at Halifax, one of his intimate friends, about the quarrels. The letters have not been preserved.

47. Ralph Bice in conversation with the author, July 25, 1990.
48. Mark Robinson stated in 1953 that he had known for a fact that Thomson "twitted" Blecher about being a deserter. And Noble Sharpe would report that Winnie Trainor once contacted him (when he was conducting the investigation into the skeleton that had been found in Thomson's original Canoe Lake grave), and he learned that, "their [Thomson and Blecher] altercations reached a climax when Tom accused the other man of being a deserter from the American Army." Source: Dr. Noble Sharpe, "The Canoe Lake Mystery," *Canadian Society of Forensic Science Journal*, June 1970.
49. William T. Little, *The Tom Thomson Mystery*, (Toronto, Ontario: McGraw-Hill, Toronto, 1970).
50. Library and Archives Canada/Bibliotheque et Archives Canada, MG30 D38, "Blodwen Davies Fonds," George Thomson, Letter to Blodwen Davies, June 8, 1931. Note: Original document withdrawn from circulation. Copy Available on microfilm C-4579.
51. According to Robert P. Little, Blecher never reported the upturned canoe to anyone; rather the canoe had been spotted in the Blecher boathouse by Thomson's friend and fellow guide Charlie Scrim, and it was Scrim who then made the news of its location public; Robert P. Little, "Some Recollections of Tom Thomson and Canoe Lake," *Culture* 16 (1955), 210–222. The reader will further recall that Emily Thomas had reported that, "Martin Blecher saw the canoe floating, he went out and took it to Fraser's. No one heard anything till Mr. Fraser came down Monday morning with the mail." Letter to Ottelyn Addison from Mrs. Edwin Thomas, Kish-Kaduk Lodge, Algonquin Park, February 16, 1956 and excerpted in the book *Tom Thomson: The Algonquin Years*.
52. "Then again Tom did not care for Martin Blecher." Library and Archives Canada/Bibliotheque et Archives Canada, MG30 D284 'Tom Thomson collection', Vol. 1 File 5, Winifred Trainor, Letter to [George?] Thomson, September 17, 1917

53. Tape recording of Mark Robinson, circa 1953, in conversation with Alex Edminson. Robinson states:

> Across the left temple here there was a mark, it looked as it he had been struck—struck with the edge of a paddle, just up across the left temple like that . . . I may state right here that I think Thomson was struck on the head by a paddle by some person that afternoon. I don't think Tom died a natural death from drowning.

54. Harry Ebbs, Interviewed on November 26, 1975 by Rory MacKay. Courtesy of the Algonquin Park Archives.

Chapter Eleven

1. Library and Archives, National Gallery of Canada, Dr. James M. MacCallum papers, Margaret Thomson, Letter to Dr. James MacCallum, September 9, 1917.

2. Library and Archives Canada/Bibliotheque et Archives Canada, MG30 D284, "Tom Thomson Collection," Vol. 1, File 5, T. J. Harkness, Letter to J. S. Fraser, Sept. 12, 1917.

3. "Efforts Being Made to Find Him Since Sunday Last – Is a Noted Artist," *Owen Sound Sun*, July 13, 1917. The article stated: "A telegram from Canoe Lake, Algonquin Park, received by his parents, Mr. and Mrs. John Thomson, 4th Ave. E., on Tuesday announced that a canoe belonging to their son, Thomas Thomson, the well known Toronto artist, had been found on the lake and no trace of Mr. Thomson could be found. He had arrived at Canoe Lake on Saturday and the canoe had been found the following day." See also T.J. Harkness' letter to Shannon Fraser in which Harkness states: "I know what he drew from the bank when he was away, and he was guiding a few weeks and no doubt was paid for it and where do you suppose his money went to." Library and Archives Canada/ Bibliotheque et Archives Canada, MG30 D284 'Tom Thomson collection', Vol. 1 File 5, T. J. Harkness, Letter to J. S. Fraser, September 12, 1917.

4. Library and Archives Canada/Bibliotheque et Archives Canada, MG30 D284, "Tom Thomson Collection," Vol. 1, File 3, J.S. Fraser, Letter to John Thomson, July 18, 1917. In his letter, Fraser reports the following:

> Dear Sir: We found your son floating in Canoe Lake on Monday morning about nine o clock in a most dreadful condition the flesh was coming off his hands. I sent for the undertaker and they found him in such a condition [illegible] he had to be buried at once he is buried in a little grave yard over looking Canoe Lake a beautiful spot. The Dr. found a bruise over his eye and thinks he fell and was hurt and this is how the accident happened.
> Yours Truly, J. S. Fraser

5. Charles F. Plewman, "Reflections on the passing of Tom Thomson," *Canadian Camping Magazine*, 1972.

6. Fraser had been the one to receive the bill directly from Robert Flavelle, indicating that the undertaker was acting under Fraser's instructions (i.e., Fraser was the client). Fraser mentions receiving the bill from Flavelle in a letter that he wrote to T.J. Harkness. Library and Archives Canada/Bibliotheque et Archives Canada, MG30 D284, "Tom Thomson Collection," Vol. 1, File 4, J.S. Fraser, Letter to T.J. Harkness, August 6, 1917.

7. William T. Little, *The Tom Thomson Mystery* (Toronto, Ontario: McGraw-Hill, Toronto, 1970), 106–109. Dorothy Stone's recollection of Beatty and Fraser intimating that "we knew where he wanted to stay and we saw to it that he stayed there." Toward this end, it must be remembered that it was Fraser who had taken the Huntsville undertaker to and from the original gravesite on the night that Thomson's body was supposedly exhumed; Archives of Ontario, RG 4–32 'Attorney general Central Registry Criminal and Civil Files', File #2225, Blodwen Davies, "Application for the exhumation of the body of one Thos. Thomson drowned in Canoe Lake in 1917," July 27, 1931.

8. Library and Archives, National Gallery of Canada, Dr. James M. MacCallum papers, Margaret Thomson, Letter to Dr. James MacCallum, September 9, 1917.

9. Library and Archives, National Gallery of Canada, Dr. James M. MacCallum Papers, Elizabeth Harkness, Letter to Dr. James MacCallum, February 19, 1918.

10. Fraser Thomson: "There has been a lot of conjecture about how he died; whether foul play or an accident caused his death. I know that there had been ill will between a German who worked at one of the lodges and my brother. Tom had been trying to enlist and the German had said something to him. There was a quarrel. Then Tom was found dead soon afterward. Who knows what happened? His death will always be a mystery."

    Toronto Telegram newspaper interview with Thomson's younger brother, Fraser Thomson; "Unearthing of Skeleton Revives Artist Mystery," October 10, 1956.; George Thomson: "Now I want to say in passing that I have from various sources a pretty accurate account of what happened at the inquest and in common with other friends and relatives of Tom's am more firmly convinced than ever that his death was caused either by accident or foul play". Library and Archives, National Gallery of Canada, Dr. James. M. MacCallum Papers, George Thomson, Letter to J.S. Fraser, December 25, 1917.; Margaret Thomson: "Sometimes I wonder if the man did do anything to harm Tom. I suppose it is wicked to think such a thing, but if anyone did harm him, it was for the little money they could pocket." Library and Archives, National Gallery of Canada, Dr. James M. MacCallum papers, Margaret Thomson, Letter to Dr. James MacCallum, September 9, 1917.

11. Daphne Crombie quoted from her interview with Ronald Pittaway on January 14, 1977 which was recorded at her home in Toronto. Courtesy of the Algonquin Park Archives.

12. Ibid.

13. "It was rumored around Mowat Lodge in 1916–17 (chiefly by Annie Fraser) that Tom Thomson and Winifred Trainor were to be married. A letter left carelessly lying on a dresser gave some substance to this rumor"; Ottelyn Addison, in collaboration with Elizabeth Harwood, *Tom Thomson: The Algonquin Years*, (McGraw-Hill, Ryerson, 1969), 93.

14. Daphne Crombie quoted from her interview with Ronald Pittaway on January 14, 1977 which was recorded at her home in Toronto. Courtesy of the Algonquin Park Archives.

15. Ibid.

16. Ibid.

17. Ibid. "Annie told me all this and also MacCallum."

18. Library and Archives, National Gallery of Canada, Dr. James M. MacCallum papers, Margaret Thomson, Letter to Dr. James MacCallum, September 9, 1917.

19. "1910s Men's Edwardian Fashion and Clothing Guide," https://vintagedancer .com/1900s/edwardian-1910s-historical-mens-fashion-and-clothing-an-overview/.

20. Ibid.

21. "Edwardian Men's Neckties," https://vintagedancer.com/1900s/edwardian -mens-ties/.

22. "Edwardian Men's Shocs—New shoes, Old Style," https://vintagedancer .com/1900s/edwardian-mens-shoes/.

23. "1910s Men's Edwardian Fashion and Clothing Guide," https://vintagedancer .com/1900s/edwardian-1910s-historical-mens-fashion-and-clothing-an -overview/.

24. Tom Harkness had written, "And how do you account for Tom only having .60 cts when found? I know what he drew from the bank when he was away, and he was guiding a few weeks and no doubt was paid for it and where do you suppose his money went to?" (Library and Archives Canada/ Bibliotheque et Archives Canada, MG30 D284 'To Thomson Collection', Vol. 1 File 5, T.J. Harkness, Letter to J.S. Fraser, September 12, 1917).

25. Audrey Saunders, handwritten notes from interview with Molly Colson during the summer of 1944. Courtesy of the Algonquin Park Archives.

26. Library and Archives Canada/Bibliotheque et Archives, Canada, MG30 D284 'Tom Thomson Collection,' Vol. 1 File 5, Winnifred Trainor, Letter to George Thomson, September 17, 1917.

27. Tom Harkness had written to Shannon Fraser: "You told Geo Thomson that you owed Tom a small amount, but you have not given me any information about it."Library and Archives Canada/Bibliotheque et Archives Canada,

MG30 D284, "Tom Thomson Collection," Vol. 1, File 5, T. J. Harkness, Letter to J. S. Fraser, Sept. 12, 1917. See also Library and Archives Canada/Bibliotheque et Archives Canada, MG30 D284 'Tom Thomson Collection', Vol. 1 File 4, J. S. Fraser, Letter to T. J. Harkness, August 6, 1917, and also Library and Archives Canada/Bibliotheque et Archives Canada, MG30 D284 'Tom Thomson Collection,' Vol. 1, File 5, T.J. Harkness letter to J.S. Fraser, September 12, 1917.

28. Library and Archives Canada/Bibliotheque et Archives Canada, MG30 D284 'Tom Thomson Collection,' Vol. 1, Files 6, J.S. Fraser letter to Dr. James MacCallum, November 11, 1917.

29. The correspondence, such as it is, consists of the following:

> Mowat
> P. O.
> Dear Sir
> . . . i seen the Rangers and they said the canoes was worth $10.00 dollars a peace they leak pretty bad they are Pretty old canoes and full of holes so they said that was all they are worth . . . if that Price is all right for the canoes please let me know and i will send the money down right away
> hope this litter finds you all well
> Yours truly,
> J S Fraser

(Library and Archives Canada/Bibliotheque et Archives Canada, MG30 D284, "Tom Thomson Collection," Vol. 1, File 4, J. S. Fraser, Letter to T. J. Harkness, Aug. 6, 1917.)

> Mowat
> Dear Sir . . . .
> You will find in close $5.00 to make up the balance for the canoes i will send his blanket down right a way.

(Library and Archives Canada/Bibliotheque et Archives Canada, MG30 D284, "Tom Thomson Collection," Vol. 1, File 5, J. S. Fraser, Letter to T. J. Harkness, Sept. 8, 1917.)

> I asked her [Winnie Trainor] about the canoe and she said one was bought in 1915. She said she heard Tom remark one time that the old one was the best of the two. I asked her if there were any holes in them and she said there were not. She said Mr. Fraser had been renting them to their borders [at Mowat Lodge] for fifty cents a day. So he was making a dollar a day from the two of them.

(Library and Archives, National Gallery of Canada, Dr. James M. MacCallum Papers, Margaret Thomson, Letter to Dr. James MacCallum, September 9, 1917.)

Annan
Dear Sir:
Your letter received tonight with five dollars enclosed being the
balances on two canoes you claim due the Estate of the late Tom
Thomson . . . You told Geo Thomson that you owed Tom a small
amount, but you have not given me any information about it. Now
Mr. Fraser the Estate demands a full account of everything.

Surely Tom had some personal property. Had he no trunk or
grip or clothes except what you showed Geo Thomson and how do
you account for Tom only having .60 cents when found? I know
what he drew from the bank when he was away, and he was guiding
a few weeks and no doubt was paid for it and where do you suppose
his money went to?

I tell you frankly Mr. Fraser I am suspicious that you are not
dealing square and I hope you will be able to give a satisfactory
explanation of everything.

Another question I would like to ask: did you pay Tom for the
canoes he bought for you and when?

. . . I am waiting your reply.
T.J. Harkness
P.S.: I think I told you before that the family appointed me to look
after Tom's estate and I want a full list of all his belongings.

(Library and Archives Canada/Bibliotheque et Archives Canada, MG30
D284, "Tom Thomson Collection," Vol. 1, File 5, T. J. Harkness, Letter to
J. S. Fraser, Sept. 12, 1917.)

Huntsville, Ont.
Dear Mr. Thomson
Your letter received this a.m., and would say I had the pleasure of
meeting your sister Margaret in Toronto Aug 31 . . . and she asked
me about the $250.00 Tom loaned J. S. Fraser. I told her all I knew
about it and that is at the time, May or June 1915, the loan was
made—and in July 1915 Tom bought a new Chestnut canoe, silk
tent, etc. and went from Canoe Lake on a long trip coming out at
South River about Labor Day. . . . I do not think Tom got his canoe
from Huntsville. Frasers got theirs here. I also heard at the time he
[Shannon Fraser] was trying to make the raise of a loan in town and
was even asked by the agent if I would like to put it up and my reply
was no. I did not know until July 1915, that Tom had made it or I
would have said no for him not to as the thing was risky. . . . You see
the Frasers were money grabbing as usual but it will all come back
to them. . . . Never mind they'll get it yet. As far as Fraser's good
faith he has none. Mark Robinson the Ranger hates him.

Well, Tom said this spring [1917] while at our house that he had loaned Fraser $250.00 for canoes, but that he had got it all back but in little bits though. Again if I had known, I could have got them all wholesale instead of retail and Tom might have realized $50.00 on the outlay instead of nothing. I suppose Frasers thought he would board on till Fall with them. I did not know the amount until this Spring when we happened to bring up Shan's financial standing. . . . Hoping this will be some information to you. You could ask Frasers about it, saying you had come upon some correspondence about this transaction.

I am so sorry I burned my letters that I had left after our home was burned. I had this one where he left the Frasers dissatisfied but he did not tell the reason till the Fall 1915. Then again Tom did not care for Martin Blecher. . . . Mrs. Fraser I think would see you got everything should you request it. I do not think Frasers deserve one thing. Tom no doubt was paying his board well, supplying fish work & etc. His canoes can be easily stored at the Lake. Tom ploughed and planted their garden & ploughed Larry Dixon's garden too.

If you did not want the things around home you could have them sent to Annan. Anyway so as Shan Fraser could not have them around. I suppose Tom would be greened if he knew all now.
W.T.

(Library and Archives Canada/Bibliotheque et Archives Canada, MG30 D284, "Tom Thomson Collection," Vol. 1, File 5, Winifred Trainor, Letter to [George?] Thomson, Sept. 17, 1917.)

Mowat
P.O., Ontario
Dear Dr,
You will have to excuse me for not writing sooner but have been so busy this fall I can hardly find time to write. I bought Tom's two canoes and his people said to pay the men out of the canoe money that searched for Tom's body, so I am sending your $17.50 back after paying out of it $3.20 for cement and freight . . . [note: the cement and freight would have been for the construction of the cairn to Thomson's memory that was being erected at Canoe Lake by Thomson's artist friends from Toronto]
Yours Truly,
J. S. Fraser
(Library and Archives Canada/Bibliotheque et Archives Canada, MG30 D284, "Tom Thomson Collection," Vol. 1, File 6, J. S. Fraser, Letter to Dr. James MacCallum, Nov. 11, 1917.)

It is clear from the above correspondence that Fraser had in fact paid back most of the $250.00 that Thomson had originally loaned him in 1915, but that there was still money owing on that account.

30. "Artist Tom Thomson May Have Killed Self, Pallbearer, 82, Says," *Toronto Star*. While the clipping from the Toronto Star article that I cite has no date, the same information was published in the *Pembroke Observer* on Monday, February 14, 1972 in an article entitled "Predicament with Fiancé. Thomson May Have Taken Life in Algonquin Park," which would indicate that the articles were published at approximately the same time. The *Pembroke Observer*'s article contained the following information:

New information on the mystery surrounding the 1917 death by drowning of Canadian artist Tom Thomson indicates he may have taken his own life because of the desperate situation in which he found himself with his fiancé, Winnie Trainor . Shannon Fraser, operator of the lodge, confided to Mr. Plewman that he thought Thomson had committed suicide because of a predicament with his fiancé. He indicated diplomatically that the Huntsville girl could have been pregnant and "was pressing him (Thomson) to go through with the marriage."

"He (Fraser) intimated that she was coming up to see Tom and have a showdown on the fatal week. In the interview he said that many people weren't aware Thomson and Miss Trainor had been engaged the summer prior to the artist's death and had relations more intimate than was supposed.

31. Ottelyn Addison, in collaboration with Elizabeth Harwood, Tom Thomson: The Algonquin Years, (McGraw-Hill, Ryerson, 1969), 93.

32. Doug Dunford, in conversation with the author, October 1, 2016.

33. Ibid.

34. Library and Archives Canada/Bibliotheque et Archives Canada, MG30 D38 'Blodwen Davies Fond', Vol. 11, J.E.H. Macdonald, Letter to Blodwen Davies, May 21, 1931. Notes: Original document withdrawn from circulation. Copy available on microfilm C-4579.

35. A.J. Casson in conversation with the author, July 1, 1990. John Little Archive.

36. Trent University Archives, Blodwen Davies fonds, 91–001/1/16, Alex [Y. Jackson], Letter to Yvonne, September 15, 1966.

Chapter Twelve

1. Blanche Linton quoted in letter, June 5, 1971, Judge William T. Little archive.

2. Ibid.

3. However, according to Nila Reynolds' interview with Linton (nee Packard): "[Certain of the guides] commented on a possible relationship between Thomson and a ranger's wife then summering the Park which might make Thomson's removal a relief to the husband. Although Blanche did not know the people mentioned, the Colson's niece, Anne Cauldwell, did and asked her aunt [Molly Colson] if the guide's story was true. Mrs. Colson's denial was emphatic: "No, Tom wasn't a man like that."Reynolds, Nila. "Blanche Linton Remembers Tom Thomson," Early Canadian Life, February 1979 edition; page 19. Edwin C. Guillet, "Chapter III—Reflections," in *The Death of Tom Thomson, Canadian Artist: A study of the Evidence at the Coroner's Inquest, 1917* (Self-published, October 31, 1944), 1, 7–9. Note: One of only five copies.

4. Roy MacGregor, *Northern Light: The Enduring Mystery of Tom Thomson And the Woman Who Loved Him* (Random House Canada, 2010), 165–166. MacGregor states that:

    > Dr. Philip Hall, the forensic specialist at the University of Manitoba who who had long been studying the mystery . . . [and that] Hall's familiarity with a number of longtime Canoe Lake residents, including contemporaries from 1917, had convinced him . . . "that Thomson was having an affair with the wife of his murderer, and that he was killed by a man who was perhaps 'the most respected person in the community.' My sources claim that the facts were known to several people, but that everything was hushed up due to the status of and esteem for the murderer.". . . . In Hall's interpretation, Annie Fraser, whom he described as "'somewhat flighty', was the only steady female inhabitant of the lodge, and Thomson was well known as a philanderer."

5. Joan Murray, *The Best of Tom Thomson* (Toronto, Ontario: McCelland & Stewart, 1999), 17.

6. Ibid.

7. Interview with Wilfred Pocock, M.D., by Ron Pittaway, November 8, 1978, Courtesy of the Algonquin Park Archives.

8. Margaret Thomson writing to Dr. James M. MacCallum indicated that, "She [Winnifred Trainor] said that he was intending to leave there [Canoe Lake] in a week or so, and that he didn't want them [the Frasers] to know where he was going, as they were so curious about everything. (Library and Archives, National Gallery of Canada, Dr. James M. MacCallum papers, Margaret Thomson, Letter to Dr. James MacCallum, September 9, 1917).

9. Roy MacGregor, *Northern Light: The Enduring Mystery of Tom Thomson And the Woman Who Loved Him* (Random House Canada, 2010), 323–24.

10. According to Margaret Thomson, "She [Winnifred Trainor] said that Mr. Fraser was the meanest man she ever saw and that her Father detested him." (Library and Archives, National Gallery of Canada, Dr. James M. MacCal-

lum papers, Margaret Thomson, Letter to Dr. James MacCallum, September 9, 1917).

11. Interview with Wilfred Pocock, M.D., by Ron Pittaway, November 8, 1978, Courtesy of the Algonquin Park Archives.

12. Apart from the rumor appearing in my father's book (pp. 140–141), this rumor was also known by longtime Canoe Lake resident Jack Wilkinson who told Algonquin Park researcher/archivist Rory MacKay that, "Martin Blecher was accused of hitting him on the head you know, but of course they had a fight over a girl or something." (Jack Wilkinson and Rose Thomas, Interviewed at Kish-Kaduk Lodge, Algonquin Park, February 11, 1976, by Rory MacKay.) This rumor was also known by Dr. Harry Ebbs, who had first come to Algonquin Park in 1924, and who also told MacKay that, "Tom Thomson and Blecher had words on more than one occasion about the war and their part in it, and then Winnie Trainor came up with her family and lived in a little cottage in the summer there, and there was gossip that both Blecher and Tom Thomson were interested in her, and that they had words." (Harry Ebbs, M.D., interviewed by Rory MacKay at his home in Toronto on November 26, 1975).

13. Robinson's journal entry: "Edger Russell and I had lunch with Mr. and Mrs. Martin Blecher," (Trent University Archives, Addison Family fonds, 97–011, Mark Robinson, Daily Journal, September 19, 1918).

14. Mary I. Garland, *Algonquin Park's Mowat: Little Town of Big Dreams*, (Whitney, Ontario: Friends of Algonquin Park, 2015), 151.

15. Ibid.

16. Ralph Bice in conversation with the author, July 25, 1990.

17. Peter Goddard, "Rare letters reveal rowdy side of Tom Thomson, Group of Seven painter," *Toronto Star*, March 21, 2011, https://www.thestar.com/entertainment/2011/03/21/rare_letters_reveal_rowdy_side_of_tom_thomson_group_of_seven_painter.html.

18. Ibid.

19. "Death on Canoe Lake," *The Record*, January 29, 2011, https://www.therecord.com/whatson-story/2572903-death-on-canoe-lake/.

20. Audrey Saunders, *Algonquin Story* (Ontario Department of Lands and Forests, 1946), 55.

21. Doug Mackey, "Amable du Fond lived in area which carries his name," *Past Forward Heritage Limited,* June 8, 2001, http://www.pastforward.ca/perspectives/June_82001.htm.

22. Ibid.

23. Roy MacGregor, *Northern Light: The Enduring Mystery of Tom Thomson And the Woman Who Loved Him* (Random House Canada, 2010), 126–127.

Chapter Thirteen

1. Rupert Lee, "Canadian Pictures at Wembley," *The Canadian Forum* 14 (August 31, 1924): 338–9.
2. Library and Archives, National Gallery of Canada, Dr. James M. MacCallum Papers, Tom Thomson, Letter to Dr. James MacCallum, October 6, 1914.
3. http://www.heffel.ca/Artist/Buy/Canadian/Tom_Thomson.aspx.
4. Bill Henry, "Sale sets Thomson Record," *Owen Sound Sun Times*, November 27, 2009, http://www.owensoundsuntimes.com/2009/11/27/sale-sets-thomson-record.
5. Blanche Linton quoted in letter, June 5, 1971, Judge William T. Little archive. According to Linton: "He [Thomson] often sold his paintings to tourists for two or three dollars—while doing the repairs those last days he saved the end pieces of the boards he sawed off to paint on (for me this kills A.Y. Jackson's [later] theory of suicide). Blanche recalls admiring his paintings displayed in the Lodge living room and one of the falls which hung in the Guide's dining room."
6. Richard Callighen in conversation with the author, 1990. John Little Archives.
7. Thomson writes in a letter to Dr. MacCallum: "I hear that my swamp picture is down at Ottawa on appro. Hope they keep it." (Library and Archives, National Gallery of Canada, Dr. James M. MacCallum Papers, Tom Thomson, Letter to Dr. James MacCallum, April 22, 1915).
8. Library and Archives Canada/Bibliotheque et Archives Canada, MG30 D284, "Tom Thomson Collection," Vol. 1, File 5, T. J. Harkness, Letter to J.S. Fraser, September 12, 1917.
9. Library and Archives Canada/Bibliotheque et Archives Canada, MG30 D38 Blodwen Davies fonds, Vol. 11, George Thomson, Letter to Blodwen Davies, June 8, 1931. Note: Original document withdrawn from circulation. Copy available on microfilm C-4579
10. Ibid.
11. Archives of Ontario, MU583/F1066 William Colgate Collection, Files on Tom Thomson 1915–1958. File IIA – "Tom Thomson Correspondence, 1915–1943," Margaret Thomson, Letter to Dr. James MacCallum, August 2, 1917.
12. Ibid.
13. Library and Archives Canada/Bibliotheque et Archives Canada, MG30 D284 "Tom Thomson Collection," Vol. 1, File 5, Dr. James MacCallum, Letter to Thomson, September 1, 1917. Notes: Intended recipient was George Thomson, as indicated by the reply coming from George Thomson.
14. Presumably this letter resides in the Library and Archives Canada/Bibliotheque et Archives Canada, MC30 D284 "Tom Thomson Collection," Vol. 1, File 5, Dr. James MacCallum, George Thomson, Letter to Dr. James

MacCallum, September 1917. I say presumably because the author saw a transcript of the Letter at the Tom Thomson Memorial Gallery in Owen Sound.

15. If George Thomson wrote any letters to his brother Tom, none have come forth in any of the archives. Thomson's sister Margaret, writing to Dr. James MacCallum in 1917, indicates that: "Tom wrote very few letters [to his family]. It is one of my regrets now, that I hadn't written to him more often." (Archives of Ontario, MU583/F1066 William Colgate Collection, Files on Tom Thomson 1915–1958. File IIA – "Tom Thomson Correspondence, 1915–1943," Margaret Thomson, Letter to Dr. James MacCallum, August 2, 1917).

16. Library Archives Canada/Bibliotheque et Archives Canada, MG30 D284, "Tom Thomson Collection," Vol. 1, File 7, Dr. James MacCallum, Letter to T.J. Harkness, May 6, 1918.

17. Library and Archives Canada/Bibliotheque et Archives Canada, MG30 D284 'Tom Thomson collection', Vol. 1 File 7, Eric Brown, Letter to Dr. James MacCallum, August 26, 1918.

18. Tom Thomson had received $500 from the National Gallery of Canada for his painting *Northern River* that had been exhibited by the Ontario Society of Artists Forty-Third Annual Exhibition in Toronto during March 13-April 10, 1915. http://tomthomson.org/tom-thomson/a-chronology-of-tom-thomson-s-life/.

19. Library and Archives, National Gallery of Canada, Dr. James M. MacCallum Papers, T.J. Harkness, Letter to Dr. James MacCallum, September 27, 1923.

20. Library and Archives, National Gallery of Canada, Dr. James M. MacCallum Papers, Elizabeth Harkness, Letter to Dr. James MacCallum, February 19, 1918.

21. Trent University Archives, Blodwen Davies fonds, 91–001/1/16, Alex [Y. Jackson], Letter to Yvonne, September 15, 1966.

22. According to Daphne Crombie: "Anyway, they had a fight and Shannon hit Tom, knocked him down by the grate fire, and Tom had a mark on his forehead. I don't know where it was. Annie told me all this and also Dr. Mac-Callum." Daphne Crombie, interviewed by Ronald Pittaway in Toronto on January 14, 1977, Algonquin Park Museum Archives.

23. Trent University Archives, Addison Family fonds, 97–011, Mark Robinson, Daily Journal, Thursday, July 19, 1917.

24. "Tom Thomson's Last Spring," https://ttlastspring.com/2014/10/13/october-13-1917-letter-from-jeh-macdonald-to-john-thomson/amp/.

25. Tom Thomson cairn at Canoe Lake, inscription by J.E.H. MacDonald.

26. J.M. MacCallum, "Tom Thomson: Painter of the North," *The Canadian Magazine*, March 31, 1918.

27. Ibid.

28. "Peg Thomson to Minnie Thomson, July 22, 1917," https://web.archive.org
/web/20170328194615/http://tomthomsonart.com/letters/peg-thomson-
minnie-thomson-july-22-1917.

29. Ralph Bice, interviewed by the author, July 25, 1990.

Chapter Fourteen

1. According to C.A.M. Edwards's book on Taylor Statten:
   > Tom Thomson also became involved in the work that led to the
   > construction of the fireplace. He had occasionally earned a little
   > money when he needed it by clearing underbrush on Little Wap.
   > Taylor had already arranged for a party to come to the island to
   > help build the chimney, but the materials, including a supply of
   > sand, had to be on the island by the time they arrived. Taylor there-
   > fore approached Tom Thomson, for no one else was available at
   > that time. It happened that the artist was just then busily engaged
   > sketching, for it was the middle of a fine sketching season. He tried
   > to find someone else to do the work, but without avail. It was not
   > Tom's nature to refuse help where he had previously received it. The
   > job had to be done and he did it, although at some personal sacri-
   > fice. He set to work with team and scow, hauling sand from Sim's
   > Pit across Canoe Lake to the island. No one turned up to relieve
   > him, so he saw the job through to the end.
   > (C.A.M. Edwards, *Taylor Statten: A Biography*, (Toronto, Ontario:
   > Ryerson Press, 1960), 66.

2. "What is the Brent Run?" https://brentrun.me/what-is-the-brent-run/.

3. Newspaper interview, William T. Little Interview, *The Muskokan*, June 30,
   1988, 26–28.

4. Ibid.

5. Ibid.

6. Audrey Saunders, typed research notes entitled "Mark Robinson's
   Information Connected With Tom Thomson, Given In Conversation At
   Algonquin Park During The Summer Of 1944 To A.H.S., for her book
   Algonquin Story. Courtesy of Algonquin Park Archives.

7. Newspaper interview, William T. Little Interview, *The Muskokan*, June 30,
   1988, 26–28.

8. Braught, Frank, audio recording, AMP-AU-201, interviewed by Taylor
   Statten at Little Wapomeo Island, 1956. Courtesy of Algonquin Park Archives. According to Braught's account:
   > There came into Ahmek two boys who used to be associated with
   > the camp as councilors. Bill Little and Jack Eastaugh. Saturday eve-
   > ning we were sitting in the dining room and the staff or the kitchen
   > and workmen and one of these boys started to talking about Tom

Thomson and made the remark that, "It seemed too bad that we couldn't establish some definite understanding as to what had really occurred at the time Tom's body was buried at Canoe Lake". And each one began recalling incidents where others like Shannon Fraser who ran the Mowat Lodge at that time, and who was associated with the undertaker that was sent here to remove Tom's body, made the remark that he didn't think the undertaker was in the cemetery long enough to do the work that was supposed to be done in removing the body from the ground and putting it into a coffin. And the same remark was attributed to some of the trainmen who remarked when the coffin was loaded onto the train that it seemed very light. In talking about this for several minutes Jack Eastaugh said, "It seems to me that some of us ought to do something definite and try to establish the fact as to whether Tom's body is actually buried here or whether it was removed to Owen Sound." Now I have been told that the undertaker brought a steel casket here, and that it was taken out to the cemetery one evening by Shannon Fraser and he had remarked that he didn't think that the body had ever been taken up and put into this coffin that was taken back to Owen Sound. And one remark led to another, and finally Jack Eastaugh said, "You know I'd like to go over there and investigate and see if we can't find something. Now we wouldn't be committing anything illegal because we have public evidence that the body was removed and taken to Owen Sound, so if we go over there, all we'll be doing is to investigate for our own selves and find out if this is true or not." And after I had listened to them for some time the same thought had been in my mind often, but I had never found anyone who seemed willing to put the energy into it and the interest that was necessary to carry through such an investigation.

9. Ibid.
10. Ibid.
11. Roy MacGregor, "A break in the mysterious case of Tom Thomson, Canada's Van Gogh" *The Globe and Mail*, October 1, 2010. https://www.theglobeandmail.com/news/national/a-break-in-the-mysterious-case-of-tom-thomson-canadas-van-gogh/article1214427/.

    According to MacGregor: "In the fall of 1956, four men, who admitted to having had a few drinks, went exploring at the Canoe Lake cemetery with shovels and eventually dug up a skeleton with a hole in the left temple of the skull."

    See also MacGregor's comments during an interview for the documentary film *The West Wind*: "In 1956, four men, including Judge William Little, they had a few drinks, they admit it, and they grabbed their shovels, and they said, "Well, let's go off and see what we can find.""

(https://tvo.org/transcript/842259x/video/documentaries/west
-wind-the-vision-of-tom-thomson).

12. Frank Braught, audio recording, AMP-AU-201, interviewed by Taylor Statten at Little Wapomeo Island, 1956. Courtesy of Algonquin Park Archives.

13. Ibid.

14. Ibid.

15. William T. Little, *The Tom Thomson Mystery* (Toronto, Ontario: McGraw-
Hill, Toronto, 1970).

16. Ibid.

17. Ibid.

18. Frank Braught, audio recording, AMP-AU-201, interviewed by Taylor Statten at Little Wapomeo Island, 1956. Courtesy of Algonquin Park Archives.

19. Harry Ebbs, M.D., interviewed at his home in Toronto, Ontario on November 26, 1975 by Rory Mackay. Courtesy of the Algonquin Park Archives
and the Ebbs family.

20. William T. Little, *The Tom Thomson Mystery* (Toronto, Ontario: McGraw-
Hill, Toronto, 1970).

21. Harry Ebbs, M.D., interviewed at his home in Toronto, Ontario on November 26, 1975 by Rory Mackay. Courtesy of the Algonquin Park Archives
and the Ebbs family.

22. Ibid.

23. Ibid.

24. Ibid.

25. Frank Braught, audio recording, AMP-AU-201, interviewed by Taylor Statten at Little Wapomeo Island, 1956. Courtesy of Algonquin Park Archives.
This was confirmed by Harry Ebbs: "I picked him up down at the Portage
Store, and we had Frank Braught, who was living there on the lake, and
Gibby, Leonard Gibson, and who else? There was someone else there, I've
forgotten who. They brought the camp jeep around and brought 2 shovels,
they put the chain around the balsam and dragged it off, then it was very
easy to dig." (Harry Ebbs, M.D., interviewed at his home in Toronto, Ontario on November 26, 1975 by Rory Mackay. Courtesy of the Algonquin
Park Archives and the Ebbs family).

26. Frank Braught, audio recording, AMP-AU-201, interviewed by Taylor Statten at Little Wapomeo Island, 1956. Courtesy of Algonquin Park Archives.

27. Harry Ebbs, M.D., interviewed at his home in Toronto, Ontario on November 26, 1975 by Rory Mackay. Courtesy of the Algonquin Park Archives.

28. Ibid.

29. Frank Braught, audio recording, AMP-AU-201, interviewed by Taylor Statten at Little Wapomeo Island, 1956. Courtesy of Algonquin Park Archives.

30. Ibid.

Chapter Fifteen

1. "Algonquin Grave Revives Thomson Legend," Toronto Star, October 10, 1956.
2. Newspaper article, *The Leader Post*, Regina, Saturday, October 13, 1956, 13.
3. Newspaper article, *The Leader-Post*, Regina, Tuesday, October 16, 1956.
4. Newspaper article, *The Leader Post*, Regina, Saturday, October 13, 1956, pg. 13.
5. Newspaper article, *Toronto Daily Star*, "M.R. Dixon, 'I Buried Tom Thomson, No Foul Play.'" October 12, 1956.
6. Doug Dunford, in conversation with the author, October 1, 2016.
7. William T. Little, *The Tom Thomson Mystery*, "Dorothy Stone's Recollections," (Toronto, Ontario: McGraw-Hill, Toronto, 1970), 106–109.
8. "I feel rather sore at Beatty . . . I cannot for the life of me understand how he, claiming to be a friend of Tom's, can so easily swallow all Fraser's talk. . . . it makes me feel sore to think Fraser, who claimed to be such a friend of Tom's, could make all these suggestions and Beatty ready to take them all in. I cannot understand Fraser but he seems to have some subtle influence over people to make them believe in him." (Library and Archives, National Gallery of Canada, Dr. James M. MacCallum Papers, T.J. Harkness, Letter to Dr. James MacCallum, November 3, 1917).
9. Centre for Forensic Sciences, Toronto, Ontario. Documents supplied in response to Freedom of Information and Protection of Personal Privacy Act request, Dr. Noble Sharpe, Re: Human Bones Received From Unmarked Grave In Algonquin Park, October 30, 1956.
10. The undertaker Robert Flavelle's bill (sent to Shannon Fraser), revealed a charge for a shroud:
    Kearney, Aug 2, 1917
    Mr Fraser Mowat P. O.
    in account with R. H. FLAVELLE DEALER IN HARDWARE, STOVES, TINWARE, WALLPAPER, ETC.

July	17	T0 1 casket & Rough Box	75.00
"	"	1 shroud	5.00
"	"	Embalming Fees	20.00
"	"	Express on casket	0.80
"	"	Return fare	1.65
"	"	Expenses at Canoe Lake	3.00
"	"	Phone messages to Canoe Lake	0.30
"	"	Owen Sound	1.50
			107.25

(Library and Archives Canada/Bibliotheque et Archives Canada, MG30 D284, Tom Thomson Collection, Vol. 1, File 4., R.H. Flavelle, Bill for services rendered, August 2, 1917.)

11. Centre for Forensic Sciences, Toronto, Ontario. Documents supplied in response to Freedom of Information and Protection of Personal Privacy Act request, Dr. Noble Sharpe, Re: Human Bones Received From Unmarked Grave In Algonquin Park, October 30, 1956.

12. Trent University Archives, Addison Family fonds, 97–011, Mark Robinson, Daily Journal, July 17, 1917.

13. Library and Archives Canada/Bibliotheque et Archives Canada, MG30 D38, Blodwen Davies Fonds, Vol. 11, George Thomson, Letter to Blodwen Davies, June 8, 1931. Note: Original document withdrawn from circulation. Copy available on microfilm C-4579.

14. Library and Archives Canada/Bibliotheque et Archives Canada, MG30 D38, Blodwen Davies Fonds, Vol. 11, Dr. A.E. Ranney, "Letter to Blodwen Davies," May 7, 1931. Note: Original document withdrawn from circulation. Copy available on microfilm C-4579.

15. Centre for Forensic Sciences, Toronto, Ontario. Documents supplied in response to Freedom of Information and Protection of Personal Privacy Act request, Dr. Noble Sharpe, Re: Human Bones Received From Unmarked Grave In Algonquin Park, October 30, 1956.

16. Judge William T. Little interview, *Was Tom Thomson Murdered?* A CBC Television documentary, 1969.

Chapter Sixteen

1. Memorandum from the Department of the Attorney General, sent to Assistant Deputy Attorney General Mr. F.L. Wilson, from Dr. Noble Sharpe on February 20, 1967.

2. Dr. Noble Sharpe, "The Canoe Lake Mystery," *Canadian Society of Forensic Science Journal* 3 (June 31, 1970): 34–40.

3. Dr. Noble Sharpe's Final Report, Submitted on December 12, 1956 to Assistant Commissioner Jas. Barlett, Office of the Commissioner, Ontario Provincial Police, Parliament Buildings, Toronto, Ontario. (Note: The author is beholden to researcher/author Neil Lehto for providing him with copies of Dr. Sharpe's various reports and statements from 1956 to 1967 on the skeleton found in the Mowat cemetery from which this chapter draws liberally.)

4. Dr. Noble Sharpe's report to Assistant Commissioner Jas. Bartlett dated October 30, 1956, Office of the Commissioner, Ontario Provincial Police, Parliament Buildings, Toronto, Ontario; see also Dr. Noble Sharpe's Final Report, Submitted on December 12, 1956 to Assistant Commissioner Jas.

Barlett, Office of the Commissioner, Ontario Provincial Police, Parliament Buildings, Toronto, Ontario.

5. Professor Grant's Report to Dr. Noble Sharpe, sent from the Department of Anatomy, University of Toronto on 11th December 1956, to Noble Sharpe at the Attorney general's Laboratory, Report On The Canoe Lake Case, Index File No: 1036/56.

6. "Kelso Roberts, Algonquin Park Bones Not Those of Thomson," *Toronto Daily Star*, October 19, 1956.

7. Dr. Noble Sharpe's report to Assistant Commissioner Jas. Bartlett dated October 30, 1956, Office of the Commissioner, Ontario Provincial Police, Parliament Buildings, Toronto, Ontario.
    Re: Human Bones recovered from unmarked grave, Township of Peck, District of Nippissing, In Algonquin Park, File Number: 1036/56 N.S.

8. Professor Grant's Report to Dr. Noble Sharpe, sent from the Department of Anatomy, University of Toronto on 11th December 1956, to Noble Sharpe at the Attorney general's Laboratory, Report On The Canoe Lake Case, Index File No: 1036/56.

9. Dr. Noble Sharpe's report to Assistant Commissioner Jas. Bartlett dated October 30, 1956, Office of the Commissioner, Ontario Provincial Police, Parliament Buildings, Toronto, Ontario.

10. Ibid.

11. Dr. Noble Sharpe's Final Report, Submitted on December 12, 1956 to Assistant Commissioner Jas. Bartlett, Office of the Commissioner, Ontario Provincial Police, Parliament Buildings, Toronto, Ontario.

12. Both of Dr. Noble Sharpe's reports to Assistant Commissioner Jas. Bartlett, dated October 30, 1956 and December 12, 1956, respectively, contain the statement: "Water seepage would account for sand being intimately mixed with the bones (a surface depression had been noted by the original diggers). Hazel nuts (with withered contents) were present with the bones at 4 ½' level. These, I think, were due to seepage, as it seems too deep for rodents."

13. According to Dr. Sharpe: "The foot of the grave in which the bones were found was 21' due north of the corner of the fence surrounding the two marked graves. This is certainly approximately where Mr. Thomson was buried originally. There is nothing to prove that the opened grave is not the same as Mr. Thomson's and the coffin is hardwood just as his was said to be. But I feel definitely that the skeleton is not that of Mr. Thomson. I do believe, however, that this Indian was buried in Mr. Thomson's original grave, either in or on top of his empty coffin." (Dr. Noble Sharpe's Final Report, Submitted on December 12, 1956 to Assistant Commissioner Jas. Barlett, Office of the Commissioner, Ontario Provincial Police, Parliament Buildings, Toronto, Ontario).

14. Dr. Noble Sharpe interview, *Was Tom Thomson Murdered?* CBC Television documentary, 1969.

15. Judge William T. Little interview, *Was Tom Thomson Murdered?* CBC Television documentary, 1969.

16. Charles F. Plewman, "Reflections on the passing of Tom Thomson," *Canadian Camping Magazine*, 1972.

17. Aimee Bailey, Heritage and Cultural Planner, Algonquins of Ontario Consultation Office, in conversation with the author, December 6, 2016.

18. Don Delaplante, "Long a Mystery of Art World: Body May Answer Riddle of Tom Thomson's Death," *Globe and Mail*, October 10, 1956.

19. Neil Lehto, "Antoine Chouinard: An Earlier Mowat Burial?" http://www.algonquinelegy.com/Chouinard.html.

20. Dr. Noble Sharpe, Re: Human Bones Received From Unmarked Grave In Algonquin Park, Oct. 30, 1956, reproduced online at: http://www.canadianmysteries.ca/sites/thomson/investigations/1950–1965/5040en.html.

Chapter Seventeen

1. Professor Grant's Report to Dr. Noble Sharpe, sent from the Department of Anatomy, University of Toronto on 11th December 1956, to Noble Sharpe at the Attorney general's Laboratory, Report On The Canoe Lake Case, Index File No: 1036/56.

2. Reynolds, Nila. "Blanche Linton Remembers Tom Thomson," Early Canadian Life, February 1979 edition; page 19.

3. Harry Ebbs, M.D., interviewed at his home in Toronto, Ontario on November 26, 1975 by Rory Mackay. Courtesy of the Algonquin Park Archives and the Ebbs family.

4. Professor Grant's Report to Dr. Noble Sharpe, sent from the Department of Anatomy, University of Toronto on 11th December 1956, to Noble Sharpe at the Attorney general's Laboratory, Report On The Canoe Lake Case, Index File No: 1036/56.

5. Ibid.

6. According to Dr. Noble Sharpe: "Mr. Thomson is described in books, etc., as a strong outdoor type over 6 feet in height, and 40 years of age. Mention is made that he was a pipe smoker. The bones were of a shorter man of lesser age. The bones belong to an Indian."
Source: Dr. Noble Sharpe's report to Assistant Commissioner Jas. Bartlett dated October 30, 1956, Office of the Commissioner, Ontario Provincial Police, Parliament Buildings, Toronto, Ontario; see also Dr. Noble Sharpe's Final Report, Submitted on December 12, 1956 to Assistant Commissioner

Jas. Barlett, Office of the Commissioner, Ontario Provincial Police, Parliament Buildings, Toronto, Ontario.

7. M. Trotter and G.C. Gleser, 1952, Estimation of statute from long bones of American whites and negroes, *American Journal of Physical Anthropology* 10(4), 355- 356, 463–514.

8. The Trotter and Gleser formula is: (1.84 x femoral bicondylar length) + (0.94 x tibial maximum length) + 54.08 (± 3.58). When the dimensions of the femur and tibia that were removed from the Mowat Cemetery in 1956 are plugged into this formula, we get Femur x 1.84 (86.848) + Tibia x 0.94 (35.908) + 54.43 = 177.186 centimeters. This comes out to a projected height of 5 feet, 9.758 inches.

9. "Canadians still getting taller, but not as fast as others," *CBC News*, July 26, 2016, http://www.cbc.ca/news/health/height-growth-canada-1.3695398.

10. Audrey Saunders, notes from interview with Molly Colson in 1944. Courtesy of Algonquin Park Archives.

11. Dr. Noble Sharpe's Final Report, Submitted on December 12, 1956 to Assistant Commissioner Jas. Barlett, Office of the Commissioner, Ontario Provincial Police, Parliament Buildings, Toronto, Ontario.

12. Ibid.

13. Harry Ebbs, M.D., interviewed at his home in Toronto, Ontario on November 26, 1975 by Rory Mackay. Courtesy of the Algonquin Park Archives and the Ebbs family.

14. Dr. Noble Sharpe's Final Report, Submitted on December 12, 1956 to Assistant Commissioner Jas. Barlett, Office of the Commissioner, Ontario Provincial Police, Parliament Buildings, Toronto, Ontario.

15. Dr. Frederick Jaffe interview, *Was Tom Thomson Murdered?* CBC Television documentary, 1969.

16. Judge William T. Little interview, *Was Tom Thomson Murdered?* CBC Television documentary, 1969.

17. Dr. Noble Sharpe interview, *Was Tom Thomson Murdered?* CBC Television documentary, 1969.

18. Doug Lucas interview, *Was Tom Thomson Murdered?* CBC Television documentary, 1969.

19. Harry Ebbs, M.D., interviewed at his home in Toronto, Ontario on November 26, 1975 by Rory Mackay. Courtesy of the Algonquin Park Archives and the Ebbs family.

Chapter Eighteen

1. Frank Braught, audio recording, AMP-AU-201, interviewed by Taylor Statten at Little Wapomeo Island, 1956. Courtesy of Algonquin Park Archives; see also Corporal A.M. Rodger's Ontario Provincial Police Report, No:

12 District: North Bay, Burk's Falls, October 9, 1956 re: Human bones recovered from unmarked grave, Township of Peck, District of Nipissing, in Algonquin Park. First report D.H.G. File: C.R. 335–56, which states "At the present time [i.e., October of 1956], Mr. George Thomson is attempting to raise funds to have a museum erected in his memory."

2. http://tomthomson.org/visit/about/.

3. http://tomthomson.org/visit/our-history/.

4. "Tom Thomson family will bar exhumation of body," *Owen Sound Sun-Times*, February 8, 1969.

5. Ibid.

6. George Thomson: "Now I want to say in passing that I have from various sources a pretty accurate account of what happened at the inquest and in common with other friends and relatives of Tom's am more firmly convinced than ever that his death was caused either by accident or foul play." (Library and Archives, National Gallery of Canada, Dr. James. M. MacCallum Papers, George Thomson, Letter to J.S. Fraser, December 25, 1917). George Thomson also made the statement: "I think the revealing statement in the [coroner's] finding is that of the bruise over the left temple, which I believe rendered him [Tom] unconscious so that drowning ensued. Of course it is hard to say what caused the bruise. It probably was an accident— though it is possible to have been foul play." (Library and Archives Canada, MG30 D38 "Blodwen Davies fonds," Vol. 11. George Thomson, Letter to Blodwen Davies, June 8, 1931. Note: Originals withdrawn from circulation. Copies available on microfilm C-4579).

7. Fraser Thomson: "There has been a lot of conjecture about how he died; whether foul play or an accident caused his death. I know that there had been ill will between a German who worked at one of the lodges and my brother. Tom had been trying to enlist and the German had said something to him. There was a quarrel. Then Tom was found dead soon afterward. Who knows what happened? His death will always be a mystery."

    Toronto Telegram newspaper interview with Thomson's younger brother, Fraser Thomson; "Unearthing of Skeleton Revives Artist Mystery," October 10, 1956.

8. Margaret Thomson: "Sometimes I wonder if the man [Shannon Fraser] did do anything to harm Tom. I suppose it is wicked to think such a thing, but if anyone did harm him, it was for the little money they could pocket." (Library and Archives, National Gallery of Canada, Dr. James M. MacCallum papers, Margaret Thomson, Letter to Dr. James MacCallum, September 9, 1917).

9. "Tom Thomson family will bar exhumation of body," *Owen Sound Sun-Times*, February 8, 1969.

10. Ibid.

11. Ibid.

12. Ibid.
13. Ibid.
14. Ibid.
15. Ibid.
16. "Recall identifying of Tom Thomson body prior to burial here," *Owen Sound Sun-Times*, Feb. 10, 1969.
17. Robert McMichael, *One Man's Obsession* (Prentice-Hall Canada, 1986).
18. "Tom Thomson, Artist, Drowned." *Owen Sound Times*, July 20, 1917: "The body, accompanied by Mr. George Thomson, is expected in Owen Sound at noon on Friday, and in this case, the funeral, which is to be private, will leave his father's residence Friday afternoon. The remains will be interred in Leith cemetery."
19. Letter from Peg Thomson to Minnie Thomson, July 22, 1917, https://web.archive.org/web/20170328194615/http://tomthomsonart.com/letters/peg-thomson-minnie-thomson-july-22-1917.
20. Ibid.
21. Newspaper interview, William T. Little Interview, *The Muskokan*, June 30, 1988.
22. "Brother Believes Thomson's Body Buried At Leith," *Globe and Mail*, October 11, 1956.
23. Library and Archives Canada/Bibliotheque et Archives Canada, MG30 D404 'Harold Town fond,' Vol. 30 File 15, Elva Henry, Interview with Elva Henry, Harold Town, November 15, 1973.
24. Ibid.
25. Harold Town and David Silcox, *Tom Thomson: The Silence and The Storm* (McClelland and Stewart, 1977), 59.
26. When Blodwen Davies had written to Robinson inquiring if the line which was found wrapped around the artist's ankle was his own, the ranger had replied "It might have been his own line but not his regular fishing line." Library and Archives Canada/Bibliotheque et Archives Canada, MG30 D38 'Blodwen Davies fonds', Vol. 11, Mark Robinson and Blodwen Davies, Response to Blodwen Davies' questions, September 4, 1930. Notes: Originals withdrawn from circulation. Copies available on microfilm C-4579.
27. "Molly [Colson] was a wonderful healer and became the local mid-wife, prenatal counselor, setter of broken bones and even pulled teeth upon occasion. As there wasn't a doctor anywhere around the local area, she would always make house calls when anyone was sick, even in the winter. She gained local fame when she walked more than a mile from the Algonquin Hotel on Joe Lake to the Farley house on Potter Creek using two canes. There she promptly delivered one of the Farley daughters, who arrived prematurely. In another incident, a man at a local lumbering camp had fractured his leg and needed a splint before he could be moved. Molly set the bone and bound the leg using a splint that Ed made out of a piece of board. He was

eventually taken off to the doctor at Whitney who said later that he hadn't needed to reset the leg at all. It had been set perfectly." Source: http://www.algonquinparkheritage.com/profiles.php?ID=2

Chapter Nineteen

1. Harry Ebbs, M.D., interviewed at his home in Toronto, Ontario on November 26, 1975 by Rory Mackay. Courtesy of the Algonquin Park Archives and the Ebbs family.
2. Ibid.
3. Ibid.
4. Ibid.
5. Ibid.
6. Dr. Noble Sharpe, "The Canoe Lake Mystery," *Canadian Society of Forensic Science Journal* 3 (June 31, 1970): 34–40.
7. According to Corporal A.M. Rodger's report, "I recovered nearly all the bones of a human body, including the skull, jawbone with teeth still intact. There were no fillings in the teeth, and only one missing." (Ontario Provincial Police Report, No: 12 District: North Bay Burk's Falls, October 9, 1956. Re: Human bones recovered from unmarked grave, Township of Peck, District of Nipissing, in Algonquin Park. First report D.H.G. File: C.R. 335–56 Detachment File: C2E (?) 54–56).
8. According to Dr. Noble Sharpe's Final Report, dated December 12, 1956: "The absence of caries in the teeth (all present except one lower molar which was broken off) . . ." (Final Report, Dec. 12, 1956. Submitted To Assistant Commissioner Jas. Barlett, Office of the Commissioner, Ontario Provincial Police, Parliament Buildings,Toronto, Ontario. Re: Human bones recovered from unmarked grave, Township of Peck, District of Nipissing, in Algonquin Park. Our file – 1036/56 N.S).

Epilogue

1. E-mail sent from Robert Bateman to Dan Mulligan containing the content of his letter, February 5, 2002.
2. Letter from Chief Kirby Whiteduck, on behalf of the Council of the Algonquins of Pikwakanagan, to Peter A. Clark, M.D., Regional Supervising Coroner, North-East Region, Office of the Chief Coroner, Peterborough, Ontario, dated October 21, 2003.
3. Letter from Peter A. Clarke, M.D., Regional Supervising Coroner to Mr. Kirby Whiteduck, Chief Council of the Algonquins of Pikwakanagan, December 22, 2013.

4. Ellie Tesher, "Artist's Death: Offers Of Help Pour In;" *Toronto Star*, Monday, August 26 1996.
5. Ibid.
6. Letter written by Ken Danby to Tracy Thomson, November 5, 2004. Courtesy of Dan Mulligan.
7. Ibid.
8. Tracy Thomson letter to Ken Danby, November 15, 2005. Dan Mulligan Collection.
9. E-mail sent from Robert Bateman to Dan Mulligan containing the content of his letter, February 5, 2002.
10. Ellie Tesher, "Artist's Death: Offers Of Help Pour In;" *Toronto Star*, Monday, August 26 1996.

INDEX